BY THE EDITORS OF CONSUMER GUIDE®

RATING THE
DIETS

By Theodore Berland

BEEKMAN HOUSE

New York

About the Author

Theodore Berland, author of 15 books and hundreds of magazine and newspaper articles, for six years wrote a weekly newspaper column on dieting, which was also syndicated nationally. He is on the faculty of Grand Valley State College, at Allendale, Michigan, and is science writer at Michael Reese Hospital, Chicago. He has taught nutrition at Columbia College, Chicago, where he also served as chairman of the Journalism Department, and in addition, he has been on the faculties of the University of Wisconsin — Milwaukee, Bowling Green State University, Ohio, and Northwestern University. A graduate of the University of Illinois, Urbana, he holds a master's degree from the University of Chicago. He is immediate past president of the American Medical Writers Association and is a past president of the Society of Midland Authors. Among his books is the *Fitness Fact Book*.

Library of Congress Catalog Card Number: 83-60517
ISBN: 0-517-40839-2

This edition published by:
Beekman House
Distributed by Crown Publishers, Inc.
One Park Avenue
New York, New York 10016

Cover Design: Linda Snow Shum

Contents

Dieting in 1983

*Y*ou would think that in hard economic times, such as The Great Recession of '82, dieting would be last on the list of human activities in our society. Yet, while some diet clubs have experienced reduced enrollment because of the tightness of the dollar, dieting to lose weight is as popular as ever. Witness the huge sales of such books as *The Beverly Hills Diet, Never-Say-Diet Book,* and *Jane Fonda's Workout Book.*

Yet, dedicated as the public is to the concept of dieting, we don't seem to get any smarter. The few good books that present reasonable approaches to losing weight go begging, in comparison with the runaway sales of the kooky, off-the-wall, nutritionally unsound fad diet books. Still, the picture of the public is not all dismal. Very sound guides to exercise and physical fitness sell well and are closely followed.

Yet, sweating removes little fat, beneficial as exercise is for the health of heart and lungs, and for the firm tone of muscles. Instead, the interest in exercise bespeaks the desperation of the overweight, caught in the flux of opposing forces—the advertised abundance of fresh and wonderful food, and the role models of thin and energetic young men and women.

Full-page newspaper ads appeal to the overweights' despair, and offer dieters magic. The ads scream:

MAKES YOU SKINNY IN 45 DAYS...EVEN IF YOU CHEAT!!!
GRADUATE TO A NEW SLIM YOU IN JUST 4 WEEKS!
DISSOLVES STUBBORN BULGES AND WASHES AWAY YEARS OF BUILT-UP FAT

Dieters are offered magic pills, miraculous formulas, and diets with nutritionally absurd ideas. The fashion in fad diets now is to give them geographical names—The Cambridge Diet, The Beverly Hills Diet, The Southampton Diet, The Scarsdale Diet are examples. The geographical names, of course, represent locations of learning and research (Cambridge) or of wealth and social prestige where beautiful and THIN people live.

Each diet has its spokespersons, enthusiastically exclaiming the virtues of each diet on the irrepressible talk shows of radio and television and in the feature columns of newspapers and magazines. Like magicians, they promise to make something (fat) disappear through sorcery, the secrets of which they alone have mastered and which they are very willing to pass along to you for the price of a book.

So how are you, the dieter in need of help, to know which way to turn, whom to trust, which magic to buy?

The answer is in your hand: *Rating the Diets.* It is the only objective, complete up-to-date source of information on diets and other methods of losing weight. And it dares to add ratings to its data. That's possible because *Rating the Diets* has no ax to grind, no favorite diet to promote; it owes no allegiance to a guru of girth. *Rating the Diets* does not endorse the use of pills, supplements, or equipment. Instead, it helps you analyze any new diet that comes along, and it gives you an honest evaluation of the benefits and hazards of the ones that are already around.

Behind the technical jargon in the diet plans, behind the excitement and the exotic claims and counterclaims, behind the hedging about potential health problems, there are some hard facts you must know before you can choose the best diet for you. In *Rating the Diets* CONSUMER GUIDE® has put these hard facts together so you can make your own decision. After all, you are planning for *your* body and *your* future. And your decision cannot be lighthearted or made on the spur of the moment.

For *Rating the Diets* we draw upon the experiences of nutritional experts to put together all the information you need. These experts asked the same questions you yourself have asked again and again when trying to choose one diet over another.

What does "overweight" mean? How do I know if I am overweight and,if I am, by how much? What might happen if I drastically cut down on my food intake or suddenly change the kind of food I eat? Can I make sure my health will not be endangered if I start on a new diet? How can I know which diets could be dangerous? Should I join a diet group, or should I fight this battle alone? Should I try behavior modification or exercise?

As they gained the answers to these questions, the experts were able to separate the best diets from the worst and rate them accordingly. As you gain answers to these questions, you will begin to view diets in a new light. You will see some as slow-but-sure; some as providing quick and safe results but only if maintained for a short time; some as unsound; some as actually dangerous.

Once you have chosen a diet and an exercise plan that seems right for you, CONSUMER GUIDE® strongly recommends that you buy the book that describes the plan or that you join the group that oversees its own diet program. Books give explanations that may make the diet clearer and more reasonable and thus easier to stick with. Groups not only offer help in meal planning, preparing food, and coping, but they also provide the support that so many dieters need to overcome the rough spots in their reducing program. Both usually offer menus and recipes to help you stay within the limits of the diet. CONSUMER GUIDE®'s descriptions of the diets do not replace the books or groups that must be recognized as the only complete source of information, whatever the diet or program. *Rating the Diets* gives you the tools for choosing a diet; the books and groups give you the tools for following it.

Once you have chosen a diet you intend to stay with, keep *Rating the Diets* handy as a reference. The information it contains will not lose validity as long as the demands of the human body and the content of foods remain the same. With it, you can find a diet you can follow the rest of your life.

HOW TO RATE A DIET

CONSUMER GUIDE® has done most of the work for you, gathering information on the latest diets and other weight-reducing schemes, evaluating them for you, and comparing them with diets of the past that are still around. But new details will be coming up.

Here are some guidelines so you can evaluate any diet—new or old.

1. Has the author of the diet tried it on hundreds, even thousands, of overweight people, objectively compared the results against a similar

number of people on regular or other weight-reducing diets, and published the findings in a recognized and reputable nutrition or medical journal? Is the diet based on sound nutritional principles? If the answer is no, regard the diet as experimental at best.

2. Is the diet based on some "secret" no one discovered before? If the answer is yes, move on. These "secrets" do not exist. Remember though, you can lose weight, temporarily, on any diet. Just paying attention to what you eat may do it, at least for a while.
3. Is the diet nutritionally well-balanced? If the answer is no, be careful. Only well-balanced diets are safe. And a well-balanced diet includes food from the basic groups: meat/protein, dairy, vegetables and fruits, cereals and grains. Diets which are deficient in any area or based on one kind of food are not balanced. Diets with fewer than about 1000 calories a day should be medically supervised.
4. Is the person promoting the diet known, well-respected, and knowledgeable in nutrition? If the answer is no, he or she may be a fast-buck artist who has no regard for your health and safety. While many physicians have published books on diets, simply being a physician does not qualify one in nutrition.
5. How long has the diet been around? If less than five years, view it with suspicion. Anyone can invent a new diet, but only a few diets survive. At the same time, many bad old diets which are resuscitated should have been left to their eternal rest. Examples are high-fat and low-carbohydrate diets. Be aware that longevity of a diet is not a guarantee.
6. Is the proponent of the new diet challenging the recommendations of the best authorities? It's OK to challenge, but a valid challenge has to be backed by new findings, which should be available for scrutiny. Beware the diet huckster who challenges everything in sight but has no substantial scientific data.
7. Does the diet allow for individual preference, practice, and taste? The meal plan should be flexible and allow you to eat the foods you like and to eat meals according to the rhythm of your life activities. Rigid diets that tell you what and when to eat and give you no nutritional information are doomed to fail in the long run.
8. Could you live on this for the rest of your life? Weight control is a full-time, lifelong effort. One-week or 14-day diets offer temporary weight loss, at best. Then what? You need to take weight off and keep it off. That means a full-time, full-life plan.
9. Is the claim made that the diet is based on principles of another expert or a health association? If so, what do THEY think of this diet? More than one popular, best-selling diet book has been written by one person and based on another's research. In just about every case, the original proponent of the principle was not consulted and, in fact, would not have approved of the other's work, which often perverted sound principles.
10. Who recommends the diet? If the answer is your family physician and/or well-known and recognized medical and nutrition authorities, the diet is worth trying. But if it is *only* endorsed by its creator and hawker and, perhaps, some beautiful movie stars or beautiful rich people, the diet is worth avoiding.

US SENATE SELECT COMMITTEE ON
NUTRITION AND HUMAN NEEDS GUIDELINES

Sound principles of nutrition are offered by your federal government. Following is a brief summary of dietary guidelines and goals that have been promoted through various programs. Perhaps, if these guidelines and goals are actually followed, obesity will be less common in this country. After all, if you are filling up on relatively low-calorie fruits, vegetables, and whole grains, there may be less room for calorie-packed foods high in fat and sugar.

To paraphrase the US Senate dietary guidelines and goals,[1] Americans should—

1. Increase complex-carbohydrate consumption by eating more fruits, vegetables, and whole grains.
2. Lower cholesterol intake by eating less red meat, butter and eggs and more poultry and fish; also substitute nonfat milk for whole milk.
3. Reduce the total amount of dietary fat and decrease the ratio of saturated to polyunsaturated and monosaturated fats; do this by avoiding fatty foods and substituting some polyunsaturated fat for saturated fat.
4. Reduce sugar consumption by about 40 percent by eating less sugar and high-sugar foods.
5. Reduce salt intake by using less table salt and eating less salty foods.

WARNINGS

First, before starting any diet, consult your physician.

Second, the following recommendations for dieting come from US Department of Agriculture/Health and Human Services Pamphlet *Nutrition and Your Health: Dietary Guidelines for Americans:*

> If you need to lose weight, do so gradually. Steady loss of 1 or 2 pounds a week—until you reach your goal—is relatively safe and more likely to be maintained. Long-term success depends upon acquiring new and better habits of eating and exercise. That is perhaps why "crash" diets usually fail in the long run.
>
> Do not try to lose weight too rapidly. Avoid crash diets that are severely restricted in the variety of foods they allow. Diets containing fewer than 800 calories may be hazardous. Some people have developed kidney stones, disturbing psychological changes, and other complications while following such diets. A few people have died suddenly and without warning.[2]

To lose weight:
- Increase physical activity
- Eat less fat and fatty foods
- Eat less sugar and sweets
- Avoid too much alcohol

THE TRUTH ABOUT DIETING

Finally, here are some truths, stated by one of the leading nutritionists in America, Dr. Fredrick J. Stare, professor and founder of the Department of Nutrition at Harvard University:

1. No one food by itself provides good nutrition. To keep as well nourished as one's genetic potential permits, one must eat a variety of foods from among and within the Basic Four Food Groups.
2. Portion size is important and, particularly for meats and dairy products, must be adjusted to caloric output (physical activity) so that Desirable Weight is reached and maintained.
3. Alcoholic beverages are potent sources of calories. There are indications that alcohol is a carcinogen (cancer-causing agent) or cocarcinogen, especially in combination with cigarette smoking.
4. Skipping or skimping on breakfast and lunch and then having a large dinner is likely to result in intake of more total calories in a 24-hour period than having three or more smaller meals throughout the day.
5. Calories are all alike, whether they come from beef or bourbon, from sugar or starch, or from cheese and crackers. Too many calories are too many calories.[3]

Rating
the 1983 Diets

*T*his 1983 rating of diets lists mostly current but some past diets. Some ratings have been changed from those in previous editions on the basis of new nutritional evaluation. The more stars, the greater the effectiveness and safety of the diet. Within each category, diets are listed in alphabetical order.

CONSUMER GUIDE® believes that, before you go on any diet, you should have your physician assess your state of health. Be sure to ask your doctor if you should take vitamin-mineral supplements with any diet. You should also consult the original source of these diets for complete information and instructions.

★★★★

The four-star CONSUMER GUIDE® rating is given only to those diets which follow the specifications of the US Senate's *Dietary Goals for the United States* or the Prudent Diet. Both are based on the best medical and nutritional findings—that protein is an important food category; that some fats are necessary, but that excessive saturated fats are dangerous to the heart and blood vessels; and that a certain amount of carbohydrate is needed.[1,2,3]

Thus, a four-star rating is given to a balanced diet that gives you an adequate amount of protein; no more than 30 percent of calories from fat, with unsaturated fat predominant; a prominent proportion of carbohydrates (mainly complex carbohydrates), and very little sugar. A four-star diet is one you can live on healthily for the rest of your life, without vitamin-mineral supplementation.

Using these criteria, CONSUMER GUIDE® gives its highest recommendation to all of the following diets which are listed in alphabetical order.

Alternative Diet Book (University of Iowa Publication, 1976)
Appetite Control Centers diet
The Beverly Hills Medical Diet (New York: Bantam Books, 1982)
Calories In, Calories Out (Brattleboro, VT: The Stephen Greene Press, 1981)
Canadian Diabetes Association diet
The Complete Gourmet Nutrition Cookbook (Washington, D.C.: Acropolis Books, 1978)
Diet Control Centers diet
Diet Workshop diets
Dr. Rechtschaffen's Diet (New York: Random House, 1980)
Food (USDA Publication)

Food 2 (Chicago: American Dietetic Association, 1982)
High-fiber, well-rounded diets *(The Save Your Life Diet, Natural Fiber Permanent Weight Loss Diet, Eat Right—To Stay Healthy and Enjoy Life More)*
The I Love America Diet (New York: William Morrow and Company, Inc., 1983)
La Costa Spa Diet (New York: Grosset & Dunlap, Inc., 1977)
Loma Linda University diets
New York City Department of Health Diet
The Prudent Diet (New York: David White, Inc., 1973)
Prudent Diet descendants *(But I Don't Eat That Much, How to Get Thinner Once and for All)*
Redbook's "Weight-Loss Diet for Your High-Energy Life"
Scarsdale Vegetarian Diet
TOPS diet
US Army Lifetime Diet
US Senate's *Dietary Goals for the United States*
Weight Watchers diets
The Wine Diet *(The Wine Diet Cookbook.* New York: Abelard-Schwinn, 1974)
Wonder Protein Diet (West Nyack, NY: Parker Publishing Co., 1979)
The Yogurt Diet *(Dieting, Yogurt and Common Sense.* Long Island City: The Dannon Company)

★★★

Low-cal only. Because these diets are somehow deficient, except in controlling calories, they are rated only second best. Some omit a food group and emphasize others; some do not properly balance proteins, fats, and carbohydrates; some do not differentiate between saturated and unsaturated fats, or between sugar and complex carbohydrates; others require supplementation to achieve full nutrition. You can, of course, take any of these diets and tailor it to better standards.

The following diets all receive three stars and are listed in alphabetical order.

The Dachman Permanent Weight Loss Program (New York: William Morrow and Company, Inc., 1982)
Diet Center diet
Diet for Life (New York: Cornerstone Library, Simon & Schuster, Inc., 1981)
How to Eat like a Thin Person (New York: Simon & Schuster, Inc., 1982)
Jeanne Jones' Food Lover's Diet (New York: Charles Scribner's Sons, 1982)
Lean Line diet
Lose Weight Naturally (Emmaus, PA: Rodale Press, 1979)
Mary Ellen's Help Yourself Diet Plan (New York: St. Martin's/Marek, 1983)
Mayo Clinic Exchange Diet
The Revolutionary 7-Unit Low Fat Diet (New York: Bantam Books, 1981)
The Sexibody Diet and Exercise Program (Aurora, IL: Carolina House Publishers, Inc., 1982)

★★★

High-carbohydrate diets are necessarily low in protein and fat. On the whole, this group is properly headed in the direction of the US Senate's dietary guidelines and goals for Americans. However, we fear that the diets in this group are too different from the US diet to be palatable to average Americans. Fat is responsible for a significant amount of flavor; and without it, these diets may seem bland. Since one of our rating criteria is that dieters must be able to stick with the diet for a long period and must not be turned off by the blandness, we give these diets three stars.

Dr. Cooper's Fabulous Fructose Diet (New York: M. Evans & Co., Inc., 1979)
F-Plan Diet (New York: Crown Publishers, Inc., 1983)
The Live Longer Now Quick Weight-Loss Program (New York: Grosset & Dunlap, 1980)
The Pritikin Permanent Weight Loss Manual (New York: Grosset & Dunlap, 1981)
The 200-Calorie Solution (New York: W. W. Norton & Co., 1982)

★★★

Low-carbohydrate diets—those that restrict your intake of carbohydrates to a minimum and also limit calories—are effective and safe diets for most people (even diabetics, under a doctor's supervision). However, they pay little attention to the kinds of fats you eat. Fats are extremely important; saturated fats and cholesterol can adversely affect the heart and arteries. Therefore, low- carbohydrate diets also rate second best.

The following diets are all rated three-star and are listed in alphabetical order.

American Diabetes Association Exchange Diet
The Brand-Name Carbo-Calorie Diet (Garden City, NJ: Doubleday & Co., Inc., 1979)
Dr. Yudkin's Anti-Sugar Diet *(Lose Weight, Feel Great!* New York: Larchmont, 1974)
The Doctor's Metabolic Diet (New York: Crown Publishers, Inc., 1975)
Fat Destroyer Foods: The Magic Metabolizer Diet (West Nyack, NY: Parker Publishing, 1974)
New York Times Natural Foods Dieting Book (New York: Quadrangle Books, Inc., 1972)
Slimming Down (New York: Grosset & Dunlap, Inc., 1972)

★★

A high-protein diet is an effective way to lose fat, but an extraordinarily high intake of protein can also result in a high intake of cholesterol. In addition, such a diet can be used only by people who have no evidence of kidney disease. Even for people in good health, plenty of water is necessary to wash away the ketone bodies — simple acids produced by the burning of fat. Such a diet is not for pregnant women or anyone with gout (unless specially adapted). It can be used by diabetics with modification and a doctor's consultation.

A high-protein diet may cause fatigue, which can be remedied by drinking a glass of orange juice. And like starvation fasting, a high-protein diet causes bad breath.

The following diets, including high-protein diets, all rate two stars and are listed in alphabetical order.

The Berkowitz Diet Switch (Westport, CT: Arlington House, 1981)
Brand Name Carbohydrate Diet (North Miami Beach: Success
    Publications, 1977)
Canyon Ranch diet
Conway Diet Institute diet
Diet Signs (Washington, D.C.; Acropolis Books, 1982)
Dr. Blackburn's Balanced-Deficit Diet
Dr. Stillman's 14-day Shape-Up Program (New York: Delacorte Press,
    1974)
Dr. Stillman's *The Doctor's Quick Weight-Loss Diet* (New York: Dell
    Publishing, 1968)
The other Duke University diet (*Thin for Life.* New York: Baronet
    Publishing Co., 1977)
Harbor Island Spa diet (*Eat Yourself Thin.* New York: Frederick Fell, 1977)
The I Love NY Diet (New York: William Morrow and Company, Inc., 1982)
Medifast and Medifast 70 (under a doctor's supervision)
Nutrimed (under a doctor's supervision)
Optifast 70 (under a doctor's supervision)
Proti-15 (under a doctor's supervision)
Richard Simmons' *Never-Say-Diet Book* (New York: Warner Books,
    1980)
The Complete Scarsdale Medical Diet and variations, except Vegetarian
    (New York: Rawson, Wade Publishers, Inc., 1978)
The Slendernow Diet (New York: St. Martin's Press, 1982)
Southampton Diet (New York: Simon & Schuster, Inc., 1982)
TRIMS Clubs diet
Vitamin Diet for Quick and Easy Weight Loss (New York: Cornerstone
    Library, Simon & Schuster, Inc., 1982)
What Every Pregnant Woman Should Know (New York: Random House,
    1977)
Woman Doctor's Diet for Women (Englewood Cliffs, NJ: Prentice-Hall,
    1977)
You Can Be Fat Free Forever (New York: St. Martin's Press, 1974)

A high-fat diet seems to work for some people, but has inherent dangers, especially if it tells you to eat no carbohydrates during the first week and after that only the barest minimum (as in Dr. Atkins' *Diet Revolution* diet). The body actually has a low requirement for only a couple of fatty acids. Furthermore, saturated fats are potentially dangerous to men and to post-menopausal women because of the risk of heart disease.

CONSUMER GUIDE® found one high-fat diet usable because it emphasized few calories and vegetable oils or unsaturated fats.

Dr. Atkins' Superenergy Diet (New York: Crown Publishers, Inc., 1977)

A one-star rating is also given to those diets that are foolish but not outright dangerous. In some cases and under certain circumstances, they may be useful.

Adrien Arpel's 3-Week Crash Makeover/Shapeover Beauty Program
(New York: Wallaby, 1979)
Dr. Schiff's One-Day-at-a-Time Weight-Loss Plan (New York: Stein & Day, 1980)

NOT RECOMMENDED (NO STARS)

The following diets are not recommended. They are unrealistic or outright dangerous to health (except for the Rice Diet, which may be followed under medical supervision). To lose fat and keep it off, CONSUMER GUIDE® believes you need a diet you can stick with for months or years.

The following diets either do not fit the criteria for longevity or the criteria for safety. These diets are listed in alphabetical order.

The Amazing Diet Secret of a Desperate Housewife (Montclair, NY: Pegasus Rex Press, 1978)
The Best Chance Diet (Atlanta: Humanics, Ltd., 1982)
The Beverly Hills Diet (New York: Macmillan Publishing Co., 1981)
Calories Don't Count (New York: Simon & Schuster, Inc., 1961)
The Cambridge Diet
The Carbohydrate Craver's Diet (Boston: Houghton Mifflin, 1983)
Cormillot Thin Forever Diet (*Thin Forever.* Chicago: Henry Regnery, 1975)
Dr. Atkins' Diet Revolution (New York: Bantam Books, Inc., 1973)
Dr. Howard's Mini-Calorie soups
Dr. Stillman's Inches-Off Diet (*The Doctor's Quick Inches-Off Diet.* New York: Dell Publishing, 1970)
Drinking Man's Diet (San Francisco: Cameron & Co., 1964)
Fasting
Grapefruit Diet ("fake" Mayo diet)
Hollywood Emergency Diet (Millburn, NJ: Millburn Book Corp., 1978)
The Last Best Diet Book (New York: Stein & Day, 1980)
Liquid protein (Prolinn, *The Last Chance Diet*)
Passwater's *The Easy No-FLAB Diet* (New York: Richard Marek Publishers, 1979)
Paul Michael Weight-Loss Plan (New York: William Morrow and Co., 1978)

Pritikin's Maximum Weight Loss Diet (*The Pritikin Program.* New York: Grosset & Dunlap, Inc., 1978)
Rice Diet (outside hospital)
The South American Diet (Atlanta: Braswell Health Book Publishing Co., 1980)
Thin Life Centers diet
The 30-Day Way to a Born-Again Body (New York: Rawson, Wade Publishers, Inc., 1978)
The University Diet
Zen Macrobiotic Diet

Magic Mixes

*T*he formula diets are "in" again. You remember them. They come in cans and jars, already prepared or in the form of powder you have to mix with water or milk. They are "guaranteed" to "melt" fat off (albeit at low temperatures, so you won't be burned—except in the pocketbook).

A formula diet uses a liquid, powder mixture, or food bar to replace eating. Formula diets such as *Slender* differ from liquid protein because they include other nutrients besides protein. A typical formula diet, like *Slender,* contains (in one-half pound powder or 40 fluid ounces liquid) 900 calories, 44 grams of protein, 20 grams of fat, 136 grams of carbohydrate, and all the recommended daily requirements of vitamins and minerals.

With a formula diet, you do not have to measure portions or count calories: you know exactly how many calories and nutrients are contained in each "meal."[1] In addition, a formula diet keeps you away from the table,[2] thus eliminating temptation. However, you eventually must return to normal eating, and a formula diet does not help your habits.

On a formula diet, you drink 40 fluid ounces in four 225-calorie "meals" instead of eating. You must take a glass of formula in the morning, to begin the day with protein and other nutrients. Also, you should drink additional fluids such as water, coffee, and clear bouillon to prevent constipation.[3] Even so, on an all-formula diet, you may well have (besides constipation) gas, diarrhea, nausea, and abdominal cramps.[4]

A diet of liquid formula combined with a low-calorie menu is nutritionally and psychologically better than a formula diet alone. One such combination diet includes:[5]

Breakfast
Formula (one glass)
Tea or coffee

Lunch
Lettuce and tomato salad
  (any amount)
Clear bouillon (any amount)
1 cup asparagus or broccoli or
  greens
2 ounces meat or poultry
½ slice bread
½ cup skim milk or buttermilk or tea
  or coffee

Dinner
Same as lunch except add ½ cup
  of a vegetable such as peas,
  beets, or carrots, one fruit,
  and eliminate milk

Late Evening Snack
Formula (one glass)

After you have gotten used to the food intake from this combination diet, you can go on a low-calorie diet that leaves out the formula.

The first formula product was *Metrecal* in 1959. Magazines in 1964 carried ads explaining, "You'd have to avoid the sugar in about 200 cups of coffee to save the calories necessary to lose one pound. You can lose weight a lot faster with *Metrecal* dietary. You can even do it on just one or two *Metrecal* meals a day. Safely. Simply. Without feeling hungry. Over 5,000,000 dieters have been satisfied with the results."

Average weight loss in tests of the *Metrecal* liquid formula was about six pounds the first week for those who took *Metrecal* alone. For those who took *Metrecal* and followed a low-calorie diet, the average weight loss after the first six weeks was 16 pounds (ranging from 8 to 25 pounds).[6]

LIQUID PROTEIN

About a decade later came another magic liquid you drank in place of food to "melt pounds away." It, too, gave you all the nutrition its proponents said you needed.

So appealing was this fairy tale in the mid-1970s that millions of otherwise reasonable people bought the potion in hopes of becoming "the fairest of them all."

But the fairy tale turned into a horror story. The potion known as "liquid protein" did not provide enough protein on which to live, and as many as 60 dieters died as a result.

In 1978, the US Center for Disease Control described the health risk pattern associated with the use of liquid protein as the primary source of calories for more than two months: "This pattern is characterized by either sudden death or death due to intractable cardiac arrhythmias in individuals with no previous history of heart disease."[7]

Shortly after CDC's report, a widower sued the most publicized promoter of liquid protein, Robert Linn, D.O., for the sudden death of his 35-year-old wife, who had dropped from 238 to 132 pounds while taking liquid protein. This suit was just one of the rash of legal proceedings.

Until his promise of quick weight loss turned thousands to his magic elixir, Dr. Linn was simply an osteopath from Broomall, Pennsylvania, a suburb of Philadelphia. As he explained in his book *The Last Chance Diet* (written with Sandra Lee Stuart),[8] Robert Linn was fat as a child. His mother pushed her homemade noodles on him; in school, he was a junk food addict. In 1959, when he graduated from the Philadelphia College of Osteopathic Medicine, he was chubby. By 1966, when he was 32 years old, he weighed 230 pounds (at 5'11").

As he explained, "I turned to the medical texts, only to find the diet literature primitive and depressing. I began to experiment on myself. One type of dieting versus another—until finally, six months later, I was down to 165 pounds."

How did he do it? He did not really say in the book. But at some time he discovered what he called *Prolinn* (protein + Linn), which he described as "a formula composed of all the amino acids needed to form a protein molecule." In his book, Dr. Linn said, "The formula is protein extracted from beef hides." However, he told us, "Liquid protein is derived from sow underbelly as well as beef hides." (That makes it unacceptable to many Jews and Muslims.)

Prolinn was made by Wallach Pharmaceuticals, Bryn Mawr, Pennsylvania—one of the many manufacturers or distributors of liquids containing amino acids. Similar but specially formulated liquids have been used by hospitals for years to feed seriously ill patients (including those suffering from cancer).

However, the only liquid protein mentioned in either the hardcover or softcover editions of the Linn and Stuart book was *Prolinn*. And nowhere in their book did Linn and Stuart tell you where or how to buy it. (It was originally available through physicians, although it was not a prescription item.)

Perhaps the authors wanted to avoid the legal wrangle Herman Taller, M.D., incurred for promoting sales of safflower oil through his book in 1967. Nonetheless, in December 1976, the New York state's attorney ordered Dr. Linn's hardcover publisher to refund the purchase price to customers because ads "failed to disclose that a formula called *Prolinn* was an indispensable part of the prescribed diet and that it could not be obtained except through the author."

Dr. Linn then donated the *Prolinn* name to a nonprofit foundation and published the formula. As a result, *Prolinn* was no longer sold only through doctors, and other brands were made available over the counter.

Soon, *Prolinn* and *Windmill* were found on drugstore shelves. Joining these two were *Gro-Lean, Ran-Tein, T-Amino, LPP, E.M.F.,* and *Pro-Fast.* In addition, Weight Loss Centers and Shape-Up Centers that sprouted in Tampa, Philadelphia, Chicago, and other metropolitan areas sold their own brand of liquid protein, *Nu-Trim/20.* Diet Control Centers offered another version, *Multi-Protein Slim* powder.

Liquid protein became such a hot sales item that most drugstores could not keep it in stock. Druggists loved the item too; it helped sell pills. Dieters on the liquid protein diet had to take supplements of potassium, folic acid, and vitamin C, plus a multiple vitamin-mineral supplement. They also had to drink 2½ quarts of fluid a day — coffee, tea, water, noncaloric soda pop.

Liquid protein worked, according to Dr. Linn, because it was a "modified fast." He called it "protein-sparing" because it was supposed to spare the protein in muscles, glands, and vital fluids. Two tablespoons (one fluid ounce) of liquid protein provided 60 calories. Most people took it several times a day, consuming around 105 grams of protein for 420 daily calories. At this near-starvation level, the body soon used its sugar supplies of glycogen in the liver, then turned to stored fat. The modified fast was intended to prevent a serious complication of total fasting: deterioration of the muscles of the body—including the vital organs.

The idea of providing a protein-sparing formula food largely belongs to Alan N. Howard, Ph.D., head of the Lipid Laboratory, Cambridge University, England. It was Dr. Howard who organized the First International Congress on Obesity in 1974. At this meeting, nutritional scientists seemed to favor the protein-sparing, near-starvation diet, then known as the Mini-Calorie Diet.[9]

Dr. Howard explained to CONSUMER GUIDE® that "complete starvation was in vogue 15 years ago in America and Britain. But then five deaths due to starvation were reported, and many obesity centers gave it up. You can't deprive people of all food for six to nine months and not expect problems. Their bodies steal protein from their hearts."

In 1975, Dr. Howard and a colleague, I. McLean Baird, M.D., were searching for a diet between 0 and 1000 calories that would do the best and the safest job. Howard and Baird admitted five patients to West Middlesex Hospital, London, and tried them on a variety of diets. All five were started on only water, vitamins, and minerals—zero calories, in other words. The doctors monitored the patients' blood and urine to see at which point their bodies started stealing protein from tissues. It occurred at just under 25 grams of daily protein. (The National Academy of Sciences — National Research Council recommends 56 grams of protein a day for men, 44 grams for women.)

Then Drs. Howard and Baird gave their five subjects carbohydrates and a reduced amount of protein to see if there was any effect. There was, indeed. As Dr. Howard told CONSUMER GUIDE®, "There was a dramatic response. With 30 grams of carbohydrate a day, a person only needs 15 grams of daily protein." (This finding has not been widely accepted among nutritional authorities.)

In his book, Dr. Linn gave copious credit for the development of the protein-sparing modified fast to George L. Blackburn, M.D., Ph.D., of Boston. Dr. Blackburn is Associate Professor of Surgery at Harvard Medical School, Director of the Intensive Care Unit and Nutritional Support Service of the New England Deaconess Hospital, and a Senior Research Associate in the Department of Nutrition and Food Science at the Massachusetts Institute of Technology, across the river at Cambridge. He is also Scientific Director of Nutritional Management, Inc. at Boston. He had nothing to do with liquid protein.

Dr. Blackburn's idea, the protein-sparing modified fast,[10] was intended to take fat off safely, while preserving muscle tissues and other vital body protein. While liquid protein provides 75 grams of protein a day, it is deficient not only in calories, but also in vitamins and minerals; so you must supplement food with daily multiple vitamin-mineral tablets, plus calcium and potassium. The modified fast allows you to eat only lean meat, plus low-calorie bulk. But he concluded that "it is not recommended that modified fasting be used as the sole method of therapy, since the worst results occur in the patient who does not participate in a multifaceted effort."[11] As a matter of fact, Dr. Blackburn found that the patients who participated in a program of education, exercise, and diet did the best; they were more likely to take off pounds and keep them off.

Dr. Blackburn was the first to voice concern about the safety of liquid protein. And he feared that the public had bought the idea that "salvation from obesity can be found in a bottle of liquid protein. If a modified fast is an adjunct to behavior modification, nutritional education, and exercise, then I have no quarrel." Unfortunately, that's not how *The Last Chance Diet* was being marketed. He was worried that people may fast for prolonged periods on the assumption that intake of liquid protein makes it perfectly safe.[12]

It certainly was not perfectly safe. Dietitians reported on patients whose metabolism went into a tailspin with liquid protein. Others told of patients who suffered apparent kidney damage. The extraordinary, artificially high load of protein given to the body every day — approximately double the daily need for women — placed a heavy stress on the body that was already under extreme stress due to the minimal caloric intake. The body was struggling to survive in a near-fast state; then, suddenly, it had to process all that protein. Only healthy persons with healthy kidneys and livers could survive.

In addition to risking all of the evils rained upon a body not able to endure the metabolic state caused by starvation, many people risked developing or worsening gallstones.[13]

There were other hazards as well. Taking supplementary folic acid every day may hide symptoms of pernicious anemia. In other words, someone on liquid protein could have pernicious anemia but not know it, and his doctor would have no particular reason to look for it.

Another matter of safety had to do with the rather sloppy way liquid protein was derived from the hides of slaughterhouse animals and bottled. More than once in 1977, the US Food and Drug Administration and various local health authorities confiscated contaminated inventories.

Besides production problems, the big question was: Why did Linn want you to take a low-quality protein made from collagen, the same raw material used to make gelatin? Egg white, milk protein, and meat are far better, more complete sources of protein. According to Dr. Blackburn, "The most profound disadvantage of most of the liquid protein formulas is that those made with collagen are of extremely low biologic value even when fortified with the amount of [the essential amino acid] tryptophan specified and should not serve as the sole source of protein in a diet without studies confirming their usefulness."

CONSUMER GUIDE® has three major criticisms of liquid protein diets. The first concerns the quality of the protein furnished. The chart below will give you an idea of liquid protein's poor quality. Derived as it is from animal hides, it lacks the same "complete-protein" composition of muscle, not only cattle (beef), but also fish, shellfish, poultry, and other land and water animals. Protein also can be derived from soybeans, nuts (such as peanuts), and grains (wheat), as well as from milk.

All of the animal protein from muscle and milk contain the eight (nine for babies) amino acids that the human body cannot make and therefore are

PROTEIN COMPARISONS

SOURCES
(in grams per 60 grams of protein)

Essential amino acids	Daily needs of 154 lb man (in grams)	Prolinn (240 calories)	Gelatin (250 calories)	Skim milk (600 calories)	Dry beef (363 calories)	Tuna fish (272 calories)	Beans (913 calories)
Lysine	0.84	2.6	2.64	4.74	5.22	5.28	4.44
Tryptophan	0.21	0.26	0.0*	0.84	0.72	0.60	0.54
Phenylalanine	0.98	1.4	1.26	2.94	2.46	2.22	3.30
Methionine	0.70	0.44*	0.48*	1.5	1.5	1.74	0.6*
Threonine	0.56	1.2	1.2	2.82	2.64	2.58	2.58
Leucine	1.12	1.8	1.8	6.0	4.92	4.56	5.16
Isoleucine	0.84	1.44	0.84	3.9	3.12	3.06	3.42
Valine	1.12	1.4	1.5	4.2	3.36	3.18	3.66
TOTALS	6.37	10.54	9.72	26.94	23.94	23.14	23.70

*Deficient amount

called "essential amino acids." Nuts, grain, and legumes—in other words, vegetable sources of protein—are not as high in quality because they are often low or deficient in one or more amino acids.

What is important in protein as a food is that the amino acids be supplied in the proportion in which the body needs them to make its own protein. In fact, your body makes only as much protein as the smallest amount of amino acid provided. All other amino acids in food are converted to carbohydrate and are immediately used for energy or are stored for future energy use.

As the table indicates, *Prolinn* (according to the data provided by Dr. Linn in his book) is nutritionally similar to gelatin, which is derived from collagen and is processed from animal hides. Both are deficient in the amino acid methionine. Gelatin is devoid of tryptophan, but tryptophan is added to liquid collagen which is then flavored and sold as liquid protein.

If you look at the totals in the table, you will find that gelatin and liquid protein provide the lowest total amount of essential amino acids, far lower than provided by skim milk, dry beef, tuna fish, and beans.

The totals are of the essential amino acids in the same amount of protein eaten. This means that all of the rest are essentially thrown away. For instance, in 60 grams of liquid protein, only 10.54 grams are essential amino acids. And the body cannot use all that to make protein, since there is an insufficient amount of methionine.

The second major criticism of Dr. Linn's Liquid Protein Diet is that it is temporary and unreal. He has said that he wanted to remove the feel of food, the chewing sensation. However, dieters must eventually return to chewing food. And when they do, they usually return to their old nibbling, overeating habits.

Of course, Dr. Linn made the disclaimer that his diet should only be followed under a physician's guidance. But, as Marshall McLuhan said, "The medium is the message." The medium here was a paperback book sold on bookstands and newsstands. It was intended for everyone to buy and use and not just to be dispensed by doctors.

The third criticism is the serious health risk posed by a liquid protein diet plan. Even if the protein were complete, there would be dangers. Semi-starvation and modified fasting, like full starvation, severely deplete the body's stores of potassium. Muscles, especially the heart muscle, need potassium to function and are profoundly affected by its lack. Many people who bought Linn's book and liquid protein did not heed the cautions to take the vitamin-mineral supplements. These people risked becoming seriously ill on this diet.

In the final analysis, the Liquid Protein Diet was just another name for near-fasting. In fact, government researchers now believe that the 60 deaths associated with it were the direct result of starvation. At the National Heart, Lung, and Blood Institute near Washington, D.C., Jeffrey M. Isner, M.D., headed a research group studying 17 deaths associated with liquid protein. He reported that the dieters suffered "from the classic consequences of semistarvation: decreased electrical activity of the heart and [thinner and discolored fibers in the heart]."[14] Dr. Isner suggested that "extreme dieting itself may somehow alter hormonal output from the central nervous system, thereby setting these catastrophic events into motion."

The Cambridge Plan

The hottest formula diet today is the Cambridge Diet, first explained to consumers on these pages more than three years ago. It was invented by the same Dr. Alan Howard, nutritionist at Cambridge University, England (hence, the name of the diet) who originally developed the idea of a protein-sparing formula food. The diet you buy today is a third generation descendant of the mini-calorie diets he first used with patients at his university's Addenbrooke Hospital. Dr. Howard started testing his first formula on overweight hospital patients a decade ago, and published his results.[15,16] His mini-cal soup (see the chapter, Fasting It Off) evolved into a powder you could mix in a glass. Original flavors were Chicken Soup and Double Dutch Chocolate.

In 1980, Beaumark Enterprises, of Pebble Beach, California, began marketing Dr. Howard's powder formula under the name of The Cambridge Diet. Beaumark had previously been successful selling home exercise equipment by mail. Its president, Jack Feather, wanted to market an ideal diet to accompany the stretch-springs when, while visiting England in 1976, he heard about Dr. Howard's research and arranged to visit him. They struck a deal and in February 1980 Feather's company, which also employed his wife, Eileen, head of a chain of "figure salons," and their son, Vaughn, began marketing the formula by mail. Its mail-order life was short-lived, however. The US Government and the Postal Service in 1980 filed a lawsuit against Howard, Feather, Beaumark, and others, claiming the diet was a "serious risk to health," and that the defendants had conspired to defraud the public through the mails.

The legal suit was dropped when the Cambridge people agreed in a consent decree not to market by mail, to tone down claims, and to place a warning on labels and product literature. It tells you to "consult your doctor before starting this diet," and that dieters who are children, adolescents, elderly, pregnant, nursing, or have any of a list of medical conditions should either be under a doctor's care or not be on the diet. The warning also states that you shouldn't be on the diet for more than four weeks at a time, in any case.

Their problems with the government and the post office didn't frustrate the Cambridge Diet promoters. They, instead, became creative about its marketing. Instead of being sold by mail-order, it would be sold person-to-person. It would not be sold by doctors or pharmacists or grocery clerks, but by a network of "counselors" who would build up their own customer lists from friends, and fellow workers, and, in turn, *their* friends and fellow workers, and other contacts. Vaughn Feather, president of Cambridge Plan International, now headquartered just outside the airport at Monterey, California, told CONSUMER GUIDE® that his organization has 125,000 counselors. They sell the powders, which now come in ten flavors (chocolate is still the most popular), on a pyramid system. It is modeled after that of Amway Products, the multibillion-dollar household cleaning products empire.

Here's how the Cambridge system works. A person succeeds in losing weight on the Cambridge Plan. She tells friends about her success, then arranges to get some of the formula to sell to them. At this point she attends leadership training sessions sponsored by the plan, and, finally, becomes a bona fide Cambridge Counselor. As such, she distributes the total daily nutrition to her group or groups of dieters—$17.50 for a week's supply—and "counsels" them about their diets, and cooking, perhaps handing out Cambridge Plan recipes.

The pyramid forms when successful dieters in her group decide they also want to spread the word and also reap some profits. She then becomes the distributor to them. And they, in turn, form their own groups, whom they sell to; and, from them, yet another generation of counselors may be born. All the while, the profits have been filtering up to the original dieter-counselor.

Thirty-four-year-old Vaughn Feather, a 6-foot 1-inch, 185-pound model of trim fitness, says he is amazed at the phenomenally rapid growth of the Cambridge Plan. To date, more than one million dieters have been on the "program." Half of them are located in the West Coast states of California, Oregon, and Washington, but the program has moved eastward in what he calls a wave effect. "We develop counselors in an area, then the media grab hold and publicize us, and our sales explode. We develop another new area, and the same thing happens," Feather explained.

Analysis of a day's worth of the Cambridge Plan powder reveals that it supplies 100 percent of the Recommended Daily Allowances of vitamins and minerals, but only 33 grams of protein and 330 calories. Even though the protein is high quality, derived from soybeans and milk, its quantity falls significantly short of the National Academy of Science's recommendations (56 grams a day for men, 44 grams for women who are neither pregnant nor nursing). Feather and Dr. Howard say that this 33 grams of high-quality protein is adequate for dieters, as it maintains nitrogen balance (a means of determining that the body is getting enough protein). However, Dr. Howard's overweight research subjects were all studied under the dietary controls of a hospital-based weight loss plan.

Deficient as it is in protein and calories, the Cambridge Plan is an extreme way to lose weight, according to most experts and the US Food and Drug Administration (FDA). The American Society of Bariatric Physicians warns that very low calorie preparations such as Cambridge "pose a significant health hazard to dieters not under *continuous and immediate* medical supervision by a physician knowledgeable in the metabolism and nutrition of such diets. Such supervision includes appropriate laboratory evaluation at regular intervals."[17] (Italics theirs.) The American Dietetic Association issued a news release stating that "the 330-calorie-a-day diet is not a 'common sense' approach to weight loss and should not be undertaken without strict monitoring of a medical professional."[18] The publication *Nutrition and the M.D.* called Cambridge "potentially dangerous" in its August 1982 issue. An FDA consumer affairs officer said that dependence on so few calories for an extended period may result in serious adverse health effects. Serious illness and death have implicated Cambridge in several reports to the FDA and in the news media.

Defending the Cambridge Plan, its public relations agency, New York-based Hill and Knowlton, maintains that at least several such reports in 1981 and 1982 were erroneous. In three cases, involving hospitalization, the Cambridge Plan was exonerated. In a case in Oklahoma City a newspaper that linked the death of a dieter to Cambridge, was sued for libel as the woman had not been on Cambridge, according to Hill and Knowlton.

Also defending Cambridge, Vaughn Feather told CONSUMER GUIDE® that counselors are urged to inform their local medical societies of the Plan and to stress to new customers that they need to have at least a physical examination before undertaking Cambridge. If the customer doesn't have a family doctor, the counselor is supposed to offer a list of local doctors, obtained from the medical society, Feather said.

He also points to Dr. Howard's research and to four American centers where research on Cambridge is being conducted, under funding from the Cambridge Quest Foundation: University of Southern California, Stanford University, University of Denver, and University of Virginia.

CONSUMER GUIDE®'S EVALUATION

No one should go on a diet as severely close to starvation as Cambridge, unless he or she is under strict medical supervision, and then, probably only as a hospital patient. If you must use Cambridge, for some reason, use it only for breakfast and lunch, then have a protein-rich dinner and take supplementary vitamins and minerals. Rating: Not recommended. No stars.

CAMBRIDGE IMITATORS

Once a fad takes hold, it stimulates imitations. One such is the University Diet, promoted and sold by the General Nutrition Corporation. "Graduate to a New Slim You in just 4 Weeks!" scream GNC's ads for the University Diet. "Lose as much as 20 lbs. in 4 weeks or your money back! A delicious 110 calorie meal replacement and nutritional supplement with the delicious chocolate taste." (Vanilla, strawberry, and banana flavors are also available.) In addition, GNC appeals by offering a lower price in its vitamin stores than Cambridge—$14.99 for a 24.8-ounce can that contains all the nutrition you'll get for a whole week, formulated to copy the 330 daily calories of the original.

CONSUMER GUIDE®'S EVALUATION

Imitating zero gets zero. Rating: Not recommended. No stars.

Medifast, Optifast, Nutrimed, Proti-15

Even before there was a Cambridge Plan—in fact as early as 1973—there was a Medifast Program. It was started at Mt. Sinai Hospital, Cleveland, under the direction of Drs. Saul M. Genuth and Victor Vertes. They gave very overweight patients who came to the Saltzman Institute for Clinical Investigation what they called a "supplemented fast." During a week in the hospital as patients, they ate no food, but instead took feedings of a flavored powder mixed in water. Five servings gave each patient 45 grams of high-quality protein (derived from milk and egg whites), along with all the vitamins and minerals they needed, some carbohydrate, and very little fat. Total calories: 320 a day.

As a result of this hospital-supervised near-starvation, men lost an average of 5 pounds, and women 3.2 pounds for the week. After they were discharged, the patients were continued on *Medifast* for months, and were required to come to the hospital to get it. There they were weighed, tested, and counseled. Average overall weight loss was 85 pounds per dieter.

Hundreds of doctors around the country now offer overweight patients *Medifast,* which they obtain in three flavors (chocolate, vanilla malt, and orange) from the Jason Co. of Baltimore, MD. In 1982, Jason came out with a new formula, *Medifast 70,* which gives the dieters 70 grams of protein a day, and a total of 420 calories. Dieters can obtain either kind only from a doctor under whose care they place themselves. These doctors, in turn, can only offer the Medifast Program after they have been through a Medifast medical educational program.

Optifast 70, made by the Delmark Co. of Minneapolis, is a similar product, also distributed only through qualified physicians. It comes in vanilla, chocolate, cherry, and orange flavors as well as beef and chicken flavored soup and offers 70 grams of protein (derived from milk and egg whites) and a total of 320 calories a day.

Nutrimed is yet another Medifast imitator, sold in three flavors (chocolate, vanilla, orange) to diet doctors by Robard Corporation of Cherry Hill, NJ. Its protein is derived predominantly from egg white, which happens to be the best source of protein for human beings. Total calories per day, from five feedings, are 300.

Proti-15 has two flavors to choose from, chicken and pea. Made and distributed to doctors by Bariatrix International, Inc., Montreal, Quebec, Canada, each packet of powder to be mixed with water yields 15 grams of protein (from soy and milk), only a trace of fat, and three grams of carbohydrate in the chicken flavor and eight grams of carbohydrate in the pea. The calorie total is 70 for the chicken, 90 for the pea. Four such "meals" a day can give you enough protein (60 grams) for the day, but little else.

CONSUMER GUIDE®'S EVALUATION

As long as these ultra-low-calorie formulas are distributed only to physicians, for use with patients under their supervision, CONSUMER GUIDE® feels they may be non-harmful. However, two problems remain. One is the likelihood that the products will find their way to diet consumers through a gray market. The other problem is that near-starvation using formula diets, even done under a doctor's care, does nothing to help you learn how to eat properly so that you can lose weight and keep it off for life. More about that in a little bit. Rating: ★★

Formula diets were criticized by AMA spokesman Philip L. White, Sc.D., Secretary of the Council on Foods and Nutrition, soon after *Metrecal* became widely popular.[19] First, he questioned the claim that all nutritional needs were supplied by the formula. "Since the formula diets are intended to supply all of the nutrients needed by man," he wrote, "they raise the question of how much we know about man's total nutritional needs...We cannot say that the formula diets supply man with total nourishment until much more information has been gathered on individuals who have subsisted on the formula for long periods of time."

In addition, he noted that:

The formula diets by themselves do not supply enough water to meet the body's needs. If the user of a formula diet consumed no other fluids, dehydration of his body could result...

The public has been given the impression that the 900-calorie diet is a painless, permanent, perfectly safe way of losing and controlling weight. There is no question that an individual subsisting on the formula alone would lose weight. However, the Council is not convinced that the formula diets alone constitute a rational approach to weight control in the seriously overweight.

One of the most important goals in any long-term weight control program is that of educating the individual in good and bad eating habits. This type of education is best achieved by building the diet around ordinary foods. A 900-calorie formula diet is a preparation which in no way resembles the overweight person's ordinary diet. Consequently, the user of a formula diet will never learn why the foods he has been eating have caused excess weight....

And he is likely to regain lost weight.

In addition, Dr. White warned that any sudden and radical change in diet, such as to a formula, can be dangerous for people with undiagnosed diabetes, gastrointestinal troubles, liver or kidney diseases, anemia, or some heart conditions.[20]

Dr. White's point, that dehydration could occur, needs emphasis. However, most formula diets today stress the need for large quantities of liquid in the form of clear bouillon, tea, water, coffee, or dietetic soda pop.

Dr. White's final comment is very important. New eating habits — a change in your entire approach to food, cooking, mealtimes, and snacks — are absolutely necessary for a successful diet and maintenance program. A formula is not a means of learning new eating patterns, and for this reason it must not be considered anything but a temporary crutch. As a crutch, and a starting point for a diet, the formula approach seems a relatively safe one. As with every other diet, we stress the importance of a visit to your doctor before you begin—the difference between safety and danger often lies in this initial step. In particular, if you have peptic ulcer, gout, diabetes mellitus, or cirrhosis of the liver, you have no business going on this diet (or any other) without having a long talk with your doctor first.[21]

Cutting Calories

Y ou can curse them, ignore them, lie about them, believe diet pitchmen's fables about them, but they won't go away. Calories, that is. Their abundance is the reason you have gained weight; therefore, they have to be made scarce in order for you to lose weight.

Despite the fanciful dreams of "melting fat" overnight, there is no better way to lose weight than slowly, by cutting back on calories, while maintaining a balanced diet that gives you all the nutrients you need.

There. That is the secret, the essence, the Absolute Truth about dieting. All else is decoration, or fancy footwork, or sparkle to dazzle the eye, usually to extract greenbacks from your billfold.

Unfortunately, cutting calories is also the most undramatic way to diet. Some consider it downright boring. No fireworks explode, no electronics flash, no choruses harmonize. But fat comes off, slowly and surely.

To understand why calorie cut-back works, you must first learn about that entity, the calorie.

MEET THE CALORIE

Every food that your body "burns" produces some heat. This potential to cause heat is measured in calories. You burn calories just by sitting, just to provide the energy to power your body's life processes. If you perform any physical activity — shovel snow, walk around the block, swim, do housework, carry a package, play tennis—you use even more calories.

One way to look at the way to burn your calories is to think of the way you use your checking account. You start with a given amount of fat on your body, or money in the bank. Eating is like making a deposit; you add to the amount on hand. If the amount of food you eat equals the energy your body needs, or your deposits equal your withdrawals, your weight— or your bank balance—remains the same.

When you burn more calories than you consume, you start slimming down. If, for example, you eliminate one piece of bread and one pat of butter a day, you will end up not depositing 3500 calories this month. That represents a pound of fat. Easy arithmetically, but difficult in practice.

Eliminating calories can be aided by increased activity: in other words, exercise. If you decide to count calories, be sure to set up your own exercise plan. Select the physical activity that you like best and can do most frequently—be it calisthenics, jogging, cycling, swimming, or walking the dog—and do it regularly.

CONSUMER GUIDE® cautions that a low-calorie diet must include foods that are not merely low in calories, but are also nutritious. Philip L. White, Sc.D., former director of the Department of Foods and Nutrition of the American Medical Association (AMA), advised: "Foods should never be evaluated strictly on the basis of their caloric value. The inclination of the dieter is to exclude foods which appear to be of high-caloric value and to choose only those which are low. The result is frequently a 'low-calorie diet' which is limited in important nutrients."[1]

Dr. Jean Mayer, of Tufts University, wrote: "A proper diet must provide all necessary nutrients in sufficient amounts, be palatable, easily available from the viewpoints of economics and convenience, and be limited in calories so as to produce the desired caloric deficit."[2]

CALCULATING YOUR TOTAL CALORIES

Before you start counting calories, you have to find out how many calories you need per day. To be accurate, you must do some arithmetic. A small electronic calculator will help.

Here's a quick and sloppy guide: If you cut down 500 calories a day, you'll lose a pound a week. Make it 1000 calories, and you'll lose two pounds a week. This applies whether you want to lose ten pounds or 100 pounds.

Of course, this guideline assumes that your physical activities won't change much. Also, it means you have to know how many calories you were consuming before starting your diet. The best way to find out is to keep an accurate diary of what you eat, how much, and when. (If you forget food, you'll only be cheating yourself.) To lose a few pounds, just cut back on your daily calorie total. As long as you eat fewer calories than it takes to maintain your weight, you'll lose. (Unless you are very obese, that is. Markedly overweight persons maintain their obesity on surprisingly moderate caloric intakes. Still, if they decrease caloric consumption enough, they too will lose.)

Since you probably weigh more than you should, figure how many pounds you want to lose a week and do a little more arithmetic. The AMA suggests that two pounds a week is a safe rate of weight loss, one that is not liable to leave you grumpy, tired, or difficult to live with. There are 3500 calories in a pound of fat. So, if you want to lose two pounds a week, you have to cut back 7000 calories a week, or 1000 calories a day.

Now, most people want to lose a lot of weight fast. If you wanted to lose five pounds in each of the first few weeks, you'd have to reduce your food intake by 17,500 calories each week (3500 cal/lb x 5 lb), that is, take in 2500 calories a day less. This reduction would be practical only if you weighed 250 pounds or more and wanted to reduce to, say, 200 pounds. This proves that diets that promise 5-pound-a-week weight losses make false claims of fat loss for most dieters.

But this is just an arithmetic exercise. *You should not normally go below 1000-1200 calories a day, unless you do so under a doctor's supervision.* With so little food, you may not get enough minerals and other necessary nutrients.[3]

The AMA says a person leading a moderately active life needs 15 calories per pound every day. For instance, if you are a man and you weigh 150 pounds, you should take in 2250 calories a day to maintain that weight. Many more calories and you'll gain fat; significantly fewer calories and you'll lose fat.

You can calculate the number of calories you need to maintain a desirable weight by multiplying that weight by 15. Actually, 15 is an average. If you lead a very sedentary life, you should use 12 as a multiplier, in which case you need 1800 calories a day to maintain a weight of 150 pounds.[4]

Not everyone can trim down the low-calorie (or low-cal) way, but many people can—and do. A medical nutritionist at Cornell University, Charlotte M. Young, M.D.,[5] studied successful low-cal dieters, evaluated who was most successful, and came up with some valuable insights. These insights actually became criteria for success on low-cal diets. Dr. Young found that the successful calorie counters were:

• Emotionally well-adjusted
• Not overly fat
• Fat as an adult but not as a child
• On a weight-reducing diet for the first time
• People with some meaningful reason to become thin

In her study, Dr. Young found that the most successful low-calorie diets fulfill five rules. CONSUMER GUIDE® strongly suggests that you study them and be sure your low-calorie diet — either taken from a book or computed with your calorie guide—follows them.

1. The diet should provide all the nutrition your body needs, except calories.
2. The diet should come as close as possible to your tastes and habits of eating.
3. The diet should protect you from between-meal hunger, give you a sense of well-being, and not make you feel tired.
4. The diet should enable you to eat at home and away from home without feeling like a freak.
5. The diet should be one that you can live with for the rest of your new, thin life.

CALORIE-CUTTING HELPERS

Industry is responding to dieters' needs to cut back on calories, a need that pervades our society because of the popularity of the thin figure as ideal. As *FDA Consumer* magazine noted, "Pickings are no longer slim for dieters these days. The shelves in the diet section of supermarkets are now groaning under the weight of new products promising good taste but fewer calories."[6] Even the traditional no-no's such as wine and beer, pancakes and syrup, salad dressings and soda pop come in *diet* or *lite* or *light* versions. The food and beverage producers have reformulated them so as to maintain flavor as much as possible, while eliminating such calorie-costly ingredients as sugar, alcohol, fats, or oils.

FDA (the US Food and Drug Administration) in 1980 passed rules to regulate the labeling of these foods and drinks for your protection. Thus, a "low-calorie" food must supply no more than 40 calories per serving. A "reduced-calorie" food is at least a third less in calories than, but nutritionally the same as, similar, non-reduced, foods. Also, any food claiming to be "reduced-calorie" has to bear a label showing how it compares with an identical unmodified food.

Some diet foods are labeled as "imitation" because they are so modified that they cannot meet the government's standards for that food. An example is imitation margarine or imitation mayonnaise, which contain lots more water than the standard, unmodified versions.

"Light" foods are usually reduced or low in calories, but not always. Light foods may have other properties, as well. For instance, light chocolate is paler in color because of its increased milk or cream. Light whiskey is paler than regular whiskey because it is aged in new oak containers rather than in charred ones. But light cream has reduced milkfat content (18 to 30 percent).

Beer and wine are regulated by the US Bureau of Alcohol, Tobacco, and Firearms (BATF) rather than the FDA. BATF's guidelines (rather than rules) suggest labeling that compares light versions with standard versions of wine and beer. But this comparison is not required, as it is for food under the FDA. Usually, light beers are a third less in calories than standard beer; about 70 to 100 calories per 12-ounce serving. Light wines run 50 to 60 calories per wineglass (3.5 ounces), compared to 65 to 80 calories for regular dry wines. Beers and wine become light by having alcohol and/or carbohydrates removed from them. Light beers average 2.7 to 3 percent alcohol by weight (compared to 3.6 for regular beer) and light wines average 7 to 8 percent (compared to 12 percent for regular).

Diet versions of foods that are usually sweet, such as soda pop and syrups, have artificial sweetener replacing most or all of the sugar or corn syrup used in standard versions. Usually the sweetener is saccharin. Saccharin is also available in individual packets for sweetening coffee and foods. In 1981, after years of investigation and controversy, the FDA approved G.D. Searle & Company's aspartame (Equal) for sale as a tabletop sweetener and as a sweetener to be added to certain dry foods.

Electronics are also in the diet act. There is a digital readout bathroom scale which memorizes last week's weight so you can immediately tell how well (or poorly) you are doing on your diet. Its long memory accompanies a high price. (Digital Memory Scale, No. PR747, $119 plus shipping, available from The Sharper Image, Mail Order Department, PO Box 26823, San Francisco, CA 94126-6823)

There are at least several hand-size calculators with built-in programs and memories to count the calories you consume as food and expend as exercise every day. Some also have built-in height/weight charts. Three heavily advertised ones are:

Diet Trac, Olympia Sales Co., 216 South Oxford Avenue, Los Angeles, CA 90004, $59.95

Cal Count, PO Box 1600, Springfield, VA 22151, $69.95 plus postage and handling ($72.45 total)

Comus C-6, Taylor Marketing, 5851 South Vermont Avenue, Los Angeles, CA 90044, $39.95, plus $2 shipping

Simpler to use, and free, is the Slide Guide to Weekly Weight Loss offered by the Lemmon Co., PO Box 30, Sellersville, PA 18960. It comes with a thin booklet which lists low-calorie portions and menus and a useful food exchange list. You can write for it yourself, or ask your doctor to get one for you, since Lemmon is a pharmaceutical company whose representatives call on physicians.

GOVERNMENT'S CALORIE CUT-DOWN

Your federal government has, at last, recognized your need to diet to lose weight. First, there were the important recommendations from the US Senate's Select Committee on Nutrition and Human Needs. *Dietary Goals for the United States*[7] actually is not a diet, per se, but guidelines for everyone's diet. Its principles consolidate findings of the best nutritional research to date.

These are now summarized in the free pamphlet, *Nutrition and Your Health*[8], but not as well. The pamphlet is a watered-down compromise issued by the government after the considerable controversy over *Dietary Goals*. This was attacked by the meat industry, the dairy industry, the salt industry, the sugar industry, and other commercial interests, as well as by the giant of the medical establishment, the American Medical Association. But it has been staunchly defended by the American Heart Association, leading nutritionists, and others in the scientific-nutrition community.

In the judgment of CONSUMER GUIDE®, its recommendations are sound. We agree with D.M. Hegsted, Ph.D., former professor of nutrition at the Harvard School of Public Health, Boston, now in Washington with the US Department of Agriculture, who wrote in 1978, "To the best of our knowledge then, overconsumption of food but particularly fat—especially saturated fat—of cholesterol, of sugar, and salt are contributors to the most important health problems of Americans and other affluent societies.... If the proper dietary recommendations are not those specified in the *Dietary Goals*, they are certainly something very similar."[9]

Dietary Goals for the United States is a distillation of the recommendations of top food and health experts in the nation (and some from abroad) who provided written and oral testimony to Senator George McGovern (D-SD) and the Select Committee on Nutrition and Human Needs, which he headed.

The report addresses itself to the overweight, stating that "obesity resulting from the over-consumption of calories is a major risk factor in killer diseases. Therefore, it is extremely important either to maintain an optional weight or to alter one's weight to reach an optimal level."

Says the report, "Obesity is associated with the onset and clinical progression of diseases such as hypertension, diabetes mellitus, heart disease, and gall bladder disease. It may also modify the quality of one's life."[10]

In addition to losing weight and keeping it off, the committee recommends six other dietary goals:

1. Increase the consumption of complex carbohydrates (starches) and "naturally occurring sugars" (in fruits) from 28 percent of daily total calories to 48 percent.
2. At the same time, decrease the amount of refined sugar every day, to 10 percent of daily calories.
3. Eat less fat (from 40 percent of daily calories to 30 percent).
4. Balance the kinds of fats so that 10 percent of daily calories are saturated fats (such as butter or meat); 10 percent are mono-

unsaturated fats; and another 10 percent are polyunsaturated fats (such as safflower or corn oil).

5. Hold daily cholesterol consumption to 300 milligrams a day (slightly less than the amount in one egg yolk).
6. Eat no more than 5 grams of table salt a day.

To achieve these goals, the report recommends you eat more fruits, vegetables, and whole grains and eat less refined sugar, high-fat foods, especially meat, eggs, butter, ice cream, and other high butterfat dairy foods, and replace them with skim or low-fat milk.

The report also stresses that you shift from potato chips to baked potatoes; from canned fruit and vegetables to fresh; from white bread to whole wheat bread; from instant white rice to brown rice; and from sugar-coated breakfast cereals to plain cereals.

The recommended diet calls for 12 percent (by calories) protein content but increases the amount of carbohydrates beyond that in the average American diet (from 46 percent to 58 percent), while decreasing the amount of fat (from 42 percent to 30 percent).

In practical terms, on a 1200-calorie-a-day reducing diet, you would be eating: 144 calories of protein, 696 calories of carbohydrate, and 360 calories of fat. In quantity, you would be eating 36 grams of protein, 174 grams of carbohydrate, and 40 grams of fat.

You may immediately see the problem here: not enough protein. As an adult, you need more protein or a total of 44 grams for women and 56 grams for men. The calculations are all right for a 2000-calorie maintenance diet. But on a diet to lose weight, with restricted calories, you need more protein.

The solution is simple: Replace some of the fat and carbohydrate calories with protein. To do this without raising fat calories, replace meat with high-protein legumes (beans), skim milk, yogurt, and egg white.

When doing your arithmetic, remember that proteins and carbohydrates are four calories per gram; fat is nine calories per gram. Treat alcoholic beverages as carbohydrates.

CONSUMER GUIDE®'S EVALUATION

CONSUMER GUIDE® has found that the US Senate Diet is the best thing out of Washington in a long time. Rating: ★★★★

COOKING À LA DIETARY GUIDELINES

Shortly after the Senate report appeared, dietitian Margaret Dean, nutrition consultant to the American Red Cross, published a volume offering menus and recipes that follow the committee's recommendations and including a copy of the newer version of *Dietary Goals for the United States*. A sample diet from her *Complete Gourmet Nutrition Cookbook*[11] follows.

**A SAMPLE DIET FROM THE COMPLETE GOURMET
NUTRITION COOKBOOK**

Breakfast

	Calories
Hot cereal (½ cup)	84
Raisins (1 T)	44
Non-fat milk (½ cup)	44
Bread (2 slices)	176
Peanut butter (½ T)	86
Total	434

Lunch

	Calories
Chopped chicken in broth (¼ cup)	50
Cucumber salad (⅔ cup) with oil and vinegar (2 tsp)	25
Crisp lettuce (¼ head)	4
Vegetable fat (1 tsp)	38
Grapefruit (½)	82
Total	199

Dinner

	Calories
Baked tomato (1) with grated cheese	75
Creamed spinach (¼ cup) with almonds	100
Bran muffin (1)	91
Vegetable fat (1 tsp)	38
Cole slaw (½ cup)	100
Fresh fruit (½ cup)	61
Total	465
Total daily calories	1,098

CONSUMER GUIDE®'S EVALUATION

Solid and imaginative. Rating: ★★★★

Food and Food 2

Back in 1979, the US Department of Agriculture published *Food*[12] designed to be a regular magazine telling consumers the truth about food, nutrition, diets, and health. But a funny thing happened with the subsequent issues on the way to the printers. The federal government yielded to food industry pressures brought to bear on the government because the publications recommended foods lower in fats and cholesterol. To the rescue in 1982 came the American Dietetic Association, publishing *Food 2* and *Food 3*.[13] (Both are available for $7.50 plus $2 shipping from the ADA, PO Box 91403, Chicago, IL 60693.)

Food 2 is a basic dieter's guide which you may find helpful. It takes up where *Food* left off. Specifically, *Food* offered 1200-, 1800-, and 2400-calorie menus, plus details of 300-, 400-, and 500-calorie "good" breakfasts. It also had 30 pages of recipes, each tagged with total calories per serving. *Food 2* is completely devoted to dieting. It tells you the basics about calories in food, exercise, nutrients, kinds of food to eat on a diet, and how to change habits. It also offers 1200-, 1500-, and 1800-calorie daily menus, plus 22 pages of recipes—each labeled with total calories, total fat, saturated fat, and cholesterol per serving. (A sample of the diet is included at the end of the chapter.)

Food 3 deals exclusively with total fat, saturated fat, and cholesterol in foods. It explains these substances, then tells you which foods to cut back on.

CONSUMER GUIDE®'S EVALUATION

Food and *Food 2* offer solid and basic information for getting started on a lifetime diet plan. No frills or schlock here. Rating: ★★★★

US Army Lifetime Diet

Having advised the civilian population on nutrition and dieting, the federal government then turned to its military personnel. Specifically, at the headquarters of the US Army Transportation Corps, Fort Eustis, VA, about 120 miles southeast of the Pentagon, a diet, exercise, and behavior modification program was set up in 1981 for Army personnel. In a year, 300 soldiers shed a collective 6000 pounds — about 20 pounds per person, on the average.

The well-rounded Army Lifetime Diet was designed by Captain Myra Endler, a nutritionist and food-service administrator at the base. The diet provides 1200 calories per day for women, 1500 for men. The meals are not skimpy, but satisfying without being excessive in calories. (Two days' worth of the Army diet is offered at the end of this chapter.)[14]

CONSUMER GUIDE®'S EVALUATION

Follow its commands. Rating: ★★★★

US Dietary Guidelines: George Does It

When you read the promising book by the First Lady of Kentucky, Former Miss America Phyllis George, you may be put off by the initial cuteness and by ten pages of testimonials from the learned and the famous. You also may be put off by the Introduction to *The I Love America Diet*[15]:

> Hello. I'm Phyllis George Brown. I'm a career woman, a mother, and the wife of Governor John Y. Brown, Jr., of Kentucky.
> I created this book with Bill Adler because I wanted to bring you information from the United States Government Agencies that could change your life for the better. It's information about being slim and energetic...
> I'm Bill Adler. I'd like to tell you why Phyllis George Brown is the ideal person to bring this good news to you.

Other parts of this uneven book give good, basic textbook-like information on food groups and nutrients (both those that help and those that hurt you). Also, there are 57 pages of recipes, taken (with attribution) from *Ideas for Better Eating* and *Food*, both published by the US Department of Agriculture.

The strength of the George-Adler approach is that it stems directly from the *Dietary Goals for the United States* and the *Dietary Guidelines for Americans*. There is little better. In effect, the authors have gathered diet information from various government sources and put it all together in a palatable, usable form. There is a 1200-calorie reducing diet for women and a 1600-calorie reducing diet for men, as well as weight-maintenance diets — 1600 calories for women, 2400 calories for men. Makes you wonder why the US government itself didn't put this together. (A day's worth of this diet is included at the end of the chapter.)

CONSUMER GUIDE®'S EVALUATION

Everything is solid about this diet. Still, it is not as imaginative as Margaret Dean's *Complete Gourmet Nutrition Cookbook* (see above), or Weight Watchers' diet (see below). Rating: ★★★★

Dr. Rechtschaffen's Diet

Joseph S. Rechtschaffen, M.D., who has been in practice since 1945, (that's all the book tells about him) became famous for putting *The New York Times* Food Editor Craig Claiborne on a low-salt diet. He also has a book to help you lose weight. This is a direct quote: "In February 1980 the United States government issued the first federal dietary guidelines ever. The guidelines were published jointly by the Department of Agriculture and the Department of Health, Education, and Welfare. The guidelines, which may be the first step toward a national policy on nutrition, *coincide with principles of the Rechtschaffen Diet in every way*." (Italics his.)[16]

On his diet, you can expect to lose two pounds a week, according to Dr. Rechtschaffen. Also, he says, you will have a lower chance of getting cancer and heart disease. His four weeks of diets emphasize foods low in salt and fat and high in fiber. Yet they allow enough protein, thanks to tuna, chicken, turkey, veal, and yogurt—the dieter's staples. It also emphasizes use of whole-grain cereals and fill-you-up starches such as rice and baked potato.

MONDAY'S MENU

Breakfast
Grapefruit (½)
Whole-grain cereal (½ c) with plain yogurt or low-fat milk, or 1 slice whole-grain bread with low-salt, low-fat cheese
Tea, coffee, decaffeinated coffee or low-fat milk (1 c)

Lunch
Water-packed low-salt tuna (3½ oz) with scallions, lemon and salad greens
Whole-grain bread (2 slices)
Tea, decaffeinated coffee or low-fat milk (1 c)

Dinner
Pineapple Watercress Cocktail
Broiled fish
Parsley potatoes, boiled
Tossed green salad with dieter's French Dressing
Almonds or filberts (6 unsalted) with a fresh fruit
Tea, decaffeinated coffee or low-fat milk (1 c)

CONSUMER GUIDE®'S EVALUATION

Despite its strutting, this is a good diet to lose weight on and to stay on. It provides recipes and menus. Monday's menu is shown above. Rating: ★★★★

The Prudent Diet

Before the *Dietary Goals,* and after, there was and is the Prudent Diet, the mother of them all. This progenitor of all sensible, controlled-calorie diets was introduced back in 1957 by the late Norman Jolliffe, M.D. Dr. Jolliffe designed what he called the Prudent Man's Diet[17] for members of the Anti-Coronary Club, a group that met at the New York City Health Department. The thousand middle-aged members of this club were all high risk (that is, very likely to develop heart disease) when they joined. After following the Prudent Diet, their blood pressure came down, their bodies slimmed down, and the rate of heart attacks was cut in half.[18]

The Prudent Diet is a balanced, low-calorie diet which is also low in saturated fats and cholesterol. It calls for a total of about 2400 calories a day (compared to the American average of 3200), with less than 35 percent of these calories derived from fats (as compared to the national average of 40 to 50 percent), an increased proportion of protein, and a reduction in carbohydrates and salt.[19]

In their 1973 recipe book, *The Prudent Diet,* authors Iva Bennet and Martha Simon explained that the diet means "curtailing excessive intake of fat meats, high-fat dairy products, eggs, hydrogenated shortenings, and foods containing any of these ingredients; consuming more fish and shellfish; and substituting polyunsaturated vegetable oils and margarines for butter, lard, hydrogenated shortenings and other saturated fats. The top-rated Prudent Diet advocates neither excessive use of nor complete omission of any food."[20]

There are many hidden fats in foods, and fats pack the most calories per gram and ounce. For instance, 80 percent of the calories in hot dogs are due to fat content. Here are the calorie contributions of fat in some other foods: cream cheese, 91 percent; sour cream, 88 percent; American cheese, 73 percent; hamburgers, 64 percent; Danish pastry, 56 percent.[21] The accompanying chart[22] shows some visible and hidden fats.

**VISIBLE AND INVISIBLE FATS
IN THE AMERICAN DIET**

Visible fats	Pounds of fat consumed per person per year
Butter (fat content)	4.5
Lard (direct use)	5.4
Margarine (fat content)	8.4
Shortening	15.9
Cooking and salad oils	12.7
Other edible fats and oils	2.5
Total visible fats	**49.4**

Invisible fats	Pounds of fat consumed per person per year
Dairy products, excluding butter	16.8
Eggs	4.2
Meat, poultry, game and fish	41.1
Dry beans, peas, nuts, soya flour, and cocoa	6.1
All fruits and vegetables	1.1
Grain products	1.7
Total invisible fats	**71.0**
Total visible and invisible fats and oils	**120.4**

The Prudent Diet is concerned with this 120-pounds-of-fat-per-person-per-year figure. While allowing 35 percent of the daily food intake to be fat, the diet does insist on polyunsaturated fat and not for reasons of calorie count alone. In fact, saturation or unsaturation of fats does not affect their caloric content. For instance, the total calories in butter (saturated) and margarine (unsaturated) are about equal. Frying food in corn oil or shortening adds the same number of calories.

The reason Dr. Jolliffe insisted on polyunsaturated fats is that he, and many other doctors and scientists, believe the polyunsaturated fats like corn oil, peanut oil, vegetable oil, margarine, and so on, are better for, and kinder to, your heart and blood vessels than are saturated fats like butter and shortening.

In addition to *The Prudent Diet,* two books, *The American Heart Association Cookbook* and *What You Need to Know About Food and Cooking for Health,* can help you plan low-cal, low-saturated fat meals.[23, 24] Also, through your local heart association or the American Heart Association, you can obtain a free booklet of low-fat recipes and hints on how to cook to keep saturated fat at a minimum.[25]

CONSUMER GUIDE®'S EVALUATION

CONSUMER GUIDE® strongly recommends the Prudent Diet and these publications. Rating: ★★★★

The New York City Health Department Diet

The Anti-Coronary Club gave the New York Health Department a tremendous amount of data on the Prudent Diet. As a result, the diet was refined and published as a pamphlet by the Bureau of Nutrition, Department of Health, City of New York. CONSUMER GUIDE® finds the diet in this pamphlet to be a low-cal, low-saturated fat diet which is easy to live and comply with.

The pamphlet offers two exchange plans: a 1200-calorie diet for "most women and small frame men" and an 1800-calorie diet for "most men and large frame women." CONSUMER GUIDE® reprints the diet at the end of this chapter.

CONSUMER GUIDE®'S EVALUATION

This diet is top-notch. Rating: ★★★★

AFTER PRUDENT: DESCENDANTS

From the fountainhead of Jolliffe's Prudent and New York City diets came streams of diet plans. Some were good, some were better, but some were pale and pitiful imitations.

The l Love NY Diet

The newest, and worst, is *The I Love NY Diet.*[26] Written by a former Miss America and her literary agent, this diet loosely but not smartly adapts the Prudent Diet to their own uses. Bess Myerson (who is a former Consumer Affairs Director of New York City) and Bill Adler impose such twists of their own as alternating crash dieting with eating splurges or "holidays." In numbers, that's respectively 600 and 1800 calories a day. Furthermore, the Myerson-Adler diet is internally inconsistent, since it is rigid in its requirement of *what* foods you eat, but then leaves up to you *how much* of these foods you will eat. (And everyone who is overweight knows he or she lacks good judgment where quantity of food is concerned!)

Unlike the original New York City diets, Myerson's and Adler's has never been scientifically tested. Unlike the original New York City diets, Myerson's and Adler's is very rigid; the originals treated the dieter like an adult and allowed flexibility. Nor were the originals presented as tasks from which the dieter had to vacation; splurges were not included because of their preposterous implications.

Some of Dr. Jolliffe's disciples have expressed the opinion that he would be turning over in his grave to hear of this new corruption of his concepts. And the hype: "Powerful fat-destroying principles are built into the diet."

Still, there are some virtues to the *I Love NY Diet.* It *is* low in fat and high in fiber. While it tells you calorie counting is unnecessary, it does give lists of food by calories and fiber. It offers suggestions and menus for low-calorie dining out. And there is some good advice on slow eating and other modifications of your bad eating behavior.

CONSUMER GUIDE®'S EVALUATION

A Son-of-Jolliffe it is not. Rating: ★★

Redbook's Wise Woman's Diet

Redbook Magazine changed the gender of the Prudent Man's Diet, calling it the Wise Woman's Diet.® The 1200-calorie diet (there is also a 1000-calorie version for small people or those who want to lose more quickly) was originally put together by George Christakis, M.D., who had worked with Dr. Jolliffe. It has been published in *Redbook* two or three times each year since it was introduced in 1967. With it each year are new recipes approved by Dr. Christakis, who now practices in Florida and serves as consultant to that state's health department.

Over the years, other nutrition experts have served as consultants on this diet. Among them: Johanna Dwyer, M.D., director of the Frances Stern Nutrition Center, New England Medical Center Hospital, Boston; Jules Hirsch, M.D., professor and senior physician to the Rockefeller University Hospital, New York City; Myron Winick, M.D., director of the Institute of Human Nutrition, Columbia University, New York City; and Judith S. Stern, Sc.D., director of the Food Intake Laboratory at the University of California at Davis, who has supervised the preparation of *Redbook*'s 1983 version of the Wise Woman's Diet.® To obtain the latest *Redbook*'s Wise Woman's Diet® called "The Weight-Loss Diet for Your High-Energy Life," write to: Food Department, *Redbook Magazine*, 230 Park Avenue, New York, NY 10169. However, seven day's worth of menus appear at the end of the chapter.

CONSUMER GUIDE®'S EVALUATION

Redbook's diet is indeed wise. It meets the best specifications, and it is a diet that you and your family can live on for the rest of your life. Rating: ★★★★

OTHER DESCENDANTS

Dr. Christakis also authored (with the help of science writer Robert K. Plumb) an excellent pamphlet that explains the New York City Health Department Diet and its use. Simply called *Obesity*, the pamphlet is available at no cost from the Nutrition Foundation.[27]

Another of Jolliffe's former colleagues, Morton Glenn, M.D., of New York City, has written two books on dieting. The first is dedicated to the memory of his teacher, Dr. Jolliffe, who died in 1961. Both books—*How to Get Thinner Once and for All*[28] and *But I Don't Eat That Much*[29]—present a section of carefully designed Prudent Diet plans. You pick your diet according to your gender, your activity level, your weight, and how much weight you want to lose.

CONSUMER GUIDE®'S EVALUATION

It's a sensible balanced kind of diet you can follow and live on for months. Rating: ★★★★

Diet for Life

Francine Prince is a cooking authority and wife of Harold Prince, the author who helped the authors of *The I Love NY Diet* (see above). After he recovered from a heart attack, he went on the Prudent Diet, but found few good recipes to make the low-fat foods exciting or even palatable.

Working with Jolliffe's rules plus a few others, Francine put together a mighty mountain of menus which toe the line yet taste great. They are gathered in her book, *Diet for Life*.[30] The daily menus each add up to 1250 calories—with 20 percent fat, 20 percent protein, and 60 percent carbohydrates—even a bit lower in fat than the Prudent Diet. "I could begin to create," she wrote "my new haute cuisine of health using only healthful ingredients." Her diet and menu plans are even more healthy and easier to stay on that Jolliffe's, she maintains.

CONSUMER GUIDE®'S EVALUATION

Seems sensible. Rating: ★★★

Vitamin Diet for Quick & Easy Weight Loss

Francine Prince went further out on a limb in her next book, also based on Jolliffe, but with yet more twists of her own. If the title— *Vitamin Diet for Quick & Easy Weight Loss*[31]—puts you off, no wonder. If its title is slick, its premise is slippery. Yet again incanting Jolliffe's name, Prince "updates" it by adding what she calls "optimal quantities of vitamins." Call it a Super Prudent Diet, she writes. More hyperbole is offered when she calls vitamins "magic diet pills." According to Francine, your SDA (Slimming Daily Allowances) general guidelines include: 1000 milligrams of Vitamin C, a multiple vitamin product (5000 IU of A, 400 IU of D, 30 to 100 IU of E), plus B-50 complex, which contains Vitamins B_1, B_2, B_3, B_6, B_{12}, biotin, choline, folic acid, inositol, PABA, and pantothenic acid.

Great Jolliffe's ghost, how his name is misused! Nowhere is there one iota of data to show that vitamins either take off, or even help you take off, pounds or help turn down the appestat (appetite regulator), as Prince claims.

CONSUMER GUIDE®'S EVALUATION

Pay no homage to this Prince. Rating: ★★

The Wine Diet

Don't let the name of this diet fool you. It is actually a well-conceived orchestration of the Prudent Diet theme with a wine solo. Written by a physician, who has long specialized in the medicinal properties of wine, and a home economist (aided by a nutritionist), *The Wine Diet Cookbook*[32] contains 28 menus, each giving a day's total of 1200 calories, along with recipes for making each dish. Each menu's caloric total includes, of course, a glass of dry table wine at dinner. The reason, explains author Salvatore P. Lucia, M.D., professor emeritus of medicine at the University of California School of Medicine, San Francisco, is "that persons voluntarily and even unwittingly reduce the amount of food they eat when wine is served."

His premise is based not only on personal observation, but on a telling study conducted by Giorgio Lolli, M.D., president of the International Center for Psychodietetics of New York City and Rome. Dr. Lolli found that drinking wine at dinner kept dieters from raiding the refrigerator later.[33] He found that the caloric expense of dry wine (about 90 calories) was more than worth it, since wine reduced the amount of food calories consumed at the table, as well as later in the evening. He attributed this reduced food consumption to wine's natural tranquilizing effects, which also helped his subjects sleep.

Dr. Lolli says wine (dry wine only) is also beneficial for heart patients and diabetics, as well as for people with malabsorption problems. It is not for anyone with an active bleeding ulcer, however.[34]

Dr. Lolli found in his study that for best results wine should be taken with dinner or after dinner. If taken before dinner, as an aperitif, it is likely to stimulate the appetite, and you may eat more than you intended.

Using wine as a condiment for cooking foods, as well as a marinade, also will enhance the flavor of otherwise bland foods. It adds few calories, since the alcohol boils off at 172°F leaving mainly the flavor behind.

Besides watching calories, the Wine Diet also watches cholesterol and saturated fats. The authors explain that "of the 14 lunches and dinners per week, no more than five feature red meat [beef or lamb and occasionally liver or pork]. The remaining nine lunches and dinners feature fish, poultry, or veal. The reason for restricting red meats is that they contain more animal [saturated] fat than the white meats [fish, poultry, and veal]." As for eggs, "no more than three per week."

The Wine Diet dares not only to include wine in recipes and in the glass but also to offer some unusual breakfasts, such as pizza-toast, frankfurters, and sardines on rye.

Why 1200 calories? The author's answer: "Because at this calorie level it is possible to include the basic elements needed for good nutrition and still give the slimmer a chance to average as much as a two-pound loss per week."

CONSUMER GUIDE®'S EVALUATION

The *Wine Diet Cookbook* is one of the best diet books around. Because it can be used even by those who prefer not to sip or even cook with wine, it is recommended for all. Rating: ★★★★

The Yogurt Diet

Like the Wine Diet, this diet is a modification of the Prudent Diet with a special twist. Here, it is the liberal use of yogurt as the dairy dish. Yogurt happens to be good food. In every eight ounces of yogurt made from skim milk are 150 calories, 12 grams of protein, some carbohydrates, 4 grams of fat (2 of the saturated kind), a modest 17 milligrams of cholesterol, a respectable amount of Vitamin A, and lots of calcium and phosphorus.

These quantities apply only to plain, unsweetened yogurt. Yogurt with fruit has double the amount of calories, because of the added sugar. If you want flavored yogurt, buy plain yogurt and mix in some cinnamon, flavoring, or diet jelly.

The Dannon Company offers two good booklets that list yogurt diets that make sense. One—*Dieting, Yogurt, and Common Sense*[35]—offers two diets for 900-1000 calories a day and for 1500-1600 calories a day. The yogurt is built into the diet at breakfast, as the mid-afternoon snack, and, in the hearty version of the diet, as the bedtime snack.

Developed by food editor Wiletta Warberg and nutritionist Rose Mirenda, the seven-day menu plans are high in lean protein and low in cholesterol, saturated fat, and refined carbohydrates.

Here is a sample 1000-calorie-per-day diet:

Breakfast
Small glass of prune juice
Container plain yogurt
Slice whole wheat toast
Small pat margarine
Coffee or tea

Midmorning Snack
4 dried apricot halves

Lunch
4 canned sardines (drained of oil)
½ hardcooked egg
Wedge of lettuce, slice tomato
Slice whole wheat toast
Plain coffee or tea

Midafternoon Snack
Container plain yogurt

Dinner
3 slices breast of chicken (baked, broiled, or stewed) plus the liver
½ cup cooked spinach
¼ cup rice
Plain coffee or tea

Bedtime Snack
Glass skim milk

The other booklet, *The Yogurt Way to Diet*, was written by Dr. Morton Glenn (see above). Half the booklet is spent advising you how to alter your eating and exercising habits for the better. The second half offers a week of diets for men and for women. Yogurt, explains Dr. Glenn, "is a cultured milk food with a thick consistency, which tends to be filling and satisfying. It is eaten slowly with a spoon, giving your satiety mechanism a time to react properly. At lunch, between meals, or in place of a rich dessert, yogurt will help resist the temptation to overeat. It is also easy to digest."

Here is his diet for men and for women on Monday.

Breakfast

Women
4 oz. orange juice
2 oz. cottage cheese
1 slice whole wheat or whole grain toast (dry)
Coffee or tea*

Men
4 oz. orange juice
2 oz. cottage cheese
1 slice whole wheat or whole grain toast (dry)
Coffee or tea*

Mid-Morning Snack

Coffee or tea* if desired

Coffee or tea* if desired

Lunch

Women

1 container plain yogurt
1 hard boiled egg
1 slice whole wheat or enriched
   white toast
Small green salad with lemon juice
Coffee, tea, or diet soda

Men

1 container coffee, lemon or vanilla
   yogurt
2 hard boiled eggs
1 slice whole wheat or enriched
   white toast
Small green salad with lemon juice
Coffee, tea, or diet soda

Mid-Afternoon Snack

1 container plain, coffee, lemon, or
   vanilla yogurt

1 container fruit yogurt

Dinner

4 oz. tomato juice or clear soup
3 oz. broiled fish
8 spears asparagus or 8 brussel
   sprouts
½ cup carrots
Mixed green salad with lemon,
   vinegar, or diet Italian dressing
Coffee or tea*

4 oz. tomato juice or clear soup
4 oz. broiled fish
8 spears asparagus or 8 brussel
   sprouts
½ cup carrots
Mixed green salad with lemon,
   vinegar, or diet Italian dressing
Coffee or tea*

Bedtime Snack

4 oz. frozen yogurt or
   yogurt-on-a-stick
*Black or with skim milk only, no sugar

4 oz. frozen yogurt or
   yogurt-on-a-stick

CONSUMER GUIDE®'S EVALUATION

Good diet, if you like yogurt. Rating: ★★★★

Harbor Island Spa Diet

Also based on the Prudent Diet is that of the Harbor Island Spas of New Jersey and Florida.[36] In fact, Norman Jolliffe, M.D., is said to have designed this spa's original diet. Barbie Fillian contributed to the diet by creating recipes to fit its original parameters. In their book, she and Lida Livingston offer the spa's current menus, plus recipes.

If you can cut through the schmaltz at the beginning of the book, and duck the barrage of celebrity names they throw at you (Jackie Leonard, Steve Lawrence and Edie Gorme, Petula Clark, Richard Tucker, Buddy Hackett, and Olive Oyl, to name but a few of the famed thousands who have passed through these doors), then you might make it to the rather reasonable 600-, 800-, and 1000-calorie menus and recipes.

CONSUMER GUIDE®'S EVALUATION

A fairly good diet for those who like to cook. Rating: ★★

Canyon Ranch's Low, Low Diet

Yet another spa diet is that of Tucson's Canyon Ranch Vacation/Fitness Resort which is the work of diet consultant Jeanne Jones and fitness director Karma Kientzler.[37] With a wagonload of exercises, they offer a low-low diet that begins with 520 calories of liquid and moves up to 700 and 800 daily calories. After you are down to weight, you go on a 1500-calorie daily diet.

CONSUMER GUIDE®'S EVALUATION

The Canyon's dangerously low. Even if you have saddlebags, ride on by. Rating: ★★

La Costa Spa Diet

This diet was conceived for, and is used by, the La Costa Spa, located at Carlsbad, California, just north of San Diego. Offered daily to the rich and famous who frequent La Costa, the diet is also available to everybody else in book form.[38]

With the help of the late Marjorie Aichele, who was chief dietitian at La Costa, R. Philip Smith, M.D., created plans for 800, 1000, and 1200 daily calories composed of 25 percent protein, 30 percent fat (with predominantly polyunsaturated fats), and 45 percent carbohydrates.

With Dr. Smith's permission, we are including the basics of the La Costa Diet at the end of this chapter. (For the complete diet plan, see his book.) Thorough as it is, Dr. Smith's book doesn't tell you everything. Following are some secrets learned during a visit to La Costa.[39]

1. Make a meal—even a diet meal—special by putting out the linen and silver and crystal and by serving each course on china. Garnishes are very important. Use chopped parsley and cherry tomatoes and lemon slices to put color and contrast on each dish. Never serve a dry piece of meat or fish. You can do wonders with a simple sauce of natural juices, nonfat dry milk powder, and paprika. Or try blender-whipped cottage cheese as a mayonnaise substitute.

2. Dine luxuriously. That means dividing the meal into four or five courses and serving one course at a time, with plenty of time between each course. Never prepare anything at the table, even salad. Keep tea and coffee cups, water and diet soda glasses full. But don't serve alcohol; it is not permitted.

3. Serve an abundance of fresh fruits and vegetables. Crisp salads fill you, and ripe fruits satisfy the sweet tooth while yielding far fewer calories than sandwiches and pastry. Better food stores sell fresh fruit and vegetables year-round, but you have to be willing to pay the stiff off-season prices.

4. Fool the palate and please the eyes, while cutting back calories. You can make egg white omelets in a Teflon-coated pan. Make salad dressing of yogurt. Use no fat, sugar, starch, flour, or salt in cooking. Use a salt substitute, along with fresh pepper and lemon wedges.

   Keep portions down in size but serve them on a small plate resting on a nest of two larger plates. Some foods can be served on a thick bed of lettuce to achieve the same effect. Instead of a baked potato, have half a baked potato shell, garnished with a sprinkling of Parmesan cheese, chives, and caraway seeds.

5. Pamper yourself in ways other than eating. Join a health club so you will have a place to exercise regularly, get rubdowns and special baths. Splurge on a facial massage and a manicure, whether you are a man or woman. Wear nice clothes and spend the time shopping for them.

CONSUMER GUIDE®'S EVALUATION:

This is an excellent diet for home or Spa. Rating: ★★★★

Longevity Diets

While Jolliffe's Prudent Diet is the only one tested and analyzed for its effects on health, others have made similar claims without any scientific backing. The Pritikin Diet (see chapter "Losing Via Vegetarian") is one, but there are other diet proponents in this category who have jumped on the bandwagon driven by the American Heart Association.

For instance, Sidney Petrie, in his book, *The Wonder Protein Diet,*[40] agrees with the AHA about cutting calories and fats and lowering the intake of foods high in cholesterol. He means, as does Pritikin, eating egg whites rather than yolks, chicken breast without skin, some veal but no beef or pork, lots of fish, skim milk and its products, and whole-grain foods. The *Wonder Protein Diet* is quite a reversal for this author, who a decade or so ago touted a diet of whipped cream and martinis!

Kenneth S. Keyes, Jr., wrote a diet book a decade ago that also promised longer life through dieting.[41] Keyes provided instructions for devising your own weight-loss diet. And his formula of 15 percent of calories from protein, 25 percent from fat, and the remaining 60 percent from carbohydrates is still reasonable and acceptable.

CONSUMER GUIDE®'S EVALUATION

Despite their promotion, these diets are on the right track. Diets low in fat (and especially in saturated fats), moderate in proteins, and high in complex carbohydrates, which also control calories, are the best food prescriptions against heart disease and cancer. But diet can't prevent disease, nor can it prolong life. It is but one of the factors involved which you have control over. So, too, you have control over smoking, stress, and your environment. But you have no control over your heredity and only some control over your blood pressure. Only if all of the factors are in your favor will you live a long and healthy life. These books don't tell you that, but your physician will. Rating: ★★★★

The Revolutionary 7-Unit Low Fat Diet

Another low-fat approach to cutting calories was devised by two editors of Great Britain's *Slimming* magazine, Jean Carper and Audrey Eyton. In their book, *The Revolutionary 7-Unit Low Fat Diet*,[42] they explain that "you can quickly and easily lose weight—and keep it off—by doing only one thing: restricting the amount of fat in your diet." Since the highest calorie foods are those which contain fat (at nine calories per gram), the idea is to cut down, or cut out, those foods. Among them are nuts, cheese, butter, margarine, meat fat—all of which yield about 150 calories per ounce, more than double even the highest caloric starches and sugars.

The British diet allows you only seven fat units a day. You determine how many fat units are in a food by consulting a list which Carper and Eyton provide. Here's a sampling:

Food	Fat Units	Food	Fat Units
Candy, hard and mint, 1 oz.	4	Ground beef, lean, 3 oz.	3
Gelatin, sweetened, ½ cup	3	Ham, lean, 3 oz.	3
Bread, 1 regular slice	½	Milk, 2%, 1 cup	1½
American cheese, 1 oz.	3	Almonds, chopped, 1 T.	1½
Cottage cheese, regular, ½ cup	2	Chicken, light meat, no skin,	
Halibut, 3 oz.	½	3½ oz.	1½
Salmon, filet or steak, 3 oz.	2	Pretzels, 1 oz.	½
Avocado, California, ½	6½	Yogurt, low fat, 1 cup	½
Margarine, butter, 1 T.	4		

CONSUMER GUIDE®'S EVALUATION

Simple in concept, the 7-Unit Diet is a good guide for those who already have some control over their eating. The information is concise and specific. But it is not complete enough for most people who want to start on a full weight-loss program. It offers little to hang on besides the list of foods and a smattering of general advice. Therefore, a rating of mediocre, at best. Rating: ★★★ for its old low-fat approach to calorie control.

Diet for Food Lovers

Jeanne Jones, who writes cookbooks (including one on the Fabulous Fructose Diet), says she loves food, yet she is slim. Her secret? She eats everything she likes—but less of it—and few foods with fats and cholesterol. Or, to put it another way, she emphasizes complex carbohydrates and low-fat proteins. She mentions Canyon Ranch Resort of Tucson several times, which may make you suspicious of her motivation, if not backing. Essentially, *Jeanne Jones' Food Lover's Diet*[43] is a cookbook, filled with good techniques for eliminating fats and oils. A sample: "Whenever your first thought is to add butter, either for serving or cooking, think stock instead. There is nothing more delicious on a baked potato than a few tablespoons of beef or chicken stock. When using a recipe specifying butter or oil for sautéing vegetables or meats, simply substitute stock in the recipe. The same mixtures of herbs and spices and other condiments that can be added to butter can also be combined with stock for a lighter, even more delicious result..."

Here is a day's sample of the Food Lover's Diet:

Breakfast Every Day
½ grapefruit or 1 orange
Whole-grain bread or whole-grain
  cereal
½ cup non-fat milk or plain non-fat
  yogurt; or ¼ cup low-fat cottage
  cheese, hoop cheese or partially
  skimmed ricotta cheese
Coffee or tea

Monday Lunch
Raw vegetable relish tray or bag of
  vegetables
½ cup low-fat cottage cheese, hoop
  cheese or partially skimmed
  ricotta cheese
Fresh fruit
Whole-grain bread or whole-grain
  pasta
Coffee or tea

Monday Dinner
Tossed salad (as much of any of the
  fresh greens or vegetables on your
  Free-Food List as desired) with
  lemon juice, or vinegar or a Jones
  Dressing
4 ounces broiled or poached fish or
  seafood
Brown or wild rice or whole-grain
  bread
Banana or available fresh fruit
½ cup non-fat milk or plain non-fat
  yogurt
Coffee or tea

CONSUMER GUIDE®'S EVALUATION

If you're going low-fat, this is a good diet. Rating: ★★★

Mary Ellen's Diet Hints

Lots of women know of Mary Ellen, the lady with those helpful household hints. Well, this Minneapolis housewife was able to help every other housewife in America but herself, when it came to fat. When she was married at 23 she weighed just under 130 pounds. (She's 5'5"). Six months later her weight was at 160. During her pregnancy she snacked on Big Macs, so when her baby Andrew was born, she weighed 193 pounds. Five years later, she weighed 208, had high blood pressure, and a fast heart rate. In January 1982, she put herself in the care of Dr. Joel S. Holger and, with his help over the next year, lost 80 pounds.

The valid premise of Mary Ellen's approach is that you have to take charge of your own eating. She and Dale Burg, co-author of her book,[44] are quite right in saying that fad diets don't work because dieters place their complete faith in them instead of in themselves. She explains, "So I felt it was time somebody wrote a book that told the truth. No magic formula. No gimmicks. Just the assurance that it works. It takes a lot of effort, but I learned to Help Myself. And you can learn to Help Yourself, too."

Mary Ellen's eight-step plan, in brief, is to start on 1000 calorie-a-day diets and stick to them until you are within four pounds of your goal weight.

Then you switch to 1200 calories until within two pounds of goal. At goal you increase to 1400 calories. If you slide below your goal weight (you should be so lucky!!!) you increase calories.

She gives you two-weeks' worth of 1000-calorie menus, with lots of kitchen cooking hints. The self-selection diets are her own form of an exchange diet. Also in the book are her 44 Best Diet Tips, such as Quit Procrastinating, and Don't Take Guff from Waiters.

CONSUMER GUIDE®'S EVALUATION

A sensible, well-rounded low-calorie approach to dieting, but deficient in whole-grain foods. Rating: ★★★

Eating à la Canadian

The Canadian Diabetes Association has a neat approach to losing weight and maintaining weight loss. It is a simple meal plan that you could follow, even if you are not Canadian and/or not diabetic. It comes in 1200-, 1500-, and 1800-calorie versions and follows the guidelines of: carbohydrate, 45 percent or more; fat, 35 percent or less; and the rest protein; high in fiber, low in cholesterol, and moderate in sodium.

For more information, and especially the Good Health Eating Guide poster, pamphlet, or book, write: Canadian Diabetes Association, 123 Edward Street, Suite 601, Toronto, Ontario, M5G 1E2, Canada. The phone number is: (416) 593-4311.

CONSUMER GUIDE®'S EVALUATION

Tops. Rating: ★★★★

Eating like a Thinner

Jack Sprat could eat no fat—so, he was skinny. So do other skinny people know how to eat. If you imitate them, you'll be skinny, too. That's the premise of *How to Eat Like a Thin Person*.[45] After showing you how to compute your daily calorie needs, authors Lorraine Dusky and J. J. Leedy, M.D., give you some good, calorie-reducing practices to learn. For example, in a French restaurant eat an artichoke if you must be sociable and have an appetizer. In a Chinese restaurant, order steamed fish. In an Italian restaurant, order the antipasto as the main course of your meal. Everywhere, stay away from fried food—even egg rolls and tempura.

The book also encourages you to exercise and gives you some pointers on changing your behavior. Among them:

• Drink a glass of water before each meal
• Cut your food into small pieces
• Select foods which take longer to eat
• Eat large salads and use lemon juice instead of dressing

CONSUMER GUIDE®'S EVALUATION

Good information, especially if you eat out a lot. But there is not much here to hang your meal plans on. Rating: ★★★

Dachman's High, Medium, Low Choices

Ken Dachman, who lives in a Chicago suburb, managed to lose 235 pounds and get on TV and tell everyone how he did it. So then he wrote a book to give even more details.[46] First, he shows you how to compute your daily caloric needs. He then gives you choices of low-, medium-, or high-calorie diets, at, respectively, 1075, 1445, and 1775 calories per day (or, as he lists them, 7525, 10,115, and 12,285 calories per week).

The difference between his diet and all others, Dachman maintains, is that others cater to specific moods, while his is flexible enough to cover all your moods. In other words, you went on diets in the past because they appealed to you when you were in the mood for them; once the mood left, you dropped the diet. Not so with his diet.

"The 'No Excuse Diet,' which is the diet you are going to be following, is adaptable and suitable to *anyone's* needs, regardless of their age, sex, weight, bone structure or lifestyle." There is simply no excuse for not staying on his diet, says Dachman.

The Dachman Secret? Simple. Just make sure you eat the required number of portions of low-calorie foods from each of the food groups: protein, fat, fruit, vegetables, starches, grains and cereals, and dairy (skim milk). Shades of the old exchange diets!

CONSUMER GUIDE®'S EVALUATION

So what else is new? Actually, while the concept is tried-and-true, Dachman's weight loss plan is rigid, in that the choices of foods are quite limited. Rating: ★★★

Berkowitz's Miracle Diet Switch

By its authors' admissions, this diet encourages you to overeat — selectively. "Because you will, you know. Virtually everyone does. So this factor is built *into* your eating plans. Soon you'll find you're *planning your overeating!*" write internist Gerald M. Berkowitz and writer Paul Neimark, both of the Chicago area. In their book, *The Berkowitz Diet Switch*[47] they offer six diets for you to switch among: High-Protein Diet; Bare Breakfast, Little Lunch, and Deal-with-Dinner Diet; The Fill-Up-On-Salad-Or-Something-Similar Diet; The Sweet-Tooth Diet; The Six-Small-Meals-A-Day Diet; and The No-Diet Diet.

The switch trick is to keep you dieting. Dr. Berkowitz's method, which helped him lose 30 pounds, was discovered after he realized that when he grew bored with a diet, he went off of it. Rather than fall into his old weight-gaining ways of eating, he merely switched from one diet to another. By thus preventing boredom, he controlled his caloric intake. In this book, he tells you how to switch from the No-Diet (where you eat whatever you want, so long as you keep your caloric intake to your daily limit), to the Protein Diet (where two thirds of the calories you consume are of protein), and so forth, bouncing around among the six diets.

As for controlled overeating, that gets lost somewhere in the book. Like political speeches, it's heavy with hyperbole.

CONSUMER GUIDE®'S EVALUATION:

While it makes some good points, Berkowitz's method is far from being "The Miracle Diet for the 80s" it claims to be. Rather, it is a frivolous approach to a serious business — losing weight. Switch channels. Rating: ★★

Hey, It's Richard Simmons!!!

Richard Simmons, the frenetic exercise maven who has a popular exercise show on TV, once weighed 268 pounds, now weighs 138. Most of this weight loss he attributes to a vigorous exercise plan, some of it to sensible eating habits. Actually, his *Never-Say-Diet Book*[48] is not so much a diet as a philosophy of eating, glued onto an exercise program. Simmons, who has a diet restaurant and exercise studio in Beverly Hills, California, offers such homilies as: Thou Shalt Not Take Fattening Leftovers to Work with You for Lunch; Thou Shalt Eat Out Carefully.

Simmons offers three diet plans: Plan A, if you have to lose 50 pounds or more; Plan B, if you have 20 to 40 pounds to lose; and Plan C, if you have one to 15 pounds to lose.

CONSUMER GUIDE®'S EVALUATION

Hyped mediocrity. That's show business. Rating: ★★

Sexibody

Well, isn't that what everyone wants—a sexy body? Jacqueline R. Shapiro and Marion Lear Swaybill, two New Yorkers, tell you how to achieve it in their *Sexibody Diet and Exercise Program.*[49] They even offer "some simple, sensuous, gourmet guidelines [for] preparing spectacular, sexy meals with minimum effort." After the hype, it's back to the same old broiled chicken, even on "Sinfully Delicious Diet Day 1." You get 30 days of such low-cal meals—including Sexy Snacks and Passion Pasta or Chocolate Caress (no, we didn't make these up), at about 1000 calories a day.

With the diet come exercises, advice, and recipes for low-calorie dishes, heavily seasoned with sexy verbiage. If you buy the book looking for supple-body sex techniques, you'll be disappointed. Even the chapter entitled, "Sexy Is as Sexy Does" has an arms-length approach.

CONSUMER GUIDE®'S EVALUATION

A pretty good, basic low-calorie approach, schlocked up by a superficial sexy come-on. It's a tease. Rating: ★★★

Calories In, Calories Out

This very good little book (116 pages) gives you the instructions and data for designing your own low-calorie diet and exercise program for losing weight and getting firm. Author James Leisy put it all together as part of his program of recovery from a heart attack, during which he was ordered to lose 30 pounds by his doctor—and he did. *Calories In, Calories Out*[50] approaches the task with a budget-designed technique. Instead of budgeting money in and money out, you budget energy in and (more accurately) energy expended. By lowering the calories you eat, and by raising the amount of calories you expend through exercise, you can lose weight doubly fast.

CONSUMER GUIDE®'S EVALUATION

Nifty and highly profitable for the dieter who can add two and two. Rating: ★★★★

The Other Duke Diet

Most people think of the Rice Diet when they hear of people losing weight at Duke University. Actually, there is another diet associated with Duke, that of Richard G. Stuelke, M.D. Dr. Stuelke first went to Duke as a patient in 1968. On the Rice Diet, he lost 100 pounds, which he soon regained. Then he found a low-calorie diet developed by Dr. Siegfried Heyden, M.D. of Georgia. In 1972, he returned to Duke as a faculty member specializing in the treatment of obesity. He applied the Heyden diet and taught his patients how to restructure their lifestyles and change their attitudes toward food. He also taught them to exercise regularly.

After he left Duke, Stuelke enunciated these principles in the 1977 book, *Thin for Life*.[51] In *Thin for Life,* he propounded his edict that you have no milk, no alcohol, no bread. Milk, he writes, is not a drink but a food, and one that is meant for baby cows. "Milk is far from being a perfect food for humans. It lacks iron. It contains large amounts of cholesterol. It contains large amounts of sodium."

As for bread, it is "the Number One cause of problems for people who tend to be obese." And alcohol is a no-no because "drinking binges and eating binges usually go hand-in-hand."

The diet Dr. Stuelke offers essentially provides 700 calories a day. In his book, he outlines a four-week diet program and includes recipes. On Sunday, he allows you the option of breakfast and lunch, or brunch. He also gives sound advice on how to restructure your lifestyle.

CONSUMER GUIDE®'S EVALUATION

Such an extreme restriction of calories should be followed only under a physician's supervision. Rating: ★★

Natural 300 Plan

If you think you're eating a reasonable, well-rounded diet but are still not losing weight, consider this gimmick: Cut back by 300 calories a day. The idea is that of Marck Bricklin, executive editor of *Prevention* magazine. In his book, *Lose Weight Naturally*,[52] he explains, "This plan suggests that 300 calories a day is a good average figure of calorie reduction to aim for, at least during the first few months of reducing."

"Experience shows that most people can cut that much out of their daily food intake without feeling hungry, deprived, or weak. It's enough of a reduction to produce a loss of 21 pounds in 8 months," writes Bricklin. He further suggests you add 200 calories' worth of exercise—equal to 45 minutes of walking—so you have a daily deficit of 500 calories, enough to lose a pound a week, five pounds a month, and up to 35 pounds in six months.

Bricklin lists food combinations that you can avoid without noticing they're gone, including:

	Calories		Calories
½ cup beef hash	200	½ piece buttered toast	55
can ginger ale	113	large forkful apple pie	50
Total	313	2 thin pretzels	70
		slice pizza	153
Twinkie	180	Total	328
cup Hawaiian Punch	110		
Total	300		

Since *Prevention,* the magazine Bricklin helps edit, promotes "natural foods," you can be sure they are emphasized in his book. With some important exceptions, "natural foods are much less fattening than processed or convenience foods," he writes. Natural foods have no sugar or fats added and no fiber removed. For instance, a plain potato has 145 calories, while the equivalent amount of French fries has 214. The exceptions are dried fruit (loaded with sugar, even if natural) and nuts (which, in his view, should be eaten with meals rather than as snacks).

Similar cut-back tricks are detailed in the English import, *How to Lose Weight Without Really Dieting.*[53] For instance, at breakfast, you can save as much as 300 calories "by eating less toast and spreading thinner layers of butter and marmalade." Or you can cut down the size of your portions or use low-calorie substitutes.

CONSUMER GUIDE®'S EVALUATION

Good, if slanted. Rating: ★★★

The Mayo Diet—The Real One

There are several "fake" Mayo diets—and there is a real one. The real one is an exchange diet moderate in protein and high in fats and carbohydrates. And it is detailed in that institution's official diet manual,[54] which can be purchased at a medical book store or ordered from the publisher, W. B. Saunders Company. Its exchange plans are for 800, 1000, 1200 or 1400 calories. The 800-calorie plan requires vitamin and mineral supplements.

The official diet manual contains the Mayo Food Nomogram, which doctors at the famed Mayo Clinic have used since 1933. Using the Nomogram dieters can find what a 44-year-old, 150-pound sedentary writer should eat to maintain his weight: 1700 calories. For greater activity, add 30 percent. For the active writer, caloric need would be 2200 per day.

With the Mayo Nomogram, you determine your total daily calories for the first step in your diet on the basis of 15 pounds less than you actually weigh. The Nomogram helps you find the basal caloric count, according to your age and height, for the desired weight. By subtracting the number of calories you will consume on your diet, you discover your Calorie Deficit (the number of calories you will cut from the daily food intake). Multiply the Calorie Deficit by 0.002 to get the number of pounds you can expect to lose a week.

Here's how it works. If you are an inactive, 36-year-old woman weighing 230 pounds and figuring on a 15-pound loss as a start—you want to slim down to 215 pounds—your Calorie Base (using the Nomogram) is 2040. If you go on an 800 calorie-a-day diet, then your Calorie Deficit (the amount you must cut out) is 1240; multiply 1240 by 0.002 and you get 2.5, which means you'll lose 2½ pounds a week.

Now, when you compare a 2½-pound weekly weight loss against the seven-pound to 15-pound losses claimed by Stillman, Pritikin, Tarnower, Atkins, and other proponents of special diets, it doesn't seem like much. But if you can maintain a 2½-pound weight loss every week, you will have lost 25 pounds by the end of ten weeks and another 25 pounds in another ten weeks. By the end of the year, you will have lost 130 pounds (if you had that much to lose).

Under the Mayo plan, you should refigure your total daily calories, on the basis of your actual weight, every nine weeks. You should also record your weight-loss curve on a chart that has "pounds" along the vertical and "weeks" along the horizontal.

In its analysis of the real Mayo Clinic Diet, CONSUMER GUIDE® found that protein was fairly constant (60 to 75 grams) in the 800-calorie to 1400-calorie plans, while fat (mostly saturated fats) more than doubled from 30 grams at 800 calories to 70 grams at 1400 calories; carbohydrates increased from 80 grams at 800 calories to 120 grams at 1400 calories.

The real Mayo Clinic Diet, in other words, concentrates on lowering calories and keeping foods in nutritional balance. So, if you want to control carbohydrates and cholesterol, you will have to substitute certain fruits and vegetables for bread and winnow out the few polyunsaturated foods from the exchanges.

CONSUMER GUIDE®'S EVALUATION

It might be worth a try if you can control carbohydrates and cholesterol. Rating: ★★★

Unreal Mayo Diet

"Fake" Mayo diets have been passed around for years, hand-to-hand, on much-folded mimeographed or machine-copied sheets of paper. All called "The Mayo Diet," they have been otherwise known as the Egg Diet, the Grapefruit Diet, and even the Tomato Juice Diet. The most common so-called Mayo diet is sold on the fraudulent premise that grapefruit has certain enzymes which somehow subtract calories by acting as a catalyst and enhancing the fat-burning process. Actually grapefruit is just a nutritious fruit, nothing magic.

The danger in a diet that carries a respected name, such as Mayo is that too many dieters will not examine it critically but will accept the claims it makes and its directions—absurd as they may be. For example, one false Mayo diet includes, in its general eating plan, the statement that you should always eat until you are stuffed, even if this requires one or two dozen slices of bacon and as many eggs, prepared in as much butter as you wish.

CONSUMER GUIDE® cautions that this false Mayo diet does not come from Mayo Clinic—indeed the Clinic regularly denies any connection with it, or endorsement of it, in its original or present form. The situation offers simply another proof, if one is needed, of the necessity for an objective evaluation of all diets offered to the public.

So you can recognize the "fake" Mayo diet if someone hands you a copy, here is a copy of the Grapefruit Diet.[55]

Breakfast
½ grapefruit or unsweetened grapefruit juice
2 eggs, any style
minimum 2 slices of bacon—more if desired
coffee or tea, no sugar

Lunch
½ grapefruit
meat, any style, any amount
salad, any amount, with any dressing that contains no sugar
coffee or tea

Dinner
½ grapefruit
meat, any style, any amount, with gravy (no flour thickening), or fish
any green, yellow, or red vegetable in any amount
salad as above
coffee or tea

Bedtime Snack
Tomato juice or skim milk

This diet tells you to eat until full at all meals (don't omit anything listed) and not to eat between meals.

CONSUMER GUIDE®'S EVALUATION

The Grapefruit Diet is *not recommended* by CONSUMER GUIDE®.
Rating: No stars

OTHER LOW-CALORIE DIETS

Dozens of diets have been built on calorie cutting. All hold to 900 to 1200 calories a day for women, slightly more for men. Not one of them is very different from any other, except for minor differences in the amount of fat or carbohydrate included in each day's intake. None is high-fat or high-protein or low-carbohydrate; all balance the food substances and insist on some foods from all food groups.

These diets go by various names; they can be found in your library's periodical collection if you want to shop around.

DIET WORKSHOP, TOPS, WEIGHT WATCHERS

Not included in this chapter are the diets of the organizations such as Diet Control Centers, Diet Workshop, Take Off Pounds Sensibly, and Weight Watchers International.

These are all calorie-controlled diets that are based on firm nutritional principles. A further discussion of these diets is included in the chapter on diet organizations.

REFERENCE FOR COUNTING CALORIES

To count calories, you need a reliable reference that lists foods and their caloric content. A helpful and complete reference is: *The Dieter's Complete Guide to Calories, Carbohydrates, Sodium, Fats & Cholesterol,* by the Editors of CONSUMER GUIDE®. New York: Ballantine Fawcett Columbine, 1981.

CRITICISM

One of America's leading experts on obesity, Hilde Bruch, M.D., professor of psychiatry at Baylor College of Medicine in Houston, has made some important observations on dieting. "Many fat people, in particular those with personality problems, prefer rather unusual diets that will bring visible results more quickly," she wrote. "To them an extraordinary situation appears more acceptable than just a slight change in one's established habits; the great appeal of absurd fads and outlandish diets appears to be related to this. In my work with severely disturbed obese people I have found that rather monotonous, somewhat strange diets are more effective than reasonable restrictions, at least in the beginning of a reducing program. It is my impression that it is the very strangeness that makes these diets effective...These types of diets emphasize also something that is often overlooked — that dieting is a serious business which cannot be accomplished in a haphazard way. In difficult cases, it is helpful to take dieting out of the realm of ordinary living."[56]

Studies have shown that even though some doctors recommend the same low-calorie diet, they can evoke different degrees of confidence from their patients, who then diet with different rates of success.

Also important is the dieter. Some fat people lose weight no matter what diet they follow, while others may even gain weight on diets."[57]

The premise of the US Senate, Prudent, and other such diets has been criticized, mainly by the dairy industry and those the industry supports. In June 1973, the National Dairy Council issued a news release that stated saturated fats "per se, do not raise levels of cholesterol in the blood." The release quoted a scientific article by Raymond Reiser, Ph.D., distinguished professor of biochemistry and biophysics at Texas A&M University.[58] Dr. Reiser, working under a grant from the dairy council, reviewed what was known about the subject and found that cholesterol — not saturated fats — in foods caused an increase of cholesterol in the blood. "The condemnation of 'saturated fat,'" he wrote, represents "guilt by association." Dr. Reiser neglected to mention, however, that a high incidence of cholesterol and saturated fats is found in the same foods.

REBUTTAL

Dr. George Bray, M.D., of Los Angeles County Harbor General Hospital, in testimony before the Senate Select Committee on Nutrition and Human Needs said, "The ever-growing list of diets is an affirmation of the fact that no diet yet described is by itself a solution to the problem of obesity. The truth of this statement is reflected in the fact that new diets appear yearly, each claiming to be the 'ultimate solution.'...Unless caloric intake is reduced below caloric needs, the extra calories which have been stored in adipose tissue will not be burned. There is a large and convincing body of information which shows that if caloric restriction is sufficiently severe, and is maintained for a sufficiently long period of time, body weight will decline."[59]

Dr. Jean Mayer observes that "crash diets are no good. They're nutritionally unbalanced, they make you weak, irritable, and dizzy. Worst of all, from the dieter's viewpoint, they don't work. After the first thrilling plummet of the scales, the pointer inexorably creeps upward again. Looking back, the disappointed dieter knows that all she or he has accomplished is one more useless and frustrating cycle in which I call 'the rhythm method of girth control.'"[60]

The AMA's Dr. White adds: "What a person ate while becoming overweight may not resemble what he eats while maintaining the extra weight. ...In fact, the fat person may change his diet and drastically cut back his caloric intake—but not enough to lose any fat, just enough to keep it." He continues:

> The key to weight reduction is to eat less food without haphazardly eliminating any one food completely. Let quality and flavor be a guide; enjoy a little bit of all foods, but not an inordinate quantity of any one.
> Reducing diets also should be based on foods normally consumed if dieters are to lead a lifetime of successful weight maintenance. If

good eating habits are not instituted during the period of weight reduction, continuing maintenance of "ideal" weight will be most difficult, if not impossible. Important as they are, however, careful selection of food and reduction of food intake are not enough — a person must also indulge in regular physical activity commensurate with his physical condition.

Programs of proper weight maintenance, ultimately, should replace the current preoccupation with weight loss. The change from the "reducing" diet to that for weight "maintenance" is very subtle, with only minor adjustments in the amount of food eaten. Experience gained during the initial weight reduction, however, should make it possible to make whatever adjustments are needed later to reverse temporary weight-gain setbacks.

The inability of bizzare reduction diets to provide adequate weight control because of their radical departure from the normal daily diet is what contributes to their downfall. A successful weight-reduction diet is one which, with minor caloric adjustments, becomes an enjoyable way of life and provides desirable weight maintenance.[61]

CONSUMER GUIDE®'S EVALUATION

Counting calories is a well-established way to lose weight. It has three main advantages.

1. Properly done, it can be used to establish a well-rounded diet that is scaled down in calories but not in nutrition.
2. It is personal. By counting calories, you can tailor your diet to fit your present state of fatness and the state of thinness you desire in the future.
3. With a calorie guide, you can diet by the numbers and learn how to gauge portion sizes. After using a calorie guide for a while, you'll get to know which foods to avoid.

If you decide on a low-calorie diet, you'll have lots of company and lots of help. You'll probably find that most dieters whom you know are cutting back calories. Some of them are certain to stray and take up a fad diet like Beverly Hills. But eventually they will come back to calories, because in the long run cutting calories is the most durable method of weight loss.

CONS

The big disadvantage of low-calorie diets is that, in a way, cutting calories is the most difficult way to diet. You must eat a well-rounded diet but smaller amounts and the problem is the temptation to eat just a little more or just another helping. In other words, the low-calorie approach relies on your will power.

But there are some good ways to bolster your will power. Most dieters find they cannot successfully follow a low-calorie diet except with others. So, they go on a diet with their mate or with a close friend. Or, they join a club of fellow dieters, such as TOPS, Weight Watchers, or Diet Workshop.

In other words, the low-calorie diet, for most people, does require support from others.

And you may well find yourself relying more and more on commercial low-cal foods. Low-cal and dietetic foods are helpful mainly because the portions are premeasured so therefore you cannot be tempted to make the portion a little bigger or to nibble on the leftovers.

To help calorie counters who rely on commercial low-calorie prepared foods, the food industry has been expanding its low-calorie and dietetic lines. The result is a wider variety of diet foods. But as you become more and more dependent on these items, the food processor can demand higher and higher prices. Eventually, the cost of your dependency will be dear.

Overall, CONSUMER GUIDE® judges the strictly low-calorie diet method as middle-of-the-road: safe but slow. If you travel the low-calorie road, follow one of the US Senate or Prudent families of diets that is high in protein and carbohydrates and low in saturated fats and cholesterol. And, as mentioned above, you may also wish to join a diet club. CONSUMER GUIDE® does not advise restricting your calorie intake below 1000 calories a day without consulting a physician and planning your nutritional intake and expenditure carefully.

FOOD 2 DIET

1200 CALORIES

Breakfast
Branflakes, ¾ cup
with strawberries, fresh, ¾ cup
and plain lowfat yogurt, ¾ cup

Lunch
*Chef's salad, 1 serving
Salad dressing, Italian, regular,
2 tablespoons
Rye wafers, 4
Tangerine, 1 medium
Water, tea, or coffee

Dinner
*Mock beef stroganoff (with
noodles), 1 serving
Spinach, cooked, ½ cup
Whole-wheat roll, 1
Margarine, 1 teaspoon
Cantaloupe, 5-inch diameter, ¼
Skim milk, 1 cup

Snack
Banana, 1 medium

1500 CALORIES

Breakfast
Grapefruit juice, unsweetened,
½ cup
Shredded wheat, 1 biscuit
Whole-wheat toast, 1 slice
Margarine, 1 teaspoon
Skim milk, ½ cup

Lunch
Roast beef sandwich
Roast beef, cooked, lean,
3 ounces
Lettuce leaf, 1
Mayonnaise-type salad
dressing, 2 teaspoons
*Whole-wheat bread, 2 slices
Carrot strips, 6 to 8 (2½″-3″ long)
Orange, 1 medium
Water, tea, or coffee

Dinner
*Baked fish fillet, 1 serving
Baked potato, 1
Margarine, 2 teaspoons
Green peas, cooked, ½ cup
Salad
  Tomato, sliced, ½
  Cucumber, sliced, ½
  * Yogurt-dill dressing,
    2 tablespoons
French bread, 1 medium slice
Margarine, 1 teaspoon
Peach slices, fresh, ½ cup
Water, tea, or coffee

Snack
Plain lowfat yogurt, ¾ cup
  with blueberries, fresh or frozen
  (unsweetened), ¼ cup

1800 CALORIES

Breakfast
Orange juice, ¾ cup
Poached egg, 1
*Bran muffins, 2
Margarine, 2 teaspoons
Skim milk, 1 cup

Lunch
Split pea soup, 1 cup
Chicken salad sandwich
  Chicken salad, ½ cup made with
    low-calorie mayonnaise-type
    salad dressing
  Rye bread, 2 slices
Pear, canned in light sirup,
  2 small halves with sirup
Water, tea, or coffee

Dinner
*Sweet and sour pork chops,
  1 serving
Baked sweetpotato, 1 small
Broccoli, cooked, ½ cup
Fruit cup, ⅔ cup
  (apples, oranges, bananas)
Whole-wheat roll, 1
Margarine, 1 teaspoon
Water, tea, or coffee

Snacks
Skim milk, 1 cup
Whole-wheat crackers, 4

*Recipes for starred items are found in the recipe section.

US ARMY LIFETIME DIET

DAY 1

Breakfast
½ grapefruit
1 waffle square
1 tsp. butter or margarine
1 sausage or 1 oz. ham
8 oz. skim milk
Coffee or tea
(Men: 2 sausages or 2 oz. ham)

Lunch
3 oz. roast turkey
½ cup corn bread dressing
½ cup broccoli
(continued next column)

Lunch *(continued)*
Tossed salad with low-calorie
  dressing
2 peach halves
8 oz. skim milk
(Men: Add ½ cup mashed potatoes)

Dinner
1 hot dog with bun
Onions and mustard
½ cup coleslaw
12 grapes
(Men: 2 hot dogs, 1 bun)

DAY 2

Breakfast
½ cup orange juice
½ cup oatmeal or ¾ cup
  high-protein cereal
1 egg, cooked as desired
8 oz. skim milk
(Men: 2 eggs; add 1 slice dry toast)

Lunch
¾ cup Waldorf salad with chicken
  (1½ tsp. mayonnaise per serving)
6 oz. vegetable juice cocktail
6 saltines
8 oz. skim milk
(Men: Add 1 roll)

Dinner
¾ cup spaghetti sauce
½ cup cooked spaghetti
Raw zucchini and radishes
Tossed salad with rice vinegar,
  herbs
4 apricot halves
(Men: 1 cup each spaghetti, sauce)

I LOVE AMERICA DIET

THE REDUCING DIET MENUS FOR MOST WOMEN
(AND SMALL-FRAME MEN)

Breakfast
½ cup orange juice
½ cup bran flakes with raisins
½ cup whole milk (we prefer skim,
  fortified)
1 slice whole-wheat toast
Coffee, tea, or water

Lunch
(You can brown-paper-bag this one)
1 ham sandwich,* consisting of:
  • 2 ounces ham
  • 1 slice (1 ounce) cheese
  • lettuce
  • ½ medium tomato
  • 2 slices enriched bread
1 medium apple
Coffee, tea, or water

Dinner
3 ounces roast beef
1 medium baked potato
½ cup broccoli
1 cup skim milk, fortified

Snacks
1 small cucumber, sliced
3-4 strips carrot (strips are about
  2½ to 3 inches long)

*If you're watching your salt intake carefully, you can switch to any unsalted meat (turkey or roast beef, for example).

THE NEW YORK CITY HEALTH DEPARTMENT DIET

For Most Women And Small Frame Men

Breakfast
High vitamin C fruit — choose ONE from "Food Facts"
Protein food — choose ONE:
  Cottage or pot cheese, 2 oz.
  Hard cheese, 1 oz.
  Cooked or canned fish, 2 oz.
  Egg, 1
Bread or cereal, whole grain or enriched — choose ONE:
  Bread, 1 slice
  Ready-to-eat cereal, ¾ cup
  Cooked cereal, ½ cup
Skim milk, 8 oz. cup
Coffee or tea

Lunch
Protein food — choose ONE:
  Fish, poultry, or lean meat, 2 oz.
  Cottage or pot cheese, 4 oz.
  Hard cheese, 2 oz.
  Egg, 1
  Peanut butter, 2 level tbsp.
Bread, whole grain or enriched, 2 slices
Vegetables, raw or cooked, except potato or substitute
Fruit, 1 serving
Coffee or tea

Dinner
Protein food — choose ONE:
  Cooked fish, poultry, or lean meat, 4 oz.
High vitamin A vegetable — choose ONE from "Food Facts"
Potato or substitute — choose ONE from "Food Facts"
Other vegetables — you may eat freely
Fruit, 1 serving
Coffee or tea

Other Daily Foods
Fat — choose three from "Food Facts"
Milk — 2 cups skim or choose milk substitute from
  "Food Facts"

For Most Men And Large Frame Women

Breakfast
High vitamin C fruit — choose ONE from "Food Facts"
Protein food — choose ONE:
  Cottage or pot cheese, 2 oz.
  Hard cheese, 1 oz.
  Cooked or canned fish, 2 oz.
  Egg, 1

(continued)

Bread or cereal, whole grain or enriched — choose ONE:
  Bread, 2 slices
  Ready-to-eat cereal, 1½ cups
  Cooked cereal, 1 cup
Skim milk, 8 oz. cup
Coffee or tea

Lunch
Protein food — choose ONE:
  Fish, poultry, or lean meat, 2 oz.
  Cottage or pot cheese, 4 oz.
  Hard cheese, 2 oz.
  Egg, 1
  Peanut butter, 2 level tbsp.
Bread, whole grain or enriched, 2 slices
Vegetables, raw or cooked, except potato or substitute
Fruit, 1 serving
Coffee or tea

Dinner
Protein food — choose ONE:
  Cooked fish, poultry, or lean meat, 6 oz.
High vitamin A vegetable — choose ONE from "Food Facts"
Potato or substitute — choose ONE from "Food Facts"
Other vegetables — you may eat freely
Fruit, 1 serving
Coffee or tea

Other Daily Foods
Fat — choose six from "Food Facts"
Milk — 2 cups skim or choose milk substitute from
  "Food Facts"

Food Facts

Limit These Protein Foods
Lean beef, pork, lamb to 1 pound per week total
Eggs to 4 per week
Hard cheese to 4 oz. per week

High Vitamin C Fruits (No added sugar)
Cantaloupe, ½ medium
Grapefruit, ½ medium
Mango, ½ medium
Orange, 1 medium
Orange or grapefruit juice, 4 oz.
Strawberries, 1 cup
Tangerine, 1 large
Tomato juice, 8 oz.

Other Fruits (No added sugar)
Apple or peach, 1 medium
Apricots, prunes, or plums 2 to 3
Banana or pear, 1 small
Berries, ½ cup
Cherries or grapes, ¼ lb.
Honeydew melon, ½ small
Pineapple, ½ cup
Raisins, 2 tbsp.
Watermelon, ½ round slice (1 x 10 in.)

High Vitamin A Vegetables

Broccoli
Carrots
Chicory
Escarole

Mustard greens, collards, and
  other leafy greens
Pumpkin, winter squash
Spinach
Watercress

Potato Or Substitute

Beans, peas, lentils, dry, cooked,
  ½ cup
Corn or green lima beans, peas,
  ½ cup
Corn, 1 small ear

Potato, 1 medium
Rice, spaghetti, macaroni, grits,
  or noodles, ½ cup cooked
Sweet potato or yam, ½ cup

Fat

French dressing, 2 tsp.
Margarine, 1 tsp. with liquid
  vegetable oil listed first on
  label or ingredients

Mayonnaise, 1 tsp.
Vegetable oil, 1 tsp.

Skim Milk Or Substitute

Buttermilk, 2 cups (8 oz. each)
Evaporated skim milk, 1 cup
  (8 oz.)

Nonfat dry milk solids, ⅔ cup

You May Drink

Bouillon
Club soda

Coffee
Consommé

Tea
Water

You May Use

Herbs
Horseradish

Lemon, lime
Pepper

Salt
Spices
Vinegar

You May Eat Freely

Asparagus
Broccoli
Brussels sprouts
Carrots
Cauliflower
Celery
Chicory
Collards

Cucumber
Dandelion greens
Escarole
Green beans
Kale
Lettuce
Mushrooms
Mustard greens

Parsley
Romaine lettuce
Spinach
Summer squash
Swiss Chard
Tomato
Turnip greens
Watercress

You May Not Eat Or Drink

Bacon, fatty meats, sausage
Beer, liquor, wines
Butter, margarines other than
  described in "Food Facts"
Cakes, cookies, crackers,
  doughnuts, pastries, pies
Candy, chocolates, nuts
Cream: sweet and sour, cream
  cheese, non-dairy cream
  substitutes

French-fried potatoes, potato
  chips
Pizza, popcorn, pretzels and
  similar snack foods
Gelatin desserts, puddings
  (sugar-sweetened)
Gravies and sauces
Honey, jams, jellies, sugar and
  syrup

(continued)

You May Not Eat Or Drink *(continued)*

Ice cream, ices, ice milk,
    sherbets
Milk, whole
Muffins, pancakes, waffles

Olives
Soda (sugar-sweetened)
Yogurt (fruit-flavored)

REDBOOK'S "WEIGHT-LOSS DIET FOR YOUR HIGH-ENERGY LIFE."

(Reprinted by permission from "The Weight-Loss Diet for your High-Energy Life."
Redbook, *January 1983, pp.110, 135-142.)*
Calories given in parentheses

SUNDAY MENU #1: 1,205 Calories

Brunch
    ½ grapefruit (40)
    *Cheese Popovers (165)
    1 ounce cooked Canadian
        bacon (77)
    Spinach-Mushroom Salad:
        Toss 2 cups torn spinach leaves
        (28), ½ cup sliced fresh
        mushrooms (10) and 1 small
        tomato, quartered (20), with 1
        tablespoon *Creamy French
        Dressing (13)

Snack
    1 medium-sized pear (86)
    1 ounce Brie cheese (94)
    6 thin wheat crackers (54)
    6 ounces tomato juice (35)

Dinner
    *Marinated Steak (128)
    1 cup sliced mushrooms (20),
        cooked in 1 teaspoon butter or
        margarine (34)
    1 4-ounce baked potato (81),
        topped with 2 tablespoons plain
        low-fat yogurt (15) and 1 teaspoon
        chives (0)
    1 cup green beans (32)
    *Angel Food Cake with Peach
        Melba Sauce (139)

Snack
    1 cup skim milk (88)
    2 cups popcorn, no fat (46)

For 1,000 calorie diet, omit Angel
Food Cake with Peach Melba Sauce
and thin wheat crackers.

MONDAY MENU #2: 1,186 Calories

Breakfast
    1 large hard-cooked egg (82)
    1 2-inch bran muffin (104)
    1 teaspoon butter or margarine (34)
    1 small orange (57)
    1 cup skim milk (88)

Lunch
    Steak Sandwich: 2 ounces
        Marinated Steak (reserved from
        Menu #1, 80), on 1 slice
        whole-wheat bread (56), with 1
        large lettuce leaf (2) and 1 small
        tomato, sliced (20)
    1 medium carrot (30)
    1 small apple (61)

Snack
    ¼ cup cranberry-juice cocktail
        (41) with 1 cup club soda (0)
    *Trail Mix (155)

Dinner
    3 ounces roast chicken, without
        skin (142)
    ½ cup cooked rice (93)
    1 cup cooked broccoli (40)
    ½ cup water-packed canned
        plums (57)
    ½ cup skim milk (44)

For 1,000 calorie diet, omit butter
from breakfast, whole-wheat bread
from lunch, cranberry-juice cocktail
from snack and skim milk from dinner.

TUESDAY MENU #3: 1,200 Calories

Breakfast
1 cup 40% bran flakes cereal (106)
1 cup skim milk (88)
½ small banana, sliced (40)
½ cup orange juice (61)

Lunch
*Chicken Waldorf Salad (201),
    served on 2 large lettuce leaves (4)
4 9-inch bread sticks (70)

Snack
*Peanut Butter-Corn Muffin (95)
1 cup skim milk (88)

Dinner
1 3-ounce broiled lean
    hamburger (186) on ½ toasted
    English muffin (59), with 1
    tablespoon tomato catsup (16)
Crunchy Salad: 2 cups shredded
    lettuce (16), 1 small tomato,
    chopped (20), ½ cup grated
    carrot (23) and ½ cup diced
    cucumber (10), tossed with 2
    tablespoons Creamy French
    Dressing (see Menu #1, 26)
*Pineapple Tapioca (91)

WEDNESDAY MENU #4: 1,192 Calories

Breakfast
½ cup grapefruit (40)
1 2-ounce pita bread (80),
    stuffed with ½ cup 99%-fat-free
    cottage cheese (82), mixed with
    1 tablespoon raisins (26) and
    sprinkled with cinnamon (0)

Lunch
Spinach-Mushroom Salad (see
    Menu #1, 58), tossed with 1 large
    hard-cooked egg, chopped (82),
    1 medium-sized carrot, sliced (30),
    and 2 tablespoons Creamy
    French Dressing (see Menu #1, 26)
1 slice whole-wheat bread (56)
½ cup skim milk (44)

Snack
1 ounce Swiss cheese (105)
1 medium pear (86)
1 cup herbal tea (0)

Dinner
*Rumaki (401)
1 cup cooked Swiss chard (26) or
    other leafy greens
½ cup unsweetened applesauce
    (50) sprinkled with cinnamon (0)

For 1,000 calorie diet: Eat ¼ cup
cottage cheese at breakfast; ½ ounce
Swiss cheese for snack; at dinner eat
4 instead of 6 pieces of Rumaki.

THURSDAY MENU #5: 1,196 Calories

Breakfast
½ cup orange juice (61)
1 large egg, scrambled without
    added fat (82)
1 slice rye bread, toasted (61)
1 teaspoon butter or margarine (34)

Lunch
Chicken Waldorf Salad (reserved
    from Menu #3, 201), served on 2
    large lettuce leaves (4)
1 slice whole-wheat bread (56)
1 cup skim milk (88)

For 1,000 calorie diet, omit butter at
breakfast and bread at lunch; cut
snack in half.

Snack
Grape Soda: ¼ cup unsweetened
    grape juice (42) and 1 cup club
    soda (0) over ice
2 2½-inch-square graham crackers
    (55), with ½ small apple, sliced
    (30), and 2 teaspoons peanut
    butter (62)

Dinner
*Spinach-Tofu Soup with Scallion
    Dumplings (267)
Crunchy Salad (see Menu #3,
    69), with 1 tablespoon Creamy
    French Dressing (see Menu
    #1, 13)
¼ cup plain low-fat yogurt (31),
    mixed with ½ small banana,
    sliced (40)

64

FRIDAY MENU #6: 1,202 Calories

Breakfast
- 1 cup 40% bran flakes cereal (106)
- 1 cup skim milk (88)
- ½ cup frozen unsweetened blueberries (45)

Snack
- Peanut Butter-Corn Muffins (see Menu #3, 95)
- 1 cup herbal tea (0)

Lunch
- *Ham and Potato Salad (224)
- 1 small orange (57)
- 1 carrot (30)

For 1,000 calorie diet, omit second snack.

Snack
- Cranberry Spritzer: ¼ cup cranberry juice cocktail (41) and 1 cup club soda (0) over ice
- Trail Mix (see Menu #2, 155)

Dinner
- *Poached Fish with Mustard Sauce (142)
- 1 4-ounce potato, baked (81), topped with 2 tablespoons plain low-fat yogurt (15) and 1 teaspoon chives (0)
- 1 cup cooked green beans (32)
- Pineapple Tapioca (see Menu #3, 91)

SATURDAY MENU #7: 1,194 Calories

Breakfast
- ½ cup grapefruit juice (61)
- 2 4-inch pancakes (124), topped with 1 teaspoon butter or margarine (34) and 1 tablespoon Peach Melba Sauce (reserved from Menu #1, 17)
- 1 cup skim milk (88)

Lunch
- 1 cup Spinach-Tofu Soup with Scallion Dumplings (reserved from Menu #5, 123)
- 1 9-inch bread stick (18)
- 1 large tangerine (46)

For 1,000 calorie diet, eat ½ grapefruit instead of juice at breakfast, omit butter and drink ½ cup skim milk; omit bread stick at lunch; drink ½ cup apple cider and eat 1 cup popcorn for snack.

*Recipe given in complete diet

Snack
- 1 cup hot apple cider (117), with a cinnamon stick (0)
- 2 cups popcorn, no fat (46)

Dinner
- Cucumber Salad: Top 2 large lettuce leaves (4) with 1 cup sliced cucumbers (20) and 1 tablespoon Creamy French Dressing (see Menu #1, 13)
- ¾ cup cooked spaghetti (144), with *Meatball Sauce (292)
- ½ cup water-packed canned apricots (47)

LA COSTA SPA DIET

800-Calorie Plan

Breakfast
  Milk
  Meat
  Bread
  Fruit

Luncheon
  List 1 Vegetable
  List 2 Vegetable
  2 Meat Exchanges
  Fruit

Dinner
  List 1 Vegetable
  List 2 Vegetable
  2 Meat Exchanges
  2 Fruit Exchanges

(Total calories: 793)

1000-Calorie Plan

Breakfast
  Milk
  Meat
  Bread
  Fruit

Luncheon
  List 1 Vegetable
  List 2 Vegetable
  Meat
  Bread
  Fruit

Dinner
  List 1 Vegetable
  List 2 Vegetable
  2 Meat Exchanges
  Bread
  2 Fruit Exchanges

Snack
  Fruit

(Total calories: 1009)

1200-Calorie Plan

Breakfast
  Milk
  Meat
  Bread
  Fruit

Luncheon
  2 List 1 Vegetables
  List 2 Vegetable
  2 Meat Exchanges
  Bread
  Fat
  2 Fruit Exchanges

Dinner
  List 1 Vegetable
  List 2 Vegetable
  4 Meat Exchanges
  Bread
  2 Fruit Exchanges

Snack
  Fruit

(Total calories: 1200)

List 1. Vegetable Exchanges
(One cup raw measure provides 3 gm carbohydrate, 1 gm protein, and 16 calories.)

Asparagus
Bamboo shoots,
  bean sprouts
Beans
  Green
  String
  Yellow Wax
Broccoli
Brussels sprouts
Cabbage
Cauliflower
Celery, celery leaves
Chinese cabbage
Cucumber
Eggplant
Greens
  Beet

Chard
Collard
Dandelion
Chicory
Endive
Kale
Mustard
Spinach
Turnip
Kohlrabi
Mushrooms
Okra
Peppers
  Green
  Red
  Sweet
  Hot

Pimiento
Radish
Salad greens
  Lettuce
  Romaine
  Endive
  Curly Endive
  Escarole
  Watercress
Sauerkraut
Green onion, scallion
Squash
  Zucchini
  Crookneck
  Summer
Tomato
Water chestnut

List 2. Vegetable Exchanges
(One-half cup cooked measure provides 7 gm carbohydrate, 2 gm protein, and 36 calories.)

Artichoke (1 small, edible portion)
Beets
Carrots
Leeks
Onions
Peas, green (young, tender)
Pumpkin

Rutabaga
Squash
  Acorn
  Banana
  Butternut
  Hubbard
  Winter
Turnip

List 3. Fruit Exchanges
(No added sugar. One serving provides 10 gm carbohydrate and 40 calories.)

Apple (2½" diameter), 1
Apple juice, ⅓ cup
Applesauce, ½ cup
Apricots
  Fresh, 2 medium
  Cooked, ½ cup
  Dried, 4 halves
Banana (3"), ½
Strawberries, blackberries, 1 cup
Blueberries, boysenberries, gooseberries, ⅔ cup
Loganberries, raspberries, ½ cup
Cantaloupe (6" melon), ¼ section
Cherries, 10
Cranberry juice, 1 cup
Currants
  Fresh, ⅔ cup
  Dried, 1 tbsp.
Dates, 2
Figs
  Fresh, 1 large
  Dried, 1 medium
Grapefruit, ½ medium
Grapefruit juice, ½ cup
Grape juice, ¼ cup
Grapes, 12 medium to large
Guava, 1 large or 3 small

Honeydew melon (7" melon), ⅛ section
Kumquats, 3 medium
Lemons, 2 small or 1 large
Lemon juice, ½ cup
Limes, 2 medium or 3 small
Mango, ¼ section
Nectar (canned): apricot, peach, pear, ⅓ cup
Nectarine, 1 medium
Orange
  Navel, 1 medium
  Valencia, 1 small
Orange juice, ½ cup
Papaya, ⅓ medium
Peach, 1 medium
Pear, 1 medium
Persimmon, ½ large
Pineapple
  Canned, ½ cup chunks or 1 large slice
  Fresh (4 x 6½ in. fruit), ⅙ wedge
Plums, 2 medium
Prune juice, ¼ cup
Prunes, fresh or dried, 2 medium
Raisins, 2 level tbsp.
Rhubarb, cooked, 1 cup
Tangerine, 1 large
Watermelon, 4 x 1½ in. wedge

List 4. Bread Exchanges
(One serving provides 15 gm carbohydrate, 2 gm protein, and 68 calories.)

Bread: white, French, Italian, wheat, rye pumpernickel, 1 slice (25 gm)
Bagel (3" diameter), ½

Biscuit or roll (2" diameter), 1
Bread crumbs
  Dry, grated, ¼ cup
  Soft, ⅓ cup

Bread sticks (6½″ long), 2
Buns: frankfurter or
   hamburger, ½
Cake, angel food (1½″-thick
   slice), 1
Cereal
   Cooked, ½ cup
   Dry packaged, (wide variation
      in calories from 55 to 200
      per serving. Read label.)
Rice or grits, cooked, ½ cup
Corn bread, 1½″ cube
Crackers
   Graham, 2
   Oyster, ½ cup
   Holland Rusk, 2
   Saltines, 5
   Soda, 3
   Thin, 6 to 8 small
   Zweiback, 2½
Flour, 2½ level tbsp.
Barley, 1½ tbsp.

Cornstarch, 2 level tbsp.
Tapioca, dry, 2 tbsp.
Macaroni, noodles, spaghetti,
   cooked, ½ cup
Matzo (5″ square), 1
Matzo meal, 3 tbsp.
Muffin
   English (3″ diameter), ½
   Plain (2″ diameter), 1
Toast, Melba, 4 rectangles or 8
   rounds
Tortilla, corn (6″ diameter), 1
Beans, dried, cooked, ½ cup
Corn
   Ear, ½ large or 1 small
   Whole kernel, ⅓ cup
Parsnip, 1 medium
Peas, dried, cooked, ½ cup
Potato, white (2″ diameter), 1
Potato, sweet or yam (2″
   diameter), ½

List 5. Meat Exchanges
(Lean, no fat added. One serving provides 7 gm protein, 5 gm fat, and 73 calories.)

Meat, poultry, liver, fresh fish, no
   bone, 1 slice, lean*
Cold cuts (1½″ square or
   diameter x ⅛″), 1 slice
Canadian bacon, 2 thin slices (1
   oz.)
Cheese: cheddar, Swiss,
   American, 1 slice 3½ x 3½
   x ⅛ in. (1 oz.)
Creamed cottage cheese, ¼ cup
Low-fat cottage cheese, ½ cup
Parmesan, grated, 3 level tbsp.
Egg, 1 large

Anchovies, no oil, 9 thin fillets
Anchovy paste, 2 level tbsp.
Caviar, no oil, 2 level tbsp.
Clams, oysters, shrimp, 5 small
   or 3 large
Crab, lobster, ⅓ cup
Herring, pickled, 1 piece 1 x 1½
   x 1½ in.
Lox, no oil, 1 oz.
Sardines, no oil, 3 medium
Scallops, 2 to 3 (1½ oz.)
Frankfurter, 1 (8 to 10 per lb.)
Peanut butter, 2 level tbsp.

Cooked weight, 1 oz.; raw weight, 1⅓ oz.

List 6. Fat Exchanges
(One serving provides 5 gm fat and 45 calories.)

Butter or margarine, 1 pat (1
   level tsp.)
Bacon, crisp, 1 slice
Coconut, fresh, 1 piece 1 x 1 x
   ⅜ in.
Cream cheese, 1 level tbsp.
Neufchâtel cheese, 2 level tbsp.
Cream
   Light (20%), 2 level tbsp.
   Heavy (40%), 1 level tbsp.

French dressing or oil and
   vinegar, 1 tbsp.
Mayonnaise, 1 level tsp.
Nuts in shell, 6 small
Tartar sauce, 2 level tsp.
Oil or cooking fat, 1 tsp.
Olives, 5 small or 3 large
Avocado (4″ diameter) ⅛
   section

High on Carbohydrates

*A*lthough carbohydrates have been the whipping boy of many diet makers for decades past, they have suddenly become the stars of some new diets. Some diets emphasize complex carbohydrates, others certain simple carbohydrates such as fructose.

An advantage of a high-carbohydrate diet is that there is plenty of sweet to satisfy cravings for candy and confection. This is because simple carbohydrates are sugars, and complex carbohydrates are starches that saliva breaks down to sugars as they are chewed.

Another advantage of high carbohydrate foods is that they are essentially derived from plants, which means they are free of heavy fats. That means they are less calorie-intensive than any meat. (Carbohydrate is four calories per gram; fat is nine calories per gram.) Also, carbohydrates seem to pose little or no threat to arteries, certainly less of a threat than fats.

Another advantage, according to Martin Katahn, Ph.D., director of the Weight Management Program at Vanderbilt University, Nashville, is that carbohydrates provide energy "to keep you feeling zestful and to give you the increasing endurance you are trying to build." A high-carbohydrate diet, he points out, is what coaches give their top athletes so they can have maximum energy and endurance.[1] The contrast to low-carbohydrate diets is striking; as anyone who has ever been on a low-carbohydrate diet can testify, a deficit in carbohydrates makes you feel low and energy-less.

Dr. Katahn adds that there is metabolic benefit. "Compared with dietary fat, it costs the body four times the amount of energy to put excess carbohydrate calories into your fat stores. It takes about 5 percent of the energy content of dietary fat to convert it to storage. It takes about 20 percent of any excess carbohydrates to do the job."

Nathan Pritikin, popular high-carbo guru, wrote, "The benefits of a high-carbohydrate diet for weight loss over other approaches, dietary or nondietary, are numerous. Diets high in unrefined, complex carbohydrates associated with intact fiber tend to lower blood insulin levels and normalize carbohydrate and lipid (fat) metabolism. The water and high fiber content of the foods permitted provide sufficient bulk in the diet to appease the hunger of the average dieter. Because these foods are low in caloric density, the high carbohydrate diet is of great help even to compulsive eaters in controlling their weight."[2]

Furthermore, the Good Housekeeping Institute has stated, "Contrary to popular belief, those delicious high-starch foods you have probably considered forbidden ... are actually *ideal* for dieting. In fact, nutrition experts are recommending as the best diet one that's more than 50 percent carbohydrate."[3]

This chapter will examine current popular plans for losing weight on diets that derive half or more of their total daily calories from starchy foods. We'll also look at diets that push "good" carbohydrates. Be sure to also read the chapter on vegetarian diets, which is a specialized approach to the high-carbohydrate diet. Vegetarian diets are essentially derived from plant sources and are also high in fiber, since they emphasize vegetables, fruits, and whole grains. The diets discussed here may include foods derived from animal sources, and foods rich in carbohydrates from refined sources, such as wheat flour and corn syrup.

The 200-Calorie Solution

This book by Dr. Katahn (quoted above) is based on two premises. One is that you need to exercise to burn 200 calories every day. That's the 200-calorie solution. "Most overweight people in this country [US] do not fully appreciate how inactive they are," writes Dr. Katahn. The more inactive we become, the fatter. And the fatter we get, the less active." Therefore, he proposes that you exercise every day: "Adding an average of 200 calories of energy expenditure to your life each day is a good guarantee that you will not regain whatever weight you lose following temporary, moderate caloric restriction, when you start to eat 'normally' again."

To lose weight, he puts you on a 1200-calories-a-day diet (1500 for men). At that level, you should lose three pounds the first week and about two pounds every week thereafter, he says. You get most of your carbohydrates from bread, pasta, potato, fruits, and juices, and your basic protein from chicken, fish, flank steak, and lean hamburger.

Dr. Katahn emphasizes high carbohydrates not only as a substitute for fat but as a direct source of energy for your newly exercised muscles. He points to the fact that muscles have their own stores of energy, in the form of a carbohydrate known as glycogen. But these energy stores are mighty small. "Your quick energy stores total about 2,000 calories," he writes. "You can deplete your quick energy stores in a matter of hours with vigorous activity.... When you get low on stored glycogen, you get low on energy." Thus, a high-carbohydrate diet enables your muscles to replace the glycogen they have used in exercise. A similar technique is used in training athletes for competition. Known as "carbohydrate loading," this technique begins by having the athlete completely expend stored muscle glycogen and then replenish (perhaps overload) with new glycogen. To use up the muscle glycogen, the athlete exercises to exhaustion those muscles used in competition and simultaneously eats a low-carbohydrate diet. CONSUMER GUIDE® points out that while many athletes follow this regime, its usefulness and its competitive advantage have not been proved.

CONSUMER GUIDE®'S EVALUATION

While Dr. Katahn is not suggesting you deplete your muscle glycogen stores, as athletes may do, he does recommend a similar approach to carbohydrate loading, albeit for a much lower level of physical activity. Although the carbohydrate-loading premise may be spurious, the diet

plan is a good one, in that it provides adequate amounts of protein and fat.
Rating: ★★★

For Carbohydrate Cravers

Written by a researcher at the Massachusetts Institute of Technology,
The Carbohydrate Craver's Diet[4] offers an 1100-calories-a-day diet
based on carbohydrates at every meal, plus sweet and starchy snacks in
between. Naughty as the diet sounds, its author, Judith J. Wurtman,
Ph.D., maintains it works—and works better than high-protein diets that
have become so popular. The reason, according to Dr. Wurtman, is that
the chemistry of your brain, not your will, makes you crave carbohydrates,
and only carbohydrates can satisfy this craving. You will keep eating other
kinds of foods in vain efforts to satisfy the craving, but you'll only add
calories to calories. All it takes to quell the desire is some sweets, a small
amount at many fewer total calories.

Judith Wurtman, Ph.D., is the research scientist in the Department of
Nutrition, Massachusetts Institute of Technology, who made a publicity
splash in 1981 when she and her husband, Richard Wurtman, M.D., said
they discovered why some people crave sweets and other carbohydrates
and will eat them no matter how much other foods they've eaten. The
secret they uncovered was that a body chemical — tryptophan — is
released, after some chemical processes, when carbohydrates are eaten
and digested. Tryptophan controls hunger. Ergo, eat carbos and your
body sends tryptophan to turn off the appetite control center of your brain.

That's why high-protein, low carb diets fail, she says: Not enough
carbohydrates to stimulate tryptophan release.

That's the background. Now the diet: breakfast, 200 calories; lunch,
300 calories; and dinner 400 calories. That's 900 calories. The kicker is
the 200-calorie, carbohydrate-rich snack, such as a 1.4-ounce package
of M&M's, or four fig bars, or a two-ounce Milky Way, or a two-ounce 3
Musketeers bar, or an ice-cream sandwich.

"Snacks," writes Dr. Wurtman, "are at the very heart of the Carbohydrate Craver's Diet. They are not a gimmick, and they are not a
200-calorie reward for good eating behavior. They are fundamental to
the diet. A carbohydrate-rich snack, eaten at your peak craving period,
is what makes the diet work. It's also what enables you to stay with the
diet for as long as you need to."

Dr. Wurtman also encourages women who have a sweet tooth just
before their menstrual periods to snack sweetly. Sweets also alleviate
stress, so don't feel guilty if you eat candy when you are uptight, she
advises.

She adds that her diet has been tested on MIT students and WORKS!
No surprise, considering she was feeding them only 1100 calories a day.

CONSUMER GUIDE®'S EVALUATION

Dr. Wurtman's degrees are in teaching and education. Her diet will
certainly appeal to those with a sweet tooth, and will work because it
controls calories. But it ignores the lack of control sweets lovers have

when they get their hands on candy and such. Also, she does not address the phenomenon of eating refined carbohydrates—they cause a rapid rise of blood sugar, then a precipitous fall. This fall triggers hunger pangs. Rating: Not recommended. No Stars.

The Beverly Hills Medical Diet

No, no, it's not the Mazel Beverly Hills diet, it's the Beverly Hills MEDICAL Diet (BHMD) by Dr. Arnold Fox.[5] It's not only the name that fools you, it's also the fervor of the prose. Sample:

> With the Beverly Hills Medical Diet you will lose weight. As much as ten pounds, or more, in two weeks.
> With my Long-Life Anti-Stress Program you will feel better. Better than you ever thought possible.
> With my program of sound nutrition you will live longer. And you will *stay* slim.
> Too good to be true?
> Hardly.
> *I have seen the proof.*

Perhaps it's the smog that makes Beverly Hills diet gurus breathless. In any case, Dr. Fox's hype (or perhaps it is that of Cindy Turpin Owen and Stan Ginsburg, who worked on the manuscript) is highly anti-high-protein, anti-ketosis, anti-fat, and very pro-unrefined-carbohydrates. So his diet rests heavily on "a hearty feast of those Complex Carbohydrates and fiber-laden foods."

If you strip away the hype, the BHMD is surprisingly top-rate. It emphasizes whole grains, fish, and poultry, and it cuts down or eliminates beef, pork, and white-flour foods, keeping calories low.

The BHMD gives 20 percent of its calories as fat, little or no cholesterol, and minimum sodium and sugar. Dr. Fox does not tell you how many calories a day you get by eating his diet but "hints" at 1500. Nor does he provide a nutritional breakdown of his diet.

CONSUMER GUIDE®'S EVALUATION

Despite the hype and the informational shortcomings, the BHMD is worth trying. Rating: ★★★★

Your Best Chance?

The publicity touts Joe D. Goldstrich as "Nathan Pritikin's former cardiologist." Also, he was National Director of Education and Community Program for the American Heart Association. Furthermore, says the publicity release, the Dallas doctor gave up his practice and a hospital staff position in order to develop a diet for losing weight and saving your heart. Now, says a note in the book, "Dr. Goldstrich's program offers you the best of both worlds: a fully integrated approach to curing and preventing heart disease, losing weight safely and achieving true and complete health."

Wow! With hype like that, *The Best Chance Diet*[6] should take off like a rocket. Zoom! Be a best seller. Zham! On it, everyone should lose weight and keep heart trouble away. Zowie!

Dr. Goldstrich says he lost weight on Pritikin's diet (discussed below), which he feels has some good nutritional concepts. "But the diet Nathan Pritikin had developed is a very rigid diet. It is a diet which I felt many people would find difficult to follow once they left the protective environment of the Longevity Center." So he developed his own diet, which is more flexible.

His diet is low in fat, cholesterol, and salt, and high in complex carbohydrates. He gives you 14 days of it, plus recipes developed by his mother, Edythe, who lost 32 pounds on the diet. But he doesn't tell enough. He doesn't give portion size in the diet, and he gives all of the components of his formula for weight loss, except calorie count:

- protein: up to 25 percent of daily calories
- fat: 10 percent of daily calories
- complex carbohydrates: 60 to 70 percent of daily calories
- cholesterol: up to 200 mg a day
- salt: none
- alcohol: none
- sugars: none

CONSUMER GUIDE®'S EVALUATION

While Dr. Goldstrich is right about the rigidity of the Pritikin Program, he goes too far in the other direction. His diet is laid back, too general, and you have to use his recipes to make it work. Rating: Not recommended. No stars.

The Pritikin Diets

Certainly the most durable and feisty proponent of a high-carb diet is Nathan Pritikin, whose program, it seems, has as many critics as followers.

It all began in 1974, when the inventor, newly moved from Chicago to California, and his two co-authors of *Live Longer Now*[7] analyzed facts about diet and its effects on common, degenerative diseases — heart disease, diabetes, hypertension, and gout. From their survey of nutrition, they extracted guidelines for a diet to promote fitness and, presumably, to lengthen life. The diet has been used on clients in Pritikin's Longevity Center in California.

The diet changes in the 1974 book were drastic: reduction of daily fat to less than 10 percent of the total calories per day (the average level is now 42 percent, and the American Heart Association recommends 35 percent); no sugar or honey (an average American eats four ounces of sugar a day); severe limitations of daily consumption of caffeine, cholesterol, and salt; and no alcohol.

On the subject of weight reduction, the authors went lightly. They just about surrendered to the force of organically programmed body weight directed by our "appestats," pointing to the high failure rate among dieters. However, they claimed that the "appestat automatically readjusts itself to a more normal level when one switches to the Pritikin 2100 Diet and Exercise Program." In CONSUMER GUIDE®'s view, this claim is unproved.

In 1979, Pritikin published what is still a hot book in the diet market. Essentially an expanded, updated version of *Live Longer Now,* the bestselling *The Pritikin Program*[8] explains that the Pritikin Diet is low in fats, cholesterol, protein, and highly refined carbohydrates, such as sugars.

The other half of *The Pritikin Program* is exercise. "The main exercise we recommend (in fact, you don't have to do anything else) is regular, sustained walking. All sustained isotonic exercises that work your long muscles, particularly your legs, so as to pump the blood back up to your heart, are acceptable," Pritikin writes.

There are two diets in *The Pritikin Program.* One is the Longevity Diet. The other is the Maximum Weight Loss Diet.

The Longevity Diet is not designed to reduce weight, although it is called "unbeatable for safe, effective, long-lasting weight loss." And it seems inevitable that switching from the typical American high-fat, high-protein diet to spartan Pritikin fare would shed some excess poundage. It is not strictly vegetarian; it allows some dairy foods, meat, and fish although it is suggested that the dieter think of these animal products as no more than condiments to flavor the foods emphasized in the diet — grains, vegetables, and fruits.

The menu for a typical day on the Longevity Diet would look like this:

Breakfast
½ grapefruit
Bowl of cooked, whole wheat grain cereal with sliced banana, skim milk, cinnamon, and bran

Lunch
Bowl of lentil soup
Whole wheat pita bread (warmed or toasted) stuffed with raw salad greens, pickled vegetables (pepper, pimiento, onions, cauliflower, celery, etc.) and sprinkled with vinegar or lemon juice and bran
Glass of water with lemon wedge

Dinner
Oxtail soup (defatted)
Broccoli and yellow squash (steamed)
Long-grain brown rice
String bean salad
Sourdough or whole grain rye bread
Applesauce mixed with skim-milk yogurt

Snacks
Scandinavian flatbreads
A few pieces of fresh raw fruit (apples, pears, grapes, peaches, or plums)
Whole wheat pita bread stuffed with salad material, as per lunch

The Maximum Weight Loss (MWL) Diet is specifically aimed at losing weight. The Maximum Weight Loss Diet actually is two diets: one provides 600 calories per day; the other, 1000.

Pritikin calls the Maximum Weight Loss Diet, "your safest, most effective way to shed excess pounds and achieve an attractive figure." And he claims that his diet "is superior by far to any fast. A total fast, for instance, would produce only 6 more pounds of weight reduction in one month than his plan." He adds that a total fast would bring on unpleasant and worrisome side effects as well.

The Maximum Weight Loss Diet is built upon two rules.

Rule Number 1: Eat all day. To accomplish this, people on the Maximum Weight Loss Diet carry a plastic bag containing raw vegetables. The bag may contain, for example, four ounces of carrots, a half pound of cauliflower, or a half pound of radishes. Since these raw vegetables are high in bulk and low in calories, dieters can nibble on them all day to keep the stomach full and stave off hunger pangs.

Rule Number 2: Eat one portion of food a day from the grain, dairy, and fruit groups. Eat as much food as you want from his other groups, including soups, cooked vegetables, salads, and entrees such as stuffed zucchini and breaded eggplant.

Says Pritikin, experience at his Longevity Center in California shows that patients on the Maximum Weight Loss Diet can lose up to 31 pounds in the four-week period—and still eat up to four pounds of food every day. The average monthly weight loss of these patients is 13.2 pounds.

Pritikin writes, "For most dieters at most times, weighing of foods should not be necessary." Only when you can't lose ten or more pounds per month should you weigh your food portions.

The strategy behind the 600-calorie and the 1000-calorie diets is to "provide plenty of diet interest." Dieters eat a variety of vegetables, and by using Pritikin's recipes and his ideas for combining vegetables, they can prepare a number of innovative low-cal dishes. But because the diet requires eating so many vegetables, dieters have to spend a good deal of time preparing food. To save some time, Pritikin suggests purchasing a good chef's knife or a food processor or cooking large quantities of food and freezing them. A sample menu for the 600-calorie Maximum Weight Loss Diet follows:

Breakfast
  3.5 ounces cooked oatmeal
    (plus bran)
  4 ounces nonfat milk
  ½ orange

Lunch
  8 ounces Latin belle soup
  4 ounces raw bell peppers
  4 ounces raw carrots
  4 ounces raw cauliflower
  4 ounces raw cucumbers

Dinner
  8 ounces tomato-rice soup
  8 ounces shredded cabbage,
    onions, and tomatoes
  8 ounces stuffed eggplant

The 1000-calorie diet uses the 600-calorie diet as a basis and allows the addition of another 400 calories in a variety of ways. For instance, the dieter could have one baked potato (for 145 calories), eight medium strawberries (100 calories), and four ounces of fish or fowl (90 to 190 calories).

As anyone can see, Pritikin's Maximum Weight Loss Diets provide little protein and fat, but plenty of vegetable bulk.

Bowing to pressure about the protein inadequacy of the MWL diet, Pritikin inserted the following paragraph (p. 127) in the 1980 paperback edition of his book:

"The 600-calorie diet contains 30-35 grams of protein which should be adequate because high-carbohydrate diets are protein-sparing. If more protein is desired, 3 oz. of uncreamed cottage cheese each day will add 17 grams of protein, bringing the total protein intake to 50 grams and calories intake to 680."[9]

The Pritikin Maximum Weight Loss Diet is extremely spartan, or should we say primitive. Its main tenet, very low fat content (5 to 10 percent of calories), is very restrictive and initially unappealing to Americans who are used to a diet that contains 40 to 45 percent fat because flavor often accompanies fat.

The Pritikin Program diets are also low in protein; they aim for 10 percent protein (in calories). Pritikin believes, "The body's need for protein has been grossly exaggerated." He continues, "Excessive protein is quite harmful. You will find that the Pritikin Diet challenges many of the most sacred assumptions about the role of protein."

Challenge is one thing, proof is something else. Proof requires lots of data, which Pritikin has not provided. Rather, data back up the National Academy of Sciences, which has stated "nor is there evidence that [protein] intakes double or triple the recommended allowances are harmful. In fact, protein intakes that exceed RDA are often desirable, since low protein diets usually contain only small amounts of animal products and thus tend to be unpalatable and low in important trace nutrients."[10]

CONSUMER GUIDE®'s calculations show that the amount of protein in a "Typical Day's Fare" of the Longevity Diet is right on the edge — a bit more than a woman needs but not as much as a man requires. Still, it is half again as much protein as in Pritikin's Maximum Weight Loss Diet.

The Maximum Weight Loss Diet has 30 to 35 grams of protein, which is below the 44 to 56 grams of protein in the National Academy of Science's Recommended Dietary Allowances.[11]

The bulk of the Pritikin Program diets (80 percent in calories) is derived from complex carbohydrates — vegetables. The Maximum Weight Loss Diet specifies unusually large—to some people, mind-boggling—amounts of food, half a pound of this, and a quarter pound of that. True, the foods are vegetables that are low in calories, and certainly the fiber from these vegetables will help speed food through the intestines and will keep the bowels moving. But all that roughage may be dangerous for people with a bleeding peptic ulcer or active ulcerative colitis. Large quantities of such vegetables as beans are apt to produce gas.

In any case, if you do decide to take up the Pritikin Maximum Weight Loss Diet, add or double the optional cottage cheese supplement. And if you want other vegetarian diets, we suggest Loma Linda's, Weight Watchers', or the Scarsdale version.

CONSUMER GUIDE®'S EVALUATION

Still too primitive and too sparse. Rating: Not recommended. No stars.

You should also be aware of a rigorous study at another center of research that sought to objectively evaluate the Pritikin Program's claims for longevity and heart health. The widely quoted study was conducted at the University of Alberta, Edmonton, and reported in the *Journal of the American Medical Association* (October 23, 1981). Gordon Brown, M.D., who led the study of 50 patients, said the Pritikin Program offered no more relief from peripheral vascular disease than did the moderate diet proposed for many more years by the American Heart Association (AHA).

Furthermore, said Dr. Brown, there was some evidence that the Pritikin Program may lead to reduced resistance to infection and poor wound healing. For these and other reasons, the program is unsuitable for women of childbearing age.

Dr. Elizabeth M. Whelan, of the American Council on Science and Health, called the Pritikin Program "restrictive, austere, and dreary."[12]

Pritikin questioned some of the methods in the Alberta Study and said his own 1975 study showed significant improvement in peripheral vascular disease, although he did not compare his Program's results to the AHA regimen. He also charged the Canadians with not knowing his diet. Dr. Brown countered that his study center's dietitian had attended Pritikin's center, learned his methods, and found him cooperative because he wanted such a study done with a control group.[13]

Pritikin Permanent Weight-Loss Diet

In 1981, Pritikin came out with a new version of his program, *The Pritikin Permanent Weight-Loss Manual*.[14] Finally, he was putting it on the line: here was a new diet and exercise program, primarily designed to help you lose weight and to keep it off. It is based, he writes, on "the ideal regimen for both weight-loss and long-term weight maintenance." That is, a high-carbohydrate diet of 700 to 1200 calories a day. And it not only can make you slim forever but also can make you healthy all your life, he says.

The new Pritikin weight-loss diet is far better than the older Maximum Weight Loss Plan. It provides enough fish, fowl, egg white, and lean beef to give you all the high-quality protein you should need. There is also enough variety to keep you from getting bored and dropping out.

CONSUMER GUIDE®'S EVALUATION

The new Pritikin Permanent Weight-Loss Diet is probably the best high-carbohydrate diet around for losing weight. While it is still too spartan for most dieters' tastes, it might just afford the right mixture of discipline and variety for you to successfully lose weight and keep it off. Rating: ★★★

Quick Weight-Loss Program

There is another *Live Longer Now* descendant, authored by Jon N. Leonard, Ph.D., one of Pritikin's original collaborators at the Longevity Foundation. Dr. Leonard, now director of the Institute of Health in Tucson, Arizona, wrote the 1980 *Quick Weight-Loss Program*.[15] It allows you to eat all the fresh vegetables you want, but to limit your meat to a quarter pound of lean cuts a day. Fresh fruits are limited to three or four pieces a day. Allowed are egg whites (no yolks) and nonfat milk and its products. Not allowed are nuts, avocados, olives, and packaged or canned fruits and vegetables.

CONSUMER GUIDE®'S EVALUATION

Actually, Dr. Leonard describes a philosophy of eating and losing weight, rather than a diet. He also offers recipes and exercises. Rating: ★★★

Fructose, the "Good" Sugar

It's a bit of a dilemma. Tom Cooper is actually against carbohydrates. Well, all but one. That one is a sugar called fructose. Perhaps his Fructose Diet and their products ought to be in the chapter on low carbohydrate diets. Still, because he wants you to have lots of his kind of carbohydrate, fructose, it seemed logical to place it here, instead. The problem is that in either place, it will be confusing.

Fructose, in Dr. Cooper's opinion, is a "good" sugar. It is otherwise known as fruit sugar. It is found in abundance in grapes, strawberries, apples, pears, and corn. It is also a component of sucrose, or table sugar (which is derived from sugar cane and sugar beets), and honey.

In fact, both table sugar and honey are composed of almost equal portions of fructose and glucose. That other sugar, glucose, is the source of energy in the body. When ordinary sugar is digested, it is broken down to fructose and glucose. "Fructose is partly converted to glucose in the intestinal mucosa. The remaining fructose is rapidly converted to glucose or glycogen in the liver."[16] Glucose enters the bloodstream almost immediately and begins to work. Its first job is to fuel the brain and the central nervous system. Its second is to provide energy for other cells, tissues, and organs. Glucose that is not "burned" as fuel for brain or brawn converts into animal starch and is stored (glycogen) in the liver and the muscles. Excess glucose (i.e., more than that which can be stored in the liver and muscles) becomes fat and is stored on thighs, buttocks, and the abdomen.

Fructose alone usually is sweeter than table sugar. As a result, people use a third to a half the amount and get a third to a half the calories of regular sugar. For instance, a glass of sugar-sweetened pop has 92 calories, but a glass of pop sweetened with 90 percent fructose corn syrup has 46. But fructose's sweetness depends on how it is used. According to an article in *FDA Consumer,* "It can be 15 to 80 percent sweeter than sucrose, but its sweetness…decreases as temperature, amount of fructose, and acidity are decreased."[17]

Fructose health claims began a century ago when a German doctor found that it was more suitable than regular sugar for his diabetic patients. In those days, fructose was very expensive because it could be made only from a substance found in the tubers of such plants as the dahlia and Jerusalem artichoke. Fructose remained expensive until recent years because it had to be imported from Europe in pill or granulated form. Today fructose can be made rather inexpensively from corn syrup. Also on the market, new in 1982, are fructose tablets, which at eight calories per tablet, "are recommended for use between meals as an appetite appeaser," according to the label. The tablets, under their trade name *Fabulous Fructose Tabs*, are sold by Teltex Inc., of Provo, Utah (P.O. Box 1575), which also sells Dutch Chocolate, Sassy Strawberry, and French

Vanilla powders, high in fructose and vitamins, for mixing with skim milk. Sold under the trade name, *Fabulous Fructose Diet*, the milkshakes (at 130 calories per shake) are meant to replace two regular meals. The third meal should be of food, centered around some ordinary source of protein such as fowl, fish, or red meat.

Large manufacturers of sweeteners are gearing up for a fructose sales drive. For instance, Archer Daniels Midland (ADM) of Cedar Rapids, Iowa, built a $25 million plant to produce tank-car quantities of a refined corn syrup that is 90 percent fructose. ADM also has been distributing copies of the best-selling book, *Dr. Cooper's Fabulous Fructose Diet*.[18]

What is fabulous about J. T. "Tom" Cooper's diet is that you must consume about 1½ ounces, by weight, of fructose a day. Do that, says the Atlanta fat doctor, and you will not be hungry and you will be able to remain loyal to the otherwise low-carbohydrate diet he recommends.

Cooper's diet is skewed in the wrong direction, however. He offers a high-protein, high-fat diet, whereas scientific evidence urges less protein and fat and more carbohydrates. The diet, he explains, involves "the fructose supplement of 30 to 40 grams per day; a large amount of protein foods such as fish, poultry, and meat; two large salads; potassium and other minerals; and lots of liquid."

Dr. Cooper extols fructose because "it does not require insulin to enter certain of the body's cells," and it thereby avoids the "glucose-insulin trap" that causes dieting failures. By the "glucose-insulin trap," he means that "almost every carbohydrate is converted in the body into a simpler sugar, glucose." Actually, fructose is converted to glucose, too.

In an interview with CONSUMER GUIDE®, Dr. Cooper admitted that he is aware that his fructose diet is a fad. "But," he asked, "why would anyone want to go on a fad diet? Because it works. It helps them get down to the weight they want to be. Look, people who go on diets want magic, a quick weight loss. They expect something slightly different than what they are used to. So we give them this magic and then ease them into a regular maintenance diet."

Dr. Cooper offers such a diet in his book, *The Fabulous Fructose Recipe Book*.[19] It recaps his basic weight-loss diet, then offers a rather well-rounded maintenance diet of 1200 to 1500 calories per day. The unique wrinkle in the Cooper approach is that he wants you to take fructose tablets whenever you feel the need for a snack, so as to, in his words, "abort the abnormal craving for sweets." He does put a limit on the practice though: no more than ten fructose tablets a day. He also borrows a page from Stillman and requires you to drink two quarts of water during the day. Here is Dr. Cooper's Fabulous Fructose Maintenance Diet.

Breakfast
- 1 fruit portion
- 2 low- or medium-fat protein portions
- 1 starch portion
- 3 fat portions
- 1 nonfat milk portion

Lunch
- 3 low- or medium-fat protein portions
- 1 or 2 starch portions
- 2 fat portions
- 1 or 2 vegetable portions
- 1 or 2 fruit portions
- ½ nonfat milk portion

Dinner

3 or 4 low- or medium-fat protein portions
1 starch portion

1 fruit portion
½ nonfat milk portion

Lists at the back of his book describe foods to be used in the diet and specify the amount of fiber, cholesterol, and sodium in each. A fruit portion is 40 calories; a vegetable portion, 25; starch, 70; low-fat protein, 55; medium-fat protein, 75; high-fat protein, 95; fat, 45; nonfat milk, 80; low-fat milk, 125; whole milk, 170.

CONSUMER GUIDE®'S EVALUATION

If you can forget the powders, tablets, and fructose fables, and skip the first book, Dr. Cooper's maintenance diet makes sense; and his food lists are useful, too. Rating: ★★★

The Hollywood Version

The fructose fable appears in another book, written by Hollywood actor Frank Downing,[20] that came out just about the same time. While being fitted for his costume as a maintenance man in the film *Coma*, Downing noted his fat. He weighed 225 pounds and had a 49-inch waist. He also had high blood pressure and high blood cholesterol. To walk a half-mile cost him his breath.

Today, Downing weighs 180 pounds. He has normal blood pressure and a normal cholesterol level. And he runs six miles a day.

His little black book called *The Hollywood Emergency Diet* costs about a dime a page and tells you that "fat people are not like skinny people." He claims that fat people are addicted to overeating because of bounding blood sugar levels. And the way to even out blood sugar levels and calm hunger pangs is—hold on to your chair—fructose. "Fructose is the only sugar that can be assimilated directly into your muscles," writes Downing. "Fructose raises your blood sugar level without creating an insulin response!"

In addition to fructose, Downing advises eating lots of kelp. Kelp is loaded with iodine, which he thinks stirs up the thyroid and fires up the body's metabolic furnace. In fact, it only helps if you have an iodine deficiency; too much iodine *slows* the thyroid!

Other secret weapons are lecithin, which "has the property of liquifying fat globules and thereby enabling them to be more readily flushed out of the body," and brewer's yeast, "probably the most highly concentrated protein food found in nature."

CONSUMER GUIDE®'S EVALUATION

As a dietitian, Downing is a great actor. Rating: Not recommended. No stars.

Diet of a Desperate Housewife

As ads for Downing's book were running in newspapers around the country, other ads promised that in return for $10 you would receive the weight-loss secrets of a desperate housewife.[21] What you got for you money was a lot of misinformation.

"As I very clearly state in my advertising," said Nancy Pryor, author-publisher of *The Amazing Diet Secret of a Desperate Housewife,* "I am not a doctor, nor a nutritionist... I am an ordinary garden variety housewife. But in spite of all that, I sincerely believe that I have come up with a weight-loss plan that outshines all the others."

Nancy Pryor made an offer you almost couldn't refuse. She wanted to accumulate 50 stories of people who tried her diet plan and succeeded in losing weight. Some of those stories would earn $50; others, $100; still others, $500. And the one she considered the best of all would win a $1,000 reward. All would be used in future ads.

Enticed? Great! Now for the secrets:

Secret No. 1: Fructose, often known as "fruit sugar." Fructose is a remarkable substance, says Pryor. Indeed, it would be remarkable if it did all the things she says it does: It tastes like table sugar (sucrose) and has the same number of calories, but "it can be assimilated *directly* into your muscle cells" and "*raises your blood sugar level without inducing an insulin response!*" (her italics).

Secret No. 2: Dieting every other day.

Secret No. 3: Lecithin, dolomite, brewer's yeast ("ounce for ounce it is probably the most nutritious food in the world for human consumption"), yogurt, and wheat germ.

Secret No. 4: Fructose before each meal.

Secret No. 5: Kelp, because Adelle Davis says so.

Pryor offers three diet variations, all of which revolve around these secrets. She allows no snacks and suggests you hold to 900 calories a day.

Now that you've heard the secrets of an "ordinary" housewife, compare them with this quote from a biochemistry textbook:

"Fructose is partly converted to glucose in the intestinal mucosa. The remaining fructose is rapidly converted to glucose or glycogen in the liver." In other words, the body takes all the fructose it gets and converts it — as it does all carbohydrate in food — directly into either glucose, the sugar which powers brain and body, or glycogen, a starch stored for future energy use.

CONSUMER GUIDE®'S EVALUATION

The lesson with Pryor, as with others, is that just because a statement has been printed does not make it a fact. Rating: Not recommended. No stars.

CRITICISM

While there are some advantages to a high-carbohydrate diet, there are disadvantages, and, more seriously, dangers. One disadvantage is the possibility of water accumulation. The main chemical ingredients of carbohydrate are carbon, hydrogen, and oxygen. The latter two, hydrogen and oxygen, occur in roughly the same proportion as in water (H_2O). In fact, that's why it is called *carbo* (for carbon) *hydrate* (for water). So, eating a lot of carbohydrate gives you a lot of water. Couple that with salt (as, say, in popcorn) and you may accumulate the water as bloat and pounds.

Another problem with emphasizing carbohydrate over meat is that you can readily become deficient in protein, iron, and Vitamin B_{12}. Proteins that are in carbohydrates are essentially derived from plants and, hence not complete protein for human requirements. Protein is made of amino acids and your body needs to get eight of them in specific, unequal amounts. Only soy protein comes close. Wheat protein provides all eight, but you have to sock away a lot of bakery goods to get enough protein.

Finally, there is insulin. Your pancreas secretes this hormone in response to the concentration of glucose in your blood. Glucose, a simple sugar, is the basic energy source of your body. That is why all sugars and starches you eat are converted to glucose. Ditto the excess protein you eat. If your pancreas is functioning normally, you don't have to worry; it will provide enough insulin to sweep the excess glucose out of your blood and keep the blood sugar level fairly constant. But if your pancreas is on the borderline of normal, or not functioning, you may have trouble, in the form of diabetes. Diabetes is a serious disease in which the body either does not produce enough insulin or can't properly use what insulin is produced. Many people don't realize they have it until they "overdose" on carbohydrates. Then, their blood sugar level soars, and the sugar spills over into the urine. That's why the two tests for diabetes measure sugar content of blood and urine.

Diabetics have to keep the levels of insulin and of glucose in their blood in balance. A high-carbohydrate diet can easily upset that balance in dieters who have diabetes without suspecting it.

So, CONSUMER GUIDE® advises, if you are considering a high-carbohydrate diet, first consult your doctor. If the doctor is in doubt, a glucose tolerance test will probably be recommended. In addition, if you are considering a near-vegetarian diet, consult you doctor — vegetables are members of the carbohydrate group. And if you do have diabetes, the best diet for you is one that controls calories and is nutritionally well-rounded, not high or low in carbohydrates.

As for fructose: it is, after all, a sugar, and ultimately will be converted to glucose in your body. The same cautions apply to high-fructose diets as to high-carbohydrate diets.

A word about carbohydrate loading: some coaches swear by it, some at it. In athletic performance, inherited physical capabilities, inherited coordination, and the will to win, plus good training, are the key elements to victory. A well-rounded diet is still best for all people, including athletes.

Low on Carbohydrates

*A*s the previous chapter testifies, carbohydrates are becoming less and less of a villain in dieting. Still the myth persists among many dieters and diet proponents that if you cut carbohydrates you "melt" fat.

Some even regard carbohydrates—and especially sugar—as poison. Take William Dufty, who wrote *Sugar Blues*[1] after he was inspired by Actress Gloria Swanson's no-sugar approach to eating. He also colors the approach with the Oriental notion that sugar is feminine *yin*. You crave to counterbalance it with red meat, the masculine *yang*. So, he wrote, give up both red meat and sugar together.

John Diamond, M.D., an Australian psychiatrist, also considers sugar a poison. It makes muscles weak, he wrote.[2]

With such misinformation from self-styled "authorities," it's easy to become confused. Also confusing is their terminology: consider for example, "low-carbohydrate diet." Almost all weight-reducing plans call for a reduction in carbohydrates. Nevertheless, a low-carbo diet has real, important differences. It usually restricts carbohydrates to near zero for part or all of the diet, but at the same time it lets you—even encourages you — to eat unlimited amounts of either of the other major food substances — fat or protein, two nutrients federal guidelines recommend decreasing.

THE ANTI-SUGAR MAN

John Yudkin, M.D., Ph.D., is one of the world's leading sugar antagonists. In his book—*Lose Weight, Feel Great!*[3]—he states, "Reducing the amount of fat in the diet does not produce a satisfactory diet for most people, and…reducing protein is either difficult or dangerous…I am recommending a low-carbohydrate diet for slimming."

In an earlier publication, this professor emeritus of nutrition at Queen Elizabeth College, University of London, reported that a low-carbohydrate diet is "the diet of choice in the treatment of obesity. It reduces excessive caloric intake: it is likely to contain a better supply of nutrients than do other calorie-restricted diets."[4] Furthermore, it is tasty, socially acceptable, and inexpensive.

He suggests this diet is easy to live with. Dr. Yudkin gives this example of the main meal of the day: "You take no bread with your soup; you take one small potato or none with your helping of meat and vegetables, nor need you trim the fat off the meat or avoid putting butter on the string beans; you have a piece of fruit after the main course and, if you are still hungry, a piece of cheese with perhaps a small cracker. You do not, of course, take sugar in your coffee, and you avoid soft drinks unless they are sugar-free."[5]

A low-carbohydrate diet, in other words, is nothing more than a "sound nutritious eating pattern," according to Dr. Yudkin. And, he believes it is far better than a low-calorie diet. Castigating his critics, he stressed,

> My colleagues and I have demonstrated by experiment, not simply by armchair calculation, that the supply of nutrients through this method is far better than in the orthodox method that tells you to eat the same as before, only less.
>
> I have never really understood why so many doctors in the American medical and nutritional establishment have frowned upon a diet that tells you in effect to reduce only, or chiefly, those foods that give you the calories you don't need while giving you the nutrients you do need.[6]

Dr. Yudkin's chief concern—aside from the effects of all carbohydrates on the body—is sugar. Having studied the effects of sugar on the body, and the alarming increase in the use of refined sugar, he became adamant about eliminating sugar from the diet. Many health authorities agree with this attitude toward refined sugar.

He observed that the artifical sugar substitute cyclamate was banned after rats, fed amounts many times more than those a person would consume, developed disease. Rats fed normal amounts of sugar, however, suffered worse: they had "enlarged and fatty livers, enlarged kidneys, and a shortening of life span."[7]

Dr. Yudkin believes that Americans and the British are becoming addicted to sugar and are suffering ill health and obesity as a result.[8] He notes that his countrymen today eat in two weeks the same amount of sugar they ate, on the average, in a whole year two centuries ago. In the US, we eat about 95 pounds of sugar per person per year.[9] A century ago, it was ten pounds per person per year.[10]

During World War II, many nations were forced to ration food. Studies of the civilian populations showed that, with moderate food cutbacks, including a reduction in sugar, the people enjoyed better health than before or after the war when sweets were plentiful. Of course, disease and death were rampant in countries whose population suffered starvation and famine.[11]

Eliminating sugar is the core of Dr. Yudkin's low-carbohydrate diet. He insists that by cutting out sugar, people will remove other carbohydrates from the diet. He recommends reducing the daily carbohydrate intake from 350 grams to 50 grams to lose weight. This reduction in carbohydrates will produce a saving of 1000 calories or more, he maintains.[12] Of this total, sugar will account for about 450 calories, hidden as it is in syrups, juices, soft drinks, ice cream, and pastry. Because sugar "is free from any nutrients whatever, it is clearly the first choice for curtailment or elimination in a diet that is to be rich in nutrients, but reduced in calories," says Dr. Yudkin.

Dr. Yudkin is also concerned with fat. However, he believes that fat in the diet will be reduced along with carbohydrates since the two so often go together in foods, as in cake and frosting, bread and butter, and fried potatoes. And he retorts that "the low-carbohydrate diet is not a high-fat diet, a designation frequently and incorrectly ascribed to it."

One advantage he ascribes to his low-carbohydrate diet is that you don't have to count calories. In his studies, Dr. Yudkin found that when he told his patients to eat anything they wanted but to limit their carbohydrate intake to 50 grams, their caloric intake decreased 35 percent; there was no decrease in protein intake and a small decrease in fat intake. "Thus, the low-carbohydrate diet significantly reduces calories while in almost every instance improving intake of nutrients. I cannot think of any other practical regimen for reducing caloric intake that will have a similar beneficial effect on the nutrient intake," says Dr. Yudkin.

One disadvantage is that you have to count carbohydrates. But "there are lots of foods that contain no carbohydrate at all," he wrote.[13] "Meats, fish, eggs, cheese, tea, coffee, butter, margarine, cooking fats. And there are many others that contain so little that you can ignore it: for example most of the vegetables like cabbage, lettuce, spinach, onions, and cauliflower, and also such things as cream."

But other foods contain plenty of carbohydrates, and you have to keep track of them. To help you tally your carbohydrate intake, Dr. Yudkin devised a table of Carbohydrate Units. Each CU, as he calls it, equals about five grams of carbohydrate.[14] CUs work like this: eat as much or as big a hamburger as you want; but if you eat it in a bun, count six CU. Two eggs and bacon for breakfast are fine, but if you take toast, it will cost you three CU. Cheese is fine; on three crackers, it equals three CU.

Dr. Yudkin does not suggest you overeat, merely eat until you feel satisfied, and most important, keep your carbohydrates to 10 CU per day. Actually, you will be cutting some of your calories, too.

CONSUMER GUIDE®'S EVALUATION

Dr. Yudkin's vehemence about carbohydrates, and particularly sugar, seems to have blinded his scientific objectivity. His diet is mediocre; he allows lots of calories, saturated fats, and cholesterol which everyone should limit. However, the dieter should listen to what he says about excessive sugar. Rating: ★★★

Dr. Atkins' Thin Carbs

Dr. Robert C. Atkins' *Superenergy Diet*[15] promotes a handful of diets, all based on the notion that when blood sugar plummets, you feel hungry and tired and tend to add pounds.

Scarred but not beaten from his forays with the American Medical Association and the US Congress over his high-fat diet, Dr. Atkins wrote *Dr. Atkins' Superenergy Diet* in 1977 with writer Shirley M. Linde of Florida.

The basis of the book is the observation that "a great percentage of overweight people have abnormalities in the specific areas of sugar metabolism." Such people are tired and anxious. For them, a low-carbohydrate diet can "improve or correct the condition." Atkins and Linde write, "The sugar in your diet may be more dangerous than the fats or the cholesterol…amounts and kinds of carbohydrates may be more significant than calories."

Dr. Atkins' Superenergy Diet is not one diet but four:

Diet No. 1. The Superenergy Weight Reducing Diet, which Dr. Atkins claims "is far superior to the low-calorie diet in the management of obesity." With the Superenergy Weight Reducing Diet, you count carbohydrates instead of calories and live it up on protein. You start at zero carbohydrates and gradually increase the amount of carbohydrates to about 40 or 50 grams or to the level at which you feel best.

Diet No. 2. The Superenergy Weight Gaining Diet, which is of no concern to us here.

Diet No. 3. The Superenergy Weight Maintenance Diet. The secret here is fructose which, Dr. Atkins claims, does not require insulin to "burn." "Thus," suggest Atkins and Linde, "it provides a readily available carbohydrate source for energy, but one which does not evoke the insulin overreaction that characterizes the person with low blood sugar and is the most common cause of fatigue."

Diet No. 4. For special situations — pregnancy and surgery. This diet merely limits sugars, starches, and refined flour.

Atkins and Linde (as did Dr. Cooper) draw heavily on and give credit to the writing of J. Daniel Palm, Ph.D., of Northfield, Minnesota, in his book, *Diet Away Your Stress, Tension, and Anxiety.*[16] Palm's Fructose Diet is low in carbohydrates and high in protein. It requires the dieter to exchange fructose for other carbohydrates. Palm suggests that you use fructose to sweeten coffee, tea, or Kool-Aid, use it in salad dressings and desserts, and even eat it as candy. The Palm Fructose Diet specifies that you take between 75 and 100 grams (300-400 calories) of fructose a day.

Says Palm, "The trick is to eat the fructose in small amounts at regular intervals throughout the day so that the digestive system will act as a reservoir. If you start feeling fatigued, if you yawn in the middle of the day or feel sleepy, you should eat some fructose then."

Although Atkin's diet calls for the use of unsaturated and vegetable fats, it also permits fat cuts of meat and poultry so that its overall fat content exceeds the US Senate guidelines.

While on any of the four Superenergy Diets, Dr. Atkins suggests you avoid alcohol and caffeine because they adversely influence blood sugar levels. He also recommends eating six rather than three meals a day to maintain a fairly constant blood sugar level and an energetic feeling, and he advocates megadoses of vitamins and minerals.

CONSUMER GUIDE®'S EVALUATION

In his indictment of sugar, Dr. Atkins is neither original nor alone. Pure sugar is densely packed with calories and devoid of significant nutrition, as is pure fructose. And the whole fructose scheme is nonsense: The body converts fructose into glucose, the only form of sugar it can use, and glucose requires insulin. Rating: ★

Dr. Blackburn's Low-Carbo Balanced Deficit Diet

Dr. George Blackburn, whose ideas were pirated by Dr. Robert Linn for the latter's liquid protein diet, has actually designed a diet that you can follow.

Dr. Blackburn, a surgeon-nutritionist on the faculties of Harvard Medical School and the Massachusetts Institute of Technology, says "There is nothing unique with this diet except that it strictly reduces starches and sugars, and in other regards is similar to the American Diabetes Association's exchange list diet."[17]

Because the diet does not meet daily vitamin requirements, all patients should take a daily vitamin supplement with iron. And such a diet should be followed under a doctor's care, he adds. It also does not follow US Senate guidelines for increasing carbohydrates and decreasing animal fats, cholesterol, and saturated fats in the diets.

Dr. Blackburn states that this is not a crash diet you can jump on and off. You have to commit yourself for as long as it takes to get to normal weight. That may mean a year or more. He promises that once you are at normal weight some profound changes will take place in your body. Your appetite will lessen to match your thinner body. And your insulin balance will be restored so that your body will stop making so much fat.

Blackburn believes that insulin is the reason for the low-carbohydrate diet. Carbohydrates require insulin to burn, but insulin also has a role in converting unused carbohydrate to fat and storing the fat on your body. So, lower your carbohydrate intake and you also lower fat production—if only it were that simple!

This exchange diet includes meal plans and lists. For example, if the breakfast meal plan calls for a high Vitamin C fruit, go to that list and choose one with an asterisk.

Unlike other exchange diets, this one offers no snacks. Blackburn feels that insulin should be mobilized as infrequently as possible; that means eating only three meals and no snacks.

CONSUMER GUIDE®'S EVALUATION

This diet is more reasonable than most low-carbohydrate diets — and probably more palatable, too. Rating: ★★

Paul Michael's Plan

One of the first items that strikes you in Paul Michael's "confidential report" is that "bread isn't the basic food for human beings. Meat is. 'Naturally' thin people know this intuitively." As proof, Michael cites the Eskimos, who live on a diet of blubber (fat) and fish and eat essentially no carbohydrates. He sees carbohydrates as the culprit of modern-day diets, and, by his reasoning, cream is less fattening than milk, simply because cream contains less milk sugar than whole milk!

The basis of *The Paul Michael Weight-Loss Plan*[18] is a reduction in carbohydrate intake to a maximum of 60 grams a day. You can eat all the proteins and fats you want. And you can eat them whenever you are hungry. Outside of that, he suggests six meals a day instead of three.

CONSUMER GUIDE®'S EVALUATION

Pure nonsense. If your body receives more protein than can immediately be used for cell building and energy, it stores the excess as fat, and you gain weight. Rating: Not recommended. No stars.

Brand Name Carbohydrate Diet

"Besides a significant weight loss, a decrease in carbohydrate intake improved the appearance of hair and skin and added to mental and physical alertness. Prolongation of life was also indicated."[19]

If you think that statement came from a medical report, you're wrong. It was found in a little book that promotes a so-called carbohydrate diet but actually describes a low-carbohydrate diet.

Published by Success Publications of North Miami Beach (which also goes under the name of Merit Publications), the book *Brand Name Carbohydrate Diet* states that *"cutting down on carbohydrate intake can have some wonderful results"* (book's italics). It mentions "experiments at Johns Hopkins University and at the Columbia-College of Physicians and Surgeons as well as the Middlesex Hospital in England," but it provides no information on them.

The diet is simple: no less than 40 nor more than 60 grams of carbohydrate a day, plenty of fluids, three full meals, including "a good old ham and eggs breakfast," plus 15 minutes of daily exercise.

That's on the first six pages. The remaining 117 pages of the book offer an alphabetical listing of foods (some by brand name) by their size and carbohydrate content.

CONSUMER GUIDE®'S EVALUATION

This little book ("an ideal supermarket and restaurant companion" says the publisher) is successful because carbohydrates are natural fall guys. Dieters believe that if they avoid the Three Cs—cookies, candy, and cake —they'll lose weight. This advice ignores the other, "good" sources of carbohydrates: fruits, vegetables, cereals, and grains. Rating: ★★

No Carbohydrates Forever

Alberto Cormillot, M.D., is a South American; yet his diet and approach to dieting are geared to North Americans. His eating plan, he promises, "will keep you permanently satisfied and free from hunger, aroused by eating of carbohydrates.

"Once you have eliminated carbohydrates, you will see your bulging stomach disappear with surprising speed. That is, you'll lose not only pounds, but inches as well. With this plan, you'll be able to regulate your weight loss by increasing and decreasing the carbohydrates in your diet."[20]

He strays even further into fantasy when he says, "Reducing the quantity of calories...is generally not necessary. The important thing is to reduce the carbohydrates."

The Cormillot Thin Forever Diet lists as forbidden *all* cereals, grains, and nuts, as well as *all* pasta and other flour products. Among the acceptable foods are lean meat, skim milk, yogurt, ricotta cheese, and diet drinks. However, he also allows such high-fat foods as bologna and knockwurst.

CONSUMER GUIDE®'S EVALUATION

Definitely this is an unbalanced diet. Rating: Not recommended. No stars.

Doctors Kremers' No-Breakfast Diet

"Starch is to the overweight person what alcohol is to the alcoholic; the more he takes of it, the more he wants." This is how William F. Kremer, M.D., and Laura Kremer, M.D., view the making of the overweight.[21]

They provide absolution by stating that "overweight people are governed by a different hormonal make-up from people of average weight. Their (the overweights) overeating is not, in its origin, due to self-indulgence. Instead it is forced on them by an increased tendency to mobilize foods inside their own bodies. Their overeating is not necessarily founded on unusual lack of willpower or self-discipline, but might be determined by a shift of the hormonal balance."

The way to tip hormonal balance back the other way is to eat plenty of protein but few carbohydrates, says Dr. Kremer. It all has to do with glucagon, a hormone that forces the body to release its stored fat and starch for use as fuel.

The Kremers offer a basic 500-calorie dinner and let you add 100 to 300 calories from predinner drinks and soup to achieve what they believe is a reasonable number of calories, assuming no breakfast is eaten.

After dinner, apples, carrots, celery, and sugarless chewing gum are allowed until bedtime.

Lunch for the Kremer dieter consists of a 400-calorie sandwich. But breakfast is a real surprise. "The best breakfast is no breakfast." The Kremers ask, "Who says you have to eat breakfast?" And answer their own question: "Thin nutritionists who like breakfast, that's who...As a matter of fact, if you are overweight, breakfast is the worst way to start the day."

They claim that no study has proved the need for eating upon arising from night's sleep and that there is no proof that failing to eat breakfast in the morning will foster nibbling and craving the rest of the day. They point out that the workingman's breakfast, which was the norm when people went to work at dawn, was actually a hearty brunch consumed after a morning's work. Also, workers went to bed right after dinner, when the sun had set. Today, "most people eat enough between 6:00 P.M. and bedtime to see them nicely through the next morning till noon."

CONSUMER GUIDE®'S EVALUATION

While some people require breakfast, others do not. If you need breakfast,this diet is not for you. But if you prefer to skip the morning meal, this otherwise well thought-out diet may suit your lifestyle. Rating: ★★★

The Drinking Man's Diet

A low-carbohydrate diet with a gimmick is found in the The Drinking Man's Diet.[22] Perhaps the most popular diet in the mid-1960s, The Drinking Man's Diet still has its defenders. Actually a 60-gram carbohydrate diet, the program "allows you to take out your favorite girl for a dinner of squab and broccoli with Hollandaise sauce and Chateau Lafitte, to be followed by an evening of rapture and champagne." In short, the idea is to let you be sociable—even a bit wicked—eating and drinking with apparent abandon, yet taking off pounds as you maintain your health.

The 54-page booklet, which went through at least eight printings, calls low-calorie diets unaesthetic and "downright unhealthy." It even includes testimonials from advertising and insurance executives.

Written under pseudonyms by Robert Wernick, The Drinking Man's Diet actually is an adaptation of a mimeographed or handwritten diet which had been making the rounds from hand to hand, office to office. It was variously (and wrongly) called the Air Force Diet, the Airline Pilots' Diet, and the Astronauts' Diet. An insurance man, an advertising man, and a sharp marketing specialist got the idea of dressing it up with text.[23]

Wernick talked to doctors, and read books, and government publications. One doctor told him: "Hell, nutrition isn't an exact science. Cutting down on your carbohydrates can't possibly hurt you. Just be sure you get enough of them so your liver can handle the liquor you drink."

Not the subject of prolonged research, this thin pamphlet for fat drinkers was produced in one month. The public press (whose reporters are not known for their abstinence from alcohol) heralded it across the country. Some, like Time magazine however, were critical. "The book's contents are a cocktail of wishful thinking, a jigger of nonsense, and a dash of sound advice."[24]

Thirty-five of the booklet's 54 pages contain tables that list the number of grams of carbohydrates in various foods and drinks—all derived from pamphlets issued by the US Department of Agriculture. For legal reasons, the booklet contains such cautions as: eat at least 30 grams of carbohydrates a day; join Alcoholics Anonymous if you have a drinking problem; and eat "plenty of protein to protect your liver."

CONSUMER GUIDE®'S EVALUATION

Throw away your swizzle sticks; this diet is not to be taken seriously. Rating: Not recommended. No stars.

The Diabetic Diet

For years, diabetics have been counting the grams of carbohydrates they eat. They have to, since their bodies lack insulin, the hormone that breaks down sugars and starches.

Many knowledgeable doctors adapted the diabetic's diet as a reducing diet for their obese patients. You can adapt it yourself, if you have decided that low-carbohydrate is the best diet for you.

The basic diabetic diet of the American Diabetes Association (ADA) is built on the concept of controlling the *proportions* of fats, carbohydrates, and proteins by using "food exchanges." The ADA Diet relies on food exchange lists. Any food on one exchange list can be substituted for any other food on the same list to gain the same nutritional value. But you must remain within one exchange: crossing over throws the proportions out of balance. (You may write the ADA, 2 Park Avenue, New York, New York 10016 for *Exchange Lists for Meal Planning*. Or you may ask your doctor for the printed food exchange lists that are provided by some drug companies.)

If you follow the ADA Diet, you will probably have enough variety and enough food to satisfy you while you keep carbohydrates and calories down. A day's total carbohydrate allowance is usually divided into fifths. One-fifth is allowed at breakfast and the remaining four-fifths are divided among lunch, dinner, and a snack.

The ADA Diet includes milk, but you can cut that out, if you want, or drink skim milk instead of whole milk. And be sure you take a multivitamin supplement every day.

According to one diabetes researcher, Joseph B. Herman, M.D., of Hadassah Hospital, Jerusalem, "If you are too fat, you can prevent or delay the onset of diabetes by losing weight." He goes on to explain, "Since obese persons have a high level of circulating insulin, an added strain is placed on the pancreas, which manufactures insulin, eventually leading to pancreatic exhaustion in the genetically predisposed. Reduction of weight relieves the strain on the pancreas and restores normal function."[25]

CONSUMER GUIDE®'S EVALUATION

While primarily designed for diabetics, this diet can be followed by anyone. Its food exchange system is tried-and-true; its control of nutrients, unbeatable. Rating: ★★★

COUNTING CARBOHYDRATES YOURSELF

Charts such as those provided by the ADA are useful to many dieters. But if you want to count carbohydrates directly, you have to get a list of the carbohydrate content of foods. You can buy a book that lists brand-name foods and their carbohydrate content and gives you the elements of a low-carbohydrate diet. But select the book carefully. Some low-carbohydrate diet books have hundreds of pages of background and theory and only a few pages of carbohydrate content lists.

If you've already accumulated several lists of the carbohydrate content of foods, you probably have been puzzled by the lack of agreement among them. Here's just one frustrating example: One book ascribes 13 grams of carbohydrate to a fresh apricot, while another gives it 5 grams. The reason for the conflicting numbers is that some authors base their lists on independent data; others adapt the lists of the US Department of Agriculture but evaluate and transcribe the information differently.

CONSUMER GUIDE® recommends that if you are serious about counting carbohydrates the rest of your life, you should get the most complete technical government list available. It is *Nutritive Value of American Foods (in Common Units)*, Agriculture Handbook No. 456, available for $8.50 from the U.S. Government Printing Office, Washington, DC 20402. Another good guide is *The Dieter's Complete Guide to Calories, Carbohydrates, Sodium, Fats & Cholesterol* by the Editors of CONSUMER GUIDE.® New York: Ballantine Fawcett Columbine, 1981.

Counting Carbo-Cals and Carbo-Calories

Some people would like to know which combinations of calories and carbohydrates are the most fattening and, therefore, the ones to be most consistently avoided. At least two attempts have been made to combine calories and carbohydrates into a single unit. One is the Carbo-Cal, given to the public by Sidney Petrie in 1966.[26]

Petrie's Carbo-Cals are at the heart of the diet proposed by Johnny Carson's TV sidekick, Ed McMahon.[27] McMahon explains the technique in his book *Slimming Down*. "Medical authorities agree that the daily minimum requirements are 60 grams of carbohydrates. Figuring four calories to a gram we should aim at a minimum daily Carbo-Cal intake of 250 or so."

Thus, Petrie's Carbo-Cal, which McMahon lives by, simply takes the carbohydrate content of food and translates it into calories. It is based on the fact that the body burns a gram of carbohydrate to get four calories. Thus, a medium-size banana contains about 25 grams of carbohydrate and (multiplying by four) 100 Carbo-Cals. A cup of creamed cottage cheese, containing six grams of carbohydrate, is 24 Carbo-Cals.

Petrie has published another diet book with the dramatic title, *Fat Destroyer Foods.*[28] The book offers diets at several levels of carbohydrate intake, from the Free Diet to the High, Higher, and Highest Protein Diets. The ultimate, the Highest Protein Diet, is as close to 100 percent protein and fat and 0 percent carbohydrate as you can get, Petrie boasts. But he cautions you to "consult your physician before embarking on even these temporary programs."

If you do not like to count Carbo-Cals, there are Carbo-Calories, which are the invention of Beverly Hills investment manager Donald S. Mart. Carbo-Calories are explained in the newly-revised edition of Mart's book *The Brand Name Carbo-Calorie Diet.*[29] Most of the book is lists, but in the brief text, Mart explains how the Carbo-Calorie mathematically combines calories and carbohydrates. He carefully points out that the Carbo-Calorie is not a real measurement. It combines a unit of heat with a unit of weight and is calculated according to the formula:

$$\frac{20A + B}{24} = X$$

with A the carbohydrate count in grams, B the calorie count, and X the Carbo-Calorie count.

According to this formula, 100 Carbo-Calories a day will provide 60 grams of carbohydrate and 1200 calories. Mart's recommended daily minimum of 58 Carbo-Calories gives 30 grams of carbohydrate and 800 calories. For comparison's sake, a medium banana contains 26 Carbo-Calories; a cup of creamed cottage cheese, 16; a chocolate malted milkshake (8 ounces), 60; a Big Mac, 58.5; three pieces of Kentucky Fried Chicken, 171.7. Other Mart advice includes: prepare balanced menus, take vitamins, consult your doctor in advance, and "carry this book with you wherever you go ... One little mistake can wipe out your whole diet day."

CONSUMER GUIDE®'S EVALUATION

A lot of mathematics over a notion. Save yourself the trouble and find a simple diet you can live by without having to consult these lists of dubious value. Rating: ★★★

Natural Low-Carbohydrate Diet

With the trend toward "natural" foods, it was only a matter of time until someone propounded a natural foods diet for losing fat. That someone was slim Yvonne Young Tarr, a former model.

Despite the prestigious New York Times imprimatur, her book[30] makes outlandish and erroneous statements, such as "without carbohydrates you cannot gain weight!" She agrees, however, that "your body does require some carbohydrates, but not in excessive amounts. The average person attempting to lose weight should have no more than 58 grams of carbohydrates daily, and in this diet you should neither exceed nor go below that amount."

Tarr's favorite carbohydrate foods are honey, fruit, and whole wheat bread. She contends that with these and other natural foods, such as eggs and yogurt, you can lose weight and gain health at the same time. Most of her book is filled with recipes that she developed or tested. Among them are nasturtium salad, alfalfa sprout nibbles, lamb-and-eggs, and goat's cheese soup.

CONSUMER GUIDE®'S EVALUATION

The recipes may be OK, but stay away from Tarr's diet. Rating: ★★★

CRITICISM

Some experts do not believe that cutting down on carbohydrates is a healthy way to lose weight. US Senate guidelines and many health authorities call for increasing the proportion of calories you get from carbohydrates. Energy derived from other sources tends to be high in cholesterol and saturated fats which contribute to heart disease.

Walter L. Bloom, M.D. of Atlanta, reported that people complain of fatigue after two days of no-carbohydrate diet. They also experience what doctors call postural hypotension—a drop in blood pressure brought on by a change in the position of the body, as when getting up after lying on the back—which can cause dizziness. This is probably due to water loss that often accompanies low-carbohydrate diets.

Another criticism of low-carbohydrate diets is that the resulting weight loss is merely due to water loss. Dr. Bloom[31] compared seven healthy people on a protein-and-fat formula diet of 1500 calories with people on a diet of 2000 calories. Each group received only 1 gram of carbohydrate a day. Dr. Bloom found that people who were eating 2000 calories a day initially lost as much weight as those who were consuming 1500 calories a day. The low-carbohydrate diet made both groups excrete extra amounts of salt, and with it, water. This initial weight loss is deceptive, however. In the long run, all other things being equal, those who consume fewer calories lose more weight.

The theory of weight loss due to water loss was confirmed a few years later by Philadelphia researchers at Lankenau Hospital.[32] In their experiments, they, too, found that without carbohydrates, the body dumps salt and water. However, the researchers did not see this water loss as significant if dieting continues for months or years. "Over a long period of weight loss," they reported, dismissing the low-carbohydrate/water-loss theory, "a calorie is a calorie."

Dennis Craddock, M.D., of England found that the low-fat, Prudent Diet is far more successful than a low-carbohydrate diet in the long run. For four years, he studied patients who had been on either a low-carbohydrate or Prudent Diet. Only a third of those on low-carbohydrate diets successfully kept off their weight, compared to three-quarters of those on the Prudent Diet.[33]

Another charge against the low-carbohydrate diet, wrote Arthur Blumenfeld, is that it is similar to the diets fed to laboratory rats to induce such conditions as fatty liver, diabetes, and high blood fat (hyperlipidemia)![34]

REBUTTAL

Zero-carbohydrate diets have been criticized because they induce a state known as ketosis, during which the body accumulates ketones, chemicals that are the product of burned fats. Ketosis can be dangerous for diabetics, unborn babies, and gout victims.

However, Dr. Yudkin responds to the criticism of zero-carbohydrate diets by saying that is not what he is talking about. "The low-carbohydrate diet," he says, "is not the same as a highly experimental carbohydrate-free diet, and it certainly does not produce ketosis. I have no doubt that in practice the low-carbohydrate diet will be found to be the most effective and, nutritionally, the most desirable."[35]

Also, poor people who eat lots of carbohydrates, because such foods are cheap, tend to be fat, while rich people who eat fewer carbohydrates and more protein tend to be lean.

Another defender of low-carbohydrate diets, Aaron G. Saidman, M.D., who practices bariatric medicine (treatment of obesity) in Washington, D.C., claims that recent research shows a low-carbohydrate diet is the easiest way for the body to lose fat. His experience also indicates that low-carbohydrate is the easiest diet to learn.[36]

George L. Blackburn, M.D., of Harvard and the Massachusetts Institute of Technology says that eating three low-carbohydrate, low-calorie meals a day is the only way to shrink fat tissue and get your body back to a low-insulin inner environment. He disagrees with those who propose three meals plus three snacks a day. Eating between meals, Dr. Blackburn maintains, will keep the insulin level constant — which is *not* desirable because insulin deposits fat in addition to regulating carbohydrate "burning."

Dr. Blackburn says fat people are prone to diabetes because their tissue and insulin supply are out of balance. When you eat carbohydrates, that imbalance worsens. When you cut back on carbohydrates, the balance can be restored.

CONSUMER GUIDE®'S EVALUATION

If you are one of those who cannot seem to get rid of fat on a straight low-calorie diet — and you are otherwise healthy — you might try a low but not deficient carbohydrate diet. The advantage of a low-carbohydrate diet is that you can still salve your sweet tooth, while reducing the total amount of carbohydrates you eat.

The disadvantages are several. You can easily slip up and take too big a piece of watermelon or cake, especially in a social situation. You can be lulled by the temptation of low-carbohydrate alcoholic drinks such as dry wine and whiskey. But while you are being lulled, the alcohol is burning in your body, and solid foods are being converted to fat.[37] You can't lose weight if you get drunk on alcohol and gorge yourself on meats, cheeses, and fats.

There is also the plateau phenomenon. Your initial weight loss will be due to water loss. As you lose fat, it will be replaced by water in the tissues of your body. Soon you will reach a plateau during which you lose no weight at all. If you stick with the diet, however, you will dump that water in a few weeks and see some dramatic weight loss.

CONSUMER GUIDE® thus rates the low-carbohydrate diets as helpful and beneficial, if you know what you are doing and can exercise control. Recommended for satisfying your sweet tooth are artificially sweetened drinks and candies (especially hard ones to suck on).

For ease of use, CONSUMER GUIDE® recommends adapting the ADA Diet with its system of exchanges or sending for one of the Government Printing Office charts. You can make your own list of foods you like to eat and affix carbohydrate gram totals there. However, be sure you take supplementary vitamins every day.

Remember, with a low-carbohydrate diet, you also have to count calories. You cannot eat or drink 5000 calories a day and expect to slim down just because you are staying away from carbohydrates. But by lowering your intake of carbohydrates, you drastically reduce one kind of food that your body can turn to fat. You thus force your body to convert your fat stores to energy.

High-Protein Diets

*I*t seems to have lost favor in some quarters of the Diet Society, especially to its old enemy, carbohydrates. Still, protein is King. If the numbers of protein's advocates are decreasing, the vast majority of dieters yet pay obeisance to protein as the best nutrient for taking weight off. The persistence of such diets as Stillman's, Scarsdale, and Woman Doctor's attest to this.

Slendernow Diet

"Protein, protein, why protein?" asks Richard A. Passwater, chronic protein pusher in his new book, *The Slendernow Diet.*[1] "Next to water, protein is the most abundant substance in the body. It's the building material for all cells and enzymes," he explains. "Protein is needed daily for body repair and body function. The body can convert excess protein into carbohydrates and fats, but protein cannot be made from carbohydrate or fat. Protein cannot be stored in the body. Protein can only be made from protein … If your diet slips to the minimal protein level, your thought processes can be hindered.…Without sufficient protein, your skin will wrinkle and sag, and your hair and nails will suffer as well. You may remain alive on lower protein levels, but you may be healthier on more protein."

Scared? Sure! That's what Passwater wants you to be. There is some truth in what he says. You need protein, but the urgency is not as great as he indicates. Nor does your body need the 100 grams of protein a day he prescribes—unless you are not healthy, in which case you shouldn't be on a diet.

The Slendernow diet gives 1200 calories a day to women, 1500 to men. The elements of the diet are two high-protein diet milkshakes, in place of two meals, and a regular meal, balanced with real food. The 220-calorie, 24-grams-of-protein milkshakes are "spiked" with the kind of powder rich in soybean and milk proteins, that is available in all "health food" stores. The basic milkshake recipe is:

1 cup skim milk	4 to 6 ice cubes
2 rounded tsp. of protein powder	sweetener (sugar substitute,
up to 1 tsp. polyunsaturated oil	fructose, or honey)
(such as safflower oil)	

In blender, starting at low speed, add milk, then slowly pour in powder. Fruit or flavoring may be added. Next, increase blender speed. Add ice cubes last, increasing to full speed.

Passwater suggests a main meal, preferably lunch, of 750 calories for women, 1050 for men, with the main course fish, fowl, or meat (although tofu is allowed for those who want to go vegetarian). Passwater says you can expect to lose three to seven pounds the first week, 1.5 to three pounds every week thereafter.

He adds that you can do the Slendernow diet alone or join a Slendernow Neighborhood Club. To find if there is one near you, write:

Futuron Industries
Slendernow Neighborhood Clubs of America
4419 Westgrove
Dallas, TX 75248

CONSUMER GUIDE®'S EVALUATION

This diet makes more sense than the Magic Formula Diets reviewed in an earlier chapter. Still, it is an unrealistic approach, since you are unlikely to want to be drinking protein milkshakes in place of meats the rest of your life. Also, the diet overemphasizes protein, to the detrimental exclusion of carbohydrates. Rating: ★★

Passwater's No-FLAB Diet

In an earlier fit of hyperbole, Richard Passwater advised, "Don't count calories, count FLABS." He explained, in his book, *The Easy, No-FLAB Diet,*[2] that FLAB is an acronym for Fat Liquidating Activity Barometer.

Dr. Passwater, a biochemist, says calories don't count. Rather, it is the quality of food you eat that puts on or takes off fat. Therefore, he suggests that you keep eating your 100 grams or so of protein a day, and the same amount of fat, but decrease the amount of carbohydrates — especially simple sugars—you eat.

Passwater has a way of computing this food quality, which he calls FLAB units, and recommends you eat only foods having 50 or more FLAB. "The aim of the FLAB concept," he writes, "is to eliminate from the diet the poor-quality foods that upset the ideal blood sugar and insulin relationship, which promotes fat-burning without hunger."

Essentially, his diet is a third protein, a third fats, and a third carbohydrates, by calories. Sample foods and their FLAB index:

broiled fish	100	raw carrots	100
cottage cheese	84.5	popcorn, plain	100
vanilla ice cream	45	spaghetti	63.6

CONSUMER GUIDE®'S EVALUATION

The no-FLAB approach does not assure a well-rounded diet. Furthermore, it serves to emphasize protein and fat, rather than complex carbohydrates, which better serve the dieter seeking to lose weight. Finally, calories *do* count. Not even a biochemist can upset the laws of energy. Rating: Not recommended. No stars

Scarsdale: Legacy Lives On

The author's murder, and the subsequent sensational courtroom trial of the woman accused and convicted of killing him, served not to bury the already-popular Scarsdale Diet, but to insure it some sort of life everlasting of its own. There are good reasons for its survival and, indeed, its popularity among the dieting population.

The basic Scarsdale diet gives some dieters what they want. Simply stated, it (1) does not require thinking or choosing but dictates what the dieter should eat and when; (2) has as its nutritional champion the one, the only, protein; (3) is associated with some symbol of success (in this case, Scarsdale in Westchester County, New York — one of the richest communities in the US); and (4) has a thin doctor as its front man.

Actually, while the stern visage on the dustcover belongs to the late Herman Tarnower, M.D., of the Scarsdale Medical Center, the book was written by Samm Sinclair Baker, who collaborated with Irwin Maxwell Stillman on three books. Before *The Complete Scarsdale Medical Diet*[3] was distributed in December 1978 for January 1979 publication, excerpts of the diet had already appeared in *The New York Times,* and, via its wire service, in other newspapers around the country, as well as in *Family Circle* magazine. In fact, before the book was published, there was supposedly such a run on grapefruit in Westchester County that supermarkets ran out of the fruit in the summer of 1978.

Like the Stillman diet, the Scarsdale diet requires plenty of protein — essentially from "plenty of meat" — especially poultry, fish, and eggs. "Quantities are not important," said Baker and Tarnower. They also said that the diet's combination of 43 percent protein, 22.5 percent fat, and 34.5 percent carbohydrate will provide 1000 calories a day. But, in a rough estimate, Phillip White, Sc.D., secretary of the Council on Foods and Nutrition of the American Medical Association, found the diet totaled 700 daily calories.

Dr. Tarnower claimed average losses of a pound a day. Futhermore, "many report losses of 20 or more pounds in two weeks," probably because of the diet's rigidity. Dr. White points out, "This diet is extremely rigid. The dieter has few decisions to make and these are minor. This very rigidity encourages compliance for a while. There is no 'metabolic miracle' performed, just tight control of what you eat."

The diet's rigidity is reflected in its rules. The dieter is urged to eat only what is assigned, make no substitutions, never overload the stomach, and never stay on the diet more than 14 days. The dieter must give up alcoholic beverages, oil and mayonnaise on salads, and butter and margarine with vegetables. All meat eaten on the diet must be very lean, and chicken and turkey skin must be removed. Between meals, the Scarsdale dieter can eat carrots and celery, but nothing else, and he can drink only water, black coffee, tea, and club and diet sodas.

On the Scarsdale diet, breakfast every day consists of one half of a grapefruit, or other available fruit, one slice toasted protein bread, and black coffee or tea.

A different lunch and dinner menu is give for every day of the week. In addition, the dieter is allowed the option of choosing to have a "substitute lunch," which consists of low-fat pot or cottage cheese mixed with low-fat sour cream, sliced fruit, and six walnut or pecan halves. This lunch can be had any day of the week in lieu of the lunch designated for that day.

Here's the lunch and dinner diet for the week:

MONDAY

Lunch
Cold cuts of lean meat; tomatoes; coffee, tea or diet soda

Dinner
Fish; combination salad (as many vegetables as you wish); 1 slice dry protein toast; grapefruit or other fresh fruit; coffee, tea, or diet soda

TUESDAY

Lunch
Fruit salad, as much as you want, any kind; coffee, tea, or diet soda

Dinner
Plenty of steak or broiled, lean hamburger; tomatoes, lettuce, celery, olives; Brussels sprouts or cucumbers; coffee, tea, diet soda

WEDNESDAY

Lunch
Tuna fish or salmon salad with lemon-and-vinegar dressing; grapefruit or other fresh fruit; coffee, tea, or diet soda

Dinner
Roast lamb slices; celery, cucumbers, tomatoes; coffee, tea, or diet soda

THURSDAY

Lunch
Two eggs; low-fat cottage cheese; zucchini, string beans, or stewed tomatoes; 1 slice dry protein toast; coffee, tea, or diet soda

Dinner
Chicken (roast, broiled or barbecued); spinach, green peppers, string beans; coffee, tea, or diet soda

FRIDAY

Lunch
Assorted cheese slices; spinach; 1 slice dry protein toast; coffee, tea, or diet soda

Dinner
Fish; combination salad (as many fresh vegetables as you want): 1 slice dry protein toast; coffee, tea, or diet soda

SATURDAY

Lunch
Fruit salad (any kind, as much as you want); coffee, tea, or diet soda

Dinner
Cold chicken, or turkey; tomatoes and lettuce, grapefruit or other fresh fruit; coffee, tea, or diet soda

SUNDAY

Lunch
Chicken or turkey; tomatoes, carrots, cabbage, broccoli, or cauliflower; grapefruit or other fresh fruit; coffee, tea, or diet soda

Dinner
Plenty of steak; tomatoes, celery, cucumbers or brussels sprouts; coffee, tea, or diet soda

As its name states, the Scarsdale Medical 14-Day Diet (SMD) is followed for two weeks. Then you must switch to the Keep-Trim Eating Plan. The Keep-Trim Eating Plan, designed for weight maintenance, allows a greater range of foods and even a cocktail or glass of wine with dinner. If you want to lose more weight, you can return to the original SMD after two weeks on the Keep-Trim Plan.

The Keep-Trim Eating Plan has a list of 14 DON'Ts — foods to be avoided. They include sugar, cream, whole milk, desserts, candy, chocolate, potatoes, rice, avocados, pasta, fatty meats like sausage and bologna, rich salad dressings, butter, margarine, oil, shortening, and peanut butter.

It also has an extensive list of fine foods which are permissible. Among them are alcoholic beverages. Each day you may have 1½ ounces of hard liquor (Scotch, bourbon, rye, Canadian whiskey, vodka, gin, dry rum, cognac, or other dry brandies) or 4½ ounces of dry wine. Sweet cocktails like old-fashioneds or whiskey sours are not allowed, but a dry Manhattan or martini is OK. All drinks should be mixed with diet or club soda.

The Keep-Trim Eating Plan also permits the following: lean meats and poultry, fish and shellfish, three eggs a week, some cheeses, certain soups, vegetables, fruits, their juices, small quantities of nuts, and sugarless jellies, jams, and preserves.

SCARSDALE VARIATIONS

The basic Scarsdale Medical 14-Day Diet has four other versions. One is the low-budget Money-Saver Diet which answers prepublication criticism that the SMD called only for the most expensive cuts of meat and kinds of shellfish. Another variation, the Scarsdale Gourmet Diet for Epicurean Tastes, includes such items as Borscht Suzanne for Monday's lunch and Lamb à La Provençale for Wednesday's dinner. The Scarsdale International features a week's worth of menus based on foods from other lands, and the Scarsdale Vegetarian relies on dairy products for most of its protein.

For the most part, each variation follows the same rules as the Scarsdale basic diet. Each specifies the same breakfast menu and each diet is to be followed for no more than 14 days, after which you revert to the Keep-Trim Eating Plan. The authors allow you to switch back and forth from one diet variation to another, or to the basic plan, but suggest that you confine your substitutions to the menus for a single day. For example, on Tuesday, you can have the Tuesday lunch from any of the five diets, but you should not substitute Friday's lunch instead. Menus and recipes for one week are included with each variation.

CONSUMER GUIDE®'S EVALUATION

Great Dr. Stillman's ghost: The basic Scarsdale diet is much like those "grapefruit diets" passed from hand to hand in offices and beauty parlors. It is a slightly modified version of Dr. Stillman's Protein-Plus Diet since fruits and vegetables are allowed.

Actually, it should be called the Scarsdale Mystery Diet. The mystery is how Tarnower and Baker could claim that the diet provides 43 percent protein, 22.5 percent fat, and 34.5 percent carbohydrate. These percentages are calculated on the basis of the total calories consumed each day, but Tarnower and Baker didn't specify how many daily calories the diet actually aims for. More importantly, the diet is purposely vague as to quantity of foods consumed each day.

As if that weren't error enough, Tarnower and Baker committed an even greater error when they told us the diet was NOT a fad diet and that it was intended to modify behavior. Now, anyone who has ever studied fat people knows that "plenty of steak" means a far larger quantity of beef to them than it does to lean people. When the authors tell the reader to eat as much as he or she wants "as long as you avoid overloading your stomach to the point of discomfort," they are displaying astonishing naiveté.

Scarsdale's basic diet has an unrealistic approach to quantity. Except at breakfast, it specifies no quantities. Tuesday's lunch, for instance, consists of as much fruit salad as you want. Dinner on that day calls for "plenty of broiled, lean hamburger." So, while the Scarsdale diet limits the *selection* of foods, it places no restriction on the amount of food you eat. Authors Tarnower and Baker must not have been aware of, or else they ignored the fact that people with weight problems misuse and abuse food. People are overweight because they eat too much food. They don't know when enough is enough; they do not realize how much they are eating nor do they keep track of how much they consume.

Authorities such as Henry Jordan, M.D., of the University of Pennsylvania, have pointed out repeatedly that portion control is what the overweight must have. They must learn to cut back on food amounts if they are going to succeed in taking and keeping weight off. They must learn to control their eating behavior, not be given license to eat as much as they want. The overweight don't need this kind of freedom, because they don't know how to use it.

The Scarsdale Medical 14-Day Diet provides enough daily protein and carbohydrate, and it is low in fat. What it lacks is nutritional completeness. A well-balanced weight-loss diet must not only cut calories and provide the proper amounts of the top three nutrients, it must also provide adequate amounts of all the other nutrients as well. And the SMD is low in calcium and Vitamins A and D because it pays scant attention to dairy products, allowing dairy food only at lunch on Thursday (low-fat cottage cheese) and Friday (assorted cheese slices), or as a substitute lunch for any day.

Finally, there is no magic in protein. You do need it, but you only need so much. All protein beyond the minimum is not only money lost but carbohydrates gained, since that is exactly what the body makes of excess protein.

The only commendable part of the diet is that it emphasizes polyunsaturated oils and limits saturated fats as it cuts back on total daily fat intake. Other than that, the rigid Scarsdale diet is a throwback to a time when dieters were less enlightened.

To effectively lose weight and keep it off, you need a diet for a lifetime. Any diet that is designed for only two weeks is faddish, foolish, and forgettable. Rating for basic Scarsdale, plus variations (except Vegetarian): ★★

Unlike the other variations on the Scarsdale basic diet, the Vegetarian version provides some portion control through the use of recipes which suggest approximate serving sizes. In addition, with its emphasis on dairy foods as a protein source, it provides adequate high quality protein (a problem with the Pritikin diets) and is well rounded nutritionally. CONSUMER GUIDE® finds the Scarsdale Vegetarian Diet superior to both the basic diet and to all the other variations. (See "Losing via Vegetarian.")
Rating: ★★★★

The Original Stillman Diet

When Irwin Maxwell Stillman, M.D., died of a heart attack in 1975, he had the same physique he had had when he was a sprinter at Bushwick High School in Brooklyn more than 60 years before.

During the 45 years he practiced medicine in Brooklyn, Dr. Stillman had come to regard the obese as the most difficult patients to treat effectively. He worked hard to develop and perfect a weight-reducing diet during his care of nearly 12,000 patients. In 1960, after he had retired to Florida, he decided to bring his diet to the public. By 1974, he said, 20 million people had been on the Stillman diet.

Dr. Stillman emphasized, "I'm not a diet doctor, I'm just a family doctor who found the way to help people lose weight and fat." His way was to write *The Doctor's Quick Weight Loss Diet*[4] with the help of writer Samm Sinclair Baker (who later teamed with Herman Tarnower to write the Scarsdale diet book).

QUICK WEIGHT-LOSS DIET

The Doctor's Quick Weight Loss Diet book actually contains dozens of diets or diet variations. But the diet most people follow, referred to as the Stillman diet, or the water diet, is the Quick Weight Loss Diet. As Dr. Stillman explained to CONSUMER GUIDE® in 1973, his diet is based on the physiological theory that the body deals differently with proteins than it does with fats and carbohydrates. The Stillman diet leans heavily on the phenomenon known as specific dynamic action (SDA). "I didn't originate the concept," Dr. Stillman said. "I used it. I adapted it."

Stillman's mentor in physiological research was Eugene Dubois, M.D., medical director of the Russell Sage Institute of Pathology, professor of medicine at Cornell, and physician-in-chief to the New York Hospital.

Dr. Dubois explained that, according to SDA theory, the protein molecule is so big and chemically complex that the body uses extra energy to digest it. A high protein diet, Dr. Dubois wrote, costs the body some 20 to 30 percent of the protein calories just for digestion.

In his book, Dr. Stillman claimed[5,6] that his diet could cause the body to burn 275 calories more per day than a diet with the same calorie total that included carbohydrates and fats. Thanks to the SDA phenomenon, the "fires of the metabolism" are raised, he said, and fat from the body (and any in food) is burned more intensively. He added, "Studies have shown that persons on a high-protein diet such as this, with no carbohydrate intake, melt fat out of the storage or fat centers."

With the Quick Weight Loss Diet, you can eat all you want of certain foods, such as:

Lean meats and poultry	Low-fat cheeses (For example, you
Lean fish and seafood	could have cottage, farmer, pot,
Eggs	or ricotta cheeses.)

Meat, poultry, seafood, and eggs must be broiled, boiled, smoked, or otherwise prepared so as to be free of oils, grease, fats, and gravy. Some can be prepared by dry frying in nonstick pans.

Prohibited foods include breads and pastries in any form, alcohol, ice cream and sherbets, whole milk or cream, and soft drinks containing sugar.

The Stillman diet requires you to drink at least eight glasses of water per day in addition to the black coffee, tea, and diet soda pop you are encouraged to drink. And you must take vitamin supplements. The eight glasses of water, and the frequent urination they cause, result in the diet's nickname, "the water diet."

In their book, Stillman and Baker explain why all the water is necessary. It has to do with burning the fat off the body. Only 60 percent of the fat is completely burned, and the remainder, ketones, must be disposed of. The body washes ketones from the blood with water, and they leave the body in the urine. As a result, the body needs more water to replace that which is lost with increased urination.

The ketones, continue Stillman and Baker, "are also slight irritants to the kidney. In order to get rid of them the body must have plenty of water to wash them out."

On the protein diet, the authors say, you will have bad breath if you do not drink enough water. And because it is a low-residue diet, you will have few bowel movements.

One of the great appeals of the Stillman diet is its ability to make you lose a lot of weight in a short period of time; you see results fast. The authors deny, however, that quick weight loss is due to loss of water only.

Stillman and Baker encourage you to weigh yourself every day to see how you are doing. And they say you will be amazed at your progress. They cite case after case, such as the fat man who lost 112 pounds in 16 weeks. Samm Baker and his wife each lost seven pounds the first week on the diet; they stayed on it for four weeks until they reached their desired weights.

The Stillman diet does not require you to count calories or limit the amount of the recommended foods. In fact, the advice is that you eat as much of these foods as you want, until your appetite is curbed. Of course, a calorie limit is built in, as it is in the Weight Watchers Diet, by avoiding certain foods entirely. In his interview, Dr. Stillman revealed that the total daily intake ranges from 1500 to 1800 calories.

The Stillman and Baker book is not at all modest in its claims: "You'll achieve the wonderful reducing results and the slim figure you want." It assures us that "the diet will work for you — swiftly, pleasantly, surely." Furthermore, "the Quick Weight Loss Diet is the finest and best for most people who should take off excess weight."[7]

The authors claim you should lose between seven and 15 pounds the first week and five pounds every week thereafter. The five-pound figure is an average; you may lose three pounds one week and ten pounds the next.

When you get to within three pounds of your ideal or goal weight, you go on the Stay Slim Eating Diet, a calorie-counting technique. You estimate the number of calories your body needs every day and eat no more than that in any combination of foods or meals. Whenever your daily weigh-in shows you have gained three pounds, you go back to the high-protein Quick Weight Loss Diet.

14-DAY SHAPE-UP PROGRAM

Dr. Stillman's last diet scheme (see the chapter on vegetarian diets for his Inches-Off Diet), his *14-Day Shape-Up Program*[8], came out in 1974. In his book, Stillman took some gloves-off jabs at Dr. Robert Atkins and his high-fat diet, charging that it was based on fallacy, that it produced nausea, and—worst of all—that it was not effective. "I have been visited by scores of overweights who failed with (Atkins') directions," wrote Dr. Stillman. "You cannot stuff yourself with 'fattening food' of any kind and succeed in slimming down substantially and progressively. Fat is a highly concentrated food. The excuse that 'fat melts away fat' may appear valid on paper but certainly not on the scale or in your body where it counts."[9]

Doctor Stillman called his new diet the Protein-Plus Diet. You may be surprised to learn that the plus is—yes!—carbohydrate. Thus Dr. Stillman slowly came to agree with just about everyone else that the body needs a certain amount of carbohydrate every day. The Protein-Plus Diet suggests that the daily intake include 5 percent carbohydrate, in grams, 5 to 15 percent fat, and up to 90 percent protein.[10] According to our calculations, these percentages equal 25 grams of carbohydrate, 25 grams of fat, and 200 grams of protein for a total of 1125 calories a day. Although low in carbohydrate, this high-protein, low-fat diet may prevent ketosis (an abnormal increase in ketones), which is a possibility with Stillman's water diet.

To get the few daily grams of carbohydrate, you need to choose vegetables from a restricted list, including asparagus, bean sprouts (but not beans), eggplant, radishes, tomatoes, and zucchini. The diet also allows bread, buns, and custard cake — all made according to recipes in the book.

Liquids are still important in the diet, although the requirement is for ten glasses a day of water, sugar-free soda, coffee, or tea.

With this diet as well as his original protein diets, Dr. Stillman maintained that "you don't count calories or carbohydrates—you just choose the foods which I have selected for you as being high in proteins, low in carbohydrates and low in fats." He gives a food prescription for two weeks of dieting, listing the foods you should eat at each meal on each of the 14 days. He also includes a 41-page list of foods and their calorie, protein, fat, and carbohydrate content. This list is to be used, Dr. Stillman instructed, by those who have slimmed down and want to stay that way. He called it his Stay Slim Eating Plan. On the Stay Slim Eating Plan, you choose your desired weight and multiply by 12 to get the total number of calories per day. But Dr. Stillman did not tell you what proportions of proteins, fats, and carbohydrate to have each day; presumably you should stick with his Protein-Plus percentage formula.

As for the 14-day exercise program, CONSUMER GUIDE® finds it mild. Stillman (a sprinter in his youth) and Baker (an exercise buff even in his later years) suggest 15 minutes of exercise every day while viewing a television program. The exercises involve bending and stretching and should help you keep limber and improve your posture and muscle tone.

CONSUMER GUIDE®'S EVALUATION

Both Stillman diets (Quick Weight Loss, and 14-Day Shape-Up) are based on shaky premises and offer unbalanced, unrealistic nutrition. Rating: ★★

Fat Free Forever

The two New Jersey osteopaths who wrote *You Can Be Fat Free Forever*[11] have borrowed heavily from Dr. Irwin Stillman. Their Food Intake Plan, conveniently packaged in a one-page tear-out chart, lists the meat and fish you can eat. You are also allowed all seasonings, a few fruits (grapefruit, cantaloupe, apples, pears), and a few vegetables (carrots, celery). In addition, you are required to drink eight glasses of liquids a day (nonsugar and nonalcoholic).

Along with the diet comes sound advice about changing your eating habits. The most succinct is: "You are sick and cannot eat other foods. You will be well only when you reach normal weight."

CONSUMER GUIDE®'S EVALUATION

Despite the sound advice about changing habits, this diet should be used with caution because of its emphasis on high protein. Rating: ★★

A Woman Doctor's Womanly Diet

Barbara Fiedler Edelstein, M.D., is a bariatric physician (one who specializes in the treatment of overweight patients). In her book, *The Woman Doctor's Diet for Women*,[12] which has been widely excerpted in women's magazines, Dr. Edelstein lets you in on a few secrets right at the beginning. Did you know: All important diet books have been written by men? Most diet doctors are men? Men head most diet businesses? Most women go to male doctors? Most diet books offer the same diet for both sexes?

Right away you should be suspicious. What is an "important" diet book? Many diet books have been written by men, but quite a few of the most popular have been written or co-written by women. Surely it is no surprise that most diet doctors are men nor that most women go to male doctors; after all, more doctors are men. However, the foremost diet businesses and clubs — Weight Watchers, TOPS, Overeaters Anonymous, Diet Workshop, Appetite Control Centers, Diet Control Centers — were started and are headed by women. Finally, most diets do offer separate, lower-calorie diets for women.

Besides the effort to convince women to buy her book, Dr. Edelstein offers an astonishing piece of misinformation. "I'm willing to bet that a big part of the reason you're still fat is that you've never been told this simple fact: MEN LOSE WEIGHT ALMOST TWICE AS FAST AS WOMEN DO. They burn calories twice as fast for the same amount of exertion."

That claim sounds good in a mail-order pitch, and it may help sell books. But is it really true?

There are differences between the sexes that affect weight loss. The greatest is that men are generally larger and heavier — more weight can burn off calories faster. Also women's bodies contain extra amounts of fat which give the round contours to hips and breasts. More profoundly, fat is the source of energy that can be called upon during the crucial months of pregnancy and breast-feeding. Also, women take on extra amounts of water every month as part of the menstrual cycle.

Men may appear to be more effective at losing weight than women. But this difference may be associated with psychological and geographical rather than biological factors. For example, women who stay at home and cook for their families are near food and tempted to eat.

A 1981 study, conducted by researchers at the University of Southern California, concluded that "the sex of the subject had no effect on weight loss."[13] While men are usually heavier when they start their diet, and lose more weight during the first two weeks of dieting, in the long run men and women lose the same amount of weight each week, on the average, and overall.

Nontheless, Dr. Edelstein has a "secret" to help fat women lose weight. "Eat 40 to 50 percent of your caloric requirements in protein" is her answer.

The justification for her high-protein diet is that "the overweight female is able to handle protein food more efficiently than carbohydrate food. This means that her weight loss will be greatly facilitated if she eats more protein and less carbohydrate while dieting."

Also, she says, "Protein has a high specific dynamic action (SDA). This means that a great number of calories are required to break down protein for use as energy in the body. Carbohydrates, on the other hand, use very few calories to produce energy."

Dr. Edelstein does her sisters a disservice by misrepresenting the facts of nature. Carbohydrates are the main source of energy for the body. The human body, whether male or female, can use only so much protein a day (about 50 grams). All excess protein is converted into carbohydrate and either burned or stored.

Dr. Edelstein offers three diets: Core, High-Calorie, and Restart. Despite her claimed intention of letting her female readers in on all the facts, she does not reveal the total number of calories in each diet, but claims that you will lose seven to ten pounds in the first two weeks. Here is the Core Diet:

106

Breakfast
2 oz. orange juice or 1 orange
1 egg (prepared any way)
1 piece melba toast

Lunch
4 oz. meat or fish*
1 piece melba toast
1 cup salad with diet dressing or 1
   cup cooked vegetable (except
   corn or peas)
1 fresh fruit (no grapes or cherries)
   or ½ cup Jello-O (regular)

Supper
Exactly like lunch EXCEPT
1 more ounce meat and you can
   have both salad (unlimited
   amount)** and a cooked
   vegetable

Between Meals
Raw vegetables
Dill pickles
Diet gelatin
Mushrooms (raw or broiled—not
   cooked in butter)
1 can stewed tomatoes

To Drink Any Time
Tea or coffee with regular milk and
   sugar substitute
Diet soda
Tomato juice
Skim milk

Condiments
All—mustard, catsup, horseradish,
   relish, herbs, spices, soy sauce—
   as long as they contain no fat
Onions as a garnish

*Meat: Beef (including roast beef, lean hamburger, cube or minute steak, round
   steak, tenderloin), chicken or turkey (includes crisp skin and chicken roll)
Fish: Seafood, all canned fish, drained of oil. Fresh fish—may use 1 teaspoon of
   margarine in preparation.
**Salad can be plain or with vinegar. Limit diet dressing to 1 or 2 tablespoons.

CONSUMER GUIDE®'S EVALUATION

There is nothing new or special for women in this diet. It seems designed
not so much for women as for sales to women. Rating: ★★

Dr. Schiff's Protein Plan

Graying Martin M. Schiff, M.D., of Los Angeles is in love with protein. He
believes "it slenderizes. It energizes. It heals. It builds body tissue. It adds
life." He has built his *One-Day-at-a-Time Weight Loss Plan* around protein.[14] Like his medical colleague, Barbara Edelstein, Dr. Schiff does not
let his scientific education get in his way.

"The Plan's food components emphasize proteins and de-emphasize
fats and carbohydrates. The way I help you know the difference is to give
you a list of preferred foods and a list of banned foods. On the preferred
foods list is a parade of proteins. ...Just reading the list," writes Dr. Schiff
(with the help of writers, Robert Stone and Patricia Day), "will make your
mouth water."

Among the Schiff no-no foods are ham, pork, bacon, hot dogs, smoked
meats, sausage, bologna and other cold cuts, duck, goose, smoked fish,
sardines, soft cheeses, potatoes, corn, rice, "starchy" vegetables such
as peas and lima beans, avocados, bananas, cherries, dates, dried fruits,
fruit juices, milk, butter, cream, mayonnaise, yogurt (except occasionally), baked goods (including bread), cereals, pretzels, pasta, tea or
coffee, candy, ice cream, ices, nuts, seeds, coconut, chocolate, jams,
jellies, preserves, honey, and desserts.

So what's left, you ask? Aha! The wonderful protein foods not on the above list. Plus, Dr. Schiff's magical "accelerator." Ready? Liquid protein. Taken straight, or mixed with diet soda or milk, it is used as a meal once a day.

Finally, Dr. Schiff informs us that while his diet is "an eating program," you don't count calories. "Instead you keep track of your enjoyment." He suggests measuring eating enjoyment by "kiks." He explains, "The 'kik' is not based on amount of food; it is based on deliciousness. It is qualitative, not quantitative. More 'kiks' equals more food enjoyment, more personal enjoyment—and less weight."

CONSUMER GUIDE®'S EVALUATION

Take many steps away from this incredibly ignorant book. Rating: ★

The Woman Psychiatrist's Diet

Having lost 72 pounds herself, Joyce A. Bockar, M.D., wants to share her secret of success. Diets don't count, she says in *The Last Best Diet Book*.[15] What does count is your mental attitude, and protein.

"The reason for the large and initial fast weight loss is linked to the fact that the diet is totally unbalanced. On diet days you eat *only* protein, no carbohydrates at all, and a tiny amount of fat." She admits that "it is not the easiest diet in the world to stay on" as it allows only 600-750 calories a day. The highly restrictive diet has the same breakfast and dinner, with a choice of tuna or chicken or fish for lunch. The same, day after day after day. Nothing else is allowed: no vegetables, fruits, or foods made with flour.

Another feature of the unique Bockar approach is the eating binge, which is allowed after every ten pound loss. Each binge is 2000-3000 calories and includes steak, salad, cheesecake, and spaghetti.

The rest of the book is psychology: It helps you understand why you're overweight and how to overcome those attitudes.

CONSUMER GUIDE®'S EVALUATION

This diet is the end, not the last. Super-rigid and unbalanced, it merits little serious attention. The idea of an M.D. directing dieters to actually use food binges to lose weight is repugnant to us. Rating: Not recommended. No Stars.

Pregnant Woman's Diet

Gail Brewer, who works for the Metropolitan New York Childbirth Education Association, is concerned that pregnant women do not get enough protein. In her book *What Every Pregnant Woman Should Know*,[16] written with Tom Brewer, she quotes a Johns Hopkins University study that discovered even middle-income women consume insufficient amounts of protein during pregnancy. Brewer's solution: "A quart of milk and two eggs a day form the foundation of this diet for every pregnant women."

Brewer wants every pregnant woman "to have 2600 calories and 100 grams of protein a day, plus all the salt and other essential minerals and vitamins she needs." These totals are slightly more than the National Academy of Sciences recommended daily dietary allowance of 2400 calories and 76 grams of protein.

Weight control, write the Brewers, may be hazardous during pregnancy. They dispute the accepted 24-pound total weight gain during pregnancy and say another ten pounds should be added. Otherwise they warn, the baby may be small and underdeveloped, and the mother's health may be affected.

They also abhor the use of amphetamines (speed) and other drugs used to depress appetite and thereby control weight during pregnancy. Not only can the drugs be harmful to baby and mother, but they can lead to malnutrition when the daily intake of protein is too low.

CONSUMER GUIDE®'S EVALUATION

CONSUMER GUIDE® agrees that pregnant women should stay off pills and be sure they are getting enough protein and other nutrients necessary for the mother's and fetus's health. Furthermore, pregnancy is not a time for drastic weight loss. Better to diet after the baby comes. Rating: ★★

Dieting by the Stars

"Aries seldom get fat because their bodies usually burn calories efficiently," states a unique book which mixes astrology and dieting.[17]

"You tend to eat too fast, which means your stomach doesn't have a chance to tell your brain that you've eaten enough. Slow down."

For each of the signs of the Zodiac, Joanne Lemieux has a similar pitch, and a diet. But all the signs' diets are the same, essentially high-protein, high-fat, low carbohydrate.

CONSUMER GUIDE®'S EVALUATION

If you believe in the stars, try *Diet Signs,* otherwise look into yourself. There is just too much hocus-pocus in this approach. Rating: ★★

CRITICISM

High-protein diets are far from balanced; they exclude carbohydrates and fats as much as possible. Some doctors and leading nutritionists feel that excluding carbohydrates and fats is bad for the body. They contend that human beings are omnivorous and must eat all kinds of food. And they consider variety not only the spice but a necessity of life.

Accordingly, Fredrick J. Stare, M.D., professor of nutrition at Harvard University, calls Stillman's first book an "absurd volume."[18] He said the diet is "one of intentional nutritional imbalance" which "misinterpret[s] the old theory of specific dynamic action of protein, i.e., higher protein consumption requires more calorie use in digestion and metabolism. Even if this theory were valid with a mixed diet (which it is not), the extra 275 calories used per day by Stillman's own calculation are a mere smidgen of the 3500 calorie deficit which is required for the loss of one pound of body fat."

There is also serious doubt that the specific dynamic action theory itself is even valid. Late in 1973, two University of California nutritional researchers reported on experiments they had conducted to test the theory. According to their tests, SDA flunked. Robert B. Bradfield, M.D., and Martin H. Jourdan, M.D., observed that "the importance of SDA in human nutrition has been misinterpreted and overrated."[19] They found SDA—if it exists — to represent perhaps a two percent difference between high-protein and rounded diets, a difference that is so small it is insignificant.

The Californians' conclusions were based on data they obtained from feeding overweight women a rounded diet and a high-protein diet—both at the same calorie level. They also fed the same two diets to women of normal weight. During the study, careful measurements of metabolism were made to find any clues of a step-up in energy usage. They found none, which to them means that a high-protein diet does not use up or waste the calories Drs. Stillman, Passwater, and Edelstein claim it does.

A high-protein diet may also be dangerous. In 1972, Dr. White of the AMA noted that many people who restrict carbohydrate intake experience fatigue "caused by various metabolic changes," such as excessive loss of body fluids, sodium and other minerals; ketosis; and loss of nitrogen "brought on by the breakdown of dietary and body protein." He did admit that "the severity of the fatigue may lessen as the body adapts somewhat to the lack of carbohydrates."[20]

In mid-1973, Harold Yacowitz, Ph.D., of Farleigh Dickinson University reported that a Stillman-type diet may cause the breakdown of body protein and bone.[21] The New Jersey scientist based his conclusion on a study of five overweight but otherwise healthy men and women who were placed on a well-rounded diet for two weeks, then on a high-protein, low-carbohydrate diet for several weeks. During the study, Yacowitz measured certain enzymes in the blood. One enzyme (glutamic oxaloacetic transaminase) that showed up in the blood of the patients on a high-protein diet indicated the possibility of tissue breakdown (essentially muscle). Yacowitz also found that those on a Stillman-type diet excreted more calcium in the urine, and he theorized this calcium may have been drawn from bones.

In the *Journal of the American Medical Association* in 1974, a Harvard Medical School study reported that Dr. Stillman's diet may cause a dangerous rise in blood cholesterol.[22] In the study, 12 healthy, slightly overweight employees of Peter Bent Brigham Hospital in Boston had their blood tested while on their usual diet and while on the Quick Weight Loss Diet. Said the doctors who conducted the study, "The average serum cholesterol level increased significantly... during the diet." They concluded: "There seems to be very little reason for recommending the Stillman diet."

Writing in the *FDA Consumer*, Judith Willis noted that on a low-calorie, high protein diet, the body converts its metabolism to a state known as ketosis: "... in ketosis the body's mode of burning calories may be similar to that of fasting. The body's fuel comes from glucose, which is most easily obtained from carbohydrates and less easily from protein. When the body lacks carbohydrates...protein is degraded to supply the minimum level of glucose. This protein is taken from lean body mass muscles and major organs such as the liver, heart, and kidneys."[23]

There is a special caution for women planning to be, or already, pregnant. Ketosis may impair the development of the fetus's brain.

A criticism of any high-protein diet is that too much protein is unnecessary, possibly unhealthy, and certainly expensive. A British researcher stated[24] that his analysis of data from studies of starving children and the children on various diets indicate that they, and we adults, need far less protein than the "protein industry" advertises. The Senate Select Subcommittee on Nutrition and Human Needs' report states, "The average American eats daily almost twice as much protein as the Food and Nutrition Board of the National Academy of Sciences recommends."[25] Therefore, the sensible dieter should cut down on protein, especially high-fat animal protein.

REBUTTAL

Stillman and Baker met head-on some of the criticisms of their protein diet in their first book. Critics, they claimed, "ignore the fact that their so-called balanced eating habits produced the excess weight which ruins good looks and impairs health." As for the balanced diet approach as the only healthy way to diet, Dr. Stillman replies: "I have never seen or been given any proof that this is true—although I have openly challenged this concept for years."

To the criticism that his diet brought on fatigue, Dr. Stillman replied, "Whenever you break a habit, you feel let down. When you go off your regular overweight diet and do go on my diet, that is a change in habit. In some few cases, people will experience fatigue, but it soon leaves. In fact, the overwhelming proportion of people on my diet feel buoyant and full of energy. And they should. A great deal of weight is being removed from them."

We feel that Dr. Stillman treated fatigue too lightly. Part of the problem is the monotony of the diet. Also, fatigue is frequently a symptom of depression, which is common among Americans, especially dieters.

Dr. Stillman responded to Dr. Yacowitz's finding of protein loss from the body by citing a study by two researchers from the Massachusetts Institute of Technology.[26] The researchers studied seven people who fasted for a month and then went on a protein diet. They continually monitored the subjects' blood and urine and found that the protein diet caused loss of fat tissue but no loss of protein (muscle) tissue. They also found that when they gave their subjects even a little carbohydrate it brought on hunger pangs.

CONSUMER GUIDE® believes that the scientific argument on protein loss from body tissue is far from resolved. Dr. Stillman pointed out that high-protein diets have been used for many decades for patients with certain illnesses. People with gallstones, for instance, are not allowed to eat fat; and, before insulin was available, doctors placed their diabetic patients on protein-only diets. But Dr. Stillman admitted that his high-protein diet is not for anyone with kidney disease. However, he did not see this as a big issue. He told CONSUMER GUIDE®, "After all, people with nephritis [a kidney disease] know it and are already under a physician's care." Nevertheless, kidney disease is a major contraindication to the Stillman diet; so be sure your doctor tells you that you can eat large amounts of protein before you try it.

As for the Harvard researchers who found that his diet raised the level of cholesterol in the blood, Dr. Stillman asked, "How the hell do they have the nerve to make such broad statements after a study of only 12 subjects? They should test thousands, not a dozen!" In his experience with thousands of patients, Dr. Stillman found that blood cholesterol went down, not up, on his diet. He attributed Harvard's findings of 1215 milligrams of cholesterol to the daily inclusion of eggs. "Don't eat eggs, and your daily cholesterol content will be only 115 milligrams," he told CONSUMER GUIDE®.

Almost without exception, "crash" or radical diets are deficient in vitamins and minerals, some more than others. The Stillman diet was shown to be deficient in Vitamin A, thiamine, riboflavin, Vitamin D, Vitamin C, Vitamin E, folic acid, sodium, potassium, calcium, iodine, copper, cobalt, zinc, and fluorine. Dr. Stillman countered this criticism by saying that he insisted on large doses of vitamin and mineral supplements as an integral part of his diet. But forgetting to take the supplements could lead to serious health problems.

CONSUMER GUIDE®'S EVALUATION

A high-protein or all-protein diet has advantages and disadvantages. In fact, like all diets, the Stillman diet and others like it have clear-cut pros and cons that you should study before you decide if such a diet is right for you.

CONS

A protein diet may by psychologically undesirable because it tends to be monotonous. To be most effective—to follow Stillman's basic program to the letter—you must confine yourself to lean meats, a few dairy products, and lots of water. Put bluntly, this is very boring and may make the dieter feel deprived. However, there are some frills in his 14-Day Diet Plan. Nevertheless, the US Senate report[27] recommends more carbohydrates (55 to 60 percent of dietary calories) — the opposite of Stillman's 14-Day Diet.

On high-protein diets, your mouth will be dry and your breath foul unless you drink lots of water. But water is not always a solution; sugarless gum does help, as do breath sweeteners. When you do drink lots of water (eight 10-ounce glasses or ten 8-ounce glasses a day), you will urinate frequently, which may be an inconvenience in business or travel. Also, if you have any history of kidney or liver disease, a high-protein diet can be dangerous.

If your blood cholesterol level is high, you must watch what you eat. The Stillman diet is essentially an animal-protein-and-fat diet, which means you will get lots of cholesterol and saturated fats but little polyunsaturated fats. The same can be said of Dr. Edelstein's diet; however, the high cholesterol provided by these diets is not ordinarily an immediate concern to premenopausal women. But it should be, because by age 70, the rate of cholesterol-associated heart diseases in women is as great as in men.

A further difficulty arises with the so-called yo-yo type effect you may experience when you go off such diets. If you go off entirely, you may shoot back up to your original weight. This "bouncing back" phenomenon is due partly to water retention — there is no doubt that some of the dramatic weight loss from high-protein diets is due to water loss, though we at CONSUMER GUIDE® are convinced that the burning of fat is a significant aspect of the total loss of weight. Partly, the yo-yo effect is due to simply overeating the "forbidden" foods that carry high-calorie price tags. In any event, bouncing back is something to be guarded against; you cannot go back to your former diet without a quick surge of pounds.

While on a high-protein diet, you have to be extremely careful to get plenty of vitamins and minerals by means of supplements. Diets like Stillman's are severely lacking in many vitamins and minerals. If you forget or do not bother to take supplements, you can become ill, perhaps seriously. Some also lack fiber; so you might want to take bran each day.

PROS

A drastic change in your diet can by psychologically desirable because it reminds you that dieting is serious business and cannot be done haphazardly. In other words, your old ways were bad, fat ways, so your new ways must be dramatically different.

Dramatic or not, a protein diet quickly becomes monotonous. However, monotony can have positive side effects. When the food in front of you is the same as the food you faced yesterday, and is the same as the food you will face tomorrow, you tend to eat less simply because the excitement or variety is gone. And, obviously when you eat less you can lose weight more quickly and more visibly.

High protein diets seem to work for those who can manage them mostly because they restrict calories. If you choose a high protein diet, you will lose fat and lose it relatively rapidly. However, CONSUMER GUIDE® recommends Stillman-type diets only if certain conditions are met: (1) If your physician has examined you and found you fit, and (2) if you have no past or present liver or kidney ailment or diabetes.

High-Fat Diets

With medical scientists emphasizing the relationships between both cancer and heart disease and heavy amounts of fat in the diet, high-fat diets for weight loss are losing ground. Still, they are around, ready to be used by dieters desperate to achieve some results and ready to try anything.

Fats do have two advantages. One is that flavor goes with fat, so that a high-fat diet is satisfying to the palate, easy to stay on, and never boring. The other advantage of fat is that it takes a longer time to digest than do protein and carbohydrates, and it affords a more prolonged feeling of fullness. If there is one thing that dieters cannot easily cope with, it is hunger. But though fat fights hunger, it also fights slimness.

Still, these diets persist, so some history and explanations are in order and follow.

The first popular high-fat reducing diet was proposed by William Banting, coffin maker to the Duke of Wellington in Great Britain. Banting's *Letter on Corpulence*, published in 1864, became a best-seller, as thousands of Britishers read and followed the principles that helped Banting reduce to 156 pounds from 202 pounds in a year. Banting, however, was following the instructions of his ear surgeon William Harvey.[1]

Dr. Harvey had just returned from Paris where he had attended lectures by the physiologist Claude Bernard. What fascinated Harvey was Bernard's discussion on the evils of sugar and how diabetes could be controlled by a diet that eliminated sugar.

When Dr. Harvey examined the 60-year-old coffin maker, he concluded that Banting's earache was due to the pressure of fat on the eustachian tube (the narrow tunnel connecting the middle ear to the back of the throat that equalizes air pressure on both sides to the eardrum). Dr. Harvey was convinced that the only way his patient could get relief from the earache was to get rid of fat. So he placed Banting on a unique diet: meat, including mutton and bacon, and fish, with a bare minimum of sugar, bread, beer, and potatoes.

Though the first half of the 20th century saw weight-reducing diets concentrate on calorie counting and a balanced diet, the high-fat theory resurged, thanks to Alfred W. Pennington, M.D., then head of the medical division of E.I. duPont de Nemours and Company, Wilmington, Delaware. In the 1940s, Dr. Pennington studied overweight duPont employees and their health. By 1951, he had formulated a diet by which, he said, they would eat fat and get thin.[2]

The diet was based on Dr. Pennington's theory that people with tendencies to be fat have defects in their metabolisms. That is, people get fat not because of eating too much but because of what their bodies do with food—turning too much of whatever they eat into fat.[3] He felt that putting overweight people on low-calorie diets only made them hungry. Low-calorie diets did not remove fat because overweight people's bodies were breaking down carbohydrate incompletely (stopping before the final

114

breakdown into the acids and molecules required by the cells). As a result, much of the carbohydrates they were eating converted directly into fat.

The solution was obvious to Dr. Pennington: severely restrict the amount of carbohydrates overweight people eat. He also accepted the findings from experiments conducted at the Russell Sage Institute in 1928 that indicated each meal could consist of two to three ounces of fat and six to nine ounces of meat – in other words, fatty meat. Dr. Pennington's theory became popularly known as the duPont Diet. It was published by *Holiday* magazine in June, 1950, and was subsequently offered in booklet form for ten cents.[4]

Calories Don't Count

The high-fat fad quieted down for awhile, then was popularized anew by Herman Taller, M.D., with the publication of *Calories Don't Count* in 1961.[5]

Dr. Taller, a Brooklyn obstetrician-gynecologist, had fought his own weight problem for years. In 1955, after a routine medical examination, Taller's doctor told him his cholesterol level was too high. Because high blood cholesterol levels had been linked with heart disease, the doctor recommended a change in diet. Taller's doctor prescribed, as a supplement to his daily diet, oils with polyunsaturated fats (cholesterol is chemically linked to saturated fat). To his doctor's satisfaction, Taller's blood cholesterol dropped to normal. To Taller's surprise, he was losing weight even though he was consuming 5000 calories a day. It was then he began to doubt the calorie-counting theories of weight loss.

Taller dug into history and found the Banting pamphlet and the Pennington reports. They made sense to him, and he combined their conclusions with his own experience to come up with his "new nutrition principles."

"To lose fat," Dr. Taller wrote, "you must make your body consume its stored fat, a process my new nutrition principle achieves." By eating fats, he proposed, "you set in motion a process which stimulates the pituitary gland and gets this fat-burning going at a higher rate. The obese person not only burns the fat he eats; his system gets so fired up that it burns the fat he has accumulated over the years."

The key element in Taller's diet was "lipo-equilibrium," meaning fats in balance—a balance absent in overweight people. His idea was to restore it and to get the liver to convert body fat to energy. He saw that the way to restore the balance was to eat soft, polyunsaturated fats. When you eat such fats, said Dr. Taller, "you set in motion a happy cycle. You stimulate body production of certain hormones which work to release fats stored around the body." The best of these polyunsaturated fat-containing oils, in his opinion, was safflower oil; corn oil was next best. He recommended taking two tablespoons of oil before each meal.

Dr. Taller cited case after case that proved oil melted away fat. He withstood the heavy barrage of criticism from the American Medical Association and other medical organizations, but when he promoted the sale of safflower oil along with his book, the government stepped in.

On May 10, 1967, Dr. Taller was found guilty in the US District Court in

Brooklyn on six counts of mail fraud and one count of violating federal drug laws; the next month, he was fined $7000 and placed on probation for two years. Government prosecutors called his book's sales tie-in with CDC (for "Calories Don't Count") brand safflower capsules made by Cove Vitamin and Pharmaceuticals, Inc., a "worthless scheme foisted on a gullible public."[6]

Still, Dr. Taller had interested a fat-conscious public in high-fat diets and provoked reports such as that by Broda O. Barnes, M.D., of Colorado State University.[7] Dr. Barnes kept his patients on saturated-fat diets for 25 years. He reported that while his patients were eating bacon, eggs, and eggnog made with whipped cream, they were losing weight. But he wasn't surprised. After all, he noted, Eskimos live on blubber yet stay trim.

CONSUMER GUIDE®'S EVALUATION

Dr. Taller's convoluted, challenging theories were never proven. The fact is that calories DO count—and how! Rating: Not recommended. No stars.

Dr. Atkins' Diet Revolution

Robert C. Atkins, M.D., explained to CONSUMER GUIDE® that he "did not start out with the idea of writing a book. But it helped solve problems which existed. It properly explains to the public obesity, nutrition, and metabolism." He admitted that "in a sense I adapted Taller's approach," but he went on to state that "this was 13 years later after a lot of scientific evidence had linked insulin and heart disease and hammered down the case against carbohydrates. I believe the evidence overwhelmingly implicates sugar as a major epidemiological culprit."

Dr. Atkins was born in Columbus, Ohio, and was educated at the University of Michigan and Cornell Medical College. After his internship in Rochester, New York, he went to New York City for a residency in cardiology. In fact, it was as a heart specialist that he began his practice in 1959. He grew interested in diets four years later, he claims, when he became a medical consultant for American Telephone & Telegraph (AT&T). After he posed for a photograph for a company identification badge, he asked his nurse, "Do I really have three chins?"

He felt he must do something about his fat. But what? The idea of hunger scared him; he felt he had no will power. "I was looking for 'The Hungry Man's Diet,'" he said, when he started searching through medical journals and textbooks.

He soon came upon Pennington's report from duPont. It fascinated him. But even more intriguing was a report by British researchers who had found in the urine of people who were fasting a substance that mobilized fat—that is, moved it out of adipose (fatty) tissue to be burned.[8] Researchers from Middlesex Hospital, London, analyzed the substance and found that it was not growth hormone, which is known to mobilize fat, but a new substance.[9]

Dr. Atkins also read the reports of Walter Lyon Bloom, M.D., of Piedmont Hospital, Atlanta, who wrote that people on a no-carbohydrate diet of bacon and eggs and plenty of meat exhibited the same metabolic changes as people who fasted.[10] Dr. Atkins put himself on such a diet and carefully checked the ketones in his own urine, as Dr. Bloom had done for his patients.[11] (Ketones are the simple acids produced by the body when fats are burned; their presence in the urine, then, indicates that the body is burning fat.) As a physician, Atkins knew the test for ketones was easy to perform: merely buy urine test sticks or tablets in a drugstore; if urine turns the stick or tablet purple, ketones are present. In his book he notes, "I soon discovered that even if I added 10 to 15 grams of carbohydrates, after a zero carbohydrate start, the tablet still turned purple. This meant that my body was continuing to burn my fat. I could snack on cheese, cold cuts, cold shrimp, cottage cheese, and have a filling salad with each meal."

He next tried his diet on 65 employees at AT&T. So heady was his success that he put his private patients on the same diet. Before long, Dr. Atkins was no longer a cardiologist but a diet doctor. That was in 1964.

Shortly thereafter, he began treating comedians and actors, and his fame zoomed. A description of his diet appeared in *Harper's Bazaar* in 1966, and, in 1970, *Vogue* ran a 16-day version called *Vogue's* Super Diet. His practice grew with his fame. Soon his 23-room office complex was handling 350 desperately fat patients a week.[12]

It was then that Ruth West, who had written diet books of her own, asked Dr. Atkins if he'd like to collaborate on a diet book. Dr. Atkins was ready and willing. He was concerned about the federal ban on the sale and use of cyclamates as artificial sweeteners and wanted a platform to express his views. Also, he was thinking of expanding his business interests by opening a West Coast office and perhaps a string of health spas.

The book—*Dr. Atkins' Diet Revolution*[13]—was copyrighted in the names of Atkins and West, and West is thanked "for her inestimable help in the preparation of this book," but she is not listed as coauthor.

In the book, Dr. Atkins outlines an initial week of zero-carbohydrate menus that provide an abundance of fats. Recommended are such dishes as chicken salad with mayonnaise and celery, seafood with lemon butter sauce, cheese omelet with bacon, and eggs Benedict with hollandaise sauce, among others. Not recommended are fruits, vegetables, sugars, starches, breads, sweet pickles, chewing gum, ice cream, catsup, and so on. "At the end of the first week following this basic zero-carbohydrate diet," says Dr. Atkins, "most men will have lost seven or eight pounds, most women five or six pounds."

When this weight loss occurs, Dr. Atkins continues, you may go on to Level Two of the diet. Level Two allows foods with carbohydrates—about five grams per day for a week. Then you move, step by step to Level Five, adding to your diet, in moderation, such foods as grapefruit, cantaloupe, cottage cheese, pea pods, wine and alcohol, cheesecake, tomato, and other similar foods. You may consume these foods as long as your body remains in a state of ketosis—burning fat and eliminating ketones from the body. You yourself discover when to level off, for as soon as the urine test sticks stop turning purple, your body is not releasing ketones anymore. You have reached your Critical Carbohydrate Level. Dr. Atkins believes this level should not exceed 40 grams a day, too low a level in CONSUMER GUIDE®'s opinion.

Dr. Atkins advises his readers to check the urine for ketone bodies daily; keep turning the test sticks purple, he says, and you keep losing weight. He also remarks that the ketones in the urine and on the breath are sneaking calories out of the body as a negative sort of bonus. (Yes, calories, even though they are not supposed to count.)

Doctors who become alarmed when nondiabetic dieters develop ketosis, contends Dr. Atkins, "have had no experience with the ketosis induced by a carbohydrate-free diet. I have, since this is my specialty." He adds, "I have observed no ill effects...On the contrary, I have arrived at the conclusion that ketosis is a state devoutly to be desired."

On this diet, asserts Dr. Atkins, the body will have no carbohydrates to burn as fuel; therefore, it will mobilize fat from unsightly adipose tissue. Cutting out carbohydrates triggers secretion of fat-mobilizing hormone (FMH) which keeps the body's metabolic fires fueled with fat. You convert your body "from being a carbohydrate-burning engine into being a fat-burning engine," he claims. "This is the diet revolution."

CRITICISM

Like Dr. Taller's, Dr. Atkins' popular high-fat, low-carbohydrate diet was heavily criticized by members of organized medicine and authorities on nutrition. Here is a sampling:

- Fredrick J. Stare, M.D., professor of nutrition at Harvard University, said it bordered on malpractice to recommend such large proportions of saturated fats and cholesterol when the hazards to the heart are so well known.[14]
- The Council on Foods and Nutrition of the American Medical Association called it "a bizarre regimen" that is "without scientific merit."[15]
- The chairman of the board of the New York County Medical Society said Dr. Atkins' book was unethical and self-aggrandizing.[16]
- The highly respected The Medical Letter called the Atkins' diet "unbalanced, unsound, and unsafe."[17]

CONSUMER GUIDE® has analyzed the criticism aimed at Dr. Atkins' high-fat, low-carbohydrate diet and presents the arguments free of rhetoric with which they were originally presented. Among the medical journals and magazines that were opposed to Dr. Atkins' views were The Medical Letter, Medical Opinion, Modern Medicine Magazine, American Medical News and its sister publication the Journal of the American Medical Association. McCall's criticized Dr. Atkins, and newspapers around the country, including The New York Times, Washington Post, and the Los Angeles Times printed his critics' remarks.

On April 12, 1973, the US Senate Select Committee on Nutrition and Human Needs held a hearing on the Atkins' book and diet. The findings of the hearing, together with the findings of other congressional committees studying nutrition in the United States, may ultimately be used in food and drug legislation. A copy of the hearings can be obtained at your local library.

A summary of the criticisms, including those of CONSUMER GUIDE®, follows. It is followed by rebuttal from Dr. Atkins and his supporters.

1. The Atkins' diet is not based on scientific or nutritional principles. Its premise, neither new nor revolutionary, is more than a century old. Like other low-carbohydrate diets, it ignores the fact that the human being is an omnivore—people must have all four food groups (dairy, grain, meat, and fresh fruits and vegetables) in their diets. We are not yet sure if we can delete food groups without becoming deficient in necessary substances.

   A frequent criticism leveled at Dr. Atkins is that if, indeed, he discovered a new nutritional principle, the proper place to announce and explain it would have been in a medical journal or at a medical meeting. Dr. Atkins did neither. Nor did he deal with the medical aspects of water loss in weight control. Most of the weight lost on a low-carbohydrate diet is due to water loss. Studies have shown[18] that carbohydrate in the diet inhibits excretion of sodium and water. Other studies have shown that if only 600 calories of carbohydrates are given to people after they have fasted, they regain all their lost weight, mostly as water.

   In his book, Dr. Atkins makes casual references to respected researchers and cites significant studies, but he cannot document them. In our interview, Dr. Atkins was asked for complete citations for specific statements which he had attributed to other doctors and scientists. He replied that the book was written for the public; so no specific references were cited. When pressed for the reference list he used in the preparation of the manuscript, Dr. Atkins said, "It and the papers I quoted were in a briefcase I lost."

   With the help of the Illinois Institute of Technology Library Services and the Florsheim Medical Library at Michael Reese Medical Center, CONSUMER GUIDE® was able to track down the textbooks and journal articles to which Dr. Atkins alludes in his book. A shocking finding is that, in some instances, he took statements out of context to support his theory. George F. Cahill, Jr., M.D., of Harvard University Medical School, made the same discovery. He found that Dr. Atkins used "true but obviously distorted" quotations and "numerous distortions of physiologic fact....The Atkins' concept is replete with very uncritical and, in places, erroneous science and logic."[19]

2. Dr. Atkins cannot revoke the first law of thermodynamics — that the energy in any isolated system must be in balance. The calories eaten must equal the calories burned if the system (body) is to remain the same. If the body burns more calories than it receives, it burns off its fat reserves to maintain that balance. If it receives more than it burns, it stores fat to maintain the balance. Therefore, no one in a sedentary occupation can consume 5000 calories, as Dr. Atkins claims, and also lose weight, even allowing for a difference in the way the body handles fats, carbohydrates, and proteins.

   As for Dr. Atkins' belief that calories leave the body as ketones in urine and breath, these lost ketones account for only 100 calories per day or one pound a month.[20]

3. The existence of a fat-mobilizing hormone has never been confirmed say the AMA and *The Medical Letter.*

4. Diets high in saturated fats and cholesterol are hazardous to health. Atkins' and other high-fat diets go directly against the strong case built up against them by medical researchers in the last 20 years. Research

on chickens and chimpanzees, and studies in communities and clinics, have firmly nailed atherosclerosis—cause of many heart attacks—to fats in the diet.

The Atkins' diet also may seriously disturb the rhythm of the heartbeat. *The Medical Letter* quoted a British report which showed that "the starvation-like state induced by a low-carbohydrate, ketogenic diet stimulates release of free fatty acids into the plasma; in patients with cardiovascular disorders such as cerebrovascular and coronary artery disease, increased free fatty acids may induce cardiac arrhythmias."[21] In fact, in March 1973, a lawsuit against Dr. Atkins alleged that his diet led to a heart attack.[22] Joseph Kottler charged that Dr. Atkins, whose patient he had been, had treated him "recklessly and carelessly" and that the diet had led to Kottler's heart attack. One of Dr. Atkins' attorneys said the suit was without merit and that the plaintiff was "jumping on the publicity trolley car."[23] The suit was never brought to trial but *The New York Times'* account of the suit noted that a week earlier the AMA's Council on Foods and Nutrition had warned that people whose blood level of fat rises in response to unlimited eating of foods high in saturated fats and cholesterol assume increased risk of heart disease.[24]

Diets heavy in fats can bring on diarrhea, which causes loss of water and weight but also loss of vitamins, minerals, and enzymes.[25]

5. The state of ketosis (in which ketones are abundant in blood and urine) is unhealthy. These partly burned fats can irritate the kidneys. Aware of this, Dr. Stillman insisted that his dieters drink at least eight glasses of water a day. Dr. Atkins, however, advised patients to "drink as much water or calorie-free beverages as thirst requires. Don't restrict fluids… but it is not necessary to force them either."[26] Dr. Atkins would have done his readers a favor and spared their kidneys had he passed on Dr. Stillman's advice. Even with heavy intake of water, however, the AMA has warned that "ketogenic diets may also cause a significant increase in blood uric acid concentration" which would cause gout to flare up in susceptible dieters.[27]

During the US Senate Select Committee on Nutrition and Human Needs hearings, testimony indicated ketogenic diets were dangerous to unborn children. Karlis Adamsons, M.D., professor of obstetrics and gynecology at Mt. Sinai Hospital School of Medicine, New York, said, "If I were a fetus I would forbid my mother to become ketogenic." When the pregnant woman's body becomes ketogenic, the amount of glucose in her blood drops. Glucose is a major form of energy used by the brain and nervous system. If the mother's blood sugar is lowered, so is the unborn infant's; the result may be brain damage. Dr. Adamsons cited a study of 55,000 pregnancies. Analysis of the data showed that children born of mothers who had a form of ketosis known as acetonuria had lower IQ scores than children born of mothers who didn't.[28]

6. Dr. Atkins' and other high-fat diets may cause other health problems. The lack of carbohydrates brings on fatigue after two days on the diet, says the AMA. The AMA also notes that such diets may cause hypotension or low blood pressure, a threat not only to adults but also to unborn babies. The New York County Medical Society said further

that the Atkins' diet may cause weakness, apathy, dehydration, calcium depletion, lack of stamina, nausea, and fainting.[29]

Finally, the Bantam Books edition of *Dr. Atkins' Diet Revolution* contains a Publisher's Note that says, in part, "charges which have been made against the diet by the AMA and others involve the possibility of various results and effects which may be adverse to the dieter's health. We therefore reiterate and reemphasize the importance of medical supervision prior to and during the utilization of this diet."

REBUTTAL

Dr. Atkins reacts to the AMA, his County Medical Society, and other critics in one of two ways. He invites them to review the records of the 10,000 patients he claims he has successfully treated for obesity. "The data are here, and I invite all serious investigators to review and analyze them," he told CONSUMER GUIDE®. "I've made the offer time and time again, but no one has yet taken me up on it." He contends that the data on his patients are unique; that other physicians who have prescribed high-fat diets have never cut out carbohydrates completely, as he has.

The other way he replies to his critics is to criticize them for their closed minds and vested interests. He explained to CONSUMER GUIDE®: "In the history of medicine, there have been many controversies. When there were two opinions involved in the controversy, the result was further study by disinterested people. This is no controversy because the other parties haven't studied my program and its basis. They are not even entitled to participate in the discussion. What we have here is a new frontier of medicine, and the same people are giving their old opinions. If you look at the financial records of the AMA and the Harvard School of Nutrition and see the list of their benefactors, advertisers, and endowers you'll see why they insist on our eating carbohydrates." Dr. Atkins quotes reports that Dr. Stare and his department receive hundreds of thousands of dollars from food companies as well as from the food industry-financed Nutrition Foundation.[30]

Here are his answers to specific criticisms.

1. When we asked Dr. Atkins why he hadn't published the data from his 10,000 patients, he explained that it was frightfully expensive to pull that much data together and analyze it. Still, CONSUMER GUIDE® suggests it would have been far cheaper than the thousands of dollars in legal fees he has had to pay to defend his book and his theory.
2. Dr. Atkins maintains that his calorie-counting critics have never studied the amount of calories in ketones excreted in the urine or in the breath but have only guessed at them. Furthermore, says Dr. Atkins, "No one has done a scientific study of the energy balance of people who lose weight yet eat lots of calories. There are people who are not on my diet who eat 2000, 3000, 4000, and 5000 calories a day, lead sedentary lives, and yet still maintain or lose weight. Calorie excretion through ketones is the only explanation, the only way those calories can leave the body without burning."

CONSUMER GUIDE® agrees that more studies must be conducted

on ketosis and its relation to the body's energy balance. However, it is doubtful that large amounts of ketone calories are excreted; if they were, the urine and breath would be unbearably foul.

CONSUMER GUIDE® also finds that critics from the AMA and Harvard ignore some recent, significant additions to scientific knowledge about carbohydrates and fatty acid metabolism. For instance, George E. Schauf, M.D., has successfully treated more than 900 obese people by putting them on diets of lean meat and poultry, a carbohydrate intake limited to 50 to 80 grams a day, and corn and safflower oil in salads. Also revealing were studies at Oak Knoll Navy Hospital, Oakland, California, which showed that obese sailors lost more fat when on a fat-and-protein diet with few carbohydrates than they did when fasting. Dr. Schauf believes such findings strongly support the theory that the amount of fat that is lost depends a great deal on how much the fat cells can be driven to work. A diet that decreases calories alone, he says, won't make them work hard enough.[31]

3. The argument over the existence of a fat mobilizing hormone (FMH) pivots on the word "hormone." CONSUMER GUIDE® finds this an incredible bit of nitpicking on the part of Dr. Atkins' critics; at the same time, we must add that the existence of FMH is not crucial to Dr. Atkins' theory. In any case, the AMA states that "no such hormone has been unequivocally identified in man." The AMA does acknowledge, however, that growth hormone and adrenalinlike chemicals can mobilize fat.[32]

In his letter to the US Senate Select Committee on Nutrition and Human Needs, Professor Pawan said that evidence of a fat mobilizing substance (FMS) besides growth hormone and chemicals is growing. And, he said, "There is suggestive evidence that FMS may be a hormone. At present, it would be premature to designate the substance — FMS — a 'hormone,' since it has not yet satisfied the stringent scientific criteria for such a definition."[33]

Eli Seifter, M.D., of Albert Einstein College of Medicine says he has found such a substance in urine.[34] Furthermore, Maurice V. L'Heureux of Loyola University's Stritch School of Medicine, near Chicago, reported in June, 1973, that he was able to isolate FMS from the urine of fasting rats. He found that FMS stimulated the production of cyclic adenosine monophosphate, which, in turn, intensified the action of a fat-destroying enzyme named lipase.[35] In medical experiments testing its effect on obese subjects, FMS has been shown to stimulate weight loss.[36]

4. In his testimony before the US Senate Select Committee, Dr. Atkins attempted to refute Dr. Stare's criticism of the high-cholesterol content of his diet. "He knows as I do that a high-fat diet, when given in conjunction with any significant amount of carbohydrates, is capable of raising the serum cholesterol level, and usually does. But what he has not stated, despite the body of evidence, is the effect of a high-fat or moderately high-fat diet in the absence of a significant quantity of carbohydrates. This is a different metabolic situation and the results are different, and I think this is the important distinction we must make before this committee, that there is a difference between a diet of

restricted carbohydrates and high fat as compared to a diet of high fat and no restriction of carbohydrates.

"Until there is a body of evidence showing that the cholesterol levels go up or serum fat levels go up when there is this kind of carbohydrate restriction recommended in my book, then we must assume that data has [sic] not been accumulated. The only data which has [sic] been accumulated are those I personally have accumulated."[37]

During his interview with CONSUMER GUIDE®, Dr. Atkins said he had measured the blood cholesterol level of "4000 or 5000 of my patients. We are now tabulating the data from a group of 500 patients for median cholesterol level drops on a regimen of my diet with supplemental B complex and C vitamins. Our early results seem to confirm the findings of others that vitamins play a role in fat mobilization and usage. In hundreds of my patients, blood cholesterol had dropped 100 points or more; 96 percent of all my patients showed a drop in triglycerides; 75 percent of my patients showed a drop in both blood cholesterol and triglycerides."

Dr. Atkins also found fault with critics whose attacks were based on the results of laboratory studies. "The studies are not relevant," he told CONSUMER GUIDE®, "because they are in animals, not people, and because the animals haven't been living on an antecedent lifetime diet of sugar and refined flour. There have been no studies in animals living on diets comparable to the diet people have lived on before going on my diet."

5. Speaking of the charges that a ketogenic diet is dangerous during pregnancy, Dr. Atkins told the US Senate Select Committee on Nutrition and Human Needs that he recommends his diet to his pregnant obese patients because, "I believe it is safe when followed by a physician. I have stated that I do not recommend to an obese pregnant patient that she turn around and start eating carbohydrates because I am well aware that in obesity there is a high predilection to diabetes, and diabetes frequently has its onset during pregnancy and a diabetic pregnancy may be full of complications."[38] In other words, Dr. Atkins sees no reason why one of his patients, after becoming pregnant, should drop the high-fat diet and begin eating carbohydrates again.

CONSUMER GUIDE® believes that no woman of child-bearing age should go on the Atkins' or any other special diet without first consulting her physician. Since the thalidomide disaster of almost two decades ago, researchers have come to realize that the fetus is extremely sensitive to the slightest alteration in the chemical environment of the uterus.

6. In his book, Dr. Atkins wrote: "this diet is not a fad diet, nor is it designed for a quick weight loss, but it's going to be the way you eat for the rest of your life."

If you choose to follow the Atkins' diet for the rest of your life, CONSUMER GUIDE® reminds you that it can cause fatigue and depression. You may have to resort to an occasional glass of orange juice (as Dr. Stillman suggested in his diet) for some carbohydrate to counteract these effects. More importantly, you must have a thorough physical examination and laboratory testing before you start the Atkins' diet. In fairness, we must quote the same advice from Dr. Atkins in his book: "Before any patient starts with me, I take a comprehensive series of blood tests, which I recommend you have your own physician give you, particularly if you have more than 20 pounds to lose. Get a routine series of blood tests as a base line so that if anything changes, you will know where you stand. The blood count, sugar level, cholesterol, and triglycerides should improve, but the uric acid may go up. For my patients, this rarely poses a problem because I routinely prescribe a drug to prevent uric acid formation for my patients if the uric acid level is high to begin with, or if it goes above the normal range after being on the diet."[39]

CONSUMER GUIDE®'S EVALUATION

If you've been on a low-calorie diet and then begin to follow the Atkins' diet, you may think you are not dieting at all. If you gorge yourself with as many fats as Dr. Atkins recommends, you'll be eating many high-calorie foods. Yet, by restricting your carbohydrate intake, you limit some fats. Without bread, for example, you will cut down on butter and therefore on calories.

The main weakness of the Atkins' diet is the absence of scientific reasoning behind it. The ability of the body to make its own sugar from protein for immediate and stored fuel is well known. But how eating fat will stimulate the body to release stored fat is not known.

Fat stored under the skin, and around certain internal organs, is released and mobilized; so it is easy to see why some people think the body must have fat-mobilizing substances. But, despite the beliefs of Drs. Taller and Atkins, the action of a fat-mobilizing substance remains unclear and undemonstrated in experiments on animals or in trials on people.

Likewise, CONSUMER GUIDE® feels that the danger to the heart and arteries posed by high-fat diets is reason enough to stay away from them. Ketosis is another reason. Women who are not planning to become pregnant and men and women who are healthy (especially those who are free of kidney disease or gout) have no particular problems with ketosis. However, if you are pregnant (or liable to be), have any kidney problem, gout, or possible cardiovascular disease, stay away from the Atkins' diet. And while Dr. Atkins doesn't insist on it, CONSUMER GUIDE® recommends you follow Dr. Stillman's advice and consume at least eight glasses of water a day while on any ketogenic diet.

CONSUMER GUIDE® finds the Atkins' diet potentially dangerous, not well-thought-out, and not firmly based on scientific principles. Dr. Atkins has evidently taken up the fallen high-fat banner from Dr. Taller, who took it up from Pennington and other predecessors and added some colors of his own. (Dr. Taller, at least, emphasized unsaturated fats.) But the Atkins' diet is still the high-fat approach proposed by Banting and Harvey. It probably owes its appeal to the titillation of doing something we think is not right. In that sense, the Atkins' diet is self-indulgent and unscientific and should be avoided, especially when there are other safer and more effective diets to choose from. Its only value is that fat does help assuage hunger and thus may stem the compulsion to nibble.

Rating for the Atkins' and similar high-fat diets: Not recommended. No stars.

Losing
via Vegetarian

Vegetarianism is a movement whose time has come—again. It was last with us in strength in the 1930s and 1940s (you may remember that there was a Vegetarian Candidate for President in 1948, by the name of Maxwell). After that, meat predominated. Since the 1960s, with the earth-consciousness movement, more and more people have eschewed meat and consciously decided to live on what the land brings forth. Designers of diets have noted that among veggies (as vegetarians are often called) there are few fatties. Because most plant foods are not as densely packed with calories as animal-derived foods, they make effective diet foods.

At the same time, no category of diets has as wide a range of merit, from the well-thought-out, and scientifically based diets of Frances Moore Lappé and the Seventh Day Adventists to the nonsense of Judith Mazel.

Many people avoid flesh foods for moral reasons that involve the slaughter of living animals. For some, this is a religious commitment. Others have turned to vegetarianism because they agree with Lappé, who says our planet can no longer afford the luxury of raising crops to feed animals and raising animals to feed ourselves. Instead, she argues in *Diet for a Small Planet*[1], we must raise crops as food that we consume ourselves.

Other meat-avoiders are afraid of the chemicals that have found their way into livestock. Still others are afraid of germs from diseased animals, although government inspection usually prevents diseased meat from reaching the market.

Regardless of their reasons, vegetarians most often follow one of three basic diets:

1. Vegetarian (also called strict vegetarian or pure vegetarian), including only foods of plant origin: seeds, grains, nuts, fruits, and vegetables.
2. Lacto-vegetarian, including all foods of plant origin, plus foods made of milk, such as yogurt, cheese, cream.
3. Lacto-ovo-vegetarian, including all foods of plant origin, plus dairy foods, plus eggs.

Some vegetarians vary these themes, such as those who will eat the flesh of fish but not of land animals.

On its face, a basically vegetarian diet, which provides some protein from animal sources such as dairy products and eggs (number 3 above), can probably be viewed as nutritionally safe. This is because proteins from these sources are complete. That is, these sources provide balanced quantities of the eight essential amino acids needed by your body to make its own protein. But they must be eaten in sufficient quantities.

Protein in most plant sources is not complete. That is, it does not provide the proper balance or sufficient quantities of the eight essential amino acids. Soy is a notable exception. So is wheat but you have to eat large quantities (about a cup-and-a-half of wheat germ, for instance) to get enough of the amino acid it is lowest in—methionine.

However, there are tried-and-proven, and scientific, ways of mixing complementary plant proteins so that you do indeed get enough—even plenty—of the necessary amino acids, as well as enough iron, calcium, and B vitamins in which red meats are rich.

If you are considering strict vegetarianism, think twice. We human beings change habits slowly. We resist giving up the high-calorie foods we have eaten all our lives. Becoming a vegetarian may take a year or two or even a decade. The speed with which you change life-long habits depends on your motivation, your environment, and other factors over which you have some but not total control.

If you have already decided to become a vegetarian, be sure to consult a good source of information on the subject. One of the best sources is the Seventh Day Adventist Dietetic Association (Box 75, Loma Linda, California 92354). You can also purchase any one of a number of books on vegetarian menus and cooking. Among them are *Recipes for a Small Planet*,[2] *The Forget-About-Meat Cookbook*,[3] *Eating for Life*,[4] *The New Vegetarian*,[5] *The Vegetarian Family*,[6] and the *It's Your World Vegetarian Cookbook*.[7]

Unfortunately, vegetarianism still carries a stigma of cultism. For example, followers of the Zen Macrobiotic Diet combine vegetarianism with philosophy. However, the stamp of approval was given to vegetarianism in 1980 when the American Dietetic Association published its Position Paper on the subject.[8]

In this statement, the ADA said it "recognizes that well-planned vegetarian diets are consistent with good nutritional status. In contrast, poorly planned or unplanned diets increase the risk of diet-related nutritional disorders and, therefore, should be avoided... a vegetarian diet can be planned to be nutritionally adequate, if attention is given to specific nutrients which may be in less available form or in lower concentration or absent in plant foods."

The Alternative Diet

To help you make the transition to vegetarianism, you may want to follow the plan found in the University of Iowa's *The Alternative Diet Book*.[9] The plan has three phases to help you change from a high-meat (155 pounds per person annually) diet to a low-meat diet.

Phase I eliminates egg yolk, butterfat, lard, and liver and other organ meats, all of which are laden with cholesterol. Substituted are egg whites, margarine, and skim milk.

Phase II gradually reduces the daily portion of meat to six to eight ounces, while emphasizing vegetables, legumes, and whole grains. The quantity of fat and cheese is lessened, and foreign dishes abound.

Phase III reduces the daily serving of meat to three to four ounces. Meat, fish, and poultry become condiments to spice up vegetable-rice-cereal-legume dishes.

The *Alternative Diet Book* also offers meal plans, recipes, and an exchange list. Ideas for sandwich fillings, for instance, include the following combinations: lima beans and catsup, red beans and sliced tomato, cottage cheese and chopped egg whites, peanut butter and raisins.

The authors point out that "most of these new recipes will be different in taste and texture from accustomed recipes because they contain about one-half the amount of fat of current American recipes. If you try to go from 40 percent fat to 20 percent fat quickly, you will find that the taste is unfamiliar. However, if you change gradually, you will come to like the taste and texture of foods lower in fat." At the end of this chapter is a one-day menu from Phase I.

CONSUMER GUIDE®'S EVALUATION

A properly designed vegetarian diet is an excellent and healthy way to lose weight and keep it off. It provides chewy foods that work the jaws and stimulate the intestines. It provides bulk to replace the densely packed calories of meat and pastries, and it is low in saturated fat and cholesterol. Two cautions: first, be sure to take supplementary Vitamin B_{12}, and, for women, supplementary iron. Second, be sure your doctor confirms that you do not have a peptic ulcer or other inflammation of the digestive tract. Rating: ★★★★

Vegetarian à la Weight Watchers

In January 1981, Weight Watchers International, or WWI, stuck out its corporate neck and introduced its Vegetarian Plan. (For a discussion of WWI and its other diet plans, see "The Group Experience.") The new plan, says WWI, omits poultry, meat, and fish and "has been scientifically designed to provide a wide variety of nutritious foods."

The WWI Vegetarian Plan is lacto-ovo in that it provides animal protein in eggs and dairy foods to supplement the protein in such plant sources as peanut butter, tofu (soybean curd), beans, peas, and lentils.

As in the other new diets introduced by WWI in 1981, beer and wine are allowed occasionally, and even catsup and low-calorie gelatin desserts can be eaten once in a while.

For the convenience of the reader, this diet is reprinted at the end of this chapter.

CONSUMER GUIDE®'S EVALUATION

This is a well-thought-out, nonboring lacto-ovo-vegetarian diet that can be eaten by all, and is especially helpful for dieters with heart and cholesterol problems. Rating: ★★★★

High Fiber for Low Weight

Early in this century, food faddists urged us to eat roughage and become "regular." We were told to eat dishfuls of green vegetables and cereals. It was to become "regular," in fact, that breakfast flakes were originally marketed. It was also this obsession with being "regular" that started the laxative craze in America. Regularity was espoused to rid the body of "poisons" that might affect your "system." Later, doctors told us that we did not have to move our bowels daily to be healthy.

Then along came Denis Burkitt, M.D., a British doctor who conducts research in Africa. In trying to find out why so few African natives, as opposed to Europeans and North Americans, have colon cancer, he compared the diets of African villagers with those of Englishmen. He also compared bowel movements. The rural Africans, who were lean and rarely suffered colon cancer, eliminated about a pound of fecal material a day. The Englishmen, who were overweight and far more likely to develop colon cancer, eliminated less than four ounces a day.

Obesity was, Dr. Burkitt stated, "largely a modern phenomenon" that came with the development of "fiber-depleted starchy carbohydrate foods."[10]

Dr. Burkitt's research inspired David Reuben, M.D., who had told us everything we wanted to know about sex but were afraid to ask. In 1975, he gave us *The Save Your Life Diet*.[11]

Based on Dr. Burkitt's research, Dr. Reuben proposed that we increase bowel movements by correcting our dietary lack of natural fiber.

But what is natural fiber? Fiber is found in plants. Although the word "fibrous" may be applied to meat, that refers to the meat's texture, not to its composition.

Fiber is composed mainly of cellulose, plus a few other constituents (lignin, hemicelluloses, and some polysaccharides) and its best sources are unprocessed miller's bran, parsnips, peppers, artichokes, and seaweed. The next best are beans, cabbage, Brussels sprouts, and carrots. All fruits, berries, and nuts have adequate amounts of fiber. The potato, usually a weight-loss villain, has virtue in the fiber it contains; the sweet potato has even more fiber than the white potato.

Cows can digest fiber, but people cannot. If people could, the total caloric content of vegetables like celery and lettuce would be enormous. But because we cannot digest their carbohydrates, they give us few calories.

Fiber proponents like Dr. Reuben, the late Barbara Kraus (author of *The Barbara Kraus Guide to Fiber in Foods*), and osteopath Sanford Siegal insist that natural fiber will not only stave off colon cancer – the number two cause of death from cancer in America – but also can help you reduce. According to them, adding fiber to the diet will make the intestines absorb less fat and other nutrients from foods. Also, fiber will fill the stomach and intestines with bulk and add far fewer calories than refined carbohydrate foods and meats. Claims Dr. Siegal, "The fiber will decrease the transit time of food through the intestinal tract, thus lowering the number of calories your body receives from the food you eat."[12]

In keeping with these beliefs, Dr. Reuben prescribes a diet for losing weight, but he does not specify any quantities of food, except for bran. There are two reasons for that, he tells us. "First, anyone who really wants to lose weight will eat as little as necessary to feel 'full' so that [he] can reach [his] goal. Secondly, within sensible limits, as long as the diet is high in roughage, one cup or two cups of all-bran cereal or an extra helping of meat or brown rice is not going to make that much difference over the long run."[13]

Dr. Reuben's *Save Your Life Diet* offers basic food, snack, and beverage lists. But the diet does not indicate how food should be prepared (except that visible fat should be removed) or how much should be served.

Dr. Siegal is more specific; he helps you find out how much bran to eat daily. He suggests that you eat some unpopped popcorn kernels and then determine how much time elapsed between swallowing them and defecating them. A transit time of 24 to 36 hours in the digestive system is ideal, he says.

Losing weight with Siegal's *Natural Fiber Permanent Weight Loss Diet* sounds easy: "Eat a minimum of 10 to 12 grams of fiber daily and eliminate all refined carbohydrates."[14]

Not a physician, the late Barbara Kraus was far more moderate in her claims for fiber than Drs. Reuben and Siegal. Instead of proposing a diet, she merely listed the fiber content of thousands of foods and stated: "Several studies have shown that an increased consumption of fiber-rich foods helps us to lose weight. Fiber displaces part of the energy-yielding nutrients (protein, fat, carbohydrate); longer chewing time required by fibrous foods slows down the intake of food."[15]

But says Peter G. Lindner, M.D., a well-respected diet doctor, "Fiber is just one part of a properly balanced diet. Undue emphasis on fiber, and especially adding it as a *food supplement* (e.g., bran) to an otherwise poor diet, will probably cause more problems than it solves" (his italics).[16]

He warns that a "high-fiber diet is often associated with flatulence (gas), borborygmi (rumbling noises), frequent defecation, soft bulky stools, and a constant *awareness* of bowel activity."

Evidence indicates that high-fiber diets may help lower blood cholesterol levels.[17] But a diet high in fiber should not be given to children. Fiber contains a substance that renders insoluble calcium, iron, and zinc, and may lead to deficiencies of some of these minerals.[18]

As though putting in the last word, 69-year-old Dr. Burkitt in 1979 published his own popular book on fiber. Rather than offering a diet, his *Eat Right—To Stay Healthy and Enjoy Life More*[19] lists fiber quantities in common foods (adapted and included at the end of the chapter). He offers this important insight: "slimming foods contain much fiber, a fact that is rarely mentioned."

On a recent visit to the US, Dr. Burkitt told CONSUMER GUIDE® that the best high-fiber diet in America is that devised by James W. Anderson, M.D., chief of the Endocrine-Metabolic Section of the Veterans Administration Hospital, and the University of Kentucky Medical Center, Lexington, Kentucky, originally to control obesity in diabetic patients.

CONSUMER GUIDE®'S EVALUATION

The addition of natural fiber to the diet certainly speeds up the passage of semidigested and digested food through the intestinal tract. In so doing, it might well contribute to the health of the organs of digestion. Furthermore, a high-fiber diet decreases the amount of energy absorbed from digested food by a percent or two. That doesn't seem like much—only 40 calories out of a daily total of 2000 calories. But that amount adds up over the long run—to four pounds a year. This rate accounts for the 40 pounds that creep up on many people during the first ten years of marriage. Also, high-fiber foods are bulky, fill the stomach, and contribute to a "full feeling" or satiation, which usually makes you stop eating. Furthermore, high-fiber diets, by their vegetarian nature, crowd out fat-laden meats and other foods that are densely packed with calories. In short, providing that you have no digestive problem that prevents it and that you get enough proteins and other essential nutrients, a high-fiber diet is recommended for you to consider. Rating: ★★★★

The F-Plan Diet

Audrey Eyton, founder of Britain's *Slimming Magazine*, and herself slim, has put together a diet that in 1982 took Europe by storm. Called *The F-Plan Diet*,[20] it echoes many of the findings of her countryman, Dr. Denis Burkitt, about the value of fiber in the diet.

The point is that a lot of fiber will help you lose weight three ways:

1. The bulk will move digested food rapidly enough through your intestines that not every last calorie will be absorbed.
2. The fiber binds up nutrients in the food—especially protein and fat—so that not all of them can be absorbed.
3. The bulk fills your stomach and makes you feel "full."

The result is that your body absorbs about 10 percent less than the total amount of calories you eat. The calorie shortfall winds up in your stool. To quote Eyton: "Tests indicate that the increased calorie content of the feces amounts to nearly 10 percent."

She adds, "In one scientific experiment it was found that a daily increase of 10 grams of dietary fiber, by the addition of more fruit, vegetable, and whole-wheat bread to an ordinary Western diet, increased the number of calories excreted in a bowel movement by nearly 90. With still more additional dietary fiber, 32 grams a day, the stools were found to contain 210 calories on average."

Eyton wants you to take between 35 and 50 grams of fiber a day. You get 20 of these fiber grams by taking her Fiber-Filler every day, along with two pieces of fruit and a cup of skim milk. To make it easy, you take half a portion for breakfast, the other half as a snack. Because the total calorie count of this combination is 400, you need to deduct that amount from your daily diet total of 1000 or 1250. And Eyton gives you sample menus for diets at those caloric levels.

The rest of the fiber you get in foods that you include in your meals. To help you, Eyton offers a list of foods with their calories and grams of fiber per portion. To make it easier yet, she tells you which 20 foods offer the highest concentration of fiber. They are (in descending order): dried beans, peas, and other legumes; bran cereals; lima beans; green peas; dried figs, apricots, dates; fresh raspberries, blackberries, strawberries; sweet corn; whole wheat and other whole-grain cereal products; broccoli; potatoes; fresh and frozen beans; apples, pears, plums, raisins and prunes; greens of various kinds; nuts; cherries; bananas; carrots; coconut; brussels sprouts.

Here is her recipe for eight days' worth of Fiber-Filler:

2⅔ cups Bran Flakes (40 percent)
1½ cups bran meal
1½ cups Bran Buds or All-Bran

1 cup sliced almonds
8 large pitted chopped prunes
16 chopped dried apricot halves
½ cup raisins

There is a fourth benefit from a high-fiber diet, which is shared by vegetarian and near-vegetarian diets as well: a high-fiber diet requires a lot of chewing. This satisfies much of the overweight person's passion for eating. But the food you eat here is low in calories. That's the difference. As Eyton expresses it,

> From the moment you put fiber-rich foods into your mouth it starts to give you both physical and psychological advantages in filling you, satisfying you, protecting you from feeling hungry again soon, and speeding your weight loss. The slimming benefits of the F-Plan Diet start in the mouth, continue in the stomach, extend to the blood, and reach a grand finale with that final flush.

The disadvantages are that you ARE eating a lot of bulk. You may find an increase in the amount of gas (flatulence) in your intestines. Also, if you have any bleeding or open sores or ulcers in your intestinal tract, a high-fiber diet may exacerbate your condition; see your doctor first.

Most of *The F-Plan Diet* book contains recipes for hi-fiber dishes. While some include eggs, beef, and shellfish, these foods are offered in moderation. Even a little butter is used here and there. In general, the diet is high in carbohydrates and low in fat. Its protein content may be a problem. The 1000-calorie diet is slightly deficient, while the 1250-calorie diet is barely adequate for women. CONSUMER GUIDE® recommends—especially if you are male—that if you do go on the F-Plan, you opt for the higher calorie number and perhaps add some protein every day, in the form of dry cottage cheese or tofu, in order to meet the recommended daily protein allowances of 44 grams a day for women, 56 grams a day for men.

CONSUMER GUIDE®'S EVALUATION

Perhaps the best hi-fiber diet around. But while it is high in F (fiber) it is borderline in P (protein), so use it with care.
Rating: ★★★

The Advent of Losing Weight

One of the best vegetarian diets for losing weight is offered by the nutritionists of Loma Linda University's School of Health. While their motivation is to follow the dietary laws of Leviticus, they go one step further and avoid all flesh foods. These nutritionists have doctorate degrees in nutrition and come on with much less missionary zeal than such unschooled-in-nutrition proselytizers as Judith Mazel.

Dr. Ella Haddad, of Loma Linda's nutrition department, explained to CONSUMER GUIDE®, "After all, the original diet in the Garden of Eden did not include meat. However, vegetarianism is not a doctrine of our Adventist church. So-called 'clean meats' are acceptable. But there are fewer rules to follow as a vegetarian. Also, many people choose vegetarianism for health reasons."

"However," Dr. Haddad pointed out, "We promote a diet which includes two animal products—eggs and milk foods. This is to allow dieters to get their protein in a minimum amount of calories. It is, of course, possible to obtain all the protein one needs on a strictly vegetarian diet, but that requires taking in a larger total of daily calories than is consistent with weight loss."

Dr. U.D. Register, who holds a doctorate in biochemistry from the University of Wisconsin, and who heads the nutrition department at Loma Linda, explained that the main reason vegetarian diets work so well to take weight off is their caloric density. Because plant foods are full of fiber, the calories are dilute, compared to foods derived from animal sources. A vegetarian diet contains at least twice as much fiber as a diet that includes animal products.

The Loma Linda reducing diet, a two-day sample of which is offered at the end of this chapter, is not that low. It is a reasonable 1200 calories a day, with a low but reasonable fat content — about 20 percent. Studies have shown that you should be able to lose about 15 pounds in 30 days on this diet.

There is another vegetarian low-calorie program connected with Loma Linda. It is called the Weight Management Program run at the university by health educators Gunther Fuchs and Barbara Dickinson. It is a ten-week program for the overweight conducted at the university. The program, begun in 1975, is comprehensive and screens entrants by physical examinations, stress tests, and interviews. Dieters learn how to eat, how to shop, how to cook, and how to achieve a proper attitude. Fee is $220.00. For information, contact the Weight Management Program, Center for Health Promotion, Loma Linda University, Loma Linda, CA 92350.

CONSUMER GUIDE®'S EVALUATION

The Adventist Diet is one of the best ways to lose weight via vegetarian. It is safe and effective. However, there are two cautions. One is that the diet relies on soy protein products that resemble such meat foods as hamburgers. These are easily obtained in supermarkets, under Loma Linda's own brand name or Worthington Foods Co. (900 Proprietors Road, Worthington, OH 43085). Other manufacturers include Archer Daniels Midland Co., Cargill, and Ralston-Purina. However, the problem with such soy-based diets, according to dietitian Mary Lou Johnston of Virginia Polytechnic Institute and State University, who studied such diets, is that "they become monotonous after a while."[21]

Another potential problem is gas. Beans, including soy beans and baked beans, contain polysaccharides, which are not digested, and as a result produce in the gut hydrogen gas, which eventually must be expelled. Also, many people are not able to digest the milk sugar, lactose, which — undigested — produces gas in the colon. Furthermore, certain foods such as onions, lettuce, and cabbage produce bloating and distension of the intestines, which feel like gas.[22] These considerations aside, the Loma Linda diets are a good way to go, if you want to go vegetarian. Rating: ★★★★

Scarsdale Vegetarian

Not nearly as popular as the basic 14-day Scarsdale Medical Diet (SMD), the Scarsdale Vegetarian Diet is the best in the book.[23] It is well-rounded nutritionally and provides enough high quality protein. Except for the proviso concerning meat, the rules for the vegetarian version are basically the same as those for the SMD. The Scarsdale Vegetarian Diet also omits avocados, dry beans (except soybeans), sweet potatoes, and yams. For protein, this version of the Scarsdale diet relies on dairy products (cheese and cottage cheese) and soybeans. For example, for lunch you might have a tomato stuffed with rice and cheese, along with broiled mushrooms, zucchini and carrots, and a slice of protein bread. For dinner you could have a casserole of vegetables cooked with low-fat cheeses, applesauce with raisins, and a tomato and lettuce salad. (See "High-Protein Diets" for more information on Scarsdale diets.)

CONSUMER GUIDE®'S EVALUATION

This diet is both low-cal and well-rounded. Rating: ★★★★

Fructose Vegetarian

Like Pritikin, Dr. J. T. Cooper of Atlanta wants dieters to return to a third-world diet heavy in vegetables and light on meats. He doesn't adequately explain why he calls it *The South American Diet*[24] except to state that "nowhere on earth is the [obesity] problem more severe than in the affluent South American countries of Peru and Venezuela. A combination of...related factors have had the effect of producing a more than average number of significantly obese women and men."

Three years ago, related Dr. Tom (as he's known), "a new method of treating obesity was developed that has swept our southern neighbors by storm." Patients were reported shedding up to 5 pounds a week.

What was the miracle diet? Answer: "A simple combination of naturally occurring compounds and foods used in a certain, special way." The diet itself is heavy on vegetables, both raw and cooked, and fruit, and it allows lean cuts of meat. Dr. Cooper recommends you use fructose as your sweetener, and that you take "lipotropics," which supposedly mobilize fat off your body. These are choline, methionine, and inositol. Further, he recommends you take mood-altering substances to calm your nerves. These are the amino acid tryptophan and some sedatives and antidepressants which are only available with a doctor's prescription.

CONSUMER GUIDE®'S EVALUATION

There's no magic here. The basic diet is OK, but we oppose the routine use of such drugs. Rating: Not recommended. No stars.

The Beverly Hills Diet

The newest crazy vegetarian diet, conceived by a guru to movie stars, was characterized in an article in *The Journal of the American Medical Association* (JAMA) as "the latest, and perhaps the worst, entry in the diet-fad derby. The diet's major tenets fly in the face of all established medical knowledge about nutrition."[25] The diet is all explained in Judy Mazel's book, *The Beverly Hills Diet*.[26] By her own admission, "the diet... first exploded into reality in the heart of Beverly Hills among the movie stars, the jet-setters, and the ultra body conscious who are hardened to flimsy fads. The diet embraced by everyone from *Dallas* star Linda Gray, actress Sally Kellerman, and singer Englebert Humperdinck to hundreds of skinnies shouting the praises of the Beverly Hills diet—a way of eating that has turned slimhood into a reality."

Wow! How could anyone resist a diet like this?

"I do not purport to be a medical doctor," she wrote, "I have simply pulled together scattered facts and synthesized them into a viable, logical program, a program whose very success testifies to its validity."

The facts? First envelope, please. "Most enzymes can't work simultaneously and...many cancel one another out in our digestive systems."

Second envelope, please. "In simplest terms, fat means indigestion, or undigested food. Undigested food means fat. When your body doesn't process food, doesn't digest it, that food turns into fat."

Third envelope, please. "Protein foods are the hardest to digest because they require triple enzymatic action — hydrochloric acid, then pepsin, and then the two in combination."

Fourth envelope, please. "When you mix proteins and carbs, the carbs will usually be trapped in your stomach with the proteins. Your poor stomach can only do one thing at a time, either work or empty. And as long as the protein is there, it has no choice but to work."

Of course, all of the above are false. In order, here are the truths:

1. Humans are omnivores, able to eat all foods; our digestive system has an army of enzymes that facilitate the chemical actions necessary to break foods down into their components; these various enzymes are all capable of acting simultaneously.
2. Undigested food — like the cellulose in celery — goes through your body virtually untouched. The process of digestion breaks down foods so they can be absorbed. Thus only foods that are digested can become fat.
3. Protein is digested in the stomach by a chemical process involving the one enzyme pepsin, which becomes operational in the presence of hydrochloric acid, also secreted in the stomach.

4. The stomach, during digestion, sends liquefied foods on, and holds back the rest until it has liquefied them. It is smart enough to do both.

Of course, the list of inaccuracies and unscientific premises goes on. The Baltimore doctors who wrote the JAMA critique found 21 scientifically inaccurate statements in the book, in addition to its basic premise.

Even without these inaccuracies upon which it is built, the Beverly Hills Diet is absurd. You start out by eating only one kind of fruit—and nothing else—for each meal. Day 1 it's pineapple and bananas. Day 2 it's papaya and mango. Day 3 it's papaya, pineapple, then papaya again. Day 4 it's watermelon only. And so forth. Except for some bread or bagels and some corn on Day 11, you get no food of substantial protein content until Day 19, when you can have lobster or steak.

If the content were not absurd enough, look at the suggested quantities. Two pineapples on Day 1; six to nine papayas on Day 2; and an entire big watermelon on Days 4 and 7!

This is healthy? No way, say the JAMA authors. It presents hazards, among them possible hair loss and severe diarrhea, which can result in hypovolemic shock, potassium deficiency, and arrhythmia (erratic heart rhythm). They describe the symptoms of hypovolemic shock, which can result from profuse water loss and low body levels of salt that comes with diarrhea, as fever, muscle weakness, rapid and thready pulse, a feeling of impending doom, and poor skin tone.

Another critic of the Beverly Hills diet is the AMA's Dr. Philip L. White, director of its Department of Foods and Nutrition. He called it "a terrible book. Its effort at medical or scientific backing comes directly from the 19th century. There is very little in the book in the way of explanation of nutrition, biology or digestion that is in fact the truth."[27]

Dr. Fredrick J. Stare, professor emeritus and founder of the Department of Nutrition at Harvard University, commented, "There is nothing wrong with fruit, but nothing but fruit for ten days is not very good nutrition. The diarrhea that most people would develop during that period would help in the weight loss."[28]

He told of being on several TV shows with Mazel and telling her "that if she were a physician recommending this dietary nonsense, she would most likely be sued for malpractice, and not being a physician she has a good chance of experiencing the same fate as the late Adele Davis...who was sued for practicing medicine without a license, lost, and had to pay a considerable sum."

He explained "that there are no 'Conscious Combinations' of foods (the options were all tested at least 50 years ago)—that we eat mixtures of foods called diets, that there are essentially hundreds of different combinations of foods, and that the enzymes pouring into our digestive tract from several body tissues, particularly the pancreas, don't get confused. The starch enzymes work on the starchy foods, the protein enzymes on the protein, the fat enzymes on the fats, the sugar enzymes on the sugar—all at the same time without any problems. One does not need 'Conscious Combinations' of foods for effective utilization of foods."

Medical World News, a physician's magazine, polled leading nutritional experts who all agreed the Mazel diet was nonsense.[29]

Despite the cautions and criticism, Mazel in 1982 followed up her first diet book with yet another, *The Beverly Hills Diet Lifetime Plan*.[30] Also written with Susan Schultz, this second volume is an expansion of her earlier ideas about Conscious Combining — eating only foods that use, in her view, the same enzyme of digestion — plus quotes from herself. Plus success stories. Plus a history of her success. Plus recipes.

CONSUMER GUIDE®'S EVALUATION

Mazel seems to be riding high on only one fact: that desperate people will go on any diet, no matter how drastic and unsound, to lose weight. How long? And, how healthily? Those are essential questions. This diet is dangerous for most people and has no saving grace. It is totally tinsel, simply schlock. Rating: Not recommended. No stars.

Born-Again Diet

For Joy Gross, vegetarianism is a religion. In *The 30-Day Way to a Born-Again Body*,[31] Gross, the slim, attractive co-director of Pawling Health Manor in Hyde Park, New York, says you can lose eight to 20 pounds in a month. In addition to slimness and well-being, she promises born-again desire. "Healthy sex is like healthy food," she writes. "Premature sexual dysfunction, like premature aging, is brought on by a poor diet." But the 30-day diet she proposes should take the starch out of any desire. It lacks flesh foods, and does not provide enough food. First, you fast, drinking only water, for three days. Then you can eat some fruit (she's heavy on grapes). Day 6 calls for 12 raw cashew nuts and Day 8, some ricotta cheese — and that's all!

CONSUMER GUIDE®'S EVALUATION

Too low in protein to be safe, let alone make you sexy. Rating: Not recommended. No stars.

Holy Cow Diet

Adrien Arpel has a good dieting idea that is also safe. She follows the dieting rituals practiced in India. In other words, she believes the cow is sacred and recommends eating no beef at all.

As she explains in *Adrien Arpel's 3-Week Crash Makeover/Shapeover Beauty Program*,[32] "Beef (and its cousins, lamb and pork — avoid them, too) may well be a good source of protein, but it contains too much fat."

CONSUMER GUIDE®'S EVALUATION

Holy Cow! This is more of a philosophy than a diet. Rating: ★

Inches-Off Diet

One poorly planned vegetarian diet was introduced in 1969, by protein-pushers Irwin Maxwell Stillman and Samm Sinclair Baker as a diet that would take off inches rather than pounds.[33]

This diet, for normal, healthy adults, is a six-week, low-protein diet. Essentially, it provides a minimum amount of protein and little else. For instance, you can eat your fill of certain vegetables and fruits, soups and juices, and breakfast cereal and small amounts of high-calorie foods such as spaghetti and butter. But you can eat no meat, poultry, seafood, milk, cheese or other high-protein foods. Vitamin supplements are a must.

The Inches-Off Diet, according to Stillman and Baker, can take away six to ten inches from the waist. They say it "pulls extra fat from between the muscles."

In his interview with CONSUMER GUIDE®, Dr. Stillman explained that the Inches-Off diet is essentially a vegetarian approach. "Look, there are only 900 calories in 14 pounds of vegetables," he explained. "So you get plenty of bulk and enough protein to maintain health."

CONSUMER GUIDE®'S EVALUATION

This diet is unbalanced and unsound. It provides *no* opportunities to eat protein. In fact, while small amounts of breakfast cereals are permitted, it forbids those that contain protein. Nor are cheeses, chicken, eggs, fish, meats, milk, nuts, poultry, or beans permitted. This Stillman diet is unbalanced and unsound because it gives you only carbohydrates. Amazingly, it is exactly the opposite of Stillman's Quick Weight Loss Diet, which gives you little or no carbohydrates! Stay away. Rating: Not recommended. No stars.

ALTERNATIVE DIET

One-Day Menu

Breakfast
Orange Juice
Oatmeal with Raisins
Cracked Wheat Toast

Lunch
Fruit and Nut Cottage Cheese
  Sandwich
Fresh Pear

Dinner
Bean Sprout Tuna Chow Mein on
  Fluffy Rice
Dilled Tomato Slices
Hard Roll
Lime Sherbet
Peanut Butter Cookies

Reprinted by permission of William E. Connor, Sonja L. Connor, Martha M. Fry, and Susan L. Warner; from The Alternative Diet Book. *Iowa City, IA: University of Iowa Publications, 1976.*

WEIGHT WATCHER VEGETARIAN DIET

*With the permission of Weight Watchers International, CONSUMER GUIDE®
magazine reprints this diet from the Weight Watchers New Program Handbook
(Weight Watchers International, Inc., 1981).*

Breakfast
Fruit or Fruit Juice
Egg, 1, or Cheese, soft, ⅓ cup, or
Cheese, semisoft or hard, 1 oz.,
or Cereal, ¾ oz. with Milk, or
Peanut Butter, 1 T, or Legumes,
3 oz.
Beverage, if desired

Lunch and Dinner
Eggs, 2, or Cheese, soft, ⅔ cup, or
Cheese, semisoft or hard, 2 oz.,
or Peanut Butter, 3 T, or
Legumes, Women—6 oz.,
Men—8 oz., Youth—6 oz.
Beverage, if desired

Daily, at Any Time
Fruits, Women—3 servings,
Men—4-6 servings, Youth—4-6
servings
Vegetables, 2 servings (minimum)
Milk, Women—2 servings, Men—2
servings, Youth—3-4 servings
Bread, Women—2-3 servings,
Men—4-5 servings, Youth—4-5
servings
Fats, 3 servings

Women—3 servings daily
Men—4-6 servings daily
Youth—4-6 servings daily

apple juice or cider, ⅓ cup
grape juice, ⅓ cup
*grapefruit juice, ½ cup
*orange juice, ½ cup
pineapple juice, ⅓ cup
prune juice, ⅓ cup
*tomato juice, 1 cup
mixed vegetable juice, 1 cup
apple, 1 small
applesauce, ½ cup
apricots, 2 medium
dried, 4 medium halves
banana, ½ medium
berries
blackberries, ½ cup
blueberries, ½ cup
boysenberries, ½ cup
cranberries, 1 cup
loganberries, ½ cup
raspberries, ½ cup
*strawberries, 1 cup
*cantaloupe, ½ small or 1 cup
chunks or balls
cherries, 10 large
dates, 2

Fruits
fig, 1 large
dried, 1
fruit cocktail or salad, ½ cup
*grapefruit, ½ medium
*grapefruit sections, ½ cup
grapes, 20 small or 12 large
*honeydew or similar melon, 2"
wedge or 1 cup chunks or balls
*kiwi fruit, 1 medium
kumquats, 3 medium
mandarin, 1 large
*mango, ½ small
nectarine, 1 small
*orange, 1 small
*orange sections, ½ cup
*papaya, ½ medium
peach, 1 medium
pear, 1 small
persimmon, 1 medium
pineapple, ¼ small
plums, 2 medium
prunes, 3 medium or 2 large
raisins, 2 tablespoons
rhubarb, 1 cup
tangerine, 1 large
*ulgi fruit, 1 medium
watermelon, 3" × 1½" triangle or 1
cup chunks or balls

Program Pointers: Select one
serving at Morning Meal. Choose
at least one daily from fruit
marked with an asterisk (*). Vary
selections.

Use fresh, dried, canned or frozen
fruit or fruit juice with no sugar
added.

The serving size for all canned fruit
is ½ cup or the fresh equivalent
with 2 tablespoons juice. Two
slices of canned pineapple with 2
tablespoons juice is 1 fruit
serving.

Vegetables

Women—2 servings daily
(minimum)
Men—2 servings daily (minimum)
Youth—2 servings daily (minimum)

One serving of raw or cooked
vegetables is equal to ½ cup or ½
medium (e.g., tomato)

Select from vegetables such as:
broccoli
cabbage
carrots
cauliflower
celery
cucumbers
eggplant
green beans
lettuce
peppers
spinach
tomatoes

Limited: If desired, the following
vegetables may be selected
daily, up to a combined total of ½
cup:
artichokes
beets
Brussels sprouts
Chinese pea pods
leeks, onions
okra
parsnips
peas
pumpkin
rutabagas
salsify
scallions
shallots
water chestnuts
winter squash
yellow turnips

Program Pointers: Vegetables
may be selected at any time.
Vary selections.

Milk

Women—2 servings daily
Men—2 servings daily
Youth—3-4 servings daily

milk, nonfat, dry, ⅓ cup
milk, skim, 1 cup
buttermilk, ¾ cup
yogurt, plain, unflavored, ½ cup
milk, evaporated skim, ½ cup

Program Pointers: Select
servings at any time.
The skim milk may be made from
nonfat dry milk or may be
commercially prepared liquid
skim milk containing up to 90
calories per cup.
Milk Substitutes—One serving of

the following items may be
substituted once daily for one
milk serving:
flavored milk beverages, low
calorie, 1 packet or serving;
flavored milk puddings, low
calorie, ½ cup

Grains

Women—2-3 servings daily
Men—4-5 servings daily
Youth—4-5 servings daily

Bread Substitutes

Omit 1 serving of bread and select
any item from this list up to 3
times weekly, if desired.

cereal, ready-to-eat, (not presweetened), ¾ ounce
cereal, uncooked, ¾ ounce

bagel, enriched, small, ½ (1 oz.)
bread or rolls, enriched or whole grain, 1 oz.
bread crumbs, dried, 3 T
cereal, ¾ oz.
crispbread, ¾ oz.
English muffin, ½
flour, enriched or whole grain, 2½ T
frankfurter roll, ½ (1 oz.)
graham crackers 2 (2½″ squares)
hamburger roll, ½ (1 oz.)
matzo, ½ board
melba toast, 6 rounds or 4 slices
oyster crackers, 20
pita, 1 oz.
saltines, 6
tortilla, 1 (6″)

Program Pointers: *Cereal*—
Cereal at the Morning Meal must be eaten with at least ½ milk serving. *Bread*—Select servings at any time. Use breads containing up to 80 calories per ounce.

Eggs, Breakfast, 1
Eggs, Lunch and Dinner, 2
Select 4-6 eggs a week
Soft Cheese, Breakfast, ⅓ cup
Soft Cheese, Lunch and Dinner, ⅔ cup
Semisoft and Hard Cheese, (Limit to 6 ounces weekly.)
Breakfast, 1 oz.
Lunch and Dinner, 2 oz.
Peanut Butter, breakfast, 1 T (omit 1 serving Fat)
Peanut Butter, Lunch and Dinner, 3 T (omit 2 servings Fat)
Legumes, Breakfast, 3 oz.
Legumes, Lunch and Dinner, Women—6 oz., Men—8 oz., Youth—6 oz.
Beans
broad
butter
kidney
lima
red
soybean

barley, 1 oz. uncooked, ½ cup cooked
buckwheat groats (kasha), 1 oz. uncooked, ½ cup cooked
corn
ear, 1, whole kernel or cream style, ½ cup
cornmeal, enriched, 1 oz.
uncooked, ¾ cup cooked
cracked wheat (Bulgur) 1 oz. uncooked, ½ cup cooked
hominy, enriched grits or whole, 1 oz. uncooked, ¾ cup cooked
legumes, 1 oz. uncooked, 3 oz. cooked
pasta, enriched macaroni or spaghetti, 1 oz. uncooked, ⅔ cup cooked
noodles, 1 oz. uncooked, ½ cup cooked
popcorn, plain, 1 oz. uncooked, 2 cups cooked
potato, white, 4 oz.
rice, enriched white or brown or wild, 1 oz. uncooked, ½ cup cooked
sweet potato or yam, 3 oz.

Protein
white
Lentils
Peas
black-eyed (cowpeas)
chick (garbanzos)
split
Tofu (soybean curd)—If tofu is selected at Breakfast, increase legume serving size by 1 ounce. If selected at Lunch or Dinner, increase serving size by 2 ounces.

Program Pointers: Select Protein at mealtime only. *Cheese*—
Examples of *soft cheese* are Cottage, Pot, Ricotta (part skim).
Examples of *semisoft cheese* are Bleu, Brie, Camembert.
Examples of *hard cheese* are Cheddar, Muenster, Swiss.
Legumes—Select fresh, frozen, canned or dried legumes. Weigh legumes after cooking.

Women—3 servings daily, Men—3
servings daily, Youth—3
servings daily

margarine, liquid vegetable oil, 1
level tsp.

margarine, reduced calorie, liquid
vegetable oil, 2 level tsp.

mayonnaise, 1 level tsp.

mayonnaise, reduced calorie, 2
level tsp.

vegetable oil
safflower, 1 level tsp.
sunflower, 1 level tsp.
soybean, 1 level tsp.
corn, 1 level tsp.

Fats

cottonseed, 1 level tsp.
sesame, 1 level tsp.
peanut, 1 level tsp.
olive, 1 level tsp.

Program Pointers: Select
servings at any time.
Fat servings may be used to
sauté and stir-fry; mixed with
other ingredients and baked in a
casserole; spread on a cooked
food item and broiled until
heated. Nonstick cooking sprays
are allowed in an amount not
exceeding 10 calories per day.

Optional

Beverages
water
club soda
coffee
mineral water
tea
Condiments
(Select in reasonable amounts.)
artificial sweeteners
baking powder
baking soda
browning sauce
dehydrated vegetable flakes
extracts and flavorings
herbs
horseradish
hot sauce
lemon juice
lime juice

mustard
pepper
pepper sauce
rennin tablets
salt
seasonings
seaweed
soy sauce
spices
vinegar
Worcestershire sauce
seeds: caraway, poppy, sesame,
sunflower, ½ level tsp.
sugar, fructose, honey,
molasses, syrup, ½ level tsp.
wheat germ, 1 level tsp.
wine (for cooking), 2 level tsp.
yeast, 1 level tsp.

Bonus
(Select up to 1 serving daily, if
desired.)
mixed vegetable juice, 1 cup
tomato juice, 1 cup
tomato paste, ¼ cup
tomato puree, ½ cup
tomato sauce, ½ cup

Occasional Substitute
One of the following may be
selected up to 3 times weekly.
On the day this selection is
made, do not select a Bonus.
beer, 8 fluid oz.
beer, light, 12 fluid oz.
gelatin, fruit flavored, ½ cup
wine, red, white, or champagne,
4 fluid oz.

Extras
(Select up to 3 servings daily, if
desired.)
bacon bits, imitation, 1 level tsp.
barbecue, chili and steak sauce,
2 level tsp.

bouillon and broth:
bouillon cube, 1 cube
homemade, ¾ cup
instant broth and seasoning
mix, 1 packet

cocoa or carob, unsweetened, 1
   level tsp.
coconut, shredded, 1 level tsp.
flour, cornstarch, arrowroot, 1
   level tsp.
gelatin, unflavored, ½ envelope
   (about 1½ level tsp.)
ketchup, 2 level tsp.
olives, 2 medium
Parmesan or Romano cheese,
   grated, 1 level tsp.
pickle relish, 1 level tsp.
seafood cocktail sauce, 1
   level tsp.

Specialty Foods
   If desired, select up to 20
   calories per day from any low-
   calorie products.
   Check labels carefully for calorie
   count.
   Do not use if label does not
   indicate calories.

Program Pointers: Examples of
Specialty Foods:
beverages, carbonated or
   noncarbonated or dry mix, low-
   calorie
ketchup, salad dressings,
   gravies or sauces, low-calorie
gelatin, flavored, low-calorie
jams, jellies or preserves, low-
   calorie
syrups or toppings, low-calorie

DIETARY FIBER FOOD VALUES (g/100g)

Grains
Wheat bran (miller's bran)	44.0
Wholewheat flour (100% unrefined)	9.6
White flour (72% refined)	3.0
Soya flour (low fat)	14.3
Sweetcorn, canned	5.7
Corn-on-the-cob, boiled	4.7
Rice, white polished, boiled brown, unpolished, boiled	5.6

Breakfast cereals
All Bran	26.7
Puffed Wheat	15.4
Shredded Wheat	12.3
Cornflakes	11.0
Grapenuts	7.0
Sugar Puffs	6.1
Special K	5.5
Rice Krispies	4.5

Bread & Crackers
Wholewheat	8.5
Brown	5.1
White	2.7
Crispbread rye (Ryvita)	11.7

Nuts
Almonds	14.3
Coconut, fresh	13.6
Brazil	9.0
Peanuts	8.1
Hazel	6.1

Leaf Vegetables
Spinach, boiled	6.3
Broccoli tops, boiled	2.9
Brussel sprouts, boiled	2.9
Cabbage, boiled	1.8
Cauliflower, boiled	1.8
Celery, raw	1.8
Lettuce	1.5

Root Vegetables
Horseradish, raw	8.3
Carrots, boiled	3.0
raw	2.9
Parsnips, boiled	2.5
Beets, boiled	2.5
Potatoes, baked in skins (flesh only)	2.0
boiled (new)	2.0

Legumes

Peas, frozen, boiled	12.0
Beans, baked and canned	
in tomato sauce	7.3
Peas, canned	63
fresh, boiled	52
Lentils, split, boiled	3.7

Desserts

Apple crisp	2.5
Fruit pie	2.4
Rhubarb, stewed-no sugar	2.4
Shortbread	2.1

Fruits

Dates, dried	8.7
Blackberries	7.3
Raisins	6.8
Cranberries	4.2
Bananas	3.4
Pears, fresh, eating	3.3
Strawberries	2.2
Plums, raw, eating	2.1
Apples	2.0
Oranges	2.0
Tomatoes, raw	1.5
Pineapple, fresh	1.2
Grapefruit	0.6

Reprinted by permission of Denis Burkitt; from Eat Right—To Keep Healthy and Enjoy Life More. *New York: Arco Publishing, 1979.*

LOMA LINDA VEGETARIAN DIET

Day 1

Breakfast

Orange juice (frozen)	4 oz.
Banana, small	1 sm.
Rolled wheat	4 oz.
Raisins	2 tsp.
Milk, nonfat	8 oz.

Lunch

Baked potato, small	1 sm.
* Almond nut loaf with	4½ oz.
**Tomato gravy	¼ cup
Tossed salad:	
Tomatoes	1 lg.
Head lettuce	¼ head
Lemon-juice dressing	2 Tbsp.
Whole wheat bread	1 sl.

Supper

*Minestrone soup	1 cup
Celery sticks (5″ long ×	
¾″ wide)	3
Whole wheat bread	1 sl.

Total:	
Calories	1202
Protein	52.0
Fat	20.1
CHO	218.5

Day 2

Breakfast

Grapefruit	½
Fresh apple	1 med.
Roman Meal Cereal	¾ cup
Dates chopped	2
Milk, nonfat	8 oz.

Lunch

*Tostada Casserole	¾ cup
Mustard greens/	
lemon juice	¾ cup
Yellow squash	1 cup
Whole wheat bread	1 sl.

Supper

*Soybeans Americana	1 cup
**Cornbread	1 piece 2x3¼″
Peaches, canned	2 halves

Total:	
Calories	1197
Protein	55.0
Fat	20.9
CHO	215.4

Indicates recipes adapted from It's Your World Vegetarian Cookbook
**Indicates unpublished recipes

The Group Experience

Most people who want to lose weight need the help and support of others, especially of others who have gone through the same torture and who have succeeded in losing weight and keeping it off. Such help can be found in one of the many diet groups. Some groups are businesses; others are non-profit community efforts. In any form, they have helped millions of overweight people over the years. Mostly women, these members have walked in cautious and fat, and walked out confident and lean. They found in the groups the magic ingredient missing in diets followed from a book: human care and concern. In the group were others who could lend support. After all, no one knows the problems of a person who is overweight as well as a person who was overweight.

But the hard economic times fell on groups as they did on every other business. The combination of inflation and recession meant less disposable income. When the decision came to food on the family table versus fat off mother's hips, the family always came first. So, many diet groups experienced drops in attendance and income.

Still, they survive. Two top organizations celebrate anniversaries: For Diet Center, it was ten years in 1982; for Weight Watchers, it is 20 years in 1983. The anniversaries are significant testimony to the high priority that weight loss has among many millions of persons in our society. However, in hard times, the basic decision is reached after much agonizing and budget searching and, perhaps, readjustment. So, first, the basic decision.

IS A DIET GROUP FOR YOU?

Although they work for so many, diet clubs are not for everyone. Psychiatrist Hilde Bruch noted that "in recent years almost every patient who consulted me had at least considered going to Weight Watchers, or had gone to one of their meetings but had found them too unsophisticated and had felt turned off." What kind of person can successfully lose weight as a member of a diet club? Dr. Bruch said, "It seems that people with a more secure self-concept accept...the immediate goal, namely for achieving weight loss, and for them these group efforts seem to offer a helpful solution."[1]

The only way to decide if you should join a diet club is to attend a meeting or two and see for yourself. CONSUMER GUIDE® recommends that you read the synopsis of each diet group presented in this chapter and then find a local chapter. If the club meets in your city or town, you can get its telephone number from the directory or from directory assistance. If you live in a small town or rural area, look in the telephone directory of the closest big town or city under "Reducing and Weight-Reduction Services." Or, ask your doctor; he or she may have the address and phone number at hand. Or write to the group's national headquarters.

Albert J. Stunkard, M.D., professor of psychiatry at the University of Pennsylvania, studied TOPS and concluded that the self-help approach "provides an effective mechanism for the weight loss of obese persons." He found that one of the keys to the success of the approach is that members "regard each other as intelligent persons who have the power, if they so desire, to overcome their emotional problems. During the meetings, for example, they often tell each other (and outside observers) that losing weight is something you yourself must do, something which nobody can do for you, and something which requires self-mastery." He also noticed healthy competition among members to see who could lose the most fat, as well as "cooperation and group solidarity."[2]

There are many reasons for the success of these groups. Internist Richard C. Bates, M.D., of Lansing, Michigan, a contributing editor to the magazine *Medical Economics,* thinks the evangelist fervor is contagious. "One evangelist can be pretty persuasive; a roomful can overpower the strongest sinner," he wrote.[3] Once a member helps a newcomer, "he'll be much less likely to backslide himself."

Psychologist William G. Shipman, Ph.D., agrees that groups are among "the most successful techniques to date in treating obesity."

To lose weight and keep it off, a dieter has to achieve changes in several areas of his or her life at once, points out Dr. Richard B. Stuart of the University of Utah. "The achievement of these adjustments requires supportive contact extending through months of gradual weight reduction, encouraged by exposure to successful models who can accurately portray the experience of changing core aspects of daily living. For most mildly to moderately overweight people, the low cost of self-help groups may be the optimal format for service delivery," he wrote.[4]

DIET CENTER, INC.
P.O. Box 160
Rexburg, Idaho 83440
(208) 356-9381

Hers is typical among success stories in the diet club business. She was an overweight woman who had tried every fad diet that had come along. Eventually she began to research diets and developed her own, based on "sound nutrition." It restored her health as she lost some 50 pounds. She then helped friends lose weight. Soon a local physician was sending her his overweight patients. Thus it was in 1970 that Sybil Ferguson started the business known as Diet Center, Inc., and two years later, in 1972, started selling DC franchises. In 1974, her husband, Roger, joined the business. With her as founder and him as president, DC has grown to 1700 franchises across the US and Canada (plus one in England) which have thus far served three million dieters. DC headquarters is now a complex of buildings with 180 employees, including its own advertising and public relations firm, printing plant, and offices. (Franchises are still available for purchase, at $24,000 each.)

In January 1982, *Entrepreneur Magazine* rated DC as the nation's No. 1 weight-loss program, and said it was one of the Top Ten franchise opportunities of any type still available. Approximately five new DC centers open EVERY WEEK. DC's growth in 1982 was 28 percent over the previous year.

What is the secret of DC's phenomenal success? Sybil Ferguson told CONSUMER GUIDE®, "The Diet Center Program is much more than just a diet. It is the most comprehensive approach to total weight control on the market today. Diet Center teaches dieters how to be their own nutritionists and how to make permanent changes in eating habits and related behavior. These changes set the pattern for the rest of their lives." DC's in-house statistics show that past dieters enjoy a 64 percent rate of success in keeping weight off. (That compares with an overall 5 percent national rate.)

As in other diet groups, the counselor, or leader, is key. Formerly overweight herself, Ferguson teaches nutrition, self direction, relaxation, stress management, and exercising. She also teaches dieters how to set and achieve realistic goals. The DC program is constructed of five phases.

Phase I, Conditioning. This lasts two days and is designed to "prepare the body for dieting." In effect, it is a transition from the dieter's old, high-calorie ways to a more restricted diet of 2000 calories in preparation for the reducing phase.

Phase II, Reducing. While DC dieters don't count calories, they do eat a limited-calorie diet, 950 to 1200 calories a day for women, 1350 to 1500 for men. In addition, they take daily doses of DC's special nutritional supplement (more about this a bit later). They meet their counselors EVERY DAY to discuss problems, to weigh-in, and to assess their progress.

Phase III, Stabilization. This is the critical phase, designed to serve as another transition, a transition to maintaining control. Dieters are allowed to eat larger quantities of more varieties of food. Counselors, seen twice weekly, work to help the dieter adjust to a new self-image and work to reinforce newly-learned eating behavior. Dieters stay on this phase one week for every two weeks spent on the reducing phase (up to a maximum of three weeks).

Phase IV, Maintenance. Volume and selection of foods are increased yet again, and dieters work out with their counselors their ideal plan for life. Then they see their counselors once a week, for a year, or whenever their weight increases by two pounds or so.

Phase V, Nutritional Education and Behavior Modification Program. Weekly classes teach dieters how to change the habits that created their weight problems. They are also taught how to exercise, relieve stress, relax, visualize food portions, and improve themselves. This instruction starts during Phase II, Reducing.

Ferguson emphasizes that "Diet Center is a non-medical program. We do not diagnose or prescribe. Instead, Diet Center Counselors work closely with each dieter's personal physician. If there are any pre-existing health problems or if the dieter is extremely obese, a physical examination is required before the Program can begin. Such an examination is recommended for every dieter. Another examination is recommended after a 20-pound weight loss and one is required after a 40-pound reduction. Each subsequent loss of 40 pounds requires another physical examination before continuing."

In addition to the fee for your personal physician's examination, the DC program cost averages about $225 for six weeks, or about $37.50 a week, during the reducing phase. Included in the package are 36 daily consultations with your counselor, three weeks of twice-a-week consultations, and an additional year's worth of weekly private consultations, plus a 42-day supply of nutritional supplement, plus all the classes.

To help you estimate how long you'll need to be on the DC program, here is its average weight-loss chart:

TO LOSE	IT WILL TAKE AN AVERAGE OF
6 to 10 pounds	2 weeks
10 to 17 pounds	4 weeks
17 to 25 pounds	6 weeks
25 to 30 pounds	8 weeks
30 to 35 pounds	10 weeks
100 pounds	7 months

These data apply to women, says DC. Men lose faster, about a pound a day on the DC program.

DC emphasizes that you don't have to sign any business contracts. Also, if you lose weight in less time than was estimated, you'll get a refund on any advance payment. Note that not all centers require full advance payment; also, rates vary by location—usually higher in the cities, lower in rural areas.

CRITICISM

The DC approach sounds quite reasonable, until you get to the diet. It is a uniquely high-protein, high-carbohydrate diet, with a low (but not too low) proportion of fats. By percentages, the DC diet gives 23 percent protein, 53 percent carbohydrates (with the emphasis on complex carbohydrates), and 24 percent fat (of which a whopping 80 percent is unsaturated).

By grams, the DC diet gives 75 to 140 of protein, 110 to 170 of carbohydrate, and 25 to 52 of fats—all for men. For women, the gram totals are: 55 to 106 of protein, 90 to 156 of carbohydrate, and 22 to 34 of fat.

There are four quirks to the diet:

1. You must eat two teaspoons of unheated vegetable oil each day.
2. You must drink eight (8-ounce) glasses of water each day.
3. The reducing diet contains NO dairy products, despite the fact that such foods—rich as they are in calcium, phosphorus, Vitamins A and D, and high-quality protein—constitute one of the major food groups that medical and nutrition authorities recommend as part of the daily diet.
4. You must take some DC Supplement daily during the reducing phase. (You do not buy it; it is furnished as part of the DC service.)

REBUTTAL

Ferguson explained that her supplement contains "isolate protein and invert sugar which helps keep the blood sugar level stable and provides energy. Dieters do not crave sweets nor do they feel hungry and starved.

As a result they experience an overall feeling of well being while on the Diet Center Program. The supplement contains Vitamin B-complex that helps to calm the nerves and eliminate stress, while aiding in the digestion of foods among other important functions. This is a totally natural food supplement.... By the way, we purchase our high-quality calcium supply [used in the calcium supplement] from Holland and assays show less than 2 parts per million of lead content. Other calcium suppliers offer products as high as 20 parts per million. Such high demands for quality are placed on all raw materials from which Diet Center products are formulated."

Her calcium supplement, said Ferguson, "brings the calcium levels into optimum range as evidenced from thousands of blood analyses."

She explained that the reason dairy products are shunned during the reducing phase is that their high lactose (milk sugar) content inhibits weight loss. At the same time, she explained, "we do not, however, support lifelong dietary supplementation of any type. We encourage and teach dieters to derive all necessary nutrients from natural sources once ideal weight is reached." She added, "Dr. Mark Hegsted, as Director of Nutrition, USDA, stated that even a 1600 calorie diet needs to be supplemented to meet the RDA's requirements." (She cited an article in *Health,* for November/December 1981 as the source of the quote, which deals primarily with women of childbearing age.)

CONSUMER GUIDE®'S EVALUATION

There is no scientific evidence that we know about to support Ferguson's claim that lactose inhibits weight loss, or that the form of sugar known as invert helps stabilize blood sugar. As we've explained elsewhere, the body converts all carbohydrate ultimately to glucose, the form of sugar that is the body's primary source of energy. The advantage of complex carbohydrates is that they require more time to digest and to be broken down to sugar. Also, while it is true that the nervous system requires certain B vitamins, there is no evidence that the reverse is true, that the more B vitamins you eat, the calmer your nerves will be. Furthermore, no vitamin will eliminate stress, nor can it aid in digestion. Including such health-food dogmas in explanations of an otherwise sound dieting plan serves to cheapen it and to hoke it up.

Furthermore, there is a contradiction between DC's practice and ideals. On the one hand, it claims to teach its dieters how to eat more reasonably and more healthily than they did during all the years they were eating to gain weight; on the other hand, DC requires its dieters to take food supplements. There is almost unanimity among nutritionists and dietitians that people should be taught how to eat a well-rounded diet which DOES NOT require supplements of vitamins and minerals.

Having stated this, we observe that a reducing diet is *not* a normal way to eat and does impose some stresses on the body. Therefore, reasonable supplementation is all right. Also, we note that many adults are lactose intolerant, which is not saying what Ferguson said, but merely points up the fact that one *can* survive nicely without milk products, providing that the nutrients that milk products normally provide are obtained in other ways.

148

Summing up, despite the diet's quirks and principles based on misconceptions, Diet Center is a good, although expensive, group to join to lose weight and keep it off. Rating ★★★

WEIGHT WATCHERS INTERNATIONAL, INC.
800 Community Drive
Manhasset, New York 11030
(516) 627-9200

Another giant among commercial diet clubs, Weight Watchers International (WWI) is far more difficult to examine, since it is a subsidiary of the giant food company, H.J. Heinz. However, it is clear that WWI is suffering from increased age and decreased revenues. In the diet business, as in baseball and boxing, youth is an advantage. Fad-worn dieters are seeking the new and exciting. That's why they fall for the latest diet books and seek to join the latest new kind of group or exercise center. Diet Center is fresh; Weight Watchers has been around for 20 years—so what else is new?

What is new is that WWI in 1981 introduced a totally revised diet plan, just a year after introducing PEPSTEP, an exercise program designed by the top cardiac physiologist at Montefiore Hospital, New York City, and author of several exercise textbooks. This year, WWI has repackaged, with the help of Psychological Director Richard B. Stuart, its Personal Action Plan, more about which later.

During the score of years of its existence, WWI has been an up-to-the-moment, professionally backed commercial diet club that offers the latest techniques in weight control. Its effectiveness is mirrored by its members' attendance. For example, in 1976, its last publicly accountable year, WWI had 1,655,000 registered members in the US. Actually, somewhere during its 20-year history, more than 13 million people have made contact with the operation. A spokesman for the corporation explains that "it is difficult to do any studies or statistical analysis since people come, lose weight, and don't return." He told CONSUMER GUIDE® that "about half a million people come through our doors every week." About 15,000 total classes are held every week in the US and 23 foreign countries and territories.

This great volume has made money for Weight Watchers—for WWI's originators, stockholders, franchises, and now for its holding company H.J. Heinz Co.

Losing weight with WWI is cheap. To join, you must pay a registration fee of between $8 and $12 and weekly meeting fees of between $4 and $7. However, if you skip a meeting and want to attend one the following week, you have to pay for the meeting you missed as well as the one you attend.

If you want to attend a meeting just to decide whether or not to join WWI, you have to pay. However, many franchises periodically hold free, open meetings to recruit members.

Aside from its profit motive, WWI feels that dieters should pay because the fees represent a commitment that will not be forgotten in a week or two. "Economic sanctions will ensure that people participate in the program. If you're out of town, you can attend any other class in the program," explained Warren Adamsbaum, WWI's vice-president for domestic company-owned operations.

THE WEIGHT WATCHERS DIETS

WWI in 1981 introduced a diet it said was "in keeping with the lifestyle of the '80s." The food plan is designed "to give you more freedom in social settings. Remember, portion control is the key to success," explains a brochure.

Essentially, WWI's medical consultant, the eminent Dr. Henry Sebrell, former head of nutrition at Columbia University, and Dr. Reva T. Frankle, WWI's director of nutrition, came up with a handful of diet plans which represent a spectrum of choices, from no-choice to full-choice to vegetarian. "In a nutshell," explains Joanna Green, WWI's public relations manager, "the most important factor is the addition of a whole range of innovative new foods, that includes favorites traditionally off limits for weight loss. Wine, peanut butter, popcorn, olives, additional bread, and beer are just a few of the highlights."

WWI's spokesperson says the diets were developed in response to the recommendations of the federal government for dietary changes. The newest ones, the *Dietary Guidelines,* issued by the US Department of Agriculture, came as a follow-up to the *Dietary Goals for the United States,* issued by the Senate Select Committee on Nutrition and Human Needs.

What WWI's spokesperson didn't say, but can be inferred, is that the No-Choice Plan is included in response to the continued success of such no-choice diets as *The Scarsdale Diet.* Furthermore, WWI's Vegetarian Plan is offered in response to the increasing popularity of vegetarian diets, both generally and especially among people who want to lose weight.

The *Full-Choice Plan* includes foods which WWI's members said they loved and missed. Wine topped the "want" list, with peanut butter running second. WWI added beer as well to "make it easier for members to function in contemporary situations." Other foods added to the Full-Choice list include tofu, apricots, figs, raisins, cider, sweet potatoes, honey, and barbecue sauce. Furthermore, the use of beef has been expanded from once to three times a week, and stir-frying and sautéing have been added to the permissible cooking techniques. In addition, portions have a range of sizes, for example, meat, three to four ounces. Here are the other choices:

The *Limited-Choice Plan* keeps all food portions at the low end and does not include the newly added foods.

The *No-Choice Plan* permits the lowest size of food portions and the fewest exceptions to its rigid two-week menu.

The *Vegetarian Plan* is actually an ovo-lacto-vegetarian diet which offers protein in the form of eggs, cheese, peanut butter and legumes— beans, lentils, peas, and tofu (soybean curd). The lists of fruits and vegetables are long and varied.

Also new in 1981 was a simplified, expanded Weight Watchers Maintenance Plan, which—a WWI first—lists food by calories instead of "units." The reason for this, explains WWI, is to help the successful dieter who wants to keep a constant weight find the right daily calorie level. The brochure explains, "The plan consists of eight food groups, listed on separate cards. We will teach you to gradually add these foods to your basic menu plan (which supplies approximately 1200-1700 calories daily, depending on whether the plan is for women, men or youth.)" You keep adding calories until your weight is stable. The food groups are 100, 150, 200, 250, 300, 350, 400, and 500 calories, represented by, respectively, 1 tablespoon peanut butter, 1 ounce potato chips, 1 beef taco, 1 cup oyster stew, 8 ounces Irish coffee, lox and cream cheese on bagel, tuna fish sandwich, and a piña colada (8 fluid ounces).

You see, says WWI's Green, "the unique character of the Weight Watchers new food plan lies in its ability to make dieters feel as though they're not following a diet at all. In fact, it is really more common sense dieting than anything else."

Samples of the Weight Watchers diets are printed at the end of this chapter.

WEIGHT WATCHERS PEPSTEP PROGRAM

To add exercise to its weight-loss program, WWI commissioned one of the best people available: Lenore R. Zohman, M.D. She started the Cardiopulmonary Rehabilitation program at Montefiore Hospital and Medical Center in New York. She has served as chairman of the New York Heart Association's Committee on Exercise, as a consultant to the American Heart Association and the President's Council on Physical Fitness and Sports. And the program she designed is called PEPSTEP, introduced in 1980.

PEPSTEP is optional. WWI members must check with their doctor before starting the program. Then they examine their own physical fitness. In the first of three booklets, a Weight Watcher totals each day's physical activities according to their intensity of effort and duration of time.

After the members have determined their fitness scores, they then can begin to build up physical endurance and activity levels by climbing stairs or walking briskly. The PEPSTEPpers monitor the intensity of activity by the pulse rate. Beginning with some warm-up exercises, they then continue with stair climbing or walking or a combination of both. (More details about the PEPSTEP program are included in "Sweating It Off.")

The WWI pamphlet explains that "the stair-climbing program is modeled after a research study which was done in an insurance company in Finland. The elevators in this 11-story building were purposely 'out of order,' and the physical fitness of employees walking up various distances was compared. Those who climbed 25 flights of stairs daily, in any combination (going up counted, not down), were the ones who attained fitness and lost the most fat."

As for walking, says WWI, "Among women in a research study, walking more than 30 minutes daily for over a year, an average weight loss of 22 pounds occurred without dieting."

But how well does PEPSTEP work? To answer the question, WWI had its psychological director, Richard B. Stuart, Ph.D., field-test the exercise program. In the field test, Dr. Stuart selected 1500 people on the WWI diet who were considered to be representative of the WWI population as a whole. He placed half on PEPSTEP and half on no exercise program. At the end of the six weeks, the PEPSTEPpers lost an average 5.29 pounds; the others lost an average 3.22 pounds.

After reviewing the PEPSTEP field-test results, WWI concluded that stair climbing and/or walking:

- Helps the dieter control hunger and stay on the diet;
- Makes the dieter feel confident and cheerful and less likely to be depressed;
- Helps the dieter feel energetic and fit;
- Hastens weight loss.

An exerciser on PEPSTEP can follow the program at home or at the office and without bothering with special clothing or equipment. Also, like WWI's diet and behavior modification, he or she can readily incorporate PEPSTEP into his or her life.

PERSONAL ACTION PLAN

Diet is one fourth of the WWI plan, exercise the second fourth, and positive group support the third fourth. The final component is behavior modification—changing bad eating habits into good ones.

Weight Watchers International calls its behavior modification program the Personal Action Plan (PAP). It works, according to a study of 7623 members conducted by Dr. Stuart. Members on the diet and behavior modification plan lost an average 1.6 pounds per week, a 15 percent greater average weekly weight loss than that for Weight Watchers International members on the diet alone. A study of 721 of the members found that, 15 months later, 53.5 percent were within 5 percent or less of their goal.

The Personal Action Plan is a series of day-to-day techniques that overweight people can use to help them overcome the obstacles to losing weight. It helps them, in other words, to cope with the problems that made them fat and to conquer their problems by altering their bad habits. The behavior modification program is taught in "modules." Each WWI member studies the information in a pamphlet, then completes an action form before the next class.

Last year, WWI packaged the PAP into 52 "mini modules" cards, each of which can be carried for a week in pocket or pocketbook. The cards are, in effect, cue cards to remind the dieter of the major points learned in class that week. The cards are topical:

New Year's: How to Change Some Important Ideas about Yourself.
Week 21: Getting Set for Summer Eating.
December: How to Succeed on the Weight Watchers Program at
    Christmas/Chanukah; and Getting Set for the Holidays.
Week after Christmas: How to Build on New Behaviors.

As a means of keeping the dieter on his or her behavioral toes all year long, this succeeds well.

152

A SUCCESS STORY

The Weight Watchers International success story is built on a solid foundation of experience. As Warren Adamsbaum explained to CONSUMER GUIDE®, "It has been a long time since we have depended upon evangelical fervor at our meetings to help our members lose weight. We pride ourselves on the scientifically advanced approach we have taken to losing weight and maintaining it." Weight Watchers sessions have gone well beyond the praise-and-blame, show-and-tell kind of meetings started back in 1963 by its founder Jean Nidetch.

In the beginning, Nidetch insisted that all meetings follow the same format. Each meeting began with a weigh-in followed by a lecture, question-and-answer session, and socializing. She started the meetings, she said, because it wasn't enough for her to diet and lose weight; she was compelled to tell people about it.[5] And she has been telling people about it ever since.

But the format of meetings has changed, thanks to innovations from Dr. Stuart. Sessions still begin with the obligatory, private weigh-in, but they continue with a discussion led by a lecturer who has been trained in group discussion techniques. She (most lecturers are women, and all are former Weight Watchers International members) discusses ways to change bad eating habits. If she is skillful at leading the discussion, members will bring up their problems. Then, the lecturer and other members of the group can examine them.

Explained Adamsbaum, "Motivation and inspiration are still part of Weight Watchers, but woven into the lecturer-to-member and member-to-member dialogue. Certainly, neither punishment nor reward [is] a part of our concept. Rewards are the rewards of self-esteem and of a sense of accomplishment."

In many ways, the Weight Watchers diet has come a long way from the basic diet of the New York Obesity Clinic, which helped Mrs. Nidetch on her road to figure and fortune. The first big change came in January 1972 as a result of hiring, as WWI medical director, William H. Sebrell, M.D., one-time Assistant Surgeon General of the US, director of the National Institutes of Health, former director of the Institute of Human Nutrition, and now professor emeritus of Nutrition, College of Physicians and Surgeons, Columbia University, New York.

It wasn't long before Nidetch realized she was a better inspiration for overweight sisters than she was a businesswoman, so she incorporated WW, moved to Los Angeles, and turned over the reins to Albert Lippert, a successful businessman who parlayed a homey handful of diet groups into the world's most successful diet business.

THE WWI BUSINESS

As a profit-making organization, Weight Watchers International has been a phenomenal success, astounding not only to admiring businessmen, but to doctors as well. In mid-1978, WWI reported 12-month total revenues of close to $50 million, with a net income of nearly $5 million. Weight Watchers is a commercial corporation. It was purchased in 1978 by Heinz

Foods for $71 million. The revenues come from 10 percent of the gross income of the 103 franchises, as well as company-owned clubs. When Heinz bought WWI, it also acquired Foodways National Inc., which sells WW Sweetener and Frozen Foods, for close to $50 million. Comargo, which marketed WW soft drinks, thin-sliced bread, "ice cream," and cottage cheese, was a Bristol-Meyers subsidiary. It now operates as the Nutrition Products Group of Heinz USA and will soon add more diet products. This latest purchase, states Heinz's 1980 Annual Report, "rounds out our position as a major supplier to the diet-control market." WWI also publishes *Weight Watchers* magazine, which reaches, through subscription and newsstand sales, 4.5 million dieters. It also publishes books, such as the *Weight Watchers Food Plan Diet Book*[6] by founder Jean Nidetch. And it franchises camps for dieting youngsters and adults at California, Wisconsin, Pennsylvania, Connecticut, and North Carolina.

CONSUMER GUIDE®'S EVALUATION

Join It! Rating: ★★★★

THE DIET WORKSHOP, INC.
111 Washington Street
Brookline, Massachusetts 02146
(617) 739-2222

International director and co-founder, Lois Lindauer says Diet Workshop (DW) has finally discovered calories. She explains: "For the dieter, ignorance of calories is not bliss, it is the stage for disaster." DW now has an Official Calorie Counter for its members. "After all, calories DO count," Lindauer adds. Her franchises are also counting—their income, she says. That's because business has kept up despite the recession. The big reason, she claims, is the DW philosophy, explained to CONSUMER GUIDE® as follows: "At its conception, we determined that Diet Workshop would always offer its members the latest and best possible tools for quick, sure, and safe weight loss and control. Our entire staff is committed to the 'We Care' motto."

The DW program has four integral parts, she went on to explain, mild toning exercises, simple behavior changes that can change lives, information about nutrients and nutritional requirements, and varied diet plans so each member can lose weight at a rate comfortable to her. Each class is run by a DW-certified instructor who herself has lost weight and who has been trained in helping-skills. At each week's meeting, interesting case histories are presented and discussed and recipes handed out.

Known for diets which allow wide ranges of choices for its members, DW in mid-1979 offered a new, rigid diet to compete with the popular strict diet plans such as the Scarsdale diet and the Pritikin program. As Lindauer explains, "Dieters want to give up something in order to achieve results. They don't want to make choices, because they feel they will probably make the wrong ones. When you ask them to make choices, they spend most of their time thinking about what to eat."

Lindauer says she understands why rigid diets like the Scarsdale and

Stillman diets work. "Dieters like—no want—rigidity when they start out. They also want a quick weight loss. They want to see results in a short time. Once they have lost weight, and kept it off, they can deal with making choices."[7]

Because of this realization, Lindauer redesigned the DW diet into seven cycles.

Cycle 1, The Super Starter, is a 750-calorie menu plan, a sort of balanced version of the Scarsdale Diet, that is designed for quick initial weight loss during its one-week run.

Cycle 2, The Super Slimmer, is a 900-calorie, small-choice diet. It, too, is designed for quick loss, and it lasts a week.

At 1000 calories, *Cycle 3, The Super Mini,* is a scaled-down version of the Board of Health Obesity Clinic diet and is followed for one week.

Cycle 4, The Super Maxi, is a well-balanced base diet. It provides 1200 calories and allows choices among a so-called bonus group that includes alcohol, wine, pasta, rice, potato, and extra bread. DW members stay in Cycle 4 until they are within five pounds of their goal weight.

Cycle 5, The Super Leveler, introduces a "Mindless Eating Day" on the day of the week that is most convenient. "Mindless Eating" means restricted eating, and, in this case, the restrictions are cottage cheese or chicken, tomato juice or low-calorie cranberry juice. Because of the low-calorie count (900) of Cycle 5, the last five pounds are easier to lose.

Cycle 6, is *The Super Maintainer,* and the dieter may choose among three Super Maintainer Plans. The Super Maxi Plus is a continuation of Cycle 4 but has additions, substitutions, and exchanges. The Calorie Counter is a straight calorie measure method. And the Wild Weekender calls for five days on Cycle 4 and two days "off."

Late in 1980, DW introduced Cycle Zero, a 600-calorie daily diet to start the dieter off on a quick-loss diet that immediately feels like a diet. (See end of chapter.)

The philosophy behind the 7-Cycle Super Weight Loss Program is that a progressive diet program will keep the dieter's interest high and will induce quick weight loss.

The first five cycles of the DW program are rigid like the Scarsdale and Stillman fad diets. But unlike these fad diets, the DW program is well-balanced.

The newest DW diet is designed for women. Men should substitute another source of protein for the almost-daily egg ration, and they should stay away from shrimp because of the high cholesterol content of such seafood. Lindauer advises men to add two ounces of protein along with two ounces of bread and two fruits to the daily diet.

Both men and women may experience some hunger pangs while on the first two cycles. Hunger pangs signal that the diet is working. They last for only 20 minutes.

If you don't like the 7-Cycle Diet, DW has another, called the Success Diet.[8] Also, late in 1981, DW introduced the three-level Beacon Hill Diet (a sample is at the end of the chapter).

There were two other new items introduced in 1982. One is the Person-to-Person® Rapid Weight-Loss System. Actually, this concept isn't new.

DW was the first to have individual counseling, as well as group counseling, which is also still available. Some centers, such as that in Brookline, outside Boston, encourage dieters to come by anytime during the day, and to listen to instructional tapes, meet with other dieters, or to meet with a counselor. "Our goal is to provide the specialized support to our clients to become thinner and healthier and to learn how to acquire and maintain their new images," DW states.

Also new in 1982 was Diet-Tabs, a chewable soy protein-and-vitamin/mineral supplement, in a sweet fructose/dextrose base. "This combination," explains Lindauer, "helps to control hunger and to avoid the problems of rapid sugar level drop as well as providing some vitamin support." The chewable pills sell for $4 to $5 a package (depending on the franchise) and are available only once a week in DW class.

The original DW Diet was developed by Morton B. Glenn, M.D., Chief of the Obesity Clinic at New York City's Knickerbocker Hospital. With Dr. Glenn's help, Diet Workshop has compiled recipes which are sold in booklet form at its headquarters. The recipes also are found in the paperbacks, *It's In to Be Thin* and *The Diet Workshop Success Diet.*

DW combines diet with group support and, in most instances, provides each dieter with personal attention. Unlike any other diet group, you can stay in the program even if you are a diet dropout. DW is not a pure behavior-modification operation nor a pure exercise program. It places emphasis on its Feeling Good program for improving self-image. CONSUMER GUIDE® advises you to attend a DW session to be sure that you like the instructor and that the program suits your life-style.

CONSUMER GUIDE®'S EVALUATION

Plenty to choose from, and all top rate. Rating: ★★★★

DIET CONTROL CENTERS
1021 Stuyvesant Ave.
Union, NJ 07083
(201) 687-0007

Another housewife-started chain of diet groups, Diet Control Centers (DCC) is also a franchise operation, begun in 1968. This publicly-held company boasts 23 franchises and 250,000 members. As its franchise-recruiting brochure points out, "This is the opportunity of a lifetime. . . . You start out with all these 'pluses'—your cash investment is low; your overhead is low; you do not have to buy real estate; you do not need a costly inventory; you do not need expensive equipment; you operate on a strictly cash basis. You do not have to extend credit; you are supported every step of the way; you are part of a nation-wide family with a proven success record."

The "nation-wide family" includes suburban locations in DCC's home state of New Jersey, plus New York state, Pennsylvania, South Carolina, and Florida.

For the $10 registration fee and a $5 weekly fee, DCC dieters get to go to a weekly class (usually held in public-meeting rooms at churches, hospitals, or companies) where they learn the three-part total weight-control program. The parts:

1. *Body Awareness,* through in-place isotonic exercises, which can be done while seated.
2. *Mind Awareness,* a behavior modification program composed of ten eating-habit reeducation techniques.
3. *Food Awareness,* through the diet known as the 1200-calories-a-day, "7-Day Formula for Happy Living."

Dieters first go on the 14-day "Stage One Blast Off Diet" (a sample of which is reprinted at the end of this chapter). "Accomplishing a short-range goal of successfully losing weight for a 14-day period will highly motivate members and contribute to their future success," DCC Nutrition Director Ann C. Newswanger explained to CONSUMER GUIDE®.

The DCC diet is unique in that it permits just about all foods, even alcoholic beverages. It emphasizes ethnic dishes particularly, since in DCC's experience, "restriction of ethnic foods had only produced 'food binges.'" Control, not selection, is the byword of DCC. Explains Newswanger, "Unlike other addictions that are cured by total abstinence, overeating can be cured only by learning to control the urge, within boundaries, while you continue to eat."

DCC also emphasizes food preparation, which is much discussed at weekly meetings. Furthermore, the DCC "bible," *Slim Forever,*[9] is one-third recipes. It also contains DCC diets and a short history. In the introduction, co-founders Jacqueline Greenspan, Ruth Landesberg, and Ruth Lipp explain, "We began to experiment within the framework of a medically sound diet provided by the New York Health Department. ...Working with a professional nutritionist, we studied ways to improvise, to add greater variety, and to include favorite ethnic foods. ...We lived on our own program....We were the proof....we collectively lost 150 pounds of unwanted fat."

Like Diet Workshop and Diet Center, Diet Control Centers has gone to one-to-one counseling. The DCC version is called Personal Weight Center and is especially designed for those who have more than 15 pounds to lose. For the $60 registration fee and $25 a week (no contracts), you get a custom-tailored program, a high-fiber diet, and daily monitoring. (DCC is starting to franchise Personal Weight Center operations in other locations.) Like DW and DC, Personal Weight Center is offering dieters a chewable tablet, which is essentially composed of fiber to "aid in the elimination of hunger pangs and assist in maintaining normal body functions."

Summing up, DCC offers a well-rounded program and an adequate diet.

CONSUMER GUIDE®'S EVALUATION

One of the tops in the East. Rating: ★★★★

CONWAY DIET INSTITUTE
P.O. Box 20915
Columbus, Ohio 43220
(614) 451-5464

Ten years after he graduated from Fordham University, Patrick J. Conway was a successful marketing executive whose potbelly resulted from the rich lunches and dinners it took to get him there. He tried fasting with no success, nor did he have success on many fad diets, so he researched nutrition and designed his own diet, which in 1979 he decided to share (at a price) with the public. He calls it the Ideal 1000 Calorie Diet. It goes with a weekly Insight Seminar at his CDI locations in 25 states in the East, South, and Midwest. You can also obtain the unastounding Conway diet in his cookbook,[10] written in collaboration with his first client, Mary Ellenwood Pittenger, who went from 250 to 135 pounds.

CONSUMER GUIDE®'S EVALUATION

The CDI diet is far from ideal. Not only is it a too-low 1000 calories, but it is also high-protein and low fat. It yields 92 grams of protein and the proportion of fat in the diet is a scant 21 percent. Rating: ★★

TOPS
4575 S. 5th Street   P.O. Box 07489
Milwaukee, Wisconsin 53207
(414) 482-4620

The 35-year-old TOPS organization is nonprofit and based on the principles of Alcoholics Anonymous. It is well-organized, in large part, because of the efforts of the founder, 75-year-old Esther S. Manz, an energetic woman with a sharp mind and skillful organizational abilities. Her aides say, "She is as ordinary as mashed potatoes." When you meet her, she says, with a sparkle in her eye, "Welcome to Topsy Land."

Started in 1948 as a coffeeklatch composed of Manz's friends, Take Off Pounds Sensibly (TOPS) is now the largest and the oldest nonprofit diet club organization. It was incorporated in Wisconsin in 1952. In 1955, KOPS (Keep Off Pounds Sensibly) was launched for those who had lost weight and wanted a maintenance program—and support—to stay thin.

TOPS has 336,050 members in 12,420 chapters in the US, Canada, and 24 other countries. There are 45,000 active KOPS members. And in 1981, TOPS members collectively lost more than two million pounds of fat.

Members pay dues of $12 for each of the first two years and $10 thereafter. There are no other fees, although contributions are welcome. Membership permits you to attend meetings, to receive the monthly magazine (news, recipes, and songs), and to write in for specific information. Its income not only funds the communications functions of TOPS computerized headquarters but helps support the Obesity and Metabolic Research Program at the Medical College of Wisconsin in Milwaukee.

Research is one of the Five Facets of TOPS. Medical supervision of each member's diet is another. Third is the group therapy process, with each chapter electing its leaders and running its own meetings.

Keen competition over lost pounds is another important facet of TOPS. Each year, every chapter crowns a queen, whose royalty stems directly from her success in the program. (There are also a few men's clubs, which crown kings.)

An International King and Queen are crowned every year at the International Recognition Days. In 1982, at the convention in Cedar Rapids, Gregory Pietrucha of Chicago, and Linda Haack of Milwaukee were crowned. He lost 213 pounds; she lost 198 pounds.

Every chapter decides how to conduct its weekly meetings. Sometimes a speaker, usually a doctor or nutritionist, contributes his or her time. Sometimes, the meetings are spent singing from the TOPS songbook. Other times, there are contests, recognition programs, or a member presentation of discussion materials.

Before each meeting, TOPS members, in private, are weighed on a scale, otherwise known as The Monster or The Lie Detector. Even members who cannot stay for the evening's program will weigh-in. Weight records are kept at the chapter and the TOPS headquarters in Milwaukee. The records do not report total weight in pounds but the number of pounds gained or lost since the last meeting.

In a survey of 22 TOPS chapters,[11] Dr. Stunkard, then of Stanford, found that chapter members spend most of their time at weekly meetings talking about dieting techniques, discussing self-improvement ideas, and telling anecdotes about obese people.

The average TOPS member, he found, is a 42-year-old housewife who weighs 166 pounds when she joins. She stays in the club about a year-and-a-half and loses 15 pounds toward her goal of 119 pounds. Of course, admits the psychiatrist, these numbers represent a numerical average, not a typical person. "Chapter records show weight losses ranging from mediocre to remarkable." In fact, Dr. Stunkard found that "the results achieved by the single most effective TOPS chapter were better than those of any of the reported medical studies. The five most effective chapters ranked with the best in the literature. The average for all 22 chapters was similar to the average achieved by medical treatment."

He concluded that "these comparisons offer strong evidence of the effectiveness of TOPS." Since TOPS has added instruction in behavior modification, its results are expected to multiply.

The newest aspect of TOPS is the retreat, which affords a member the opportunity to get away from everyday pressures and concentrate solely on herself or himself and dieting. TOPS retreats are held throughout the US and Canada.

The TOPS diet, while not spectacular, is solid, having been designed by Ronald Kalkhoff, M.D., professor of medicine at the Medical College of Wisconsin, in Milwaukee. He has been the recipient of funds from the organization since 1967, as director of the TOPS Clubs, Inc., Obesity and Metabolic Research Program. Unique in this respect, the TOPS organization has contributed $2.2-million to medical research into various aspects of obesity.

Officially, TOPS considers the Kalkhoff diet "a practical guide for meal planning; it does not provide an official diet since TOPS maintains that each member of the organization should receive his own program from a physician." Nevertheless, the TOPS guide for meal planning comes in three versions: 1200 calories, 1500 calories, and 1800 calories.

In the book[12] containing the diet, which is sold only to members, Dr. Kalkhoff explains that while the Senate Select Committee's recommendations are still somewhat controversial, "they do make sense." As a compromise, he and his collaborator, Marlea Krueger, a registered dietitian who works at the Milwaukee County medical complex, designed the TOPS diet to be midway between what people actually eat and what the Senate Committee suggests they eat. Thus, the TOPS diet is (by calories) 20-22 percent protein, 40-44 percent carbohydrate, and 35-38 percent fat. As Dr. Kalkhoff and Mrs. Krueger explain, this is "somewhat lower in carbohydrate and higher in dietary fat than recommended by the Select Committee."

The TOPS diet is keyed so that you can select low-, medium-, or high-fat meats; and it points out foods high in salt.

CONSUMER GUIDE®'S EVALUATION

The TOPS diet is solid, having been adapted from the venerable exchange diets of the American Diabetes Association and the American Dietetic Association. Its special attention to refined carbohydrates, saturated fats, and cholesterol lifts it above the old ADA-ADA standard. In short, the new TOPS diet *is* tops. Rating: ★★★★

OVEREATERS ANONYMOUS
2190 190th Street
Torrance, California 90504
(213) 320-7941

While the commercial diet clubs have slipped, the growth of the no-diet, nonprofit Overeaters Anonymous (OA) has been spectacular. Today, 6000 groups in the US and 32 other countries serve about 100,000 members. Most groups are located in major metropolitan areas and are listed in the phone book. The Chicago area has 90; the New York City and the Los Angeles areas have more than 200 each.

Founded in 1960 by three Los Angeles housewives, OA is frankly and closely patterned after Alcoholics Anonymous. In fact, Rozanne, one of the founders, attended a meeting of Gamblers Anonymous in 1959 when she realized that the self-help approach (adapted from Alcoholics Anonymous) would work for compulsive overeaters.

OA says it is dedicated to the radical overthrow of conventional ideas about dieting and weight loss. It believes "that compulsive overeating is an illness, a progressive illness, which cannot be cured but which, like many other illnesses, can be arrested. . . ."

Like GA and AA, OA preserves the anonymity of those who come for help, referring to everyone by first name only. Another similarity is the strong spiritual basis for the method. "If we have no willpower of our own, it follows that we need a Power outside of our own to help us recover."

While OA expects members to get general guidance from their own doctors, it does offer a choice of eating plans and suggestions about eating, including these two points:

1. Three moderate meals a day with nothing in between but low-calorie or no-calorie beverages.
2. Avoidance of all binge foods.

However, points out an OA spokeswoman, "What OA is doing, actually, is moving closer each year to a policy of no diet recommendations." Rather, the OA emphasis is on behavior control.

In a 1981 OA pamphlet,[13] a member who is a licensed psychologist in Washington, DC, wrote, "We commonly talk only of weight problems — almost a national pastime — and our treatments revolve around weight and its control to the point of faddism. Medically, this baffling disorder is referred to as obesity, which is only the symptom. It is as insufficient to label the compulsive overeating disorder simply as obesity as it is to label the problem of alcoholism merely as the problem of being stoned ... I believe the compulsion is only controllable, not curable."

The strength of OA is in the regular meetings, where members can openly and safely share their successes and failures, their problems and solutions. "We have learned that regular meetings are essential in encouraging self-discipline," says an OA brochure. Between-meeting phone calls also help to keep members from succumbing to temptation.

Diet doctor Peter G. Lindner, M.D., of South Gate, California, found that "although the disciplines of the program are strict, there is no coercion. The spirit of cooperation is positively reinforced throughout meeting proceedings." He confirmed that "many OA members are former participants (and dropouts) from commercial weight control groups."[14]

A survey of OA members by a Fordham University graduate student shows that 95 percent are women; 65 percent had tried commercial weight-loss groups and failed; a like amount had no success following diets prescribed by their family doctors. About two thirds are in the 30-year-old to 50-year-old age group.

Survey data indicate, says OA, that it is six times more successful than other diet organizations. The average weight loss per member is 50 pounds.

Unlike other diet clubs, OA has no monetary requirement for membership — it requires only the desire to stop eating compulsively. OA charges no dues or fees for membership. Contributions can be made at each meeting. The only charges are for literature, with most leaflets costing 15 cents. You can also spend $6 ($7.50 in Canada) for a year's subscription to the magazine *Lifeline*.

Insights into the workings of OA can be found in a 1978 book by George Christians.[15] However, OA did not officially sanction the book; one reason is that the author broke OA's rule of anonymity. In *The Compulsive Overeater,* he says, "I am powerless over food. Like drug addicts, sexual deviates, kleptomaniacs, and a host of other afflicted, I have a compulsion — overeating — that has harmed my career, shamed my family and damaged my health beyond any hope of complete recovery. Yet I have hope. ... It seems like an almighty long and lonely distance from the bottom of my despair to the place where I stand so proudly. You're damn right I want to live! I like myself! And I could never, never kill a thing I love."

Another journal of a compulsive eater is the 1979 book *That First Bite*.[16] Once a skinny kid from Brooklyn, Karen R. found herself in size 40 pants and size 44 blouses in her 30s. "By the time I began this journal, I weighed 140 pounds, having been up to 160 and down and up in the previous years, and before I could come to terms with the whole thing I hit 200. I'm five foot two," she wrote.

Sick of overeating and trying fasts, diets, psychiatrists, and gurus, Karen found OA. "I have heard that when you hit bottom you go to OA," she wrote. At her first meeting, she heard and was inspired by a 28-year-old woman who said, "I don't want to die alone, in bed, with a ham sandwich." Once on the OA program, Karen lost weight. Today, she's an OA evangelist.

CONSUMER GUIDE®'S EVALUATION

OA differs from group to group in intensity of therapy and skill of its leader. Nevertheless, its approach is to get to the heart of the compulsion and deal with it. If your eating is out of control, you may well find success in controlling it by joining and sticking with OA.

APPETITE CONTROL CENTERS
1131 Route 52
Fishkill, NY 12524
(914) 896-9292

Frankly based on the New York City diet, "with inclusions to appeal to the American Diabetes Association Diet as well as the American Heart Association Diet," the ACC diet not only allows cocoa and chocolate, it also names brand names in its food lists. Started by bookkeeper Linda Mayer in 1969, ACC boasts 125 groups conducted by franchisees in New Jersey; New York state; Tucson, Arizona; and Fairfield County, Connecticut.

An ACC spokesman told CONSUMER GUIDE®, "While we feel that exercise is important to one's overall well being, it is not part of the Appetite Control Centers Program. Rather, we use dieting alone, to lose weight. The average daily consumption…is about 900 to 1200 calories."

Weekly ACC classes, which typically are attended by 25 people, cost from $4 to $6. Since 1969, more than 140,000 dieters have attended ACC.

CONSUMER GUIDE®'S EVALUATION

While ACC does not offer as complete a program as WWI or DW, it makes up for its lack in hominess. Rating: ★★★★

LEAN LINE, INC.
151 New World Way
South Plainfield, NJ 07080
(201) 757-6446

Founded in 1968 by two New Jersey housewives who loved to cook and eat ethnic dishes (Italian and Jewish), Lean Line takes a down-home practical approach to dieting. Rather than make its dieters bend to a diet shorn of Old World influences, it provides meal plans and recipes which embrace ethnicity. Its groups (which meet in New Jersey, New York, Pennsylvania, Connecticut, and Texas) teach sound behavior modification techniques. Fees are $10.50 to join, and $5 per week.

CONSUMER GUIDE®'S EVALUATION

Lean Line provides a real-life answer to ethnic dieting, which takes into account its members' love of lasagna and lox. Rating: ★★★

THIN LIFE CENTERS
151 New World Way
South Plainfield, NJ 07080
(201) 757-6446

An offshoot of Lean Line, Inc., Thin Life Centers are aimed at "problem dieters." Instead of getting Lean Line's reasonable and balanced diet, they get an 800-calorie high-protein, no-carbohydrate diet. Says a Thin Life news release, "Controversial, yes, but it works."

To get into this questionable program, dieters have to cough up $290 each for a complete physical examination, four weekly monitorings of blood and urine chemistry, and four weeks of sessions. After that, they pay $35 a week for "monitoring, support group participation, and professional consultation with a physician and lab work, when deemed necessary." Once the dieter has reached her goal weight, she pays another $130 for four more weeks of transition and reintroduction to "problem foods." Then she can continue to return weekly, for the rest of her life, at no fee.

Thin Life has seven phases: consultation, the physical exam, the semi-fast until goal weight is achieved, the four-week transition, six weeks of special group sessions, a maintenance program using ethnic and gourmet foods, and finally, maintenance control.

Lean Line boasts that Rutgers University Nutrition Department Chairman Hans Fischer supervises all of its diets. Perhaps. But that is a far cry from supervising the design of a diet to supervising (or failing to) dieters eating only 800 calories a day. This flies in the face the advice of leading nutritionists, dietitians, and physicians that no one should be on such a restricted-calories diet unless personally supervised by a physician.

CONSUMER GUIDE®'S EVALUATION

A potentially dangerous, and frightfully unbalanced diet. Rating: Not Recommended. No stars.

TRIM CLUBS, INC.
1307 South Killian Drive
Lake Park, Florida 33403
(305) 842-9411

Though Trim moved its corporate headquarters to the West Palm Beach area late in 1979, it still has its greatest concentration of clubs around

Chicago, where the organization was founded 25 years ago. That was after Marcella Debs dropped from 222 to 111 pounds and cut her name in half, to Marcy. When she started the first Trim Club for the overweight, Debs relied on her background in dieting and nutrition. She had learned about dieting while working at the obesity clinic of Duke University and about nutrition while receiving her master's degree.

From the first club in Chicago, the Trim organization moved into 12 other states (Florida, Tennessee, West Virginia, Ohio, Pennsylvania, Indiana, Michigan, Wisconisn, Minnesota, Iowa, New Mexico, and California) and claims 50,000 members.

Along the way, Debs, now a 65-year-old grandmother who weighs 111 pounds (her highest was 229 pounds), brought her husband into the business, as well as her sons: One is president of the corporation; the other runs the Nashville, Tennessee Club.

Trim concentrates on individual counseling. As Debs sees it, Trim is "an adult-education experience. We teach members about nutrition for weight reduction, as well as about behavior modification and about exercise. All of our instructors are specially trained to work with members." The emphasis is on cognitive behavior modification that was developed by consultants such as Dr. Richard C. Nelson of Purdue University. Fees are $15 to join, $4 to $4.50 (depending upon location) per weekly session. Mail-order courses are also available.

The Trim's diet, developed by Debs, follows a 21-day cycle. While serving sizes are not stated, the diet is supposed to provide 1200 calories a day, 66 grams of carbohydrate, and 60 to 80 grams of protein, as well as low totals of salt and cholesterol. The diet, she claims, "restores the chemical balance of the body." At each weekly conference, the members receive a menu plan, a study guide, and advice.

Unfortunately, Ms. Debs goes beyond the hyperbole of enthusiasm when she tells members in her study guides that the Trim's diet will "restore the chemical balance of the body," or when she writes about "fat enzymes," or tells how the fat will be liquified in the body and lost in the urine.

This approach reflects what is perhaps the most serious drawback of Trim: It does not adequately educate, as other self-help groups do, in nutrition or in serving sizes and nutrient quantities so the dieter can go it alone someday.

Furthermore, the diet does not specify food amounts, except to state that a lunch portion is half of a dinner portion. Nor are calorie totals indicated. You only follow the weekly menus which move you up in calories until Menu 12.

Also, Trim has developed a food value handbook that rates foods on a scale of 1 to 4. "A food having a Trim Value of 1 is excellent for inclusion in meal planning and can be used as a daily part of your menu," says the guide. "A food listed as having a value of 4 is not to be used under any circumstances." Prime example of a "1" food is bacon and of a "4" food is chicken livers. Also, poached egg (listed as a dairy food!) rates a 1 while beans and lentils rate 4. Amazing, considering the fact that most nutritionists consider liver to be one of the most nutrient-packed foods and beans and lentils to be excellent low-fat protein sources, while bacon and eggs are loaded with fat.

CONSUMER GUIDE®'S EVALUATION

The Trim's approach is too rigid and maternalistic. It doesn't treat you as the adult you are, or need to be. Low-cal, the diet lacks balance. Rating: ★★

CONSUMER GUIDE®'S EVALUATION OF DIET GROUPS

Going on a diet is not enough for most dieters. To lose weight successfully, they benefit from the help and support of fellow dieters in the warm atmosphere of a group. Many groups probably are available to you. Shop around and visit as many as you can, then stick with the one you choose. CONSUMER GUIDE® found TOPS to be basic and friendly; OA heavy on group therapy; Appetite Control Centers strong in nutrition; Trim, Diet Control Centers, and Diet Center good for the timid; and Diet Workshop and Weight Watchers International the most complete and the best organized.

WEIGHT WATCHERS FULL CHOICE PLAN MENU

Food		Quantity
Morning Meal		
Women, Men, and Youth		
Fruit or Fruit Juice		1 serving
Choice of Egg		1
or Cheese, soft		⅓ cup
or Cheese, semisoft		
or hard		1 ounce
or Cereal		1 serving with Milk
or Peanut Butter		1 tablespoon (omit 1 serving Fats)
or Poultry, Meat, or Fish		1 ounce*
or Legumes:		
Beans, lentils, and peas	Women and Youth	3 ounces*
	Men	4 ounces*
Tofu	Women and Youth	4 ounces
	Men	5 ounces
Tempeh	Women and Youth	1½ ounces
	Men	2 ounces
Beverage, if desired		
Midday and Evening Meal		
Women, Men, and Youth		
Choice of Eggs		2
or Cheese, soft		⅔ cup
or Cheese, semisoft		
or hard		2 ounces
or Peanut Butter		3 tablespoons (omit 2 servings Fats)
or Poultry, Meat, or Fish	Women and Youth	3 to 4 ounces*
	Men	4 to 5 ounces*

or Legumes:		
Beans, lentils, and peas	Women and Youth	6 ounces*
	Men	8 ounces*
Tofu	Women and Youth	8 ounces
	Men	10 ounces
Tempeh	Women and Youth	3 ounces
	Men	4 ounces
Beverage, if desired		

Daily, at any time

Fruits	Women	3 servings**
	Men and Youth	4 to 6 servings**
Vegetables	Women, Men, and Youth	2 servings (minimum)
Milk	Women and Men	2 servings
	Youth	3 to 4 servings
Bread	Women	2 to 3 servings
	Men and Youth	4 to 5 servings
Fats	Women, Men, and Youth	3 servings

*Cooked Weight.
**Includes fruit at Morning Meal.

WEIGHT WATCHERS LIMITED CHOICE PLAN MENU

Food		Quantity

Morning Meal

Women, Men, and Youth

Fruit or Fruit Juice		1 serving
Choice of Egg		1
or Cheese, soft		1/3 cup
or Cheese, semisoft or hard		1 ounce
or Cereal		1 serving with Milk
or Poultry, Meat, or Fish		1 ounce*
or Legumes:		
Beans, lentils, and peas	Women and Youth	3 ounces*
	Men	4 ounces*
Tofu	Women and Youth	4 ounces
	Men	5 ounces
Tempeh	Women and Youth	1½ ounces
	Men	2 ounces
Beverage, if desired		

Midday and Evening Meal

Women, Men, and Youth

Choice of Eggs		2
or Cheese, soft		2/3 cup
or Cheese, semisoft or hard		2 ounces
or Poultry, Meat or Fish	Women and Youth	3 ounces*
	Men	4 ounces*

(continued)

166

or Legumes:

Beans, lentils, and peas	Women and Youth	6 ounces*
	Men	8 ounces*
Tofu	Women and Youth	8 ounces
	Men	10 ounces
Tempeh	Women and Youth	3 ounces
	Men	4 ounces

Daily, at any time

Fruits	Women	3 servings**
	Men and Youth	4 servings**
Vegetables	Women, Men, and Youth	2 servings (minimum)
Milk	Women and Men	2 servings
	Youth	3 servings
Bread	Women	2 servings
	Men and Youth	4 servings
Fats	Women, Men, and Youth	3 servings

*Cooked Weight.
**Includes fruit at Morning Meal.

SAMPLE OF WEIGHT WATCHERS NO CHOICE PLAN

DAY 1

Morning Meal
Broiled Spiced Orange, 1 serving
Cereal, 1 serving
Skim Milk, ½ serving
Beverage

Midday Meal
Tomato Juice, 1 serving
Tuna Salad, 1 serving
Melba Toast, 1 serving
Skim Milk, ½ serving
Beverage

Evening Meal
Roast Turkey, 3 ounces
Spinach, 1 serving
Tossed Salad with 1 serving Herb
  Vinaigrette Dressing
Bread, 1 serving
Beverage

Planned Snacks
Fruit Cocktail, 1 serving
Yogurt, 1 serving

DAY 2

Morning Meal
Grapefruit, 1 serving
Cottage Cheese, ⅓ cup
Melba Toast, 1 serving
Skim Milk, 1 serving

Midday Meal
Cooked Chicken, 3 ounces
Carrot Sticks with Green Bell
  Pepper Strips
Mayonnaise, 1 serving
Bread, 1 serving
Beverage

Evening Meal
Stir-Fried Liver and Vegetables,
  1 serving
Green Salad with 1 serving
  Vegetable Oil plus Vinegar
  and Herbs
Orange, 1 serving
Beverage

Planned Snacks
Banana, 1 serving
Skim Milk, 1 serving

DAY 3

Morning Meal
Tomato Juice, 1 serving
Scrambled Egg, 1 serving
Bread, 1 serving
Skim Milk, ½ serving
Beverage

Midday Meal
Vegetable
Cottage Cheese, 1 serving
Melba Toast, 1 serving
Margarine, 1 serving
Fruit Cocktail, 1 serving
Yogurt, 1 serving
Beverage

Evening Meal
Broiled Sole, 3 ounces
Green Beans, 1 serving
Tossed Salad with 1 serving
   Vegetable Oil plus Vinegar
   and Herbs
Beverage

Planned Snacks
Applesauce, ½ cup
Skim Milk, ½ serving

THE DIET WORKSHOP CYCLE ZERO 600-CALORIE DIET

Breakfast
Egg
Whole Wheat Toast, ¼ slice
Orange, ½
   or
Cottage Cheese, 2T
Protein Bread, toasted, 1 slice
Grapefruit, ½

Dinner
Salad of leafy greens;
   Dressing: tomato juice, vinegar,
   lemon juice, herbs, and spices
Chicken (white meat), 4 oz.
   cooked, or Shellfish, 4 oz.
   cooked, or White-type fish, 4 oz.
   cooked
Carrots, 1 cup, or String Beans, 1
   cup, or Zucchini, 1½ cup, or
   Broccoli, 1 cup, or Cauliflower,
   1½ cup

Lunch
Tuna, 3½ oz. can in water
Whole Wheat Bread, 1 slice
Berries, ½ cup
   or
Cottage Cheese, ½ cup
Melba Rounds, 6
Cantaloupe, ¼

Beverages
Water
Tea
Coffee
Diet Soda
Skim Milk, ½ cup per day

Extras
Mustard
Herbs and Spices, all
Artificial Sweetener
Salt and Pepper
Vinegar
Lemons and Limes
Pan Spray

THE BEACON HILL DIET

Monday

Breakfast
fruit
¼ cup cottage cheese
6 Melba rounds

Lunch
3 ounces tuna, water packed
DAY TIME SALAD
1 ounce (small) pocket bread

Dinner
4 ounces chicken
2 teaspoons cranberry sauce
1 cup lo vegetables

Tuesday

Breakfast
fruit
1 poached egg on a
½ English muffin, toasted

Lunch
⅓ cup cottage cheese
DAY TIME SALAD
6 Melba rounds

Dinner
4 ounces fish
1 cup lo vegetables

Wednesday

Breakfast
fruit
1 slice diet American cheese
1 slice protein bread

Lunch
3 ounces turkey breast
DAY TIME SALAD
1 slice protein bread

Dinner
4 ounces chicken
2 teaspoons cranberry sauce
1 cup lo vegetables

Snack Time: Each day in addition to your menu plan you should have 8 ounces of skim milk and 1 fruit.

DIET CONTROL CENTERS' BLAST OFF—STAGE 1 DIET

DAY 1

Breakfast
Orange juice, 4 oz.
Egg, 1
Bread, 1 oz.
Beverage

Lunch
Tuna or Salmon, 3 oz.
Tossed salad with 1 T diet dressing
Bread, 1 oz.
Beverage

Snack
Skim milk, 8 oz.

Dinner
Roast Turkey (white meat), 4 oz.
Cooked carrots, ½ cup
Lettuce/Tomato
Apple, 1 medium
Beverage

DAY 2

Breakfast
Grapefruit, ½
Dry cereal, ¾ cup
Skim milk, 4 oz.
Beverage

Lunch
Tomato Juice, 4 oz.
Chicken (white meat), 3 oz.
Tossed salad with
    1 T Diet Dressing
Bread, 1 oz.
Beverage

Snack
Apple, 1 medium

Dinner
Broiled Fish, 4 oz.
Asparagus, ½ cup
Mushrooms, ½ cup
Gelatin, sugar-free flavored,
    ½ cup
Yogurt, 4 oz. plain or skim milk, 4 oz.
Beverage

DAY 4

Breakfast
Orange Juice, 4 oz.
Cooked Cereal, ¾ cup
Skim Milk, 4 oz.

Lunch
Tomato Juice, 4 oz.
Egg, 1
Cottage Cheese, 1 oz.
Bread, 1 oz.
Lettuce, Tomato, Celery
Beverage

Snack
Applesauce, ½ cup

Dinner
Fish, 4 oz.
Zucchini, ½ cup
Sliced Onions, Lettuce, Tomato
Diet Salad Dressing, 1 T
Sugar-Free Flavored
    Gelatin, ½ cup
Plain Yogurt, 4 oz.
    or Skim Milk, 4 oz.
Beverage

DAY 3

Breakfast
Orange, 1
Cottage Cheese, 2 oz.
Bread, 1 oz.
Cinnamon, dash
Beverage

Lunch
Broiled Ground Beef (lean), 3 oz.
Tossed Salad, 1 T
    Diet Salad Dressing
Bread, 1 oz.
Beverage

Snack
Skim Milk, 8 oz.

Dinner
Chicken (white meat), 4 oz.
Carrots, ½ cup
Green Beans, ½ cup
Sugar-Free Peaches, ½ cup
Beverage

DAY 5

Breakfast
Grapefruit, ½
Cottage Cheese, 2 oz.
Bread, 1 oz.
Dash Cinnamon
Beverage

Lunch
Salmon or Tuna, 3 oz.
Tossed Salad
Diet Salad Dressing, 1 T
Bread, 1 oz.
Beverage

Snack
Skim Milk, 8 oz.

Dinner
Steak, 4 oz.
Beets, ½ cup
Cabbage, ½ cup
Fresh Orange, 1
Beverage

DAY 6

Breakfast
Grapefruit, ½
Dry Cereal, ¾ cup
Skim Milk, 4 oz.
Beverage

Lunch
Tomato Juice, 4 oz.
American Cheese, 1½ oz.
Tossed Green Salad
Diet Salad Dressing, 1 T
Bread, 1 oz.

Snack
Bouillon, 1 cup

Dinner
Fish, 4 oz.
Broccoli, ½ cup
Mushrooms, ½ cup
Sugar-Free Pears, ½ cup
Plain Yogurt, 4 oz.
  or Skim Milk, 4 oz.
Beverage

DAY 7

Breakfast
Orange Juice, 4 oz.
Egg, 1
Bread, 1 oz.
Beverage

Lunch
Fish, 3 oz.
Tossed Salad
Diet Salad Dressing, 1 T
Bread, 1 oz.
Beverage

Snack
Skim Milk, 8 oz.

Dinner
Lean Veal, 4 oz.
Spinach, ½ cup
Wax Beans, ½ cup
Sugar-Free Pineapple, ½ cup
Beverage

Diet Guidelines
Follow the Diet accordingly. No
  substitutions or additions.
No alcoholic beverages.
Prepare all foods without the
  addition of oil.
Carefully weigh and measure each
  portion.

All canned fruits and juices are
  SUGAR-FREE.
Beverages include: coffee, tea, or
  decaffeinated coffee. Diet drinks
  are allowed. Artificial
  sweeteners are allowed.

Doctors, Pills, and Surgery

*I*t was everything you've always wanted, but were afraid to ask for. You love those wonderful-tasting starchy foods — bread, pasta, pancakes, and cake. You also have heard for decades that starchy foods make you fat and to get lean you have to give up all starches.

Then along came a pill that let you eat a reasonable amount of starchy foods *and* lose weight. Zounds, it was magic!

And thus the pills known as starch blockers were launched as the newest, out-of-this-world fad. But it would by only months before starch blockers would plummet to earth and crash.

While it is no longer on the market, the starch blocker serves as yet another example of how gullible and careless are those who want to lose weight.

To explain, starches are complex chemicals composed of sugars. During digestion, starches are broken down to sugars, which are absorbed in the blood stream and sent off to various organs of the body, either to be used as energy or to be converted to other chemicals. As it does in the breakdown of other kinds of complex chemicals, the body uses enzymes to ease the starches' dismantling. In the case of starches, a key enzyme is amylase, which is secreted with pancreatic juice into the small intestine.

Enter the starch blocker. It is an anti-enzyme, a chemical which grabs on to amylase and prevents it from helping the digestive process break down starches to sugars. It is derived from northern beans and sometimes called northern bean extract.

To work its magic, you take one capsule of starch blocker in the middle of each meal. The capsule joins the food you eat in your stomach and dissolves, releasing the anti-enzyme, which moves along with the food to the small intestine where it can fight off the amylase enzyme.

You take the capsule with every meal (a week's supply costs about $15), and you follow a diet that balances the amount of starches you eat with the amount of anti-enzyme that just neutralizes the amount of enzyme the body puts out to break down those starches into "nasty" sugars. In other words, each capsule is supposed to neutralize about 400 starch calories. (By coincidence, the Starch Lover's Diet[1] happens to be a high-protein diet with a limited quantity of starchy foods.)

Some physicians who introduced starch blockers considered the concept investigational and felt that the capsules should be administered only by physicians.[2] However, companies that made the northern bean extract began selling it over-the-counter in drugstores and health food stores, on the basis that it is a food and not a drug and therefore need not be reviewed by the Food and Drug Administration. When the starch blocker idea was presented to the annual convention of the American Society of Bariatric Physicians in Las Vegas late in 1981 by Dr. Peter G. Lindner of California and Dr. J. Tom Cooper of Georgia, there was considerable controversy, since the concept had never been extensively tested for efficacy or safety. In fact, a copy of a letter to the FDA, backed by inches-thick documentation, was circulated at the meeting. It was unsigned, which only aggravated the controversy.

At the outset, three brands of starch blockers were put on the market for direct sale to dieters: Amylex (R-Kane Products, Inc., Pennsauken, NJ 08110); Starch Block (GNC, General Nutrition Centers, Pittsburgh, PA 15222); and Natural Starch Blocker (American Family, Los Angeles, CA 90502). The number would grow to 100, as capsule sales skyrocketed.

However, the FDA wouldn't go for the food argument. Apparently the anonymous warning letter had hit its mark and alerted that federal agency. Also, isolated reports of starch blocker takers suffering from nausea, stomach pains, diarrhea, and vomiting began to stream in.

In the meantime, Dr. Lindner, in an editorial in *Obesity/Bariatric Medicine,* warned fellow physicians that raw northern beans "also contain at least three anti-nutritional factors, which must be carefully separated and removed from the final preparation during the extraction process." Therefore, Dr. Lindner wrote, "I would urge any physician who wishes to utilize these inhibitors on his patients to use extreme caution, and to do so strictly in a *clinical investigational* setting. . . . Self-treatment, with untested over-the-counter type preparations, can only be condemned during this developmental stage of the clinical use of alpha amylase inhibitors."[3]

In July 1982, the FDA made its move and announced that manufacturers and distributors had ten days to discontinue marketing starch blockers. Those that wished to sell in the future must provide data proving the capsules were both safe and effective. In August, the FDA said starch blockers were "unapproved and possibly dangerous drugs." They were drugs because they "may affect the body's normal metabolic functions." In the meantime, 19 promoters of the starch blocker filed legal suits challenging the FDA ruling. In October, federal marshalls seized more than a million starch blocker capsules in five states. That same month, a federal district court ruled on the suit against the FDA by seven manufacturers of the starch blocker. The verdict: It is a drug and not a food. Therefore, it must be tested as a drug, and the data must be submitted to the FDA for approval. In the meantime, starch blockers may not be marketed. However, the FDA order was stayed as the companies filed an appeal to a higher court.

Finally, in December 1982, a Baylor University medical team reported in *The New England Journal of Medicine* that the starch blocker doesn't work. While it may work in the laboratory, tests on human volunteers who took the capsules with hearty spaghetti dinners showed the anti-enzyme did not prevent the digestion and absorption of starch, as it was supposed to do.

THE FISHY SMELLS OF SPIRULINA AND GLUCOMANNAN

At about the same time as the starch blocker was foisted on the public, people also were beginning to talk about spirulina. A dark green powder or pill, high in protein, spirulina is blue-green algae that grows in brackish ponds and lakes throughout the warmer sections of the world. It is certainly neither exotic nor magical, but it could be a supplementary source of protein.

However, claims were made that phenylalanine, an amino acid that "acts on the brain's appetite center to switch off your hunger pangs," was an ingredient of spirulina. Since this amino acid is found in most other protein sources, the FDA was dubious. It asked an advisory panel to review the claim. The panel found no reliable scientific data to demonstrate this amino acid's effectiveness or safety as an appetite suppressant.[4] Still, it sells—as much as five tons a day in the US.

Then there is glucomannan, advertised as "The Weight Loss Secret That's Been in the Orient for Over 500 Years." Well, as a derivative of the konjac root, it has been used as food for many years in Japan and other Oriental countries. But there is no medical literature here or there to indicate its value in losing weight. To be sold as such in the US, glucomannan has to be approved by the FDA, as a drug or as a food additive.

DIET DRUG GUIDE

In addition to such items as starch blockers, spirulina, and glucomannan, dieters are likely to encounter a variety of drugs used as diet aids. For this reason CONSUMER GUIDE® here publishes a diet drug guide. We make no attempt to sugarcoat the facts.

But first, some general cautions. Whenever your diet doctor—or any doctor — prescribes a drug, be sure to ask the drug's name, intended action, and common side effects. And ask the doctor to instruct the pharmacist to label the container with the drug's name, dosage, and directions.

If you are pregnant, take no drugs under any circumstances without first checking with your obstetrician. Many of the drugs given by diet doctors are teratogenic—that is, they can harm unborn children.

As for nonprescription diet drugs, CONSUMER GUIDE® advises you that these are only temporarily helpful crutches.

If you have any questions about drugs, consult *Prescription Drugs*[5] or *People's Drug Guide*.[6]

If you think a doctor is pushing dangerous drugs in excessive quantities, call the local office of the US Food and Drug Administration or the Bureau of Narcotics. If he or she also is charging an exorbitant fee for what little personal attention is given you, give the doctor's name to the ethics committee of your local medical society. These societies are slow to act, but if they receive enough complaints, they will at least question the doctor.

Especially be aware of doctors who give what are called "rainbow drugs"—a handful of pills of different colors which you are instructed to take several times a day. Combining drugs — such as digitalis-amphetamine-thyroid—can be particularly dangerous.

There are four main categories of prescription diet drugs. CONSUMER GUIDE® has organized drugs under their appropriate categories, giving both generic and trade names, as well as identifying features and side effects.

All tablets and capsules have the manufacturer's name or identification. Amphetamines and similar drugs are mixed with sedatives such as barbiturates, with vitamins, with sedatives and vitamins, with bulk-producing agents for regularity, and with thyroid hormone.

PRESCRIPTION DRUGS

Appetite Suppressants (anorexiants) are drugs that supposedly curb your appetite and create a sense of exhilaration. Because they give you a pepped-up feeling, they often are called pep pills. They are also known on the black market as "uppers" or "speed."

Amphetamine is the most widely used diet drug. It was discovered in 1932 by Gordon Alles of the University of California and synthesized in 1939 by M. H. Nathanson. Alles turned over his patents to the Philadelphia pharmaceutical firm of Smith Kline & French (SKF) Laboratories. Before the federal government stepped in to control the manufacture and sale of amphetamines, SKF was selling $30 million worth each year in the US, a figure that represented 45 percent of the company's prescription drug sales.[7]

By 1966, half of all amphetamines made in the US were estimated to have gone into illicit drug traffic at a rate of ten cents to $1 per pill.[8]

In its *Drug Evaluations,* the AMA says of amphetamines and similar drugs: " ... the prolonged use of these drugs may cause psychic or physical dependence and reinforces a drug habit rather than proper eating habits." The guide tells physicians to give them only for temporary use—four to six weeks to see if they are effective. If they are, use should be limited to 12 weeks.[9]

A California psychiatrist who had treated youngsters "freaked out on speed" reported that amphetamine abusers experience profound appetite suppression—so profound they often have difficulty swallowing. And long-term users often develop paranoid psychosis, which is characterized by intense feelings of persecution.[10] Such reports are reason enough for the federal government to classify amphetamines for limited use only under the Controlled Substances Act.

The amphetamines are usually coupled with adrenergic drugs, which have similar appetite-suppressing action. The most usual form of amphetamine is dextroamphetamine. Trade names for this drug fill more than two pages of the US Public Health Service's *National Drug Code Directory.*[11] Other forms are benzphetamine, chlorphentermine, diethylpropion, phendimetrazine, phenmetrazine, and phentermine. Common trade names for these drugs are Dexedrine, Desoxyn, Biphetamine, Delcobese, Obetrol, Tenuate, Tepanil, Ionamin, and Preludin.[12]

Dexedrine, the pep pills that thousands of overweight women carried in their purses in the 1950s and 1960s, comes in orange-colored triangular tablets (5 mg) and in dark brown/transparent capsules that contain multicolored pellets (timed-release in 5, 10, or 15 mg).

Abbott Laboratories' Desoxyn comes in white (5 mg), orange (10 mg), and yellow (15 mg) tablets. The Upjohn Company's Didrex comes in yellow (25 mg) and pink (50 mg). Pennwalt produces Biphetamine as a black-and-white (12½ mg) or black (20 mg) capsule. Delco Chemical Company's Delcobese comes in tablet or capsule form (5 mg, 10 mg, 15 mg, 20 mg). Obetrol Pharmaceuticals produces Obetrol as a blue (10 mg) or a pale orange (20 mg) tablet.

Merrell-National Laboratories' Tenuate comes in two forms: a 25 mg round, white tablet and a 75 mg long, white sustained-release tablet. Parke-Davis' Pre-Sate comes in blue tablets (65 mg). Boehringer Ingelheim, Ltd.'s Preludin comes in three forms: square, white (25 mg), round, white (50 mg), and round, pink (75 mg). They also have a timed-release capsule — Prelu-2 — which is celery-green and contains an amphetaminelike drug.

Another appetite-suppressing drug is fenfluramine (Pondimin, A.H. Robins Company), an amphetamine derivative. Its side effects are drowsiness, diarrhea, and dry mouth.[13]

Another drug, which also is related to amphetamines, is Fastin (phentermine hydrochloride, Beecham Laboratories). This blue-and-white capsule should not be taken by people with heart disease, high blood pressure, or glaucoma. It also may impair your ability to drive a car, and it may reduce libido or sex drive.[14]

Still another appetite suppressant is Sandoz Pharmaceuticals' Sanorex, which resembles an aspirin tablet. Chemically called mazindol, Sanorex has many properties in common with amphetamines. Its main side effects are dry mouth, nervousness, constipation, and insomnia.[15]

Use of appetite-suppressing drugs, says the AMA, "may cause nervousness, irritability, insomnia, decreased sense of fatigue, increased alertness and ability to concentrate, and euphoria...dryness of the mouth and blurred vision and mydriasis [dilation of the pupil of the eye], dizziness and light headedness, tachycardia and palpitations, hypertension, and sweating." It adds that "susceptible patients may develop psychic dependence and physical dependence."[16]

In other words, appetite suppressants can make you feel as though you were jumping out of your skin. And you can get hooked on them.

Alvan R. Feinstein, M.D., a recognized expert on obesity from the Yale University School of Medicine, found that appetite suppressants are inferior to dieting. The newer drugs "often compare poorly with the older ones whose deficiencies they presumably were intended to correct."[17]

An eminent authority on drugs, Louis Lasagna, M.D., of Rochester (New York) School of Medicine, wrote that "the traditional academic line has described the amphetamines and newer compounds as drugs of limited utility, with a weak initial effect to which tolerance develops rapidly, and with a considerable potential for inducing psychologic dependence. This attitude contrasts with the national sales figures of appetite suppressants, which indicate a considerable prescribing by physicians."[18]

Digitalis is a drug originally intended to help failing hearts. Some unscrupulous doctors prescribe it for weight loss because one of its side effects is loss of appetite. Here's what the AMA has to say about it: "The anorexia (loss of appetite) produced by digitalis is a symptom of potentially fatal intoxication."[19]

Examples of common trade names for digitalis: Sandoz Pharmaceuticals Co. makes Cedilanid, a round, pink tablet; Burroughs Wellcome Co. makes Lanoxin, which comes in yellow (0.125 mg), white (0.25 mg), and green (0.5 mg) tablets.

Metabolic Medication works to heat up your body's fires to burn more food as fuel. Thyroid hormone is the most commonly prescribed metabolic medication. Usually it is used when a person's thyroid gland does not make enough of the hormone called thyroxine, or after surgical removal of the gland. Herbert Gershberg, M.D., of New York University School of Medicine, said: "Giving thyroid hormone to obese patients has been a common practice for many decades. The aim is to increase basal metabolism and energy output and theoretically to promote lipolysis [breakup of fat]... It is apparent that thyroid hormone has little effect on weight loss unless it is given to very obese subjects in a hospital and on a restricted diet."[20]

The AMA *Drug Evaluations* notes, "Thyroid preparations act as anorexiants but may suppress endogenous thyroid secretion and have potentially dangerous effects on cardiac function."[21]

Thyroid hormone is available as Proloid (Parke-Davis), a small, gray tablet; Synthroid (Flint Laboratories), orange (0.025 mg), white (0.05 mg), yellow (0.1 mg), blue (0.15) mg), pink (0.2 mg), green (0.3 mg); Armour Pharmaceutical Company thyroid, white tablets small to large with from ¼ grain to 5 grains thyroid; Cytomel (SKF), gray tablets (5 mcg to 50 mcg liothyronine sodium); Euthroid (Parke-Davis), orange, brown, purple, and gray square tablets; S-P-T (Fleming), green (1 gr), brown (2 gr), red (3 gr), or black (5 gr) capsules; and Thyroid and Thyroid Strong (Marion), white or red tablets ranging in size from ½ grain to 3 grains.

Thyroid hormones are especially dangerous for people with heart disease. They also can disrupt the entire endocrine (hormone) system of your body.

Diuretics—drugs that withdraw water from the body—are often given first by diet doctors so the patient can experience a quick weight loss. "Diuretics are undoubtedly among the agents used occasionally by those physicians who refuse to divulge the contents of the 'magical' injections for weight reduction," said Dr. Feinstein.[22] According to the AMA, "diuretics are of little use in decreasing adipose tissue, although they cause transient fluid loss."[23]

Diuretics stimulate the kidneys to draw water from the blood and excrete it in the urine. (Caffeine is a diuretic, as is evidenced by how it stimulates urination.)

The most commonly used chemicals for diuresis (water loss) are the *thiazides*. And among the more common thiazides are Diuril (Merck Sharp & Dohme) which comes as a white tablet in two sizes, 250 mg and 500 mg; HydroDIURIL (Merck Sharp & Dohme), in peach-colored tablets of three sizes, 25 mg, 50 mg, and 100 mg; Esidrix (CIBA Pharmaceutical Company), pink (25 mg), yellow (50 mg), blue (100 mg); Anhydron (Eli Lilly and Company), a long pink tablet (2 mg); and Abbott Laboratories' Oretic, a small or large white tablet (25 mg and 50 mg), and Enduron, orange or pink square tablets (2.5 mg and 5 mg respectively).

Thiazide diuretics can cause "dizziness, weakness, fatigue, and leg cramps."[24] Because they rid the body of potassium, along with water, one should also take potassium supplements or eat raisins and bananas (which are loaded with carbohydrates, too, unfortunately). Diabetes can worsen under thiazide diuretic therapy.

Laxatives or **cathartics** are given by diet doctors in an effort to speed food through the intestines so nutrients are not absorbed and turned to fat. Laxatives include drugs that directly stimulate the nerves of the bowels (such as castor oil); mineral oil, which eases the feces through the colon; and bulk-forming agents, which fill the colon and make it contract.

According to the AMA, "laxatives used in doses large enough to produce diarrhea can result in loss of water, but hypokalemia [low levels of potassium] and/or dehydration also may occur after prolonged administration and are potentially fatal. Bulk-producing agents cause gastric distention, inducing a transient sensation of satiety. Methylcellulose and water given together relieve hunger briefly but may cause gastrointestinal disturbances. Antispasmodics have no effect on body fat or caloric balance. Therefore, use of any of these agents as an aid to weight reduction is unjustified."[25]

Gentle laxatives taken once in a while can't hurt you. But strong prescribed laxatives frequently can harm the body.

NONPRESCRIPTION DIET DRUGS

From time to time, your local drugstore may advertise diet pills, or you may see ads for them in national magazines. You'll recognize them by such headlines as "TAKE UGLY FAT OFF," "LOSE UGLY FAT," "LOSE WEIGHT," or "GET RID OF FAT." Time and again, the federal government has prosecuted mail-order weight-reducing pill advertisers for fraud.

So-called miracle pills that can be bought at the drugstore without a prescription, or through the mails, usually are of two types. One kind is sugar candy, with instructions that you take it just before you eat to curb your appetite. CONSUMER GUIDE® finds these pills, though not dangerous, of only slight benefit. The other kind is a combination of benzocaine and methylcellulose. Benzocaine is used in ointments to deaden pain. Its effect in a diet pill is to deaden your taste buds and subdue the craving for food. Methylcellulose expands by absorbing water from your stomach; it gives you a feeling of fullness to fool you into thinking you have had a meal. Even if the premise of the actions of these two chemicals were accurate, the amounts that could be sold legally in a nonprescription drug are too small to be effectual.

Then came phenylpropanolamine. Marketed under such trade names as Appedrine, Dexatrim, Control, Dietac, and Prolamine, it is an over-the-counter drug for suppressing appetite. Its sales were phenomenal, especially after 1979 when an FDA panel of experts called phenyl-propanolamine (PPA) "safe and effective." Again, in 1982, an FDA review panel found PPA, alone and in combination with caffeine, safe and effective as an appetite suppressant and an aid to weight loss, when taken as directed. The president of Thompson Medical Co. in New York City, a leading distributor of PPA diet aid products (four of the five brands mentioned above), said PPA "will soon be accepted as one of the most important diet aid support tools available to the American consumer."

There is nothing new about PPA. It has been used for more than half a century as a nasal decongestant. Its value in suppressing appetite was first noted in 1939. A synthetic derivative of the asthma drug ephedrine, it works on the nervous system, yet is not considered habit-forming. But in

178

late 1982, three Oregon doctors reported in the *Journal of the American Medical Association* two cases in which PPA was linked to kidney failure and muscle tissue injury. This was added to the earlier reports of the adverse effects of PPA on high blood pressure. Doctors worry about patients with high blood pressure who are getting double doses of PPA by taking it as a diet aid and, unknowingly, in cough or cold medicine.

CONSUMER GUIDE®'S EVALUATION

CONSUMER GUIDE® feels that diet drugs should not be taken except under a doctor's supervision. Even then, it is important to recognize that a diet drug is only a temporary crutch.

DR. SIMEONS' "TECHNIQUE"

HCG (human chorionic gonadotropin) once was the most widespread medication given in the United States to patients to lose weight, but it has been discredited by organized medicine and the federal government. It has been the basis of the treatment given by the 80 Weight Reduction Medical Clinics in California, as well as the basis for treatment at the Simeons and Kennedy Centers in the East and Midwest.

British-born and Heidelberg-trained Albert T. Simeons, M.D., first used the hormone in India in the mid-1930s.[26] HCG is a form of growth hormone which is extracted from the urine of pregnant women. (It is this hormone, in fact, that is tested for in home pregnancy test kits.) The hormone was the accepted treatment for young boys suffering from a condition known as Froehlich's syndrome. Injections of HCG helped reduce the accumulations of fat on hips, buttocks, and thighs which made boys with Froehlich's syndrome look like girls.

Dr. Simeons moved to Rome in 1949, set up his practice at the Salvator Mundi International Hospital, and started using his regimen of HCG injections and 500 calories to treat overweight adults. In his first report, in 1954, Dr. Simeons announced to the medical profession that HCG "is in some way specifically concerned with the control of obesity in both sexes and at all ages. Although gonadotropin alone does not reduce weight, it does make a very drastic calorie curtailment possible."[27]

In Dr. Simeons' *Pounds and Inches—A New Approach to Obesity,*[28] he stated that obesity is the accumulation of an abnormal kind of fat which is not usually lost with dieting. Many fat people, frustrated because they don't lose fat on severe diets, "become indignant and decide that modern medicine is a fraud and its representatives fools, while the weak just give up the struggle in despair."

The answer, he claimed, is HCG. He was careful to explain that while HCG is produced by the placenta (the afterbirth) under direction of the sex glands, it is not a sex hormone. It does not affect the endocrine hormone system.

In his book, Dr. Simeons also outlined the principles of his 500-calorie daily diet. Breakfast consists only of tea or black coffee, sweetened, if necessary, with saccharin. Lunch and dinner are essentially the same:

100 grams (3½ ounces) fish, seafood, poultry, or red meat from which all
visible fat has been carefully trimmed; a green or root vegetable or
tomato; a breadstick or piece of melba toast; and an apple, orange, half
grapefruit, or handful of strawberries. Cooking is done without using fat. In
addition, patients drink at least eight glasses of water a day. And no other
medication is allowed.

The only cosmetics permitted are lipstick, powder, and eyebrow pencil.
The Simeons theory is that no oils should be applied to the skin because
they will be absorbed into the body and add to the fat already there.

HCG CENTERS AND THE LAW

Organized medicine became suspicious of the clinics giving HCG. One
factor that made medical associations wary was the high salaries for
part-time doctors who examined potential subscribers and prescribed
HCG injections. Some of these clinics offered $50,000 to $100,000 a year
in return for working only an afternoon or an evening each week.[29] Such
tactics closed the doors of many of these clinics.

IS HCG EFFECTIVE?

Aside from legal considerations, the essential questions are: Does HCG
melt away fat? Is Dr. Simeons' technique an effective way to slim down? Is
it safe?

In 1973, the US Food and Drug Administration put it succinctly: "There
are no scientifically adequate well-controlled clinical studies appearing in
the medical literature which establish the safety and efficacy of HCG in
the treatment of obesity."[30]

In December 1974, the US Food and Drug Administration announced it
would require producers of HCG to label it as follows: "There is no
substantial evidence that it increases weight loss beyond that resulting
from caloric restriction, that it causes a more attractive or 'normal' distribu-
tion of fat, or that it decreases the hunger and discomfort associated with
calorie-restricted diets."

In 1975, the FDA declared HCG ineffective and warned Simeons-styled
clinics against making claims about HCG's ability to take fat off the body.
Nonetheless, some clinics are still open, and some doctors still adminis-
ter HCG injections.

Since then, HCG injections have been tested against salt-water injections. Neither the doctors giving the injections nor the patients knew who
received HCG or salt water until the experiment was over. The conclusion
was that there was no difference "in weight loss, body measurements,
hunger appeasement, and various metabolic measurements."[31]

CONSUMER GUIDE®'S EVALUATION

After objectively reviewing the pros and cons of the Simeons' technique,
CONSUMER GUIDE® can only conclude that it is an expensive and
dangerous way to lose weight.

DIET DOCTORS

In the case of bariatric physicians (*barios* is Greek for weight; *iatrics* is Greek for medical treatment), the situation is happily improving. Those who call themselves that and can show you they have been certified by the American Society of Bariatric Physicians (ASBP) are far and away the kind of diet doctor to care for you. If you have a doctor in mind, you can contact the ASBP and find out if he or she is a member. The address of the ASBP is Suite 300, 5200 South Quebec Street, Englewood, CO 80111.

If the diet doctor is not a member of ASBP, there is a good chance that, at best, he or she doesn't know much about treating obesity and, at worst, he or she is disreputable, dangerous, and only out for the fast buck. Sadly, for the desperate dieter, there are many more disreputable diet doctors who have never even attended an ASBP meeting than there are those who do attend and who do use the best and safest scientific techniques to get weight off their patients and keep it off. American Medical Association investigator Oliver Field has said, "Many weight specialists practice a sophisticated form of quackery." And investigative journalists have uncovered greed and assembly-line tactics.

Twenty years ago authors Lester and Irene David concluded that "self-styled 'obesity specialists' are the newest health menace in America."[32] A woman reporter for *Life* magazine—at 5 feet 5 inches a trim 123 pounds—visited ten diet doctors around the United States and had some shocking experiences. A Kansas City doctor simply handed her a box with 140 pills, charged her $10, and told her to return in a month. In Decatur, Illinois, a diet doctor conducted a battery of medical tests, asked if she took vitamins, and gave her something he called "gland substance." A Gardena, California, doctor gave her an appetite depressant, a laxative, a protein supplement, and his own medicine (which turned out to be prednisone, a cortisonelike hormone usually used to treat inflammation). In Los Angeles, a diet doctor filled her purse with amphetamines, the pill used to curb appetite and classified by the federal government as dangerous. A Denver doctor gave her appetite depressants, too, as well as thyroid hormone. In Manhattan, she visited "one of the most prosperous 'fat' doctors in the country. He has 19 offices and grosses just under a million dollars a year." He gave her the amphetamine-thyroid combination. At Falls Church, Virginia, a doctor gave her 150 amphetamine-thyroid-barbiturate combination pills. A Miami Beach doctor gave her the same combination plus diuretics and laxatives, told her she could eat 4000 calories a day and lose weight, and asked her to return in a week.[33]

Many diet doctors use anything that works. They leave their hard-won medical educations behind, attend high-priced weekend cram courses, then apply the latest technique to the next overweight patient who comes along. In many ways, the marginal diet physician is the most despicable of doctors; he often produces results—weight loss—but at a terrible price to the body and health. Too many of these doctors ignore the first part of the Hippocratic Oath—"Do no harm"—in order to line their pockets.

FEW CONTROLS

There are few legal controls over diet doctors. Those who have an M.D. (medical doctor) or D.O. (doctor of osteopathy) degree can treat their patients according to their best judgment. This judgment may dictate prescribing a safe and effective diet (as legitimate and concerned doctors will) or prescribing appropriate or even inappropriate medications. State and federal laws do not govern the way a doctor practices medicine. Of course, he may be liable to a malpractice action, but if he prescribed a drug, he may pull the drug company into the lawsuit as a codefendant. His defense may lean on the patient's failure to call him at the first sign of ill effects. Or he may present a statement, signed by the patient, that outlines the possible dangers of drugs and that absolves him from responsibility.

In some instances, the federal government has taken action but only against physicians who stockpile dangerous or addictive drugs. A case in point is the Kansas City doctor visited by the *Life* magazine reporter. Only a month before her visit, a deputy US marshall and agents of the US Food and Drug Administration's Bureau of Drug Abuse Control confiscated 2.5 million pills and barbiturates, from his office.

The AMA has been slow to take action. Its position has been that it "does not recognize any 'obesity' or 'reducing' specialty. Nor does overweight require a 'special' type of physician. Obesity should always be treated by a doctor as part of the patient's general health problem."[34]

However, pressures for regulation are increasing. Recognizing the problem, the American Society of Bariatric Physicians has issued "Bariatric Standards of Practice." The society hires its own inspector who visits members unannounced and unanticipated. Doctors who pass (meet the standards) receive the society's seal of approval. Others could appeal. As a result of ASBP's efforts, AMA now refers inquiries on obesity treatment to ASPB.

However, "diet consultants" are unregulated. Chiropractors, podiatrists, their assistants — anyone can be a "diet consultant." Everyone is getting into the act. They do not need a license to practice yet may call themselves "doctor." While they cannot legally prescribe medication, nothing can stop them from advising you about the diet you should follow, even if that diet can adversely affect your health.

At times people who go to diet doctors and consultants lose only dollars. Only their wallets become thin. They seek a magic cure for their problem because they don't want to admit that losing weight requires a long-term effort to change the way they eat, the foods they eat, and, to a lesser extent, their physical activity. The 200-pound West Coast secretary, who died because she took too many pills prescribed by her diet doctor, and hundreds of other diet-doctor victims pay a heavy price for their fantasies.[35]

CONSUMER GUIDE® advises you to consult your family physician, internist, or obstetrician-gynecologist first, if you feel you need medical help in losing weight. You may be referred to an endocrinologist to be sure you don't have a metabolic problem (few overweight persons have such problems). If you don't have such a doctor to turn to, find a reliable bariatric physician, either through your local medical society or the ASBP. Or, go to the obesity clinic of a large hospital, if there is one in your community.

On the following pages are short summaries of some of the techniques used by diet doctors. CONSUMER GUIDE® reminds you that not all of these are effective, and not all of them are dangerous.

EAT LESS—ACUPRESS

Acupressure, a cousin of acupuncture (see below), is a technique you can safely perform to control appetite, according to Dr. Frank Bahr of Munich, West Germany.[36] The technique involves rubbing an area of the skin with your thumbnail until the skin is red but not broken. A point midway between the breastbone and navel controls hunger pangs; other points on the elbow and the knee control the emotions that lead to overeating.

The main pressure point, though, is on the upper lip (a pressure point that escaped classic Chinese acupuncturists) and is stimulated by pinching. "When you are in the bathtub in the morning, and have just cleaned your teeth and thoroughly washed your hands, then why don't you try pincer acupressure?" asks Dr. Bahr. But, he cautions, don't expect results for three days, "at which time the reflex passages to the brain have become programmed."[37]

Along with the acupressure secret, Dr. Bahr provides stickers that say "Eat Less, Acupress," and an 800-calorie diet. This appears to be a psychological crutch which may help some dieters.

ACUPUNCTURE

Many people have lost weight by having needles inserted into the skin of the ear. The needles are placed in position according to ancient Chinese medical principles that few modern Westerners understand.

Acupuncture is based on the way nerves branch within the body. Nerves to inner organs have smaller branches that emerge just under the skin at distant parts of the body. According to acupuncture theory, when the nerve branches are stimulated, they send signals to the main part of the nerve and, thus, to the organ. To help lose weight, the acupuncture needles are placed in the area of the external ear known as the concha. The vagus nerve, which extends from the brain, down the neck and chest, to the stomach, branches to the concha. When the sharp point of a needle finds this branch of the vagus nerve, it acts to inhibit the contractions of the stomach.[38]

Acupuncturist and anesthesiologist Anastacio T. Saavedra, of Chicago, explained that the acupuncture treatment to the ear does not cause a person to lose weight. Instead, it allows him to stave off appetite. Dr. Saavedra does not use long needles; he inserts a stainless steel surgical staple and instructs his patients to jiggle it with a clean finger every time they feel the urge to nibble and just before sitting down to a meal.[39] If a staple in one ear does not work, he suggests another staple in the opposite ear.

Dr. Anastacio Saavedra has performed this acupuncture treatment on one hundred of his patients and claimed a success rate of approximately 70 percent,[40] which is similar to the nationwide figures.

Frank Z. Warren, M.D., a well-known researcher in acupuncture, says the key to success lies in the way the nerves develop in the human embryo. Further study, he wrote, will "enable us to bridge the gap between what we see and what we know as concerns ear acupuncture."[41]

Dr. Warren admits that ear acupuncture, now also done with a tiny spiral needle which remains in place, is not magic. Instead, it is a method to help control hunger pangs. No weight is lost unless dieters go on, and stay on, a diet.[42] In effect, ear acupuncture is an aid, a crutch to help the dieter stick with the food called for on his diet. Acupuncture helps control nibbling and helps limit the amount of food eaten at meals. A potentially serious side effect is the possibility of infection.

Although acupuncture has been around for thousands of years, the AMA states: "The practice of acupuncture in the United States is an experimental medical procedure that should be performed only by a licensed physician or dentist or under his direct supervision."[43]

CONSUMER GUIDE® recommends that, if you want ear acupuncture treatment, go to a physician who has been trained in the procedure. This training should include a course offered by the National Society for Acupuncture Research. Acupuncture may work for you; then again, it may not.

BYPASS SURGERY

The most drastic way to lose fat is by means of bypass surgery. According to one estimate, 50,000 Americans submit themselves to such surgery every year, usually losing about a hundred pounds each.

There are two types of bypass operations today. One is technically known as the jejuno-ileal bypass. In this operation, the surgeon severs the intestines at the jejunum and reconnects them at the ileum, bypassing most of the small intestine which normally absorbs nutrients from digested food. The operation, in essence, places the patient on a fast—a permanent one at that.

This operation stirred a wave of interest late in 1973 when United Press International carried the story of a 30-year-old California man who had reduced to 181 pounds from 587 pounds in 30 months.[44] The operation received attention again in 1976, when jazz trumpeter Al Hirt told the press that he had thinned from 340 pounds to 260 pounds after the bypass operation.[45]

Yet the operation is, to quote Medical World News, "beset by controversy and doubt."[46] In fact, it is still considered experimental. Because it is experimental, only the severely obese are candidates, and then only when obesity is a greater risk to their health than is the surgery.[47] A surgeon explained: "It isn't like taking out a diseased gall bladder. One is operating on normal intestines to achieve secondary metabolic change… Therefore, the surgeon assumes a responsibility he doesn't have to assume in other procedures."

And the surgery itself holds risks. In a study of 40 patients who underwent bypass surgery at the University of Florida, Edward R. Woodward, M.D., and Patrick O'Leary, M.D., found that many patients suffered infections, kidney stones, or liver failure. The most persistent problem was diarrhea and foul-smelling excrement, the result of the surgery's artificial creation of the *malabsorption syndrome*—which means the body cannot absorb fats from foods.[48] The operation severely alters the body's metabolism and can cause liver disease.[49] It can also lead to serious intestinal infections that may require additional surgery. And it may even affect the brain's functions,[50] in addition to causing gallstones and kidney stones.[51]

OTHER SURGERY

Less drastic and more popular now is the operation known as the gastric bypass, promoted by George L. Blackburn, M.D., of Harvard University. When he operates, Dr. Blackburn does not cut into the stomach. He uses surgical staples to close off nine-tenths of the stomach. The operation reduces the size of the stomach so the patient feels full after eating less food.

However, Dr. Blackburn doesn't perform the operation on any and all who ask.

First, you must enter his Center for Nutritional Research and prove that you can stick to a diet, exercise regularly, and learn behavior modification techniques.

"Given the state of this disease [obesity], therapy is a privilege, not a right," Dr. Blackburn said. "We aren't going into partnership with any rip-off artists. If they don't listen, if they don't work at losing weight, if they don't try, they don't deserve the operation. I see it as taking the place of weak will power, but only temporarily, for those who mean business. And I won't do it on their say-so. Every patient I operate on must have an advocate, an internist, who has to convince me that the surgery won't be the end, but instead will be part of a total effort."

Surgeons surveyed by CONSUMER GUIDE® told how expensive bypass surgery is. A surgeon's fee for the three-hour to four-hour operation ranges from $2500 to $5000. Then, there is the hospital bill and, perhaps, additional costs for tests at the doctor's office after recuperation. In round numbers, the operation may total well over $10,000. Insurance companies, such as Blue Cross-Blue Shield, will pay for the surgery on patients in some states but not in others (a lot depends on how the surgeon describes the operation on the insurance forms). One patient estimated a cost of $53 per pound lost. She felt it was worth it, even though she still had diarrhea a year after the operation.

Plastic surgery can be helpful to women with pendulous breasts, but operations to remove layers of fat from hips, trunk, and thighs are not effective.[52] Moreover, the appetite resumes after surgery, as do the same eating patterns; so no real, long-term change has occurred.

CONSUMER GUIDE® advises against surgery for obesity. *Unless* you weigh 500 pounds and are desperately *ill*, stay away from the surgeon's knife. From our perspective, the procedures are highly experimental; their risks far outweigh their temporary relief.

Sweating It Off

*N*o one can remember when exercise books last topped the best-seller lists, as they do now. This indicates that there is a segment of the public that believes more and more that vigorous exercise is not only THE means of staying young and healthy and sexy, but is also one of the most important ways to get and stay slim.

This popular view was enhanced in 1982 by a report of a University of California-Berkeley study that showed that the bodies of people who are physically active process the foods they eat more efficiently. In other words, they get more nutrients out of the food they eat than do sedentary persons. As a result, their bodies crave less food, which means they eat fewer calories.[1]

Another California study, conducted at Stanford University, showed that body fat starts decreasing after only three months of jogging—that's 45 minutes' worth, five days a week. The subjects were middle-aged men who were originally sedentary.[2]

There is general agreement that exercise can help you stay on a diet. Says Frank Konishi, professor of nutrition at Southern Illinois University, Carbondale: "The energy we burn in moving our muscles around — in *exercising* them — that's the important ingredient in keeping our weight where it ought to be."[3] More enthusiastic is exercise expert Charles Kuntzleman, who considers exercise "the best package deal ever invented. With it, you'll lose weight, firm up muscles, gain a more attractive body, have greater energy, feel less stress and tension."[4]

But until recently, many of us more or less stopped renewing our lease on life in our mid-20s. As Neil Solomon, M.D., explained in the 1976 book *Doctor Solomon's Proven Master Plan for Total Body Fitness and Maintenance,* people start to move less around age 25, but they don't compensate by eating less. "On into middle age," he says, "(many of us) continue to eat like adolescents. We fast-food it for lunch, load up on drinks and desserts, and totally ignore the fact that after 30 we require about 1 percent fewer calories each year. We sit in our comfortable grooves, moving only the same small group of muscles through repetitive patterns of action, day after day and year after year, overlooking the fact that there are approximately 639 muscles in the body, not to mention 208 bones, and that all of them should be given the opportunity for a little fun and motion every 24 hours."[5]

Ten years ago, few people were putting their muscles into motion every day. According to nutritionist Jean Mayer, the typical American businessman in the late 1960s "(got) up, and, after briefly standing in front of his mirror using his electric toothbrush and his electric razor, (sat) down at the breakfast table, (went) on to sit in his car, in his office, at coffee break, at lunch, in his office, in his car, at dinner, and in front of the television set, and after lying in a warm bath for awhile, (went) on to lie in bed."[6]

Today, however, many American businessmen run several miles at the track before breakfast. Or they may put in a few fast sets at the racquetball court at lunch or work out for several hours at the gym before settling in front of the television set. And more and more people are casting aside some misconceptions about the value of exercise in slimming down and staying slim.

FALSE CONCEPTS

In the past, people didn't exercise because they were sold on one of a number of misconceptions about exercise. First, they believed that exercise would increase the appetite and make them eat more. But Fredrick J. Stare, M.D., and his colleagues at Harvard found that exercise does not stimulate the appetite in the overweight — only in the very lean. The researchers also discovered that if you exercise until you are exhausted, you lose your appetite for a while.[7]

Though such fears are groundless, women often avoided physical activity because they thought they would develop a masculine build.[8] And men and women kept from exercising because they felt they had to join a club or buy special and expensive exercising equipment. Yet none is necessary. You can exercise without leaving your home; you can walk or run around the block; you can bicycle by yourself or with friends.

HOW EXERCISE HELPS

"The value of exercise is over and above the cost of the activity," according to Dr. Judith Stern of the University of California, Davis.[9] In some people, exercise combined with a low-calorie diet not only burns up calories and often reduces the appetite but also speeds up the chemical processes in the body so that weight is lost more efficiently.[10]

Experiments at the Exercise Physiology Laboratory of the University of Louisville, Kentucky, showed that cutting calories and exercising not only reduced the proportion of body fat more than either could alone, but they also reduced blood cholesterol and high-density lipoproteins![11]

Exercise benefits the body's metabolism and even its bones. A pair of St. Louis researchers observed that exercise mobilized fat and spared the body's protein.[12] Other studies indicated that bones will remain strong during aging when people exercise regularly.[13]

THE EXERCISE FOR YOU

What kind of exercise is best? Physical fitness leaders suggest a "regular activity that utilizes many parts of the body. The activity should be vigorous enough to tax the power of the muscles and should be done long enough and strenuously enough to produce a sense of healthful fatigue."[14]

This "regular" activity may be a sport or a program of exercises. The problem is matching the vigor of the exercise with your physical condition. And that's where your doctor comes in.

Before beginning a strenuous exercise program — especially if you haven't engaged in any sort of physical conditioning for some years — check with your family doctor and have a complete physical examination. No physical condition, other than one that confines you to bed, will prevent you from doing some sort of exercise. And after he or she examines you, your doctor should have a good idea of what exercise level is right for you.

If you want to judge your physical condition for yourself, get a fitness calculator from the US Government.[15] With a fitness calculator, you can determine your fitness rating in 15 minutes. If you are past middle age, get the US Government Printing Office's pamphlet *The Fitness Challenge in the Later Years.*[16] The pamphlet will help you assess your fitness level and choose an exercise program designed to raise that level. Another way to help you choose an exercise program is to consult the *Fitness Fact Book.*[17] The *Fitness Fact Book* is a handy guide to sports and exercises. It ranks physical activities by a dozen criteria, including the number of calories expended as well as convenience and sociability.

Once you have decided on a particular sport, be sure to start slowly. If you plan to get back to basketball, try shooting baskets first, then build up your wind by jogging a little. And be realistic. Riding from hole to hole in a golf cart is not much exercise. Walking through 18 holes will rack up four to five miles of exercise.

Dr. Konishi singles out six exercises and lists them in order by the amount of energy expended: walking, bicycling, stepping, swimming, jogging, and running.[18]

Walking is a great activity because you can do it alone or with someone, in just about any weather and on any terrain. You can walk at home, at work, or on trips. In fact, in *The Complete Book of Walking,* Charles Kuntzleman provides 27 walking tours of cities from New York to San Diego.[19]

Bicycling, especially at a racing clip, is also a good exercise, but one that is limited by weather and terrain. Again, start slowly and gradually increase speed and distance.

Stepping can be done anywhere that a 12-inch high step or bench is available. To step, you lift one foot at a time onto the bench, stand fully erect, and then lower yourself one foot at a time. In addition to improving cardiovascular fitness, this exercise is great for leg and derriere muscles.

Swimming requires participation by just about every skeletal muscle of the body, and it gives the heart and lungs a good workout. But it has its drawbacks in terms of place and time. So try to find a good indoor pool, Olympic or regulation size. Then, pick a time when the water is not churning with kids, so you can travel unhampered from one end of the pool to the other. Begin with the sidestroke, if necessary, and build up your endurance from a couple of pool lengths to 10, 15, 20. Increase to at least a half mile or a mile. And never swim alone.

Despite its advantages, jogging is not an all-body exercise. It challenges the heart and some leg and lower abdominal muscles, but it does little for other muscles of the body.

A prerequisite to jogging is a good pair of running shoes. Select a pair that has soft, nonirritating upper material, durable soles, and adequate toe room. Check to see that the heels are a half-inch higher than the toes and that they are well padded.

Not required is a heavy jogging suit or rubberized clothing. Such outerwear can be expensive, and it can promote excessive sweating.

At first, you probably won't be able to jog a full mile. So measure off a one-mile course and cover the distance in a combination of jogging and fast walking. Gradually build up to jogging the full distance; then start decreasing your time to go a mile—from 15 minutes to about eight.

Before each jog, warm up with a few stretching exercises. Try to jog a mile or more at least three times a week, and jog on grass or earth, not pavement.[20]

Running is more vigorous than jogging. And to get off on the right foot, you might want to consult copies of *The Runner's Almanac, The Running Book,* and *The Complete Book of Marathon Running,* by the Editors of CONSUMER GUIDE® and published by Beekman House/Crown, New York.

If solo activities are not for you and you want to return to team sports, go to your local Y, a community center, or a park fieldhouse. Any of these facilities is a good place to get back into the swing of things. There, you can get instruction in improving your basketball game or your volleyball smash.

But whether you want to be on a team or go it alone, make sure you exercise regularly. Make an appointment with yourself and keep it.

FIGURE CONTROL

Exercises can help control your figure by enlarging some parts, slimming others, and firming. Here are some good books for each.

Flatten Your Stomach, by the Editors of CONSUMER GUIDE®, Beekman House/Crown, New York, 1979.
Shaping Your Legs, Arms, and Bust, by Ann Dugan and the Editors of CONSUMER GUIDE®, Beekman House/Crown, New York, 1980.
Slimming Your Hips, Thighs, and Butt, by Ann Dugan and the Editors of CONSUMER GUIDE®, Beekman House/Crown, New York, 1980.
New 7-Day Program to Flatten Your Stomach, by Ann Dugan and the Editors of CONSUMER GUIDE®, Publications International, Ltd., Skokie, IL, 1983.
New 7-Day Program for Slimming Your Hips and Thighs, by Ann Dugan and the Editors of CONSUMER GUIDE®, Publications International, Ltd., Skokie, IL, 1983.

EXERCISE PLANS

If you want to do more than select one activity, or work on more than one part of your anatomy, you might consider an exercise plan. There are some good ones available now.

One of the most popular is in TV star Richard Simmons' book, *Never-Say-Diet.*[21] It starts with breathing exercises and then moves on to graded exercise plans.

Equally popular is *Jane Fonda's Workout Book.*[22] The workout begins with a warm-up and then has plans for various parts of the body (arms, waist, and so forth), for various levels of fitness (beginner's, advanced, special problems). You may want to delete her views of diet and her statements about video display terminals, and add her voice instructions from a record, cassette, or video cassette you can buy at record shops.

Many more details about exercising, sports, conditioning, and preventing athletic injuries are in the less-jazzy but more detailed book, *Sportsfitness for Women*[23] by Sandra Rosenzweig, a California journalist who jumps rope for an hour a day. She not only tells you how-to-do-it, but also evaluates each activity and helps you design your own exercise/sports program. CONSUMER GUIDE® highly recommends this book for women who want to get, or are already, active.

Another good exercise book for women is *The Sexibody Diet & Exercise Program*[24]; the diet is rated elsewhere in this book. The exercises are oriented by area of the body.

Or, take up dancing or dancercising or jazz dancing. Call it what you will, the idea is to use music to inspire your body into motion.

No, you don't have to audition. You don't even have to know how to dance. This is not the kind of dancing that you do at a ball or prom. Instead, this is vigorous, graceful exercising to music, inspired by disco dancing; it not only gets the blood moving, but the muscles firmed up. For more on the subject, see *The Complete Guide to Aerobic Dancing* by Beth A. Kuntzleman and the Editors of CONSUMER GUIDE®, Beekman House/Crown, New York, 1980.

You can also exercise at your desk, in your car, while working in the kitchen. Tips on these activities can be found in *No Sweat Exercise Program,* CONSUMER GUIDE®, Skokie, IL, 1981.

For a 10-minute calisthentics program, you might check out *10-Minute Total Shape-Up,* by the Editors of CONSUMER GUIDE®, Beekman House/Crown, New York, 1981.

Traditional exercise manuals can be obtained from the US Government, the YMCA, or Diet Workshop.[25,26,27] But for a more exotic kind of exercise, you might look at books on yoga. More and more Europeans and Americans are turning to yoga as a way of getting and staying physically fit. It has a built-in reward; the more svelte you become, the more advanced positions you can assume. Other Eastern traditions are also becoming popular, especially t'ai chi ch'uan. These meditative exercises help relax the mind and make the body supple, but they do not burn many calories.

Another inducement to exercise regularly is to have a "master plan." And that's just what Dr. Solomon and his sister Evalee Harrison did in their 1976 book. In *Dr. Solomon's Proven Master Plan for Total Body Fitness and Maintenance,*[28] Harrison, a member of the staff of the Department of Human Nutrition at the University of California, Berkeley, and diet doctor Solomon, illustrate various exercises and point out the areas of the body that have become "frozen" from disuse.

In their 1976 bestseller, *Total Fitness in 30 Minutes a Week,*[29] Laverne Morehouse and Leonard Gross wrote that the key to losing weight was "to use 300 activity calories a day above your normal level." That requires some exercise but also much cutting back on food. They also divulged the key to being fit: a slow heartbeat at rest and a slow heartbeat during exertion. That requires physical training. "The primary goal of your training will be to lower your resting heart rate 5 to 10 beats a minute, *regardless* of what it was at the outset," wrote Morehouse and Gross. They emphasized that "Total Fitness" is not exercising but a way of getting you fit to exercise. One way is their 30-minute-a-week program, which consists of leaning forward pushups, modified sit-ups, hopping, and limbering movements.

And an exercise plan fit for the boardroom is contained in *The Executive's Handbook of Balanced Physical Fitness*.[30] The handbook features 18 dancelike, balancing exercises staged from easy to difficult. In his *You Can Be Physically Perfect, Powerfully Strong*,[31] Vic Boff, America's most famous exponent of buff winter bathing, gets back to the basics with traditional calisthenics and weight-lifting drills. *Slimnastics*[32] by Pamela Nottidge and Diana Lamplugh, presents a course of exercises that start gently and work up in vigor. And so does *How to Keep Slender and Fit After 30*.[33] Written by 57-year-old exercise instructor Bonnie Prudden, the book provides creative exercises that vary from mild to strenuous. It also includes "sexercises" which can enhance your sexual activities. As author Prudden writes, "An attractive body is only one of the requisites for more pleasurable and meaningful love-making. Another is your ability to make that body function as it can and should."

Abraham I. Friedman, M.D., sees sex as a means rather than an end. In *How Sex Can Keep You Slim*,[34] he asserts that sexual activity can slim you in two ways: by using energy and by keeping your mind off food.

PEPSTEP

In 1979, Weight Watchers International, Inc. (WWI), kept pace with the growing exercise movement by adding PEPSTEP to its weight loss regimen. It's too bad PEPSTEP hasn't caught on. It is an excellent exercise plan that was designed by Lenore R. Zohman, M.D., chairman of the Committee on Exercise of the New York Heart Association and originator of the Cardiopulmonary Rehabilitation program at New York's Montefiore Hospital and Medical Center. And it intends to help weight watchers lose weight, decrease their risk of illness, and lose inches.

With PEPSTEP, a dieter has a choice of two Personal Exercise Plans—one involving brisk walking; the other, stair-climbing.

The PEPSTEP walking program requires that you stretch your legs for one hour a day, five days a week. But, since you can't stride through deep snow, "it is not quite the sport for all seasons," says WWI.

WWI says you can fulfill the stair-climbing exercise at work or at home. All you need is access to at least two flights of stairs and enough level space at the top of each flight to allow a brisk walk for 100 feet. Altogether, the WWI stair-climbing program requires less than half an hour a day, five days a week for ten weeks.

During the ten weeks, the PEPSTEPper gradually increases the number of flights he climbs until he can manage 24 short flights (eight to ten steps) or 15 long flights (13 steps). But he does not scale all of them at once. He climbs only one or two flights at a time to avoid breathlessness, and he takes no more than 100 steps per minute. He follows each climb by walking for about a minute; then, he repeats the climb.

Descending a flight of stairs burns up only a third as much energy as ascending it; therefore the descent, like walking, is considered a rest between climbs.

In the PEPSTEP stair-climbing program, the climb-rest sequence forms a pattern. For example, in the first week of PEPSTEP, the climber walks up a total of four flights at home in an up-and-down pattern. He climbs up one flight, walks around on the floor, then walks down. He repeats the pattern twice. Finally, he climbs the fourth flight but does not walk around; he just returns to ground level.

If the climber is at work, his first week of PEPSTEP calls for two consecutive two-flight climbs. He climbs two flights and walks for a minute. He climbs another two flights, walks for another minute, then descends two flights.

The PEPSTEP stair-climbing program adds one or two flights each week. When the climber has reached the ten-week level, he moves on to the fitness maintenance plan, which does not change the number of flights climbed—just the number of times to climb them each week. If the PEPSTEPper has achieved his goal weight, he need take to the stairs only three times a week. If not, he should have five stair-climbing sessions a week. This is an excellent program for city dwellers.

EXERCISING AWAY FATTENING FOOD

To burn off the 209 calories in a chocolate bar, you'd have to walk 40 minutes, jog 21 minutes, or swim 25 minutes. To get rid of a martini's 140 calories, you'd have to walk 27 minutes or jog 14 minutes. You'd have to bicycle 52 minutes to burn up the 345 calories of a waffle with butter and syrup, and a slice of pecan pie would cost you almost an hour and a half of swimming. And that's just a sample. At the end of this chapter, CONSUMER GUIDE® presents the exercise equivalents of certain fattening foods. Excerpted from Dr. Konishi's book *Exercise Equivalents of Food*,[35] the charts tell you how much time in minutes you would have to spend walking, bicycling, stepping, swimming, and jogging to expend the calories in some popular foods. The charts are a handy reference, but only the book provides all the information you need. It also helps you decide how much pedaling or swimming (or whatever) to do a day to lose a given number of pounds.

THOSE COMMERCIAL EXERCISE SALONS

In some cities they are known as health clubs; in others, body shops. They are commercial salons that sell you a series of "figure-improving" treatments that often include exercises. Too many overweight innocents have signed up to pay the $500 annual membership fee only to find the exercise facilities nonexistent, but ultraviolet tanning lamps abundant.

Many health clubs are legitimate. Others are frankly commercial grab-the-money-and-run operations that change ownership as fast as they change the towels. The unscrupulous ones advertise some free exercise time but provide only a five-minute tour of the facilities, a high-pressure sell, and inviting "discount offers."[36]

CONSUMER GUIDE® advises you to tread carefully when selecting a gym or an exercise salon. If a YMCA, YWCA or community center is convenient, try it. If not, ask friends for their recommendations. Visit several facilities yourself but don't sign anything until you're sure of what you're signing. If you feel you have been taken, consult the Better Business Bureau or the Consumers' Fraud Bureau in your state.

Exercise Equivalents of Food Calories in Minutes

ALCOHOLIC BEVERAGES	weight gm.	calories kcal.	walking min.	bicycling min.	stepping min.	swimming min.	jogging min.
Ale 8 oz. glass	230	100	19	15	13	12	10
Apricot brandy 1 cordial glass	20	65	12	10	9	8	7
Beer 8 oz. glass	240	115	22	18	15	14	12
Benedictine 1 cordial glass	20	70	13	11	9	8	7
Brandy-California 1 brandy glass	30	75	14	12	10	9	8
Brandy-cognac 1 brandy pony	30	75	14	12	10	9	8
Cider, fermented 6 oz. glass	180	70	13	10	9	8	7
Cordial-Anisette 1 cordial glass	20	75	14	12	10	9	8
Crème de menthe 1 cordial glass	20	68	13	10	9	8	7
Curacao 1 cordial glass	20	68	13	10	9	8	7
Daiquiri 1 cocktail glass	100	125	24	19	17	15	13
Eggnog 4 oz. punch cup	120	335	64	53	45	39	34
Gin, dry 1½ oz., 1 jigger	43	105	20	16	14	12	11
Gin rickey 1 glass	120	150	29	23	20	18	15
High ball 8 oz. glass	240	165	32	25	22	19	17
Manhattan, cocktail 3½ oz.	100	165	32	25	22	19	17
Martini, cocktail 3½ oz.	100	140	27	22	19	16	14

One ounce has been rounded to equal 30 grams.
Values based on data from C.F. Church and H.N. Church *Food Values of Portions Commonly Used.* 11th ed. (Philadelphia J.B. Lippincott, 1970): B.K. Watt and A.L. Merrill, *Composition of Foods.* USDA Handbook No. 8 (Washington, D.C., 1963): USDA *Nutritive Value of Foods,* Home and Garden Bulletin No. 72. USDA, ARS (Washington, D.C., 1971) Calories listed are in kilocalories.

Exercise Equivalents of Food Calories in Minutes

ALCOHOLIC BEVERAGES	weight	calories	walking	bicycling	stepping	swimming	jogging
	gm.	kcal.	min.	min.	min.	min.	min.
Mint julep 10 oz. glass	300	215	41	33	29	25	22
Muscatelle, port 3½ oz. glass	100	160	31	25	21	19	16
Old fashioned 4 oz. glass	120	180	35	28	24	21	18
Planter's punch 1 glass	100	175	34	37	23	21	18
Rum 1 jigger, 1½ oz.	45	105	20	16	14	12	11
Sauterne, California 3½ oz. glass	100	85	16	13	11	10	9
Scotch 1 jigger, 1½ oz.	45	105	20	16	14	12	11
Sherry 2 oz. glass	60	85	16	13	11	10	9
Tom Collins 10 oz. glass	300	180	35	28	24	21	18
Vermouth, French 3½ oz. glass	100	105	20	16	14	12	11
Vermouth, Italian 3½ oz. glass	100	170	33	26	23	20	17
Whiskey, bourbon, rye 1 jigger, 1½ oz.	45	120	23	18	16	14	12
Wine, Burgundy 4 oz. glass	120	110	21	16	15	13	11
Wine, champagne 4 oz. glass	120	85	16	13	11	10	9
Wine, port 4 oz. glass	120	210	40	32	28	25	21
CANDY							
Almond bar, chocolate 1 bar, 1¼ oz.	38	310	60	46	41	36	31
Butterscotch 5 pieces (90 pieces/lb.)	25	100	19	15	13	12	10
Candy, hard (all flavors) 1 oz.	30	110	21	17	15	13	11
Caramel 1 oz.	30	118	23	18	16	14	12
Chocolate cream 1 piece (35 lb.)	13	50	10	8	7	6	5

Exercise Equivalents of Food Calories in Minutes

	weight	calories	walking	bicycling	stepping	swimming	jogging
CANDY	gm.	kcal.	min.	min.	min.	min.	min.
Chocolate fudge 1¼" square	30	118	23	18	16	14	12
Chocolate mint 1 small (45/lb.)	10	40	8	6	5	5	4
Forever Yours 1¾ oz.	52	192	37	29	26	23	19
Gum drops 8 small	10	33	6	5	4	4	3
Hershey bar 1⅜ oz.	40	209	40	31	27	25	21
Hershey chocolate kisses 7 pieces	28	152	29	23	20	18	15
Jelly beans 10 beans	28	66	13	10	9	8	7
Lollypops 1 med.	28	108	21	16	14	13	11
Mars bar 1⅜ oz.	40	212	40	32	28	25	21
Marshmallow 1 ave. (60/lb.)	8	25	5	4	3	3	3
Milky Way 1¾ oz.	52	192	37	29	26	23	19
Mints, cream 10 mints	15	53	10	8	7	6	5
Mr. Goodbar 1⅝ oz.	48	250	48	38	32	29	25
Peanut brittle 2½ X 2½ X ⅜"	25	110	21	16	15	13	11
Peanut butter, chocolate covered 1 oz.	30	135	26	21	18	15	14
Snickers 1⅝ oz.	48	174	33	26	23	20	17
Three Musketeers 1¹⁵⁄₁₆ oz.	58	207	39	31	27	24	21
ICE CREAM							
Ice cream ⅙ qt.: 5 rd. tbs.	90	186	36	28	25	22	19
Ice cream bar, choc. coated 1 bar	60	195	37	30	26	23	20

Exercise Equivalents of Food Calories in Minutes

	weight	calories	walking	bicycling	stepping	swimming	jogging
ICE CREAM	gm.	kcal.	min.	min.	min.	min.	min.
Ice cream bar, sherbet coated 1 bar	60	96	18	15	13	12	10
Ice cream cone 1 dip	72	160	31	24	21	19	16
Ice cream sandwich	75	208	40	32	28	25	21
Ice cream sundae 2 dips	75	326	63	49	43	39	33
Ice milk ⅙ qt.: 5 round tbs.	90	137	26	21	18	16	14
Ice milk bar, choc. coated 1 bar	60	144	27	22	19	17	14
DESSERTS							
Banana split	300	594	114	89	79	71	59
Boston cream pie 1 serving	110	332	64	50	44	39	33
Brownies, with nuts 1 piece (2″ x 2″ x ¾″)	30	146	28	22	19	17	15
Cakes:							
Angel food 1 piece, 1/12 of 10″ cake	53	135	26	20	18	16	14
Caramel with icing 1 piece, 1/12 of 9″ cake	55	208	40	31	28	24	21
Chocolate with icing 1 piece (2″ x 3″ x 2″)	55	205	39	31	27	24	21
Cupcake with icing 1 (2½″ diam.)	36	130	25	20	17	16	13
Fruitcake 1 slice (3″ x 3″ x ½″)	40	152	29	23	20	18	15
Plain cake with icing 1 piece, 1/12 of 9″ cake	50	186	36	28	25	22	19
Pound cake 1 slice (3″ x 3″ x ½″)	30	142	27	21	19	17	14
White cake 1 piece, 1/12 of 9″ cake	50	186	35	28	24	22	19
Cake with ice cream 1/12 of 9″, 1 dip	110	301	57	45	39	36	30

Exercise Equivalents of Food Calories in Minutes

DESSERTS	weight	calories	walking	bicycling	stepping	swimming	jogging
	gm.	kcal.	min.	min.	min.	min.	min.
Cheesecake 1 slice, 1/12 of 9″ cake	50	160	30	25	21	19	16
Custard, baked 1 custard	157	205	39	31	27	24	21
Doughnut 1 average	32	125	24	19	17	15	13
Doughnut, jelly center 1 average	65	226	44	34	30	27	23
Eclair or cream puff 1 average	105	296	57	44	39	35	30
Ice cream 1 dip	60	115	22	17	15	14	12
Jello, plain 1 serving (5/pkg.)	65	65	13	10	9	8	7
Jello, with whipped cream 1 serving	80	117	23	18	16	14	12
Parfait, coffee 1 serving	107	258	50	39	34	30	26
Pies (1/6 of 9″ pie) Banana custard	160	355	68	53	47	42	36
Butterscotch	160	430	83	64	57	51	43
Chocolate chiffon	160	525	101	79	70	62	53
Chocolate meringue	150	380	73	57	50	45	38
Coconut custard	155	365	70	55	48	43	37
Fruit pies	160	400	77	60	53	47	40
Fruit pies, ala mode	220	515	99	77	68	62	52
Pecan	160	670	129	100	89	78	67
Lemon chiffon	107	335	64	50	45	39	34
Pumpkin	150	320	62	48	42	38	32
Popsicle	95	70	14	10	9	8	7
Pudding, bread with raisins 3/4 cup	165	315	61	47	42	37	32
Pudding, chocolate 1/2 cup	130	192	36	29	25	23	19
Rice pudding with raisins 3/4 cup	145	212	41	32	28	25	21

From Exercise Equivalents of Foods, a Practical Guide for the Overweight, by *Frank Konishi:* Copyright© 1974 by *Southern Illinois University Press.*
Reprinted by permission of Southern Illinois University Press.

Psyching It Off

*Y*ou know why you weigh more than you want to, or than you should—you ate too much over the years. Now, you want to lose the excess weight overnight.

It never happens that fast. You have to be patient. You have to cut back on the amount of calories you eat, and at the same time make sure you are getting enough nutrients.

That's the mechanical problem and its solution.

Your emotions and your psychological needs are what causes the mechanical problem—putting too much food into your mouth.

So, it is not enough merely to diet. You also have to change your bad old eating habits and replace them with good "thin" ones. It is not easy, but it can be done. It takes lots of motivation, of wanting, *really* wanting to lose weight (not reacting to others wanting you to lose weight). It takes lots of psychological pain, because you have used food for comfort for so long.

Many people need a health professional or a group to help them "get their head straight." Some people, on the other hand, are more successful by themselves. In fact, studies at Columbia University that were reported in 1982[1] indicate that about two thirds of the total number of persons who try, on their own, to lose weight and change their eating habits, succeed. The combined statistics of two studies show that these successful dieters lost, on the average, more than 34 pounds each, and stayed within a few pounds of their new weight for over 11 years.

Dr. Maria Simonson, director of the Weight Clinic at The Johns Hopkins Medical Institutions, listed some of the many psychological factors associated with obesity that have to be overcome if weight is to be taken off and kept off. The overweight, she wrote, "are influenced by non-nutritional needs for food: feelings of boredom, loneliness, insecurity, inadequacy, fear, and hostility, unsatisfied sexual urges, and frustrations in job achievements. Eating for them may be a tranquilizer, a reward....Some persons overeat as a defense against unwanted responsibilities and activities, fearing that too much would be required of their thinner selves."[2]

Sandra Edwards, a former 220-pounder, wrote in her book, *Too Much is Not Enough*,[3] that "Food is a lousy lover." However, "food was easier to get along with than a lover. With food, gratification was immediate. Gratifying sexual experiences required someone else, they took time and they were risky....Food was the excuse I used to avoid knowing a lover."

Another observer of overweight people's feelings, New York social worker Mildred Klingman, noted, "Somewhere inside, being fat was more important to you than anything else in the world. Whatever you needed, whatever it was you got from being fat, far outweighed the benefits of being thin. When that equation shifts in your head, you will be able to lose weight. When you want something more than you want to be fat, and when getting it requires that you lose weight, you will lose weight. When losing weight is its own reward, you will lose weight."[4]

Family social scientist Francie M. Berg, of North Dakota, in her book for teenagers offers advice that is appropriate for adults as well. "Habits are not easy to change. Did you ever try to stop chewing fingernails, smoking, or sucking your thumb? Many people try off and on all their lives to change such habits as these," she wrote in *How to be Slimmer, Trimmer, & Happier.*[5] "The three most serious eating habits of overeaters are usually thinking too much about food, eating too often, and not being able to stop eating once started. Taken together these habits mean such people are eating, or wishing they were, much of the time. Their lives become an emotional tangle of wanting to eat, resolving not to eat, and feeling guilty for eating."

Berg offers her Action plan for becoming "Slimmer, trimmer, and happier…"

A—begin an aerobic exercise program
C—begin a creative project
T—touch others through a helping activity
I—improve your identity, like yourself
O—omit no meals
N—no snacking, and practice forgetting food.

Fat people psychologically split their bodies from their minds. Sociologist Marcia Millman, of the University of California at Santa Cruz, explained, "Fat people often think of themselves solely in terms of the 'neck up.' Their bodies are disowned, alienated, foreign, perhaps stubbornly present but not truly a part of the real self. The body is regarded as an unwanted appendage of the head-self [and] is a source of pleasure only in the act of doing the very thing, eating, that creates the alienation."[6]

Former fatty Carole Livingston, in her confessions, wrote, "The first step in losing weight isn't to read all the diet books you can find. It isn't going to the doctor. It isn't filling your house with low-calorie beverages and throwing out all the pretzels. The first step is admitting to yourself that you need to reduce."[7] This means, she explained, you have decided "to take your life in your own hands. You have made the decision to have control over food and not the other way around…*you* are the boss now."

More and more, *control* is the issue taught to dieters. "I have come to see that my diet has less to do with weight than with making decisions and choices, accepting and rejecting, taking control—more to do with growing up than growing thin," wrote Joan Scobey.[8]

Nancy L. Bryan, Ph.D., explained that "losing weight is the only self-improvement endeavor in which achieving the goal requires not only the decision to stop the undesirable behavior but also the passage of a good deal of time. A smoker is an ex-smoker the moment he puts down his last cigarette…a drinker becomes a teetotaler merely by abstaining from one moment to the next. An overweight person, on the other hand, has to make that same kind of heroic choice, then wait however long it takes to lose all the excess weight before claiming success."[9]

Family counselor Eda LeShan suggests that dreams can give you special insights to yourself and your fight against fat. "Dreams," she wrote, "are another form of conversation with oneself." Most important of all, dreams can reveal anxieties about dieting, about food, and your ambivalence about losing weight. But you may have to work at remembering last night's dreams. As this facility sharpens you'll notice that certain themes repeat themselves. You'll also discover that some dreams are wish-fulfillments, others express feelings you dare not express when you are awake.[10]

Another kind of insight dieters need deals with self-sabotage. This refers to the hidden need for failure inside each of us. Meridee Merzer offers these ways to combat self-sabotage:

1. Accept the fact that weight loss doesn't occur consistently. It's natural to lose weight one week and not the next.
2. It is not realistic to expect perfect dieting every day.
3. Sit down and decide what you want from your weight loss.[11]

Once you have achieved some personal insight, you have to work to change your bad eating habits to good new ones. The most popular school of techniques used to change habits continues to be behavior modification. Various combinations of these techniques are being taught by the big diet organizations such as Weight Watchers, Diet Workshop, and TOPS.

CHANGE THE EATING ENVIRONMENT

The first successful program to modify behavior to lose weight was devised by Richard Stuart, M.D., at the University of Michigan. Today, Dr. Stuart is psychological director and director of motivational research at Weight Watchers International and professor of psychology at the University of Utah. But in 1967, he was at the University of Michigan.

Then, though eight of Dr. Stuart's patients each lost more than 20 pounds over a one-year period,[12] he didn't know what he had discovered. Psychiatrist Albert J. Stunkard gives some perspective: "Stuart had no thought of breaking any records. And because at that time he didn't know a great deal about obesity, he did not at first realize how remarkable his results really were."[13]

Later, Dr. Stuart did more research on behavior modification among the obese and wrote what is still the best guidebook on the subject, *Slim Chance in a Fat World.*[14] In that book, he said people must understand "that environmental forces have a greater influence upon the amount we eat and the food we eat than do inner forces like hunger."

In other words, many people are prompted to overeat not because they are hungry but because their family pushes food, or because they are tempted by food ads on television or in magazines, or some other reason.

Dr. Stuart's idea was to make overweight people aware of troublesome eating situations and learn to get the upper hand to make changes where they are needed—"in the situation instead of in the person."

THE START OF A HABIT

Eating habits start forming a day or two after birth. And bottle-feeding may be the most crucial factor. According to some doctors, "bottle-feeding may...predispose infants to obesity."[15] Researchers in Great Britain in 1974 weighed 250 six-week-old babies who had all been born normal after full-term pregnancies. Of those fed by bottle, 60 percent were overweight; of those fed by breast, only 19 percent were overweight. Another British study found that 40 percent of 300 bottle-fed babies were overweight.

The theory behind these findings is that bottle-feeding does not provide the solace that breast-feeding does. The vicious cycle leading to obesity begins with the unsatisfying bottle: anxiety provokes eating, which provokes anxiety.

Also, the breast-fed baby apparently gets an eating cue in the milk its mother provides. While nursing, a baby removes the richest portion of the milk with the highest fat content in the breast, then stops.[16] By this natural mechanism, the breast-fed baby learns when to stop feeding, and this knowledge presumably carries over into childhood and adulthood.

Malcolm Martin, M.D., of Georgetown University Medical Center, maintains that "those predisposed to becoming obese, as a result of bottle feeding, establish the wrong kind of control feedback mechanism and henceforth tend to require more calories to satisfy their, as it were, hunger feeling. They are continuously set in sort of a gear which stimulates them to take in more calories than they actually expend."[17]

BAD TABLE HABITS

Besides starting their babies on bottles, parents may be leading their children to obesity by fostering bad table habits. One of the worst arises from the command, "You will not leave this table until you have cleaned your plate!" This rule often forces children to eat even after they are full. Another bad habit starts with the command, "Eat, you'll feel better!" This fosters the habit of eating to allay emotional tension and promote well-being. Such a delusion is often reinforced by the parents' own habits.

"Long after we've forgotten what it is like to be a child, we continue to follow the food habits we learned at an early age. In childhood we learn not only the *kind* of food we prefer but also the eating *circumstances* we require: where, when, how, and with whom we will eat," says Richard Stiller, author of *Habits: How We Get Them, Why We Keep Them, How We Kick Them.*[18]

COMPULSIVE NIBBLING

Food habits — not hunger pangs — make people fat. And compulsive or unconscious nibbling is just one food habit.

According to New York psychiatrist Leonard Crammer, if you overeat, you are obsessive-compulsive and eat addictively. You also have poor self-esteem. And "because in your eyes you are repulsive anyway, 'Why fight it? It won't help.' Your psychological problems, as unresolved as the alcoholic's, generally relate to the void of love or whatever else is lacking in your emotional diet. Food is your substitute. Or you may be the compulsive dupe of bad habits who must cater to your appetites for sensuous dishes and drink...you eat for sheer pleasure."[19]

In *Habits,* Richard Stiller writes, "The difference between human eating, which sees food simultaneously as a symbol, a cultural or religious experience, and a sensual experience, as well as a necessity, and the eating behavior of animals, which is limited to fulfilling survival needs, is the difference between appetite and hunger.[20]

The sad truth is that since fat people seldom feel real bodily hunger, they seldom are satisfied by what they eat. An experiment by Stanley Schachter, M.D., of Columbia University supported this contention.

Dr. Schachter invited four groups of people, two lean and two fat, to his laboratories to evaluate several kinds of crackers. They were specifically instructed not to eat before they came. One lean group and one fat group were given sandwiches when they arrived and were told to eat so their stomachs would be full for the test. After they ate the sandwiches, they were presented with various kinds of crackers and told to eat as many as they wished to rate them. The other two groups evaluated the crackers on empty stomachs.

What they did not know was that the "cracker testing" was a sham. Dr. Schacter's real purpose was to compare the eating patterns of lean and fat people. As it turned out, the lean people who had not been offered the sandwiches first ate far more crackers than those who had first filled up on sandwiches. However, the fat people ate the same number of crackers whether or not they had eaten sandwiches previously.[21]

The researchers' conclusion was that the obese do not know when they are hungry or when they are full; thus, an empty stomach is not the reason they eat. They may eat because they are bored or lonely. Dr. Stuart gives an example: "Nighttime eaters often eat alone because other members of their family are either occupied or asleep. They often feel let down at the prospect of long nighttime hours with little stimulation....They may also find that they are particularly bored and lonely at night when there are fewer activities that can compete with food for their attention."[22]

"That compulsive eating is overwhelmingly a woman's problem suggests that it has something to do with the experience of being female in our society," believes Susie Orbach, cofounder of the London Women's Therapy Center and author of *Fat Is a Feminist Issue*.[23] "Getting fat can thus be understood as a definite and purposeful act; it is a directed, conscious or unconscious, challenge to sex-role stereotyping and culturally defined experience of womanhood."

Being fat is a woman's way of defying male society that expects her to be "the perfect mom, sweetheart, maid, and whore," maintains Orbach. "Many women remain fat as a way of neutralizing their sexual identity in the eyes of others who are important to them as their life progresses. In this way they can hope to be taken seriously in their working lives outside the home." As one woman told her, "The fat made me one of the boys."

CHANGING BEHAVIOR

Psychologist William G. Shipman has found in his treatment of overweight women that teaching them how to change their behavior is more successful than group psychotherapy. In terms of weight loss, women in behavior therapy lost twice as much as those in psychotherapy.[24] The women were taught by Dr. Shipman to follow six principles:

1. Remove temptations. Keep food out of sight and store a minimum amount of food in kitchen cabinets and pantry. Never store any favorite

foods. Keep on hand only those foods that require preparation before they can be eaten.
2. Make illegal eating unpleasant. Deliberately overeat your favorite food until you are disgusted with it. Or think about something unpleasant as you eat your favorite treat so that eventually you will associate the two.
3. Learn to relax. Remove the tensions that induce overeating.
4. Divert the eating compulsion. When you feel you just have to have that piece of cake, go out for a walk, chew gum, or do something else.
5. If you absolutely must eat something immediately, reach for celery or something else that is safe.
6. Learn self-control. Practice self-control in small ways, such as: stop eating for two minutes during a meal; learn to eat only when sitting down; limit your eating time.

By making use of these principles, the women in behavior therapy developed techniques to keep from overeating. And the same techniques could be adapted to withstand pressures from family members and from daily living. These new techniques showed women how to change their behavior patterns, and many women continued to lose weight even after their group disbanded.

In September 1975, Diet Workshop compared the weight lost by members in the regular program against the weight lost by members on behavior modification. Members on behavior modification lost 55 percent more weight than those on the regular program after six months. Regular dieters lost 13 pounds, on the average. Those who practiced behavior-modification techniques lost an average of 23½ pounds.[25]

Albert Stunkard, M.D., former head of psychiatry at Stanford University, reached similar conclusions after studying TOPS. He found that members taught by professionals to modify their behavior stayed with TOPS longer, and lost more weight, than did TOPS members who followed the conventional program.[26]

Psychologist G. Terence Wilson of Rutgers University, recently concluded that "behavioral treatment has been significantly more effective than alternate methods in producing weight reduction on a short-term basis....Behavioral treatment also appears to result in a lower drop-out rate and significantly fewer negative side-effects."[27]

LEARNING ABOUT YOUR EATING HABITS

You don't have to join a group to change your eating habits. You can change them on your own. Before you start, however, you should find out which aspect of your eating behavior needs the most work.

A good way to find out about your eating behavior, says Dr. Stuart, is to keep a diary recording when you eat and under what circumstances plus your feelings at eating times. With the diary, you soon will be able to recognize your eating patterns. Then, you can begin to modify them, if necessary.

Keeping an eating record is the cornerstone of the Learn to Be Thin 13-step program.[28] "Once you start keeping this record, you will be able to follow your diet in a way that will change your eating behavior and lead to a permanent thin you," says author Shirley Simon.

In his book *Forever Thin,* Theodore Isaac Rubin, M.D., tells you to get to know yourself by learning when you are most vulnerable to the problems that cause your obesity. He says most obese people are vulnerable during "periods of unusual excitement, aggravation, changes (of job, home, school, friends), physical sickness, boredom, parties, pregnancy, premenstrual periods, aloneness, loneliness, sexual excitement, any frustration, break-up of relationships, news of tragedy, unusual success or joy, examinations or any period of pressure, fatigue, overwork, contact with threatening people, contact with anger-provoking people, celebrations, being in restaurants."[29]

Frank J. Bruno, M.D., suggests eating in front of a portable mirror.[30] When you are alone, place a portable mirror in front of you so you can watch yourself eat. You'll notice whether you take big or small bites, whether your cheeks fill up, whether you wolf down your food or chew it endlessly. Then, make notes on your mannerisms. Some people say that when they use a mirror they see double chins they never saw before or notice how wan their complexions are, how fat their faces have become, how grossly they shovel food into their mouths. Dr. Bruno believes that if you see yourself eat, you'll discover things about yourself that will motivate you to change your eating behavior.

CHANGING YOUR EATING HABITS

Once you have discovered your eating habits, you can do something about changing them. And books on behavior modification offer many ways from which to choose.

Now, not all habit-changing techniques work for all people, but certainly some work for some people. CONSUMER GUIDE® suggests that if you try one of these techniques and it doesn't work, try another. You may well find one that works for you.

In *Slim Chance in a Fat World,* Dr. Stuart suggests these ten steps.[31]

1. Keep a record of the conditions under which you eat.
2. Manage the feelings that are related to eating.
3. Think through expected events of the day to translate obstacles into opportunities.
4. Control the availability of tempting foods.
5. Restrain your urge to eat.
6. Record what you plan to eat before you eat.
7. Control the amount you eat.
8. Control the size of the portion you take.
9. Build support for your successful actions.
10. Record your successes.

Edwin Bayrd presents 24 rules in *The Thin Game.*[32]

1. Shop only from a prepared list.
2. Shop only after eating.
3. Shop first for produce.
4. Keep a boring refrigerator.
5. Snackproof your shelves.

6. Never skip meals, especially breakfast.
7. Always eat in the same place.
8. Do nothing else when you eat.
9. Eat from a small plate, drink from a small glass.
10. Chew everything very carefully; never gulp your food.
11. Deliberately set your fork down between every other bite.
12. Come to the table last and leave first.
13. Never finish what you are served; never take seconds.
14. Eat only off your own plate.
15. Serve plates and portions, not family style.
16. Make food changes slowly.
17. Spoil (e.g., oversalt) foods that tempt too strongly.
18. When you are angry, drink water.
19. Plan to fail; prepare for slip-ups.
20. Horrify yourself to reinspire yourself.
21. Go to the bathroom when the "coffee wagon" comes.
22. Take a walk during commercials—and not to the kitchen.
23. Punish and reward yourself.
24. Enlist help from a friend or club or group.

Stiller's book lists five approaches to breaking a habit.[33]

1. Create a new, competing habit to take the place of the old one.
2. Wear out the old habit—repeat it until disgust and exhaustion weaken its hold.
3. Associate the bad habit with an unpleasant sensation or experience (aversion therapy).
4. Get used to an unpleasant stimulus, learn to tolerate it.
5. Change the setting of the habit or interrupt its sequence to disrupt its patterns.

Ronald Jay Cohen, Ph.D., a psychologist at New York University — Bellevue Medical Center, suggests preparing a "Reward List," naming things you'll like to have—a bottle of expensive perfume, perhaps, or a massage. From this list, you can select one item if, at the end of the week, your average caloric intake has stayed within limits. Dr. Cohen calls this "making a deal with yourself." And he cautions: "Do not make rewards contingent on weight loss! This is a major mistake that many weight-program leaders and therapists make early in weight-control programs. Making rewards contingent on weight loss in the beginning of treatment may be building into the program unnecessary feelings of frustration."[34]

The way to begin, according to Sandra Edwards (quoted earlier) is to start, and to take one day at a time. "Because food and you are not a trivial matter, it is important to be as kind to yourself as you would to a friend who has lost someone close," she wrote.[35] "I have been a fairly reliable friend to myself, partly because I knew that 25 years of using food to cope weren't going to be reprogrammed in a jiffy.... Life now, unclogged by overfeeding or thoughts about it, is more fully nourishing, more thoroughly satisfying than any food has ever been."

Some tips to start dieting, by removing temptations:

- "Give your remaining high-calorie foods to your neighbors, your favorite charity or your worst enemy"; or "throw them in the garbage!"
- "Resist saving snack foods for him, for her, or the kids."
- "Use up your cake mixes and all other fattening foods and have a farewell-to-fat party, or bring them to the office, or give them to a scout troop."[36]

A way to reduce frustration, writes Dr. Rubin in *Alive and Fat and Thinning in America*,[37] is to "keep in mind that we can, if we choose, put the weight back....It reduces anxiety and thus aids the cause immeasurably, because it offers an 'out' if desired. In effect it sustains psychological (and physical) freedom of movement."

Remember, unless you change them, your habits will be with you for the rest of your life. That is why psychologists D. Balfour Jeffrey, Ph.D., and Roger C. Katz, Ph.D., stress that "firmly establishing new eating, exercise, and lifestyle habits, and finally reaching your weight goal will probably take a long time. For this reason, keep rewarding yourself along the way for each small change, for each new success. After all, you've worked hard and stuck to your commitment so far. You deserve a kind word."[38]

Jean Allen and Emily S. Mix, who have been through it themselves, offer this advice in *Build a Better and Slimmer You*: Get away from craving situations immediately—get busy, take a walk, do something. If you can't, talk it out with a friend or take a breath and regain your composure. If you fall back into your old habits, begin to rebuild your confidence. Think of your goal and begin dieting again at the next meal. Keep your "before" photos where you can see them. Try on one of your "fatty" outfits to see how well you have done. Look at yourself in the mirror and smile.[39]

The authors of the *California Weight Loss Program*[40] also advocate making a contract with yourself. It should state the number of pounds you intend to lose and the rewards you will give yourself along the way. The contract is valuable, they say, because "you must separate yourself from your problem. You must solve your problem objectively."

Psychiatrist Albert J. Stunkard, now at the University of Pennsylvania, asks each dieter to sign a contract with him or with her own family. One approach is to deposit the sum of $100 with him; in return, the dieter gets a stated amount of cash for every pound lost.[41]

Two clinical psychologists, Michael and Kathryn Mahoney, recommend that you "focus on patterns, not pounds; you must emphasize pattern changes, not weight loss."[42] Also, you must engineer the environment in which you live so it provides cues for *good* eating habits rather than *faulty* eating habits. In their book, *Permanent Weight Control,* the Mahoneys counsel you to solicit your family's and friends' help in your slimming program, to keep food out of sight, and to exercise.

The authors of *Take Charge* suggest you shop on a full stomach "to resist the call of all that seductive garbage on the supermarket shelves."[43]

Jack Osman, Ph.D., a Baltimore health science professor, notes in *Thin From Within* that "how you feel about yourself will play a great role in how you feel about weight control. The key to winning at losing is getting yourself together—getting thin from within."[44] One of his hints for dieting is to write down a few catch phrases and place them in conspicuous spots—on a mirror or the refrigerator door.

Alberto E. J. Cormillot, M.D., whose diet is analyzed in the chapter on low-carbohydrate diets, has a better behavior modification plan than a meal plan. One of the best pieces of advice from this Argentinian physician is: "The next time you go to a restaurant, ask the waiter for a menu to take home. There you will study it, but on a full stomach! No one can study a menu thoroughly on the spot. The temptation is too great, the odors too strong. At home you'll be able to see what type of foods you should select ...*and make your own list for this restaurant.*"[45]

Dr. Henry Jordon and two other University of Pennsylvania obesity specialists say *Eating Is Okay,*[46] provided you know how to do it. Follow their advice for 20 weeks and you'll lose 40 pounds, they say. Their advice: make food invisible. Buy small food packages, even if they are not as economical as large ones. Throw out uneaten food: better that leftover spaghetti ends up in the garbage disposal than in you.

Art Ulene, M.D., a Los Angeles physician and the *Today* program's "family physician," offers a 20-day program to help change your ways in *Feeling Fine.*[47] On Day 17, for example, he advises you to relax before a meal. "Take a complete break for every meal, even if it is only a brief one. Devote that small amount of time completely to eating. To concentrate fully on the joy of eating, there should be no other distractions. Don't hunch over reports or letters with a sandwich. Don't watch TV while you are eating. Give all your attention to one activity or the other."

Leonard R. Pearson, Ph.D., a clinical psychologist, and Lillian R. Pearson, M.S.W., a psychiatric social worker, claim to have perfected a behavior modification system on 2000 overweight people at their Pearson Institute at Berkeley, California. In *The Psychologist's Eat-Anything Diet,*[48] they say you can throw away your scale and your calorie guide, eat your favorite foods, and thin down (and stay down) by following their system. The secret is to eat only satisfying food. They separate food into two categories: those that "hum" to you, foods you crave and love; and foods that "beckon" to you, call out and ask to be eaten. Foods that hum drive you to them even though they are nowhere near. Beckoning foods aren't on your mind; they just appear—such as when you see a dessert served at the next table in a restaurant.

The Pearsons urge you to eat only foods that hum, because they are satisfying; foods that beckon do not satisfy you and only make you hungry for more. The body, they believe, has built-in wisdom guided by the hypothalamus. They contend that you should mind your hypothalamus rather than your eyes and eat only when the hypothalamus tells you to—that is, to follow your own body signals not the clock, a schedule, or other people. You also should be free to eat where you want; if you want to eat lunch at your desk, go ahead.

Mary Catherine and Robert Tyson, a physician and a psychologist, believe you must regard the number on your scale as the most important number in your life. In *The Psychology of Successful Weight Control,* they list the steps for launching and waging your campaign against fat.[49] Use your scale and chart your weight loss, they instruct, for your weight is reality. Also, set realistic goals and realistic means to achieve them.

"Overweight people eat too fast," according to two psychiatrists, Walter

H. Fanburg, M.D., and Bernard M. Snyder, M.D., in *How To Be A Winner at the Weight Loss Game.*[50] They say, "Eat each meal in no less than 20 to 30 minutes. Develop a definite *rhythm* to your eating. Approach each meal from the standpoint of 'How am I going to pace myself?' This is a crucial step you must make to successfully lose weight and maintain the weight loss."

Drs. Fanburg and Snyder also suggest that you always eat in the same place. "Select one place where you will eat all your meals — either the dining room or the kitchen. Eat at a specific seat in this room and do not vary this position. Remember, to limit the number of cues that suggest eating, you must limit the number of places connected with eating," they write.

Dr. Joyce Brothers applied some of her psychological know-how to herself and described it in *Better Than Ever.*[51] She served half portions on small plates to fool herself into thinking she was eating a full meal. After she lost three pounds, she rewarded herself by buying something she considered "silly" but wonderful. She also bought an expensive dress — purposefully a size too small. She had her husband take photographs of her in the nude "before" and "after" every five-pound loss.

"Friends, relatives, and lovers can be an immense help in your program of personal growth and weight control," advise two Colorado psychologists. They explain, in *The Psychological War on Fat*[52] that "more effective eating patterns include educating those close to overweight people to give positive reinforcement. When close relatives or friends start rewarding overweight people for making progress rather than nagging and criticizing them for their inappropriate eating, the overweight people are well on their way toward learning new eating behaviors. Positive reinforcement leads to a positive self-image and good feelings about self rather than to self-hate and binge-induced feelings," write Franklin D. Cordell, Ph.D., and Gale R. Giebler, Ph.D.

As you start on your diet and your new behavior of eating, you need to provide yourself with a transition in attitude, advises Bob Schwartz, who gives seminars in dieting and runs health spas. In his book, *Diets Don't Work,*[53] he advises that you should "be patient with yourself, give yourself plenty of time and leave room for error. Expect things to be different—don't be surprised when people treat you differently, for instance. And keep your sense of humor. Remember, I've never met anyone who became thin by being grim and serious about it...concentrate wholeheartedly on living and eating like a thin person."

Foods for Moods in Southampton

Foods and moods have been intertwined for as long as people have sat down to meals. We eat with every expression of emotions, from celebrations to grief. Likewise, eating some foods—like pastries—makes us happy. Coffee wakes us up, alcohol relaxes us.

Dr. Stuart Berger took off on this principle and, according to full-page newspaper ads for his book, *Southampton Diet,*[54] "what Dr. Berger discovered is the 'missing link.' Research studies in the rapidly developing field of neurochemistry indicate that natural chemicals in the foods we eat regulate chemical activity in the brain. Feelings of stress, lethargy, even sudden hunger can actually be triggered by the *last meal eaten;* feelings of well-being, energy and satisfaction are equally dependent on mood-controlling foods. Every *meal* on Dr. Berger's program takes these biochemical factors into account. By controlling self-destructive mood swings, Dr. Berger's unique mood/food approach to weight loss helps you succeed where other diets may fail."

In his book (written with Marcia Cohen, editor of the *You* Section of the *New York Daily News*), Brooklyn-born, Harvard-educated, and Southampton-based Dr. Berger talks about foods and moods as though they were scientific fact. He sugar-coats his classification by calling them "happy foods" and "sad foods."

But when you finally get to the basic Southampton Diet, it's difficult to find it much different from other low-calorie, high-protein diets that rely heavily on turkey meat and tuna, skim milk and yogurt. Not that anything is very wrong with that diet. It's just that you may wonder why all the moods/foods baloney when a simple description of the diet is all that is needed.

Dr. Berger quotes research that shows how certain neurotransmitters—which carry signals along nerves—are made by the body from specific amino acids (which, you remember, are components of proteins). According to Dr. Berger, not enough tryptophan and you are liable to be depressed. On the other hand, lots of tyrosine fights depression.

What it all comes down to is that you need to eat lots of the right kind of protein to keep your spirits up. Thus, thanks to Dr. Berger, our culture has gone from the Mood Rings of the 1970s to the Mood Foods of the 1980s.

CONSUMER GUIDE®'S EVALUATION

Under the high-class Long Island name is just another high-protein diet. You still have to learn to change your eating habits, even as you cut calories. Rating: ★★

THE URGE TO SNACK

One of the most difficult eating habits to control is snacking. Everyone snacks; so the way to approach that problem is to prepare for it, writes John E. Eichenlaub, M.D., former director of the weight-control clinic at the University of Minnesota. His snack-control program in *A Minnesota Doctor's Guide to Weight Reduction and Control*[55] follows this outline.

1. Go without snacks for a week and note your cravings.
2. Write down every feeling you have when you eat and when you are hungry.
3. Try taking a snack when you feel bad and note whether or not eating alleviates the symptom.
4. For a few days, rate how ravenous you feel at the beginning of each meal.
5. Set the conditions of your snacking by place, time, and company.
6. Pick a nutritious snack, such as yogurt or cheese.

Even after you've learned how to control your eating, you may revert to your old ways on occasion. In a 1977 survey, Diet Workshop members reported that frequent triggers for returning to bad habits were holiday meals, a party at someone else's house, and celebrations. To handle these situations, L. Melvin Elting, D.O., and Seymour Isenberg, D.O. (also authors of the 1978 version of *The Nine-Day Wonder Diet*) suggest in *You Can Be Fat Free Forever,*[56] "When you know that you are going to be present at any party where eating is a must—such as weddings, bar mitzvahs, funerals—eat at home first. You will be able to exercise a lot more control on a full stomach. Don't let hunger strike when your appetite is fully aroused and there is a lot available. And, above all, don't eat just because it is expected of you. Remember, it is you who will be going home with the extra pounds."

Six steps toward maintaining your slim, new figure are offered in a new book[57] by Dr. Robert Linn (of *The Last Chance Diet*):

Mirror: Every day for the rest of your life, you should take a few seconds in the morning to look at yourself—with no clothes on—in a full-length mirror.

Food diary: Keep a food diary and every evening look it over and evaluate how you fared; you'll see patterns to work on.

Activities planned: Each day make sure you plan to do something in the evenings, not to mention those few empty hours when you get home from work, and especially during the weekends.

Sports: Plan a weekly schedule that includes your favorite sport at least twice a week.

Refrigerator: Remove the lightbulb to discourage late-night snacking, and wrap and mark all foods. There should be no leftovers, and low-calorie snacks should be placed in front.

Weigh-in: Before breakfast every day, weigh yourself and mark it on a daily chart. Your weight may rise for a day or two, but if it stays up longer, it's time to cut back food intake and increase physical activity.

CONTROLLED CHEATING

Larry (formerly Fats) Goldberg learned how to stay on the New York City Health Department Diet and control his cheating in eating. He passes this information (including the New York City Health Department Diet as well as his own diet) along in his book, *Controlled Cheating.*[58] The idea is that you set aside one day for cheating. You must then eat everything you love. "Be red hot about everything you gorge on," advised Goldberg. "This is *your* fun day. You can eat your way through the Dolly Madison cake plant or you can have five fettucinis in 40 minutes or you can walk around your favorite enclosed mall going from Dairy Queen to Taco Bell to Topsy's Popcorn to Kentucky Fried."

Ah, but what about other days? According to Goldberg, you stick to your diet. And you wait for the next cheating day and there is no changing the date of that day. It is certain. It is anticipated. It is a sure 3000 to 4000 calories. But then, the first cheating day comes only after you've dieted for 14 days, so it's not like eating that much every day, as you used to.

THE MARSHALL PLAN

Dr. Edward M. Marshall of Beverly Hills, California, says diets don't work and what you have to do is learn to eat like a thin person. That means you eat when you are hungry and stop eating when your hunger is satisfied. You eat your favorite foods. It's just a question of having the proper attitude, of learning to use food for nutrition, not for emotional hunger. But *The Marshall Plan For Lifelong Weight Control*[59] is shorter on techniques than on philosophy.

THE BUDDY SYSTEM

Dr. William Rader agrees that diet is not the answer to losing weight. He suggests you get a buddy and work on changing your behavior through mutual support. He borrows many techniques from Overeaters Anonymous, meetings of which he suggests you and your partner attend in your community. In his *No-Diet Program for Permanent Weight Loss*,[60] Dr. Rader offers a ten-week program for two people with weight problems, who are willing to support each other's efforts to change habits and lose weight. You look at each other's food diary, talk about the influence of parents, spouses, and others close to you; about cheating at eating; and just about everything else. Essentially, you use the other person as a mirror to reflect the personal problems you try to solve by eating too much.

If you can't succeed alone, and you don't want to join a group like OA, find a buddy. It might well work.

FINDING A BEHAVIOR MODIFIER

If you have tried behavior modification on your own and failed, or don't think you can do it alone, you may want to seek professional help. But finding it may be a challenge. Smooth operators and fast-money boys are moving into the behavior modification field. They have taken advantage of almost every other opportunity to make money off susceptible, desperate fatties, so expect them here, too.

"Seminars," "counselors," and "institutes" are probably listed under "Reducing and Weight Control Services" in your telephone directory, but your telephone directory will not indicate the qualifications of the professionals involved. In fact, when CONSUMER GUIDE® examined the behavior modification scene, we came away with mixed opinions. As a result, caution is advised.

Usually, you can spot the flim-flam men by the lack of educational degrees or the lack of degrees from legitimate, accredited universities. Beware of such "professionals" as well as those whose only credentials are certificates of completion at workshops for behavior modification leaders.

Behavior modification is a legal gray area. It is neither psychological counseling nor medical treatment. Some states and cities do not regulate this area.

CONSUMER GUIDE® offers these guidelines for finding a legitimate behavior modification program for weight control.

- Look for university faculty credentials. If the leader of a program is on a university faculty, call the university and check. But beware of the behavior modifier who says he "attended" a university. What does he or she mean by attend? A short workshop or several years?
- Some of the best programs are offered at university medical centers famous for their weight loss clinics. Among these are Duke University, University of Wisconsin (Adult Medicine) at Madison, Harvard Medical School, Mt. Sinai Hospital of Cleveland, Stanford, Miami University of Ohio, University of Pennsylvania, and The Johns Hopkins University.
- Do not sign your name on the dotted line of a financial contract that promises a certain number of behavior modification sessions for an astronomical price, to be paid all at once or on some sort of payout system. If you feel that the "counselor" is pressuring you, walk away, swiftly and surely. If he then lowers his price, you know you are heading in the right direction—away from a fast deal.
- Behavior modification programs that are offered by recognized organizations, such as Weight Watchers, Diet Workshop, and TOPS are professionally designed and supervised. They should be worthwhile because they have been tested.

The pioneer in behavior modification, Dr. Albert Stunkard of the University of Pennsylvania, believes that "the next few years may well see a significant increase in the ability to control the critical social influences which affect obese people, as the genius of private industry enlists them in large-scale programs of behavioral control. If this development is coupled, as it probably will be, with further increase in the effectiveness of behavioral methods, we may well witness a phenomenon unprecedented in the history of medicine: management of a major health problem passing out of medical hands and into those of private industry."[61]

Dr. Stunkard must have had in mind the behavior modification programs of Weight Watchers and Diet Workshop, which are businesses. While Diet Workshop offered its program a few years earlier than Weight Watchers, Weight Watchers has a more comprehensive program (designed by Dr. Stuart). A set of 30 or more pamphlets—called modules—is offered, one a week. Module titles range from "How To Get Set" and "How To Avoid Temptation" to "How to Change Some Important Ideas About Yourself" and "How To Deal with Disappointment at the Scale."

In 1982, Weight Watchers came out with Mini-Modules to add to their overall program of behavior modification. These are index cards that can be carried by the dieter as a reminder of the major points covered at the weekly meeting. An example of both sides of a card appears at the end of the chapter.

At each weekly meeting, the Diet Workshop member learns something new about changing eating habits. For instance, how to survive in a restaurant: plan ahead, as to type of restaurant. Take along a survival kit including artificial sweetener, diet salad dressing packets, and powdered skim milk. Once there, put your fork down between bites, take no second helpings, don't eat from other peoples' plates, exercise control by leaving food, and enjoy the company and the conversation more than the food.

TOPS, a nonprofit international diet club, teaches its members to: know themselves; change their fattening lifestyles, budget for dietary

212

breathers; waste food rather than let it go to their waists; keep junk foods out of the house; and take one step at a time.

In California, Arizona, Idaho, Oklahoma, Oregon, Texas, Utah, and Washington are the Schick Centers for the Control of Weight. These centers, which grew out of $6 million worth of research on addictions such as smoking, use "aversion therapy." Here bad habits are punished.

After individual analysis, each Schick customer learns about the right foods and good eating behavior. He also undergoes "zap sessions," during which an electrode is attached to one arm and "bad" food is placed within reach. Every time the dieter takes some "bad" food, he receives a mild electric shock. When he takes some "good" (low-calorie) food, he gets compliments.

GAMES FAT PEOPLE PLAY

In his now-classic *Games People Play*,[62] the late Eric Berne, M.D., introduced the public to transactional analysis (TA), a new way of looking at human behavior. Transactional analysis diagrams how we act with and react to others. Now two books explain the "games fat people play" to defeat their dieting efforts.

In one, *Weight Loss for Everyone the TA Way*,[63] psychological counselor Frank Bruno says that "the basic elements in a game are a con, a gimmick, a switch, a crossup and a payoff." Look, for instance, at the compulsive eater game: "The compulsive eater adopts the pose that he is neurotic, that overeating is the symptom of an underlying psychological illness. The compulsive eater...is a role he has decided to play in a game. He plays the role because it offers him certain psychological satisfactions. The role is played from the I'm not OK—You're OK position."

OK is a term common in TA literature. So, it should not be surprising to find it in the title of a book: *The OK Way to Slim* by a Canadian TA practitioner, Frank T. Laverty.[64] "We play all the roles at one time or another but have one favorite role which we assume more often," he writes. The fat person takes on the role of victim.

In TA, you must understand the game to better understand yourself. But before you can understand the game, you have to learn a whole new set of terms. In many ways, TA is its own game, with its own language. But it may help.

Another way to get your head together is called self-awareness. Elyse Birkinshaw, a self-awareness leader from California, explains: "The object is for you, yourself, to 'program' your subconscious mind. You may now have within your mind a 'fat' image of yourself.[65] She says, "Each of us has within his head a 'billion-dollar computer,' waiting and ready to be used—the mind!"

Alan Dolit, who runs Fat Liberation groups and workshops in the San Francisco Bay area (1387 Scenic Avenue, Berkeley, California 94708), writes in *Fat Liberation, The Awareness Technique*,[66] "Fat Lib is a totally different approach; the beauty is that there are no diets to follow, no pills to pop, no miles to run, nowhere to look except inside yourself. You decide when you want to wake up, when you are ready to lose weight, why you choose to stay fat, what you can do about it and how to enjoy food more while you lose weight."

Two New Jersey psychologists teach how to expand awareness of yourself by taking "mind trips." In their book *Mind Trips To Help You Lose Weight*,[67] Frances Stern and Ruth Hoch explain that mind trips are day-dreams. For instance, to learn positive self-awareness, you picture a television set on which your entire day is rerun. You pay attention to the details of the activities in which you did well—those you did with style and ease, those you enjoyed. When the "show" ends, the credits show that you were the producer, director, and actor. You congratulate yourself and say, "Bravo for me." The point the authors make is, "Let your imagination run free; unleash the power of your own mind, your own images. You can do or be whatever you want."

Self-awareness approaches are not therapy, but they are therapeutic in that they help you understand yourself better.

HYPNOSIS

Hypnosis induced by a specialist may also help control eating habits. If you try hypnosis, be sure the hypnotist is an authority.

A book on self-hypnosis, *Total Mind Power*,[68] claims you can be your own hypnotist. Its author, San Francisco physician Donald Wilson, suggests you use "mind power," a form of self-hypnosis, like this: "You can visualize your brain as a house with little people at work...direct your mind along a course that will regulate the areas that control obesity...picture in one area a little control switch that, when turned on, makes you hungry, and when turned off takes away your hunger....You now direct your mind to lose the weight you would like to lose. You direct your mind to see yourself in a mirror the way you *want* to appear."

The way to stick to a diet, agrees Peter G. Lindner, M.D., is to learn to hypnotize yourself. He tells how in his book, *Mind over Platter*,[69] and on a record by the same title.

RELAXATION AND BIOFEEDBACK

Before you can program your mind, you must relax your body, but many people don't know how. Once you are physically relaxed, says Elyse Birkinshaw in *Think Slim—Be Slim*,[70] you can reprogram your subconscious mind. Once you are relaxed, your mind can reach the alpha level, or the creative level at which "new pictures" can be formed.

At this level, the mind cannot tell the difference between real or imagined experiences, she maintains. So, if you see yourself on a scale that reads a low weight, you will look for that low weight when you are back in your frantic real life. Your mind, she says, "takes orders from these pictures in your mind, and it must bring that picture into being."

One way to achieve mind control is through *biofeedback*. To learn biofeedback, you are connected to a machine that indicates how well you are relaxing. Under instruction, and by checking the machine, you learn to control your mind and muscles in new ways.

214

MEDITATION

One of the most universal techniques to achieve complete relaxation is meditation, and the most popular form today is TM, or transcendental meditation. TM is defined as a "simple, natural, effortless technique that allows the mind to experience subtler and subtler levels of the thinking process until thinking is transcended and the mind comes into direct contact with the source of thought."[71]

It "is a process by which one contacts this source of pure creativity and intelligence at the basis of the thinking process, allowing this creative intelligence to be expressed in greater clarity of mind, greater efficiency of action, and increasingly fulfilling achievements in daily life."[72]

If you are beginning to think that meditation sounds a bit too "far out" for you, that it is something only practiced by the radical chic, you're wrong. In fact, two solid and conservative leaders in the diet field meditate every day and feel it helps them to stay trim. One is Edith Berman, partner and research director of Diet Workshop. The other is Albert J. Stunkard, M.D., professor and former head of the department of psychiatry at Stanford and the University of Pennsylvania medical schools. Berman learned meditation while on a trip to California in 1976. Dr. Stunkard learned it from Zen master Daisetz Suzuki, in Tokyo after World War II.

Meditation's main advantage is to block the usual barrage of thoughts and allow your mind to decide the direction in which it wishes to go. In some cases, TM advocates claim, the direction will be toward greater and greater happiness.[73]

To meditate, some TM supporters recommend that you simply close your eyes, relax your body, and think of a sound—a constant hum. You may actually hum softly or concentrate on the sound of your breathing. The sound will push every thought from your mind, every other sensation of the outer world from your consciousness, and leave you free to concentrate on one idea.[74]

MEDITATION DIET

If you can use meditation to change your attitudes toward food, and toward yourself, you may be able to lose weight and control it. That, in fact, is the premise of the book *The Meditation Diet*.[75] Authors Richard Tyson, M.D., and Jay Walker "firmly believe that whatever the mind can conceive, the body can achieve." Thus, if you learn to relax and deal with the everyday tensions that make you overeat, you can lose weight and keep it off. Also, the very act of going on a diet usually increases tension. For many dieters, the way to relieve the tension of going on a diet is to go off the diet as soon as possible.

With meditation, and its accompanying relaxation, the cycle can be broken. According to Dr. Tyson and Walker, meditation will "change the programming of your mind, you will notice instant changes in your feelings toward food. Eating correctly will heighten your own sense of physical well-being."[76]

They teach you a simple way to meditate as part of their weight-control program. Their meditation is not the religious kind. As they explain, "The entire rationale behind meditation consists of this, that it affords a person an opportunity to rest and relax in a simple, non-stress situation." They recommend meditation twice a day, for about 20 minutes each time.

The diet plan also emphasizes a body awareness exercise. The body awareness exercise takes about ten minutes a day, and it is intended to increase "one's respect and love for one's body,"[77] write the authors. The exercise may be done at any time of the day, while traveling to work or sitting at home.

In addition to the body relaxation and awareness techniques, the Meditation Diet presents a well-rounded diet that includes food from the four basic groups: milk, which supplies calcium, protein, riboflavin, Vitamin A, and other nutrients; meat, which yields iron, protein, thiamin, riboflavin, and niacin; vegetables and fruits, which supply Vitamins C and A; and breads and cereals which provide protein, iron, and B vitamins.

On the Meditation Diet, the eater can make his own selections from the four basic groups, or can follow some prepared menus. But the dieter must avoid fatty meats, gravies, and sauces, and should eat plain fruits and vegetables and use low-calorie or no salad dressing. The dieter should have whole-grain, enriched, and restored cereals and breads.

The diet[78] directs three meals a day, plus one or two snacks. It outlaws butter, oil, margarine, mayonnaise, yogurt, catsup, sugar, fried foods, and fat. But it allows as many as two slices of bread, two servings of fresh fruit, and up to two quarts of beverages—water, coffee, tea, or diet soda—a day.

The diet points out that skim milk and buttermilk and cheese made from it are lower in calories than other milk products, and it says[79] that hamburger should be broiled, and salmon or tuna should be packed in water.

The diet's daily requirements specify certain basics at each meal. For instance, breakfast on the Meditation Diet usually includes a glass of juice (unsweetened), a half grapefruit, or an orange; one or two eggs or cereal with whole or skim milk; and a beverage (coffee, tea, Sanka, or skim milk).

The entree at lunch is either a vegetable salad with cottage, pot, or farmer cheese or a broiled meat dish.

Dinner consists of broiled meat, fish, or fowl—no pork—vegetables, and a vegetable salad.

You use these basics as a starting point, adding bread, fruit, and beverages or making substitutions.

CONSUMER GUIDE® suggests you try meditation if other dieting methods have failed. It is a medically safe technique of relaxation that may help you lose weight. However, the recommendation comes with two cautions.

1. Some teachers of meditation proselytize new students into Oriental religions such as the Krishna movement.
2. With some forms of meditation and Oriental religions come strict dietary practices that may not be safe.

In short, meditation alone is all right. The safest place to learn it is at a recognized adult education center, not in a religious compound.

SAMPLE WEIGHT WATCHERS MINI-MODULE

51. Getting Set for Holidays

Most of us enter holiday seasons with two expectations: We hope to have a wonderful time, and we anticipate that we will overeat. These expectations may be the first two steps toward minor disasters.
1. Holidays are hardly ever "wonderful," outside of fairy tales and movies. To hope for wonders is to court disappointment and cause strong overeating urges.
2. Overeating is as much a *choice* on holidays as on any other days of the year. To choose to overeat one day is to invite guilt the next.

Steps You Can Take

1. When you think about holidays, concentrate on what you will DO, not FEEL. This helps avoid disappointment, since you can control your actions, but not necessarily your feelings.
2. Follow your Food Plan every day. If you know that you will want to eat more at dinner, lighten up on breakfast and lunch, and get in some extra activity, as well.

By Dr. Richard B. Stuart, Psychological Director

Chart

1. List some of the things you plan to do to make the holiday pleasant for yourself and others. Check off the steps as you take them.

a. _____
b. _____
c. _____
d. _____

2. List the occasions when you think you will feel a strong urge to overeat. Then plan the meals before each when you will lighten up a bit and/or increase your activity level.

Times I'll Overeat	Times I'll Lighten Up and/or Exercise
a.	
b.	
c.	
d.	

Fasting It Off

*T*he quickest way to drop pounds is to drop food—just stop eating. When you do this voluntarily, it is fasting. (When you have no food available, it is starving.) That, in fact, is what young women with *anorexia nervosa* do; and in effect, that is what the binger/purgers or *bulemics* (who gorge, then vomit) do.

But stopping all nutrition to the body can be very dangerous. And it is not so efficient a way to lose weight. You soon plateau and no longer can lose weight. And, if the fast continues long enough, you can die. That's what happened to the fasters in North Irish prisons.

As Judith H. Dobrzynski explains in the book *Fasting*,[1] "At first the weight comes off very quickly, but later the losses are less dramatic. For people who are eating nothing; this can be very discouraging. If they cannot lost more weight by starving themselves, they think, how can they lose weight?"

One reason for slowdown in weight loss, Dobrzynski says, is that fasting weakens you. You do less without realizing it, and doing less means using fewer calories. While fasting, you should be able to lose between 25 and 65 pounds in the first month. But, Dobrzynski cautions, "despite the big losses in poundage, many fasters continue to look fat, puffy, and unattractive. This occurs because the quality of weight loss is not as good as on a longer, slower diet that results in the same number of pounds lost." She believes fasting can be an effective first step in a long-pull calorie-reduction program. The quick initial weight loss makes you feel that at last you are doing something about your weight problem.

Unfortunately, too many dieters fast for too long. They are convinced by the books that tell them that fasting will remove not only pounds but also the poisons in their system. Since most of these books are written by "doctors," this advice must be sound, right? Not always!

Take *Triumph Over Disease*[2] by foot doctor (podiatrist) Jack Goldstein, D.P.M. He writes that fasting helps you lose weight and:

- "Gives the vital organs a complete rest."
- "Stops the intake of foods that decompose in the intestines and further poison the body."
- "Promotes elimination of metabolic wastes."
- "Allows the body to adjust and normalize its biochemistry and also its secretions (glandular fluids)."
- "Lets the body break down and absorb swellings, deposits, diseased tissues, and abnormal growths."
- "Restores a youthful condition to the cells and tissues and in a relative sense rejuvenates the body."
- "Permits the conservation and re-routing of energy."
- "Increases the powers of digestion and assimilation."
- "Clears and strengthens the mind."
- "Improves function throughout the body."

218

All of these, of course, are ridiculous, including Dr. Goldstein's and his followers' belief that fasting is part of a plan to rid the body of inner and outer poisons; it is the way to start the purge.

Fasting a day or two for religious or other reasons will not likely threaten your health and daily performance, unless you have some underlying serious medical problem. But fasting for longer periods of time to lose weight can have dire consequences. These consequences are spelled out in considerable detail in *Physical Performance, Fitness, and Diet*[3] by D. R. Young, M.D., a research scientist with the National Aeronautics and Space Administration. What he has to say is frightening. For instance, among "the effects of complete food deprivation and chronic semistarvation," he writes, "are a slowing of the heart rate and depression of metabolic rate." During long-term fasting, and semistarvation, physical performance declines with every 10 to 15 percent loss of body weight. The decline in physical performance is due, he says, to a profound alteration in the way the heart functions and to decreases in muscle strength and coordination.

Dr. Young emphasizes that you lose not only fat during fasting but also body protein—and not just from muscles of the arms and legs but from the heart, liver, kidneys, and skin as well.

"Decreased performance and, indeed, survival are related to the extent of body weight loss during food deprivation," Dr. Young writes. People survive losses of 50 to 60 percent of initial body weight during chronic semistarvation, and these are probably within the range of the lethal limit."

The difference between fasting and starving is intent. Thus, you are *starved* if food is withheld from you; you *fast* when you abstain from food. The distinction is rhetorical; your body cannot tell the difference. Your body only knows it must change its biochemistry drastically.

Frederick W. Smith's *Journal of a Fast*[4] offers an intimate modern view of fasting/starvation. It is a diary of his month-long self-imposed starvation. Before his 30-day fast, Smith had undergone short fasts as social and political protests. He thought fasting had some health benefits, too.

His original intention was to fast for 40 days, the period quoted several times in the *Bible*. He thought a 40-day fast was achievable; after all, Irish patriots had fasted for more than 94 days in 1920. He differentiated fasting from starving in this way: "The natural end of a fast is whenever one comes to the end of his readily available energy reserves. After that, one begins to starve." While Smith did not undertake the fast with the goal of losing weight, that was inevitable. He lost about 34 pounds during the 30 days. Each day is described in detail.

During the first few days, Smith noted, his stomach grumbled, and he was hungry. He also had the fuzzy-mouth sensation that religious fasters experience and its accompanying bad breath. He felt giddy, especially when he rose from a sitting position.

As the days droned on, he grew weak, and he was not able to do as much work on his farm as before. He became more and more depressed and even lost interest in sex.

Dry mouth was replaced by excessive salivation—so much so that he couldn't sleep at night because he began to gag on his saliva. Then came nausea, retching, and vomiting.

He had hallucinations, then episodes of unconsciousness. Smith broke his fast by eating an orange. The orange made him hungry for the first time since the beginning days of the fast. It also upset his stomach, as did grapefruit.

In a more objective, scientific view, *Fasting: The Phenomenon of Self-Denial*[5] points out that "the fast-to-lose-weight picture is not at all rosy by any means. Side effects are common, usually lowered blood pressure. If the patient's blood pressure is too high to begin with, this may be all to the good, but if it is normal or low, then he may suffer weakness, dizziness, and blurred vision. Fasting patients have developed gouty arthritis and cases of anemia and other serious conditions, and it is for this reason that physicians do not recommend fasting as a panacea or urge fatties to go ahead on their own, unsupervised."

Dobrzynski notes that "as a fast continues, the body goes through several changes: you may lose more hair than usual, your skin may feel drier, and you may get muscle cramps. Some people have diarrhea at the start of a fast. You may feel more sensitive to cold. You may feel tired and irritable. You may feel dizzy…. Some people even experience changes in personality…. The most serious side effect, however, can be caused by the higher level of fats in the blood. That is a dangerous condition for people with heart trouble or latent heart disease. Fasting can also bring on nervous tremors and cause severe headaches. Women may stop menstruating."[6]

There is nothing new about fasting, of course. It has been advocated by many religions for thousands of years. The state of ketosis it produces fosters a "high" which is considered spiritual. The "high" is caused by a flood of intoxicating alcohol-like ketones, the by-products of the mobilization of fat.

A leading proponent of nonreligious fasting is Allan Cott, M.D., a psychiatrist in private practice in New York City. He says, "Fasting may be a healthier way to lose weight than any of the diets that restrict you to one food or to an unbalanced combination of foods."[7]

In addition, he notes, "Fasting brings welcome physiological rest for the digestive tract and the central nervous system. It normalizes metabolism. Normally, the body constantly works to digest foods, eliminate wastes, fight diseases, ward off sickness, replenish worn-out cells, and nourish the blood. When there is no food to digest, it needs only a minimum of energy to carry on the other functions."[8]

Dr. Cott and Jerome Agel (who produces Dr. Cott's books) continued riding this train of thought in their 1977 book, *Fasting as a Way of Life.*[9] "Fasting is not starving," they wrote. "The body has in reserve at least a month's supply of food. It nourishes itself during a fast as if it were continuing to receive food."

Fasting as a Way of Life contains such other ludicrous statements as: "You will not be hungry. Any so-called hunger 'pangs' are simply normal gastric contractions or stomach spasms. They represent the sensation of hunger rather than true hunger."

Dr. Cott, a psychiatrist by training, believes and proposes that the best way to lose weight is to fast, and the best way to keep weight off is to fast on a regular basis for one weekend a month or a whole week twice a year.

Another fasting pharaoh was Stanley J. Rzepela, M.D., the late author of the *Zip Diet.*[10]

The program he proposed has three phases. In Phase I, Dr. Rzepela advocated putting nothing in your mouth but liquids, from water and fruit juices to broths, raw egg whites, and gelatin. He believed these liquids would provide all the fluid and protein you need in a day, for 100 to 300 calories. In Phase II, you begin a modified fast in which you eat nothing every other day and eat a complete meal (dinner is preferred) on the alternate days. Actually, that regimen is Phase II-A. After a week, you start Phase II-B, alternating two days of fasting with one day of eating one meal. When you reach your desired weight, you go on to Phase III—the maintenance phase—that places you on a low-calorie, low-fat, low carbohydrate, high-protein diet.

Dr. Rzepela, a family physician who specialized in the treatment of obesity, said that 95 percent of the 200 patients he saw each week in his Boston office successfully lost weight by following his program. He explained that his concept was based on research with 15 patient-friends.

Like Dr. Rzepela, other fast proponents try to persuade you that your body goes on vacation when you fast. But exactly the opposite occurs. The body still has to carry out its usual functions — including those performed by the central nervous system—and it must work harder. It has to gear up a new set of chemical processes to make up for the absence of food, and some of the changes are drastic.

During the first phase of starvation, the body calls up its glycogen reserves in the liver and converts them to glucose as needed by the brain. When glycogen reserves are used up, the body calls on protein, or muscle tissue. Long before the muscles are severely depleted, though, the body turns to its fat reserves and starts mobilizing them. In a miraculous feat of chemistry, the brain shifts chemical gears and runs on ketones, the fragments of fats.[11]

While fasting, the body loses tremendous amounts of water and with it, the mineral sodium. One result of this water loss is postural hypotension—a drastic fall in blood pressure when changing the position of the body, for instance, when sitting up after lying in a prone position. The fall in blood pressure causes lightheadedness and can be so serious that some fasting patients must be fed. Because postural hypotension most likely occurs in the morning, fasters should not take a hot shower or bath in the morning, and they should take a gram of bicarbonate of soda every day to minimize the effect.

During starvation, the body also loses potassium, which can worsen postural hypotension. Other minerals such as calcium, magnesium, and phosphate are also lost. In some patients, the nervous system reacts to the loss of minerals, and these patients suffer spasms of the hands.

To provide energy during a fast, the body breaks down protein, as well as fat. And it may get protein from blood or other body parts. One result of breaking down protein for energy is a lack of hair growth.[12]

In his sometimes erroneous, but occasionally accurate book on fasting, self-proclaimed expert Salem Kirban[13] states that "if you are a coffee or tea drinker or take alcoholic beverages you will get a dull headache when you fast. Why? Because you have conditioned your body to a regular stimulant. When you take this unhealthy stimulant away you will get a reaction." (These withdrawal effects occur, but he is inaccurate in implying that alcohol is a stimulant. It is a depressant.)

Another problem with fasting is bad breath, which can be alleviated somewhat by chewing sugarless gum or using mouthwash.

Perhaps the most important change in the body is caused by the mobilization of fat — the prime aim of fasting. Ketones, simple acids produced by the burning of fats, cause the state doctors call ketosis. Ketosis can lead to an acid condition of the body (acidosis) and can provoke a rise in the level of uric acid in the blood, which is associated with gout.[14] This same ketosis, incidentally, is what may curb appetite, some doctors believe.

In one study, some fasting patients suffered days of extreme weakness. A few suffered headaches and lightheadedness. A third of the people who fasted had waves of nausea, but rarely vomited.[15]

Ernst J. Drenick, M.D., has found with his fasting patients at Wadsworth VA Hospital in Los Angeles and UCLA that strenuous and exhausting exercise can be dangerous. He closely monitored his patients and noted that some developed an irregular heartbeat (arrhythmia) when they exerted themselves. However, fasters can and should walk, he said.

Another doctor who has studied starvation, Garfield G. Duncan of Pennsylvania Hospital, Philadelphia, advises that fasting is not for pregnant women or for people with peptic ulcers, liver problems, infections, or any form of diabetes. He believes that fasts should be conducted in a hospital and "are not to be used indiscriminately. Like major surgery or the use of potent drugs, they are to be employed with a high degree of selection and never without close and qualified supervision."

Under these circumstances, said Dr. Duncan, fasters can lose weight and be happy. He placed his patients, after they left the hospital for treatment of obesity, on one- and two-day fasts. The fasts made the patients happy because each "has an acceptable method within his grasp to effectively continue to reduce and to prevent recurrence of the obese state."[16]

But when Dr. Duncan studied 107 patients who had lost weight by starvation to see how well they kept fat off, he found that 40 percent gained back all of their fat, or more.[17]

A German study in 1976[18] corroborated that weight loss from fasting is not permanent. A team of University of Dusseldorf doctors placed 45 overweight patients on total fast (water and vitamins only) for 12 days. The fasters lost 28 pounds each, on the average. After the fast, none of the fasters followed the instruction to return to the obesity clinic for follow-up on a regular basis. "On the whole," wrote the Dusseldorf doctors, "the long-term results of a total-fasting regimen are disappointing." Of 42 patients contacted later, nine either regained all their lost weight or gained even more weight; 19 regained most of the lost weight; and only 14 kept the weight off or lost more.

These results paralleled findings made by Dr. Drenick: 96 of 105 patients who fasted had regained all of their weight when checked two years later.

Still, fasting can get rid of a pound a day. "Losses are greatest in the heaviest subjects and least in the lightest," according to Dr. Drenick. Women seem to lose weight more slowly than men. But for both men and women, weight loss is most rapid in the first few days of fasting. The most weight lost by any of his patients was 71 pounds the first month and 40 pounds the second from a 540-pound patient. People who weigh 230 pounds can lose 35 pounds in 30 days, he wrote.[19]

However, fasting is *not* good for the body. Jean Mayer, M.D., former Harvard nutritionist and now president of Tufts University, writes that "fasting advocates talk of substances being 'cleansed out of the blood.' What they do not understand is that those substances are actually essential vitamins and minerals, which are always lost with the breakdown and death of cells and which are not replenished since no nutrients are being consumed. Also fasting puts a great strain on the liver, which must help convert fat into energy, and on the kidneys, which must excrete some of the substances produced by the breakdown of fat and protein."[20]

Shirley Ross provides a fairly objective account of the subject of fasting in *Fasting — The Super Diet.*[21] Besides listing the cons, she soundly advises her readers not to fast for more than a day or two without medical supervision. For those who do fast, she offers these hints: drink plenty of water; get plenty of rest; do not get emotionally excited; use toothpaste, mouthwash, and sugarless gum to mask bad breath; avoid very hot and very cold baths and showers; dress more warmly than you normally do; stay away from drugs; do not worry about constipation.

CONSUMER GUIDE®'S EVALUATION

Our evaluation is in line with this statement made by the US Public Health Service: "Because of the potential hazards of starvation diets and the need for continuous medical supervision including both clinical and laboratory evaluation, such diets should never be self-administered."[22] Never, but never, fast on your own for more than a day even for religious or meditative reasons. Rating: Not recommended. No stars.

MODIFIED FASTS

Starvation by Zen

Another form of self-imposed starvation, done by steps, is the Zen Macrobiotic Diet. The Zen Macrobiotic Diet has little to do with Zen Buddhism. In fact, Buddhists find food faddism abhorrent. Nor does it bear much relationship to macrobiotic (without the "Zen") diets, which can be healthy forms of vegetarianism (see the chapter "Losing via Vegetarian"). Rather, the Zen Macrobiotic Diet has been called "an excursion into make-believe Oriental cultism" that is no more ancient than its originator, the late George Ohsawa.

More important than the Zen Macrobiotic Diet's lack of religious connection is the fact that the diet is dangerous. There have been reports that young followers of this diet have starved themselves to death.[23]

Surviving Zen defenders deny there is harm: on the contrary, they claim the macrobiotic diet will cure or prevent every disease, including epilepsy and cancer. (Such claims, of course, have not been proven scientifically). "In macrobiotics," a spokeswoman said, "the kitchen is our medicine cabinet, and the table is our operating room."[24]

The Zen philosophy sees everything in the world as composed of two parts: yin and yang. We all have yin and yang, as does every growing thing, and the yin and the yang constantly change in proportion to one another.

Zen Macrobiotic food is supposed to have a 5:1 ratio of yin to yang. Sugar and most fruits are frowned on as too yin; meats and eggs are heavily yang. The most perfectly balanced food is brown rice, and if man were perfect, he could live on brown rice and tea alone.

The Zen Macrobiotic program prescribes moving through ten diet stages, each more severe than the one before.

Dr. Stare explained the danger of the macrobiotic method when he said: "I've heard the macrobiotic diet referred to as a way to lose weight. This is valid at the stage where vegetables are substituted for fatty meat. But taking away certain elements in the usual variety of food without adequately replacing them can be extremely dangerous. At almost any stage of the diet it is possible to become anemic from lack of iron. The diet is also deficient in most vitamins. I think it is the most dangerous fad diet around."[25] Other nutritionists agree.[26]

CONSUMER GUIDE®'S EVALUATION

We agree with the nutritionists. Rating: Not recommended. No stars.

LOCKJAW

Many overweight people have turned to their dentists, rather than to their physicians, for help. If their mouths are permanently closed, they reason, they'll not eat as much and, therefore, will lose weight. This fad, largely faded, started in November 1973.

Late in 1977, an Australian medical research group reported on 17 wired-jaw dieters. Five of the 17 dropped out before reaching their goal weight. But for the others, who sipped 800 calories in liquids a day, the median weight loss was 55 pounds, and one woman lost 101 pounds during the six-month trial. Once the wires were removed, however, six regained some weight. The Adelaide research team nevertheless concluded that wiring jaws shut was effective and less dangerous than intestinal bypass surgery.[27]

Other health professionals are not so sure. Daniel M. Laskin, D.D.S., editor of the *Journal of Oral Surgery,* called it a "gimmick" whose long-term success was doubtful. Furthermore, the technique, normally used to treat fractured jaws, can cause shifts in tooth position, provoke gum disease, and promote tooth decay. There is also the danger that what a person with wired jaws coughs or vomits might be inhaled into the lungs.

Mini-Calorie Soup

The same Dr. Alan Howard who devised the Cambridge Diet, earlier devised a Mini-Calorie Soup that provided all the nutrients he thought a person needed. The soup was tested by 50 people at home. All 50 weighed more than 200 pounds at the start and lost at a rate of five pounds a week, consistently, without plateauing. Furthermore, none developed the ketosis that accompanies the Atkins, Stillman, Linn, and other low-carbohydrate diets.[28] The only problem they experienced was a complete halt in bowel movements because the soup has no residue. When they followed Dr. Howard's advice and ate a small apple every other week, they did have small bowel movements.

Here are the recipes to show you how ridiculous they are — we don't advise you to make them.

Dr. Howard's Mini-Calorie Soups
Recipe No. 1 (200 calories)
15 grams powered egg white
30 grams hydrolyzed starch
1 gram safflower oil
Artificial sweetener and flavoring
1½ pints water

Mix well in a blender. Divide into three portions, and take one portion at mealtime.

Recipe No. 2 (278 calories)
7 grams peanuts
18 grams powdered egg white
40 grams hydrolyzed starch
2 grams safflower oil
Artificial sweetener and flavoring
1½ pints water

Mix well in a blender. Divide into three portions, and take one portion at mealtime.

Recipe No. 3 (350 calories)
1 can beef consommé, broth, or stock
1 can chicken consommé, broth, or stock

3 ounces peanuts
1 tablespoon tomato purée
Lemon juice, salt, and pepper
Plain yogurt

Combine the consommés and heat gently. Pour half the amount in a blender. Add peanuts, tomato puree, lemon juice, salt, and pepper. Blend. Add other half of liquid. Blend. Divide into six portions. Heat each portion before serving, and serve with a tablespoon of cold yogurt.

CONSUMER GUIDE®'S EVALUATION

Too mini. Inadequate in calories and nutrients, this diet should not be followed for more than a day or two. Rating: Not recommended. No stars.

Starving with Rice

The Rice Diet is contrary to everything you've already learned about food and reducing. It is a high-carbohydrate, low-protein diet. It is also low in salt and moderately low in calories.

The Rice Diet was developed in the late 1930s and early 1940s by Walter Kempner, M.D., of the Duke University School of Medicine. It was designed for patients with severe kidney disease. The diet of cooked rice, fruit, sugar, and tea was devised so these patients' impaired kidneys would have a minimum of protein and salt to process. The diet proved immensely successful for the first patients whose cases were reported by Dr. Kempner in the *North Carolina Medical Journal* in April, 1944.[29] Dr. Kempner noted that the patients' blood pressure dropped to normal, and electrocardiograms showed their hearts had returned to normal size and function. Blood vessels in the retinas of the eyes also returned to normal.

Between 1944 and 1954, Dr. Kempner confirmed the benefits of his Rice Diet for 2000 patients. He wrote then, "We [his team of doctors] have also produced a complete change in the attitude of those who, a few years ago, flatly stated that diet has no place in the treatment of hypertensive vascular disease [high blood pressure] and arteriosclerosis [hardening of the arteries]."[30]

In one of his many reports, Dr. Kempner explained that "the rice diet contains in 2000 calories less than 5 grams of fat and about 20 grams of protein derived from rice and fruit."[31] Because the diet was loaded with carbohydrates, it seemed verboten, based on what was known about diabetes, for diabetics. But Dr. Kempner placed them on it anyway.

His original intention was to use the Rice Diet to relieve the problems with blood vessels that often accompany diabetes. He anticipated having to give the diabetics increased doses of insulin because of the heavy load of carbohydrates. "However, the opposite proved to be true," he said. "Not only is the rice diet well-tolerated, but in many instances the blood sugar and the insulin requirements decrease."

He tried the diet on 100 diabetics and found that in 97 there was either no sugar in the urine or a decreased amount during the three months they were on the Rice Diet. In only nine patients did insulin have to be increased in dosage during the three months. In 85 patients, the blood sugar either stayed the same or decreased. Of 48 who had the serious eye complication of diabetes known as *diabetic retinopathy,* most improved, only one got worse, and the condition cleared up completely for another patient.[32]

Along the way, as they were treating patients with kidney disease, high blood pressure, heart disease; and diabetes, Dr. Kempner and his colleagues made the discovery that the Rice Diet not only helped their patients' medical condition but also brought about weight loss. As early as 1945, Dr. Kempner started giving the Rice Diet to obese people just for the purpose of helping them thin down.[33] Here is a typical case history from Duke that describes the Rice Diet's effect on Mr. A.M., a 32-year-old Chicago man. "He had a lifelong history of bronchial asthma and had been overweight for about 16 years. He had taken considerable amounts of amphetamines. There was a history of depression. A.M. was here for 33 weeks, during which time he lost 179.9 pounds. The depression cleared; the asthma improved. He was discharged with a normal weight of 155 pounds (fully dressed) and given a maintenance diet."

Many doctors didn't believe Dr. Kempner's reports. So they visited him, intending to scoff; they remained to applaud. The Rice Diet worked, but they could not explain how.

Among Duke's more notable patients was the wife of Richard Hughes, former governor of New Jersey. Seriously diabetic and weighing 230 pounds, she said later. "I would truly have died if I hadn't gone to Duke." She dropped 80 pounds in 19 weeks and her blood sugar dropped also. "It was easy not to eat there," she told a reporter. "After a week of that unsalted rice, it began tasting like wet Kleenex."[34]

Folksinger and actor Burl Ives visited Duke twice in four years and lost 80 pounds each time. Before he went to Duke, he had tried high-protein diets, but with poor results.

Dr. Kempner admitted that "the rice diet is monotonous, but it has the practical advantage of simplicity. No elaborate directions are necessary, and it's easy to prepare."[35]

He believes that the Rice Diet is better than fasting because in fasting the body loses protein as well as fat. However, if "enough carbohydrate is taken to supply the necessary calories, the total nitrogen excretion [indicating protein loss] may drop," he explained. "This is known as the 'protein-sparing effect of carbohydrates' and is one of the principles used in the rice diet."[36]

Furthermore, a 1978 study at Stanford University School of Medicine showed that, compared to potatoes, rice produced far lower levels of blood sugar and, consequently, less insulin demand after eating.[37]

Dr. Kempner never intended his diet to be taken lightly or to be used by nonexperts. "The rice diet is either ineffective or dangerous, unless it is done under rigidly controlled conditions," he wrote in 1949.[38]

Over the years, there have been many popularizations of the Rice Diet. Here's one, from *Epicure.*[39]

Each meal consists of: 8 ounces fruit juice (minus sugar); 3 ounces fruit (raw, baked, canned, stewed) from a selected list; and 1/3 pound (raw weight) rice, cooked. Three meals can be divided into six. Mustard, herbs, horseradish, and pepper are allowed for seasoning, but absolutely no salt.

Even though the Rice Diet may be effective, CONSUMER GUIDE® cautions that its use should be only temporary. And it may not fit in with your present approach to dieting: if you are counting calories, bear in mind that a cup of cooked rice is worth about 225; if you are counting carbohydrates, the same amount of rice contains 50 grams.

There is another, less genteel aspect of the Rice Diet you should know about before you start. American GIs who were prisoners during the Korean War found that, on a diet of rice, feces became small hard balls.[40]

Heed Dr. Kempner's caution about the danger of following the diet for a long period of time, unless you are under medical supervision. Patients who stay for months at Duke are dieting under day-to-day observation. But you will not be under such close medical scrutiny, even if you see your doctor regularly. Of course, you could go to Duke, but there is usually a six-month wait; it is expensive, as well.

CONSUMER GUIDE®'S EVALUATION

This diet is effective. But it can be dangerous. Don't follow it without your doctor's say so. Rating: Not recommended (on your own). No stars.

References

DIETING IN 1983

1. US Senate Select Committee on Nutrition and Human Needs, *Dietary Goals for the United States.* Washington, D.C.: USGPO, 1977.
2. US Department of Agriculture/Health and Human Services, *Nutrition and Your Health: Dietary Guidelines for Americans.* Washington, D.C.: USGPO, 1980.
3. Fredrick J. Stare, "Nutritional Facts and Fictions as They Relate to Health and Disease," (American Society of Bariatric Physicians, Annual Obesity and Related Conditions Symposium, Las Vegas, Nevada, October 29, 1982).

RATING THE 1983 DIETS

1. Jean Mayer, *Overweight — Causes, Cost, and Control.* Englewood Cliffs, NJ: Prentice-Hall, 1968, 160.
2. Charlotte Young, "Planning the Low-Calorie Diet," *American Journal of Clinical Nutrition* 8 (December 1960): 898.
3. US Senate Select Committee on Nutrition and Human Needs, *Dietary Goals for the United States.* Washington, D.C.: USGPO, February, 1977.

MAGIC MIXES

1. *Consumer Reports,* July 1960, 383.
2. *American Journal of Clinical Nutrition* 8 (November-December 1960): 817–831.
3. Ibid., 822.
4. *Food Technology,* April 1966, 55.
5. *American Journal of Clinical Nutrition,* op. cit., 822.
6. Ibid., 825–826.
7. U. S. Center for Disease Control. "Follow-up on Deaths Associated with Liquid Protein Diets," *Morbidity and Mortality Weekly Report,* Volume 27, 7 July 1977.
8. Robert Linn and Sandra Lee Stuart, *The Last Chance Diet.* Secaucus, NJ: Lyle Stuart, Inc., 1976 (also New York: Bantam Books, 1977).
9. A. Howard and I. McLean Baird, "The Treatment of Obesity by Low Calorie Semi-Synthetic Diets," *Recent Advances in Obesity Research.* London: Newman Pub., 1975.
10. George L. Blackburn, Bruce R. Bistrian, and Jean-Pierre Flatt, "Role of a Protein-Sparing Fast in a Comprehensive Weight Reduction Programme." *Recent Advances in Obesity Research.* London: Newman Pub., 1975.
11. Peter G. Lindner and George L. Blackburn, "Multidisciplinary Approach to Obesity Utilizing Fasting Modified by Protein-Sparing Therapy," *Obesity/Bariatric Medical* 5: 1976, 198-216.
12. Philip Noble, "Last Chance for 'The Last Chance Diet'." *Midwest Magazine, Chicago Sun-Times,* 12 August 1977, 18.
13. *Medical Letter,* September 1977.
14. "Semi-Starvation, Not Liquid Protein, Seen as Cause of Deaths," *Wellcome Trends in Cardiology* I (August 1979): 5.
15. A. N. Howard *et al.,* "The Treatment of Obesity with Very-Low-Calorie Liquid-Formula Diet: An Inpatient/Outpatient Comparison Using Skimmed Milk Protein as the Chief Protein Source," *Int. J. of Obesity* 2 (1978): 321–332.
16. Ray Moore *et al.,* "Treatment of Obesity with Tri-iodothyronine and a Very-Low-Calorie Liquid-Formula Diet," *Lancet,* 2 Feb 1980, 223–226.
17. Randall B. Lee and Peter G. Lindner, "The Ultra-low Calorie Diet Revisited," *Obesity/Bariatric Medicine* 11 (No. 1, 1982): 4.
18. "ADA Cautions Against the Cambridge Diet," American Dietetic Association news release, August 19, 1982. ADA, 430 North Michigan Avenue, Chicago, IL 60611.
19. Philip L. White, "How Good Are the 900-Calorie Formula Diets?" *Today's Health* 39 (December 1961): 5.
20. *Changing Times,* January 1961, 46.
21. *American Journal of Clinical Nutrition,* op. cit., 830.

CUTTING CALORIES

1. Philip L. White (ed.). *Let's Talk about Food,* (2d rev. ed.). Chicago: AMA, 1970, 40.
2. Jean Mayer, *Overweight.* Englewood Cliffs, NJ: Prentice-Hall, 1968, 158.
3. *Food and Your Weight,* Home and Garden Bulletin No. 74, US Department of Agriculture. Washington, D.C.: USGPO, 1969 (rev.), 5.
4. Dorothea Turner, *Handbook of Diet Therapy.* Chicago: University of Chicago Press, 1965, 48.
5. Charlotte M. Young, "Planning the Low

228

Calorie Diet," *American Journal of Clinical Nutrition* 8 (December 1960): 896–900.

6. Louise Fenner, "That Lite Stuff," *FDA Consumer* 5 (June 1982): 10, 11.
7. US Senate Select Committee on Nutrition and Human Needs, *Dietary Goals for the United States* (2d ed.). Washington, D.C.: USGPO, 1977.
8. *Nutrition and Your Health, Dietary Guidelines for Americans,* Bulletin #G–232, US Department of Agriculture, OGPA, Room 507A, Washington, D.C. 20250.
9. D. M. Hegsted, "Dietary Goals—A Progressive View," *American Journal of Clinical Nutrition* 31 (September, 1978): 1504–1509.
10. US Senate Select Committee on Nutrition and Human Needs, op. cit., 7.
11. Margaret C. Dean, *The Complete Gourmet Nutrition Cookbook.* Washington, D.C.: Acropolis Books, 1978.
12. *Food,* Home & Garden Bulletin No. 228, Supt. of Documents. Washington, D.C.: USGPO.
13. *Food 2.* Chicago: American Dietetic Association, 1982.
Food 3. Chicago: American Dietetic Association, 1982.
14. Arlene Fischer, "How to Win the Battle of the Bulge," *Ladies' Home Journal,* October 1982, 71, 74, 150, 152.
15. Phyllis George and Bill Adler, *The I Love America Diet.* New York: William Morrow & Co., 1983.
16. Joseph S. Rechtschaffen and Robert Carola, *Dr. Rechtschaffen's Diet for Lifetime Weight Control and Better Health.* New York: Random House, 1980.
17. Norman Jolliffe, "The Prudent Man's Diet," *House Beautiful,* January 1961.
18. Iva Bennett and Martha Simon, *The Prudent Diet.* New York: David White, 1973 (also Bantam Books, 1973).
19. "The Prudent Diet: Vintage 1973," *Medical World News,* 10 August 1973, 34–44.
20. Bennett and Simon, op. cit.
21. Ibid., 12.
22. Adapted from Table IX, *Civilian Consumption of Visible and Invisible Fats per Person, 1959–67, Foods, Fats and Oils.* Washington, D.C.: Institute of Shortening and Edible Oils, Inc., 1968.
23. *The American Heart Association Cookbook.* New York: David McKay Co. Inc., 1973.
24. Lawrence E. Lamb, *What You Need to Know About Food and Cooking for Health.* New York: Viking, 1973.
25. *The Heart Saver Eating Style,* Chicago Heart Association, 20 North Wacker Dr., Chicago, IL 60606.
26. Bess Myerson and Bill Adler, *I Love NY Diet.* New York: William Morrow & Co., 1982.
27. George Christakis and Robert K. Plumb, *Obesity.* The Nutrition Foundation, 99 Park Ave., New York, NY 10016.
28. Morton B. Glenn, *How To Get Thinner Once and for All.* New York: E. P. Dutton, 1965 (also Fawcett Crest, 1970).
29. Morton B. Glenn, *But I Don't Eat That Much.* New York: E. P. Dutton, 1974.
30. Francine Prince, *Diet for Life.* New York: Bantam Books, 1982; New York: Cornerstone Library, Simon & Schuster, Inc., 1981.
31. Francine Prince, *Vitamin Diet for Quick & Easy Weight Loss.* New York: Cornerstone Library, Simon & Schuster, Inc., 1982.
32. Salvatore P. Lucia and Emily Chase, *The Wine Diet Cookbook.* New York: Abelard-Schuman, 1974.
33. Giorgio Lolli, "The Role of Wine in the Treatment of Obesity," *New York State Journal of Medicine* 62 (1962): 3438–3443.
34. Theodore Berland, "Wine as a Medicine," *West Med.* 7 (April 1966): 80–83.
35. *Dieting, Yogurt, and Common Sense,* The Dannon Company, 22-11 38th Ave., Long Island City, NY 11101.
36. Barbie Fillian and Lida Livingston, *Eat Yourself Thin.* New York: Frederick Fell, 1977.
37. Jeanne Jones and Karma Kientzler, *Fitness First.* San Francisco: 101 Productions, 1980.
38. R. Philip Smith, *The La Costa Diet and Exercise Book.* New York: Grosset & Dunlap, Inc., 1977.
39. Theodore Berland, "La Costa Secrets You Can Do At Home," *Chicago Sun-Times,* 2 November 1978.
40. Sidney Petrie (in association with Robert B. Stone), *The Wonder Protein Diet.* West Nyack, NY: Parker Publishing Co., 1979.
41. Kenneth S. Keyes, Jr., *How To Live Longer-Stronger-Slimmer.* New York: Frederick Fell, Inc., 1966.
42. Jean Carper and Audrey Eyton, *The Revolutionary 7-Unit Low Fat Diet.* New York: Bantam Books, 1981.
43. Jeanne Jones, *Jeanne Jones' Food Lover's Diet.* New York: Charles Scribner's Sons, 1982.
44. Mary Ellen Pinkham, *Mary Ellen's Help Yourself Diet Plan.* New York: St. Martin's/Marek, 1983.

45. Lorraine Dusky and J.J. Leedy, *How to Eat Like a Thin Person*. New York: Simon & Schuster, Inc., 1982.
46. Ken Dachman, *The Dachman Permanent Weight-Loss Program*. New York: William Morrow & Co., 1982.
47. Gerald M. Berkowitz and Paul Neimark, *The Berkowitz Diet Switch*. Westport, CT: Arlington House, 1981.
48. Richard Simmons, *Never-Say-Diet Book*. New York: Warner Books, 1980 (paperback, 1982).
49. Jacqueline R. Shapiro and Marion Lear Swaybill, *TheSexibody Diet and Exercise Program*. Aurora, IL: Caroline House Publishers, Inc., 1982.
50. James Leisy, *Calories In, Calories Out*. Brattleboro, VT: The Stephen Greene Press, 1981.
51. Richard G. Stuelke, *Thin for Life*. New York: Baronet Publishing Co., 1977.
52. Marck Bricklin, *Lose Weight Naturally*. Emmaus, PA: Rodale Press, 1979.
53. Michael Spira, *How to Lose Weight Without Really Dieting*. New York: Penguin Books, 1979.
54. *Mayo Clinic Diet Manual*. Philadelphia: W. B. Saunders Co., 1971.
55. "A Mini-Dictionary of Diets," *Epicure*, Summer 1973, 56.
56. Hilde Bruch, *Eating Disorders*. New York: Basic Books, Inc., 1973, 313.
57. Alvan R. Feinstein, "The Treatment of Obesity: An Analysis of Methods, Results, and Factors Which Influence Success," *Journal of Chronic Diseases* 11 (April 1960): 355–356.
58. Raymond Reiser, "Saturated Fat in the Diet and Serum Cholesterol Concentration: A Critical Examination of the Literature," *American Journal of Clinical Nutrition* 25 (May 1973): 524–555.
59. US Senate Select Committee on Nutrition and Human Needs, op. cit., 9.
60. Jean Mayer, *A Diet for Living*. New York: David McKay Co., Inc., 1975 (also Pocket Books, 1977).
61. White, op. cit., 39–41.

HIGH ON CARBOHYDRATES

1. Martin Katahn, *The 200 Calorie Solution*. New York: W. W. Norton & Co., 1982.
2. Nathan Pritikin, *The Pritikin Permanent Weight-Loss Manual*. New York: Grosset & Dunlap, 1981 (also New York: Bantam Books, 1982).
3. "Better than Starch-Blocker Diet," *Good Housekeeping*, October 1982, 91–94, 98.
4. Judith J. Wurtman, *The Carbohydrate-Craver's Diet*. Boston: Houghton Mifflin, 1983.
5. Arnold Fox, *The Beverly Hills Medical Diet*. New York: Bantam Books, 1982.
6. Joe D. Goldstrich, *The Best Chance Diet*. Atlanta: Humanics Ltd., 1982.
7. Jon N. Leonard, J. L. Hofer, and N. Pritikin, *Live Longer Now*. New York: Grosset & Dunlap, 1974 (paperback, 1976).
8. Nathan Pritikin and Patrick M. McGrady, Jr., *The Pritikin Program for Diet and Exercise*. New York: Grosset & Dunlap, Inc., 1979.
9. Nathan Pritikin with Patrick M. McGrady, Jr., *The Pritikin Program for Diet and Exercise*. New York: Grosset & Dunlap, 1979 (also Bantam Books, 1980).
10. *Recommended Dietary Allowances* (8th rev. ed.). Washington, D.C.: National Academy of Sciences, 1974, 38.
11. *Recommended Dietary Allowances* (rev. 1980). Washington, D.C.: National Academy of Sciences, 1980.
12. Judith Willis, "Diet Books Sell Well But ... ," *FDA Consumer* 16 (March 1982): 14–17.
13. Nathan Horwitz and Dean Havron, "Pritikin Rips Study of His Diet; Researcher Upholds Validity," *Medical Tribune*, 25 November 1981, 9.
14. Nathan Pritikin, *The Pritikin Permanent Weight-Loss Manual*. New York: Grosset & Dunlap, 1981 (also New York: Bantam Books, 1982).
15. Jon N. Leonard, *The Live Longer Now Quick Weight-Loss Program*. New York: Grosset & Dunlap, 1980.
16. William S. Hoffman, *The Biochemistry of Clinical Medicine* (3d ed.). Chicago: Year Book Medical Publishers, 1960, 66.
17. Chris Lecos, "Fructose: Questionable Diet Aid," *FDA Consumer* 14 (March 1980): 20–23.
18. J. T. Cooper with Paul Hagen, *Dr. Cooper's Fabulous Fructose Diet*. New York: M. Evans & Co., 1979 (also New York: Fawcett Crest, 1980).
19. J. T. Cooper and Jeanne Jones, *The Fabulous Fructose Recipe Book*. New York: M. Evans & Co., 1979.
20. Frank Downing with Oleg Bardoff, *The Hollywood Emergency Diet*. Millburn, NJ: Millburn Book Corp., 1978.
21. Nancy Pryor, *The Amazing Diet Secret of a Desperate Housewife*. Montclair, NJ: Nancy Pryor, 1978.

LOW ON CARBOHYDRATES

1. William Dufty, *Sugar Blues*. New York: Warner Books, 1976.
2. John Diamond, *Your Body Doesn't Lie*.

230

New York: Warner Books, 1980.

3. John Yudkin, *Lose Weight, Feel Great!* New York: Larchmont Books, 1974.

4. John Yudkin, "The Low-Carbohydrate Diet in the Treatment of Obesity," *Postgraduate Medicine*, May 1973, 151–154.

5. Yudkin, loc. cit.

6. John Yudkin, *Sweet and Dangerous.* New York: Peter H. Wyden, Inc., 1972, 57.

7. Ibid., 3.

8. John Yudkin, *This Slimming Business.* New York: The Macmillan Co., 1959, 144.

9. *Encyclopedia Britannica* 21: Chicago, 1964, 531.

10. Henry C. Sherman, *Chemistry of Food and Nutrition.* New York: The Macmillan Co., 1952.

11. Kenneth S. Keyes, Jr., *How To Live Longer-Stronger-Slimmer.* New York: Frederick Fell, Inc., 1966, 69.

12. Yudkin, *Postgraduate Medicine*, op. cit., 152.

13. Yudkin, *Lose Weight, Feel Great!*, op. cit.

14. John Yudkin, *The Complete Slimmer.* London: Macgibbon and Kee, 1964. Published as *Lose Weight, Feel Great.* New York: Larchmont Books, 1974.

15. Robert C. Atkins and Shirley Linde, *Dr. Atkins' Superenergy Diet.* New York: Crown Publishers, Inc., 1977.

16. J. Daniel Palm, *Diet Away Your Stress, Tension, and Anxiety.* New York: Doubleday, 1976.

17. Theodore Berland, "This no-magic diet is a winning proposition," *Chicago Tribune*, 5 July 1976.

18. Paul Michael, *The Paul Michael Weight-Loss Plan.* New York: William Morrow and Co., 1975.

19. *Brand Name Carbohydrate Diet.* N. Miami Beach: Success Publications (13th ed.), 1977.

20. Alberto E. J. Cormillot, *Thin Forever.* Chicago: Henry Regnery, 1975.

21. William F. Kremer and Laura Kremer, *The Doctor's Metabolic Diet.* New York: Crown Publishers, Inc., 1975.

22. Gardner James and Elliott Williams, *The Drinking Man's Diet.* San Francisco: Cameron & Co., 1974.

23. Robert Wernick, "I Wrote 'The Drinking Man's Diet,'" *Saturday Evening Post*, 22 May 1965, 84–86.

24. "The Drinking Man's Danger," *Time*, 5 March 1965, 72.

25. *Hadassah News*, No. 489, 1 March 1976, 50 West 58th St., New York 10019.

26. Sidney Petrie and Robert B. Stone, *Martinis and Whipped Cream.* West Nyack, NY: Parker Publishing, 1966 (also Warner Paperback Library, 1968).

27. Ed McMahon, *Slimming Down.* New York: Grosset & Dunlap, Inc., 1972.

28. Sidney Petrie and Robert B. Stone, *Fat Destroyer Foods: The Magic Metabolizer Diet.* West Nyack, NY: Parker Publishing, 1974.

29. Donald S. Mart, *The Brand-Name Carbo-Calorie Diet.* Garden City, NY: Doubleday & Co., Inc., 1979.

30. Yvonne Young Tarr, *The N.Y. Times Natural Foods Dieting Book.* New York: Quadrangle Books, Inc., 1972.

31. Walter L. Bloom and Gordon J. Azar, "Similarities of Carbohydrate Deficiency and Fasting," *Arch. Int. Med.* 112 (September 1963): 333–337.

32. Walter M. Bortz, Paula Howat, and William H. Holmes, "Fat, Carbohydrate, Salt, and Weight Loss," *American Journal of Clinical Nutrition* 21 (November 1968): 1291–1301.

33. D. Craddock, *Obesity and its Management.* London: Livingston, 1969.

34. Arthur Blumenfeld, "Low-Carbohydrate Diet Debate — Cons, Part 1," *Obesity/Bariatric Medicine* 3 (May-June 1974): 93.

35. Yudkin, *Postgraduate Medicine*, op. cit., 154.

36. Aaron G. Saidman, "Low-Carbohydrate Diet Debate — Pros, Part 1," *Obesity/Bariatric Medicine* 3 (May-June 1974): 92.

37. Helen T. Rebb *et al.*, "Calorie and Nutrient Contribution of Alcoholic Beverages to the Usual Diets of 155 Adults," *American Journal of Clinical Nutrition* 24 (September 1971): 1042–1052.

HIGH PROTEIN DIETS

1. Richard A. Passwater, *The Slendernow Diet.* New York: St. Martin's Press, 1982.

2. Richard A. Passwater, *The Easy No-FLAB Diet.* New York: Richard Marek Publishers, 1979.

3. Herman Tarnower and Samm Sinclair Baker, *The Complete Scarsdale Medical Diet.* New York: Rawson, Wade Publishers, Inc., 1978.

4. Irwin Maxwell Stillman and Samm Sinclair Baker, *The Doctor's Quick Weight-Loss Diet.* New York: Dell Publishing, 1968 (originally published by Prentice-Hall, Inc., Englewood Cliffs, NJ, 1967).

5. Eugene F. DuBois, *Basal Metabolism in Health and Disease.* Philadelphia: Lea and Febiger, 1936.

6. Ibid.

7. Stillman, op. cit., 36.

8. Irwin M. Stillman and Samm Sinclair Baker, *Dr. Stillman's 14-Day Shape-Up Program*. New York: Delacorte Press, 1974.
9. Ibid., 49.
10. Ibid., 44 and 53.
11. L. Melvin Elting and Seymour Isenberg, *You Can Be Fat Free Forever*. New York: St. Martin's Press, 1974.
12. Barbara Edelstein, *The Woman Doctor's Diet For Women*. Englewood Cliffs, NJ: Prentice-Hall, 1977 (also New York: Ballantine Books, 1979).
13. Laura Zahn and Albert R. Marston, "Is There a Difference Between Men and Women in Losing Weight?" *Obesity/ Bariatric Medicine* 10 (1981): 156–158.
14. Martin M. Schiff, *Doctor Schiff's One-Day-at-a-Time Weight-Loss Plan*. New York: Stein & Day, 1980.
15. Joyce A. Bockar, *The Last Best Diet Book*. New York: Stein & Day, 1980.
16. Gail Sforze Brewer with Tom Brewer, *What Every Pregnant Woman Should Know, The Truth About Diets and Drugs in Pregnancy*. New York: Random House, 1977 (also from Ballantine Books).
17. Joanne Lemieux, *Diet Signs*. Washington, D.C.: Acropolis Books, 1982.
18. Fredrick J. Stare and Jelia Witschi, "Diet Books: Fact, Fads, and Frauds," *Medical Opinion* 1 (December 1972): 13–18.
19. Robert B. Bradfield and Martin H. Jourdan, "Relative Importance of Specific Dynamic Action in Weight-Reduction Diets," *Lancet* 2 (22, September 1973): 640.
20. Philip L. White, "Let's Talk About Food," *Today's Health*, December 1972, 11.
21. *Postgraduate Medicine* 54 (July 1973): 40; and *Science News* 103 (28 April 1973): 271.
22. Frank Rickman *et al.*, "Changes in Serum Cholesterol During the Stillman Diet," *Journal of The American Medical Association* 228 (1 April 1974): 54.
23. Judith Willis, "Diet Books Sell Well But...." *FDA Consumer* 16 (March 1982): 14–17.
24. R. P. Payne, "Safe Protein-Calorie Ratios in Diets," *American Journal of Clinical Nutrition* 28 (March 1975): 281–286.
25. US Senate Select Committee on Nutrition and Human Needs, *Dietary Goals for the United States* (2d ed.). Washington, D.C.: USGPO, 1977.
26. G. L. Blackburn and J. P. Flatt, "Preservation of Lean Body Mass During Acute Weight Reduction," *Fed. Proc. Abs.* 1973. Abst. No. 3920, Nutrition.
27. US Senate Select Committee on Nutrition and Human Needs, op. cit.

HIGH FAT DIETS

1. Herman Taller, *Calories Don't Count*. New York: Simon and Schuster, 1961, 28.
2. A. W. Pennington, "The Use of Fat in a Weight-Reducing Diet," *Delaware State Medical Journal* 23 (April 1951): 79–86.
3. A. W. Pennington, "Obesity: Overnutrition or Disease of Metabolism?" *American Journal of Digestive Diseases*, September 1953, 266–274.
4. *Diet Guide*. Philadelphia: Holiday, 1950.
5. Taller, op. cit.
6. *The New York Times*, 2 May 1967, 51; 24 June 1967, 31.
7. "Diet on Whipped Cream," *Science Newsletter* 87 (24 April 1965): 259.
8. T. M. Chalmers *et al.*, *Lancet*, 1958, 866.
9. T. M. Chalmers, G. L. S. Pawan, and A. Kechwick, *Lancet*, 1960, 6–9.
10. W. L. Bloom, "Fasting as an Introduction to the Treatment of Obesity," *Metabolism* 8 (1959): 214.
11. W. L. Bloom, "Fasting Ketosis in Obese Men and Women," *Journal of Laboratory & Clinical Medicine* 59 (April 1962): 605–612.
12. Pamela Howard and Sandy Treadwell, "Dr. Atkins Says He's Sorry," *The New York Weekly*, 26 March 1973. (Reprinted in *Nutrition and Diseases—1973*, Hearing Before the Select Committee on Nutrition and Human Needs of the US Senate, 93d Congress, 12 April, 1973. Washington, D.C.: USGPO, Stock No. 5270–01835, 1973).
13. Robert C. Atkins, *Dr. Atkins' Diet Revolution*. New York: David McKay Publishers, 1972 (paperback Bantam Books).
14. Fredrick J. Stare and Jelia Witschi, "Diet Books: Facts, Fads and Frauds," *Medical Opinion* 1 (December 1972): 13–18.
15. "A Critique of Low-Carbohydrate Ketogenic Weight Reduction Regimens—A Review of Dr. Atkins' Diet Revolution," *Journal of the American Medical Association* 224 (4 June 1973): 1415–1419.
16. "When a Best Seller on Dieting Runs into Medical Critics," *Modern Medicine*, 28 May 1973, 132–133.
17. "Dr. Atkins' Diet Revolution," *The Medical Letter* 15 (1 May 1973): 41–42.
18. *Journal of the American Medical Association*, 4 June 1973, op. cit.
19. George F. Cahill, "Atkins' High Fat Diet for Weight Reduction Not Recommended," *Journal of the American Medical Association* 227 (28 January 1974): 448.
20. *Journal of the American Medical*

Association, op. cit., 1416; and *The Medical Letter* 15: op. cit.

21. M. F. Oliver, V. A. Kurien, and T. W. Greenwood, "Relation Between Serum-Free-Fatty Acids and Arrhythmias and Death after Acute Myocardial Infarction," *Lancet,* 6 (April 1968): 710–714.

22. "Diet Revolution author is sued for $7 million on heart attack," *The New York Times,* 23 March 1973 (reprinted in *Nutrition and Diseases—1973,* op. cit., 66).

23. "Suit ties Dr. Atkins' diet to heart attack," *American Medical News,* 2 April 1973, 13.

24. "AMA Panel Denounces 'Dr. Atkins' Diet Revolution,'" *American Medical News,* 19 March 1973.

25. Neil Solomon with Sally Sheppard, *The Truth About Weight Control.* New York: Dell, 1973, 122.

26. Atkins, op. cit., 138.

27. *Journal of the American Medical Association,* 4 June 1973, op. cit., 1417.

28. *Nutrition and Diseases—1973,* op. cit., 36–38.

29. *Modern Medicine,* op. cit., 132.

30. Beatrice Trum Hunter, *Consumer Beware!* New York: Simon and Schuster, 1971.

31. George E. Schauf, "All Calories Don't Count ... Perhaps," *Nutrition Today,* September-October 1971, 16–24.

32. *Journal of the American Medical Association,* 4 June 1973, op. cit., 1417.

33. *Nutrition and Diseases—1973,* op. cit., 49.

34. Solomon, op. cit., 262.

35. Roderic P. Dwok and Maurice V. L'Heureux, "Fat-Mobilizing Substance and Cyclic AMP," Great Lakes Regional Meeting of the American Chemical Society, June 1973, Paper No. 93 (also reported in *Medical World News,* 13 July 1973, 15, and *Science News,* 16 June 1973).

36. *Nutrition and Diseases — 1973,* op. cit., 19.

37. Ibid., 20.

38. Ibid.

39. Atkins, op. cit., 130.

LOSING VIA VEGETARIAN

1. Frances Moore Lappe, *Diet for a Small Planet* (rev.). New York: Ballantine Books, 1982.

2. Ellen Buchman Ewald, *Recipes for a Small Planet.* New York: Ballantine Books, 1974.

3. Karen Brooks, *The Forget-About-Meat Cookbook.* Emmaus, PA: Rodale Press, Inc., 1974.

4. Nathaniel Altman, *Eating for Life.* Wheaton, IL: Theosophical Publishing House, 1973.

5. Gary Null, *The New Vegetarian.* New York: William Morrow and Co., 1978.

6. Runa and Victor Zurbel, *The Vegetarian Family.* Englewood Cliffs, NJ: Prentice-Hall, Inc., 1978.

7. Fern Calkins, with U. D. Register and Lynn Sonnenberg, *It's Your World Vegetarian Cookbook* (rev., enlarged). Washington, D.C.: Review and Herald Publishing Association, 1981.

8. Position Paper on the vegetarian approach to eating, *J. Amer. Diet Assn.* 77 (July 1980): 61–69.

9. William E. Connor *et al., The Alternative Diet Book.* Iowa City, IA: University of Iowa Publications, 1976.

10. D. P. Burkitt and H. C. Trowell (eds.), *Refined Carbohydrate Foods and Disease.* New York: Academic Press, 1975, Chap. 16.

11. David Reuben, *The Save Your Life Diet.* New York: Random House, 1975.

12. Sanford Siegal, *Dr. Siegal's Natural Fiber Permanent Weight-Loss Diet.* New York: Dial Press, 1975.

13. Reuben, op. cit., 114.

14. Siegal, op. cit., 125.

15. Barbara Kraus, *The Barbara Kraus Guide to Fiber in Foods.* New York: Signet, 1975.

16. Peter G. Lindner, "The New Magic 'High Fiber' Diet: Grandma Called It Roughage," *Obesity/Bariatric Medicine* 7 (July-August 1978): 134.

17. Maurizio Ponz de Leon *et al.,* "Influence of Small-Bowel Transit Time on Dietary Cholesterol Absorption in Human Beings," *New England Journal of Medicine* 307 (July 8, 1982): 102–103.

18. "Serum Cholesterol, Dietary Fat ... and Children," *Nutrition & the M.D.* 4 (July 1978): 1–2.

19. Denis Burkitt, *Eat Right — to Keep Healthy and Enjoy Life More.* New York: Arco Publishing, 1979.

20. Audrey Eyton, *The F-Plan Diet.* New York: Crown Publishers, Inc., 1983.

21. William A. Check, "Switch to Soy Protein for Boring But Healthful Diet," *Journal of the American Medical Association* 247 (June 11, 1982): 3045–3046.

22. Michael D. Levitt, "Foods That Produce Gas," *Nutrition & the M.D.* 8 (April 1982): 1.

23. Herman Tarnower and Samm Sinclair Baker, *The Complete Scarsdale Medical Diet.* New York: Rawson, Wade, 1978.

24. J. T. Cooper, *The South American Diet.* Atlanta: Braswell Health Book Publishing Co., Inc., 1980.
25. Gabe B. Mirkin and Ronald N. Shore, "The Beverly Hills Diet. Dangers of the Newest Weight Loss Fad," *Journal of the American Medical Association* 246 (November 13, 1981): 2235–2237.
26. Judy Mazel, *The Beverly Hills Diet.* New York: Macmillan Publishing Co., Inc., 1981.
27. Edwin McDowell, "Judy Mazel," *New York Times Book Review,* August 23, 1981, 26.
28. Fredrick J. Stare, "Nutritional Facts and Fiction as They Relate to Health and Disease," (American Society of Bariatric Physicians, Annual Symposium, Las Vegas, 29 October 1982).
29. "The Beverly Hills Diet," *Medical World News* 22 (1 September 1981): 6–9.
30. Judy Mazel, *The Beverly Hills Diet Lifetime Plan.* New York: Macmillan Publishing Co., Inc., 1982.
31. Joy Gross, *The 30-Day Way to a Born-Again Body.* New York: Rawson, Wade, 1978.
32. Adrien Arpel with Ronnie Sue Ebenstein, *Adrien Arpel's 3-Week Crash Makeover/Shapeover Beauty Program.* New York: Wallaby, 1979.
33. Irwin Maxwell Stillman and Samm Sinclair Baker, *The Doctor's Quick Inches-Off Diet.* New York: Dell, 1970 (originally published by Prentice-Hall, Inc., Englewood Cliffs, NJ, 1969).

THE GROUP EXPERIENCE

1. Hilde Bruch, *Eating Disorders.* New York: Basic Books, 1973, 323.
2. Albert J. Stunkard, Harold Levine, and Sonija Fox, "Study of a Patient Self-Help Group for Obesity," (122d Annual Meeting of the American Psychiatric Association, Miami, Florida, 9 May 1969).
3. Richard C. Bates, "Let Problem Patients Help Each Other," *Medical Economics,* 10 July 1967, 124–136.
4. Richard B. Stuart and Christine Mitchell, "Self-Help Groups in the Control of Body Weight," in Albert J. Stunkard (ed.), *Obesity.* Philadelphia: W. B. Saunders, 1980, 347.
5. Jean Nidetch and Joan Rattner Hellman, *The Story of Weight Watchers.* New York: New American Library, 1972.
6. Jean Nidetch, *Weight Watchers Food Plan Diet Cookbook.* New York: New American Library, 1982.
7. Lois L. Lindauer, *The Diet Workshop Success Diet.* New York: Grosset & Dunlap, 1978.
8. Lois Lyons Lindauer, *It's In To Be Thin.* New York: Award Books, 1970.
9. Mary Sargent, *Slim Forever.* New York: Bantam Books, 1974.
10. Patrick J. Conway and Mary Ellenwood Pittenger, *The Ideal Diet Cookbook.* Columbus, OH: Conway Diet Institute, 1979.
11. Albert J. Stunkard, "The Success of TOPS, a Self-Help Group," *Postgraduate Medicine,* May 1972, 143–147.
12. Ronald K. Kalkhoff (with assistance from Marlea Krueger), *A Nutrition Monograph for Taking Off Pounds Sensibly.* Milwaukee: TOPS Club, Inc., 1980.
13. *Compulsive Overeating and the OA Recovery Program.* Torrance, CA: Overeaters Anonymous, 1981.
14. Peter G. Lindner, "Overeaters Anonymous — Report on a Self-Help Group," *Obesity/Bariatric Medicine* 3 (1974): 134–137.
15. George F. Christians, *The Compulsive Overeater.* New York: Doubleday, 1978.
16. Karen R., *That First Bite.* New York: Pomerica Press, 1979.

DOCTORS, PILLS, AND SURGERY

1. *Amylex Presents The Starch Lover's Diet.* Pennsauken, NJ 08110: R-Kane Products, Inc., 1981.
2. Peter Lindner and Daisy Lindner, "A New Approach to Stubborn Weight Problems. A Primer for the Use of Starch Blocker in Obesity," (American Society of Bariatric Physicians, Annual Obesity and Related Conditions Symposium, Las Vegas, Nevada, October 29, 1982).
3. Peter G. Lindner, "'Starch Blocker' for Obesity: Breakthrough or Hazard?" *Obesity/Bariatric Medicine* 11 (1982): 65–66.
4. Judith Willis, "About Body Wraps, Pills and Other Magic Wands for Losing Weight," *FDA Consumer* 16 (November 1982): 18–20.
5. Editors of CONSUMER GUIDE® with Nicola Giacona, *Prescription Drugs.* New York: Beekman House/Crown Publishers, Inc., 1983.
6. Editors of CONSUMER GUIDE® with Nicola Giacona, *People's Drug Guide.* New York: Beekman House/Crown Publishers, Inc., 1982.
7. *Economic Priorities Report* 4 (August-November 1973): 41–42.
8. George V. Mann, "Obesity, the Nutri-

234

tional Spook," *American Journal of Public Health* 61 (August 1971): 1491–1498.

9. *AMA Drug Evaluations*. Chicago: AMA, 1980, 936.

10. Edward M. Brecher, *Licit and Illicit Drugs*. Mt. Vernon, NY: Consumers Union, 1972, 285.

11. *National Drug Code Directory* (FDA 72–3027). Washington, D.C.: USGPO, 1972, 136–138.

12. *AMA Drug Evaluations*, op. cit., 938.

13. "Fenfluramine – Another Appetite Suppressant," *The Medical Letter* 15: 33–34.

14. *Physicians' Desk Reference*. Oradell, NJ: Medical Economics, 1983, 666.

15. Ibid., 1773.

16. *AMA Drug Evaluations*, op. cit., 938.

17. Alvan R. Feinstein, "The Treatment of Obesity, An Analysis of Methods, Results, and Factors Which Influence Success," *Journal of Chronic Disease* 11 (April 1960): 362.

18. Louis Lasagna, "Attitudes Toward Appetite Suppressants,"*Journal of the American Medical Association* 225 (2 July 1973): 44–48.

19. *AMA Drug Evaluations*, op. cit., 937.

20. Herbert Gershberg, "Use of Drugs in the Treatment of Obesity," *Postgraduate Medicine*, May 1972, 135–138.

21. *AMA Drug Evaluations*, op. cit., 937.

22. Feinstein, op. cit., 369.

23. *AMA Drug Evaluations*, op. cit., 937.

24. *AMA Drug Evaluations*, op. cit., 591.

25. *AMA Drug Evaluations*, op. cit., 937.

26. "HCG: Boon for the Obese – or Just a Super-Expensive Placebo?" *Medical World News* 15 (11 October 1974): 73–80.

27. A. T. W. Simeons, "The Action of Chorionic Gonadotropin in the Obese," *Lancet* 2 (6 November 1954): 946–7.

28. A. T. W. Simeons, *Pounds and Inches – A New Approach to Obesity*. Los Angeles: Simeons Medical Supply, Inc., 10.

29. *Medical World News*, op. cit., 80.

30. "'Fat Clinics' Ethics Eyed," *American Medical News* 17 (12 August 1973): 15.

31. *AMA Drug Evaluations*, op. cit., 732.

32. Lester and Irene David, "Beware the 'Reducing Doctors,'" *Coronet* 49 (December 1969): 40–45.

33. Susanna McBee, "A Slender Life Reporter Visits 10 'Fat Doctors,'"*Life* 64 (26 January 1968): 22–28.

34. David, op. cit., 43.

35. Ibid., 41.

36. Frank R. Bahr, Paula Arno (trans.), *Dr. Bahr's Acu-Diet*. New York: William Morrow, 1978.

37. Ibid.

38. Helena L. Huang (trans.), *Ear Acupuncture*. Emmaus, PA: Rodale Press, 1974.

39. Theodore Berland, "Can staple in ear help shed weight?" *Chicago Tribune*, 4 November 1974.

40. Ibid.

41. Huang, op. cit., p. X.

42. Frank Z. Warren and Theodore Berland, *The Acupuncture Diet*. New York: St. Martin's Press, 1976; *Losing Weight Through Acupuncture*. New York: Cornerstone Library, 1977.

43. *The AMA Quick Reference Guide*. Chicago: AMA, 1976, 4.

44. "'Jolly We Are Not,' Reveals Ex-Fat Man," UPI in *Chicago Daily News*, 13 November 1973.

45. *Chicago Tribune*, 26 March 1976.

46. "In Obesity Surgery, Problems Are the Rule," *Medical World News*, 7 (September 1973): 34–35.

47. Henry Buchwald, "Jejuno-Ileal Surgery: Which Patients Qualify?" *Medical Opinion* 2 (August 1973): 40–48.

48. "In Obesity Surgery…," op. cit.

49. J. M. Gold et al., "Liver Failure After Obesity Bypass," *Obesity/Bariatric Medicine* 11 (Ap-Jun 1982): 47–53.

50. "Intestinal Bypass Encephalopathy," *Obesity/Bariatric Medicine* 10 (1981): 142.

51. John D. Halverson, "The Aftermath of Intestinal Bypass," *Bulletin of the American College of Surgeons* 67 (June 1982): 8, 9.

52. Sir Stanley D. R. Passmore, *Human Nutrition and Dietetics*. Baltimore: Williams and Wilkins, 1966, 375.

SWEATING IT OFF

1. "Exercise May Boost Food Value," *UC Clip Sheet*, Berkeley, CA 94720, January 26, 1982.

2. Paul T. Williams et al., "The Effects of Running Mileage and Duration on Plasma Lipoprotein Levels," *Journal of the American Medical Association* 247 (May 21 1982): 2674–2679.

3. Frank Konishi, Judi R. Kesselman, and Franklynn Peterson, *Dr. Konishi's Eat Anything Exercise Diet*. New York: William Morrow and Co., Inc., 1979.

4. Charles Kuntzleman, *The Exerciser's Handbook*. New York: David McKay Co., Inc., 1978.

5. Neil Solomon and Evalee Harrison, *Doctor Solomon's Proven Master Plan for Total Body Fitness and Maintenance*. New York: G. P. Putnam's Sons, 1976.

6. Jean Mayer, *Overweight — Causes, Cost, and Control*. Englewood Cliffs, New Jersey: Prentice-Hall, Inc., 1968, 79.

7. Fredrick J. Stare, "Overnutrition," *American Journal of Public Health* 53 (November 1963): 1795–1802.

8. L. E. Morehouse and A. T. Miller, Jr., *Physiology of Exercise*. St. Louis: The C. V. Mosby Company, 1967, 275.

9. "How to Burn Up Fat Faster While Maintaining Muscle," *UC Clip Sheet* 55, Berkeley, CA 94720, May 20, 1980.

10. Ibid.

11. Arthur Weltman, Sharleen Matter, and Bryant A. Stamford, "Caloric restriction and/or mild exercise: effects on serum lipids and body composition," *Am. J. Clin. Nutr.* 33 (May 1980): 1002–1009.

12. Lawrence B. Oscai and John O. Holloszy, "Effects of Weight Changes Produced by Exercise, Food Restriction, or Overeating on Body Composition," *Journal of Clinical Investigation* 48 (1969): 2124–2128.

13. "Strengthening Bones," *Parade*, 21 October 1973.

14. *Exercise and Weight Control*, Committee on Exercise and Physical Fitness of the AMA, and the President's Council on Physical Fitness, in cooperation with the Lifetime Sports Foundation. Chicago: AMA, 1967.

15. *Physical Fitness Calculator*. Washington, D.C. 20402: USGPO, 1975.

16. *The Fitness Challenge in the Later Years*, DHEW Publication No. (OHD) 75–20802. Washington, D.C. 20402: USGPO, 1975.

17. Theodore Berland, *The Fitness Fact Book*. New York: The World Almanac, 1980 (also New York: American Library, 1981).

18. Konishi, op. cit.

19. Charles T. Kuntzleman and the Editors of CONSUMER GUIDE®, *The Complete Book of Walking*. New York: Simon and Schuster, Inc., 1978.

20. *First Steps to Fitness*. Mountain View, CA 94040: World Publications.

21. Richard Simmons, *Never-Say-Diet Book*. New York: Warner Books, 1980 (paperback, 1982).

22. Jane Fonda, *Jane Fonda's Workout Book*. New York: Simon and Schuster, Inc., 1981.

23. Sandra Rosenzweig, *Sportsfitness for Women*. New York: Harper & Row, 1982.

24. Jacqueline R. Shapiro and Marion Lear Swaybill, *The Sexibody Diet & Exercise Program*. Aurora, IL: Caroline House, 1982.

25. *Adult Physical Fitness*. Washington, D.C. 20402: USGPO, 1973.

26. C. Myers, *The Official YMCA Physical Fitness Handbook*. New York: Popular Library, 1975.

27. *Exercise Manual*. E. Meadow, NY: The Diet Workshop, 1974.

28. Neil Solomon and Evalee Harrison, op. cit.

29. Laurence E. Morehouse and Leonard Gross, *Total Fitness in 30 Minutes a Week*. New York: Pocket Books, 1976.

30. Thomas J. DeCarlo, *The Executive's Handbook of Balanced Physical Fitness*. New York: Association Press, 1975.

31. Vic Boff, *You Can Be Physically Perfect, Powerfully Strong*. New York: Arco Publishing Co., Inc., 1975.

32. Pamela Nottidge and Diana Lamplugh, *Slimnastics*. Baltimore: Penguin Books, 1973.

33. Bonnie Prudden, *How to Keep Slender and Fit After 30*. New York: Pocket Books, 1970.

34. Abraham I. Friedman, *How Sex Can Keep You Slim*. Englewood Cliffs, NJ: Prentice-Hall Inc., 1972 (also, New York: Bantam Books, 1973).

35. Frank Konishi, *Exercise Equivalents of Foods*. Carbondale, IL: Southern Illinois University Press, 1974.

36. Marya Argetsinger Smith, "Exercising Urban Flab," *Chicago Guide*, August 1973, 73–79.

PSYCHING IT OFF

1. Stanley Schachter, "Don't Sell Habit-Breakers Short," *Psychology Today* 16 (August 1982): 27–33.

2. Maria Simonson, "Advances in Research and Treatment of Obesity," *Food and Nutrition News* 53 (March-April 1982): 1–4, 6.

3. Sandra Edwards, *Too Much is Not Enough*. New York: McGraw Hill Book Co., 1981.

4. Mildred Klingman, *The Secret Lives of Fat People*. Boston: Houghton Mifflin Co., 1981.

5. Francie M. Berg, *How to Be Slimmer, Trimmer & Happier* (rev.). Hettinger, ND: Flying Diamond Books, 1983.

6. Marcia Millman, *Such a Pretty Face; Being Fat in America*. New York: Norton, 1980.

7. Carole Livingston, *I'll Never be Fat Again!* Secaucus, NJ: Lyle Stuart, 1980.

8. Joan Scobey, *Short Rations*. New York: Holt, Rinehart and Winston, 1980.

9. Nancy L. Bryan, *Thin is a State of Mind*. New York: Harper & Row, 1980.

10. Eda LeShan, *Winning the Losing Battle*. New York: Thomas Y. Crowell, 1979.
11. Meridee Merzer, *Winning the Diet Wars*. New York: Harcourt Brace Jovanovich, 1980.
12. R. B. Stuart, "Behavioral Control of Overeating," *Behavior Research and Therapy* 5 (1967): 357–365.
13. Albert J. Stunkard, *The Pain of Obesity*. Palo Alto, CA: Bull Publishing Co., 1976.
14. Richard B. Stuart and Barbara Davis, *Slim Chance in a Fat World*. Champaign, IL: Research Press, 1972.
15. Donald Naismith, "Bottle Feeding Makes Fat Mammas — and Fat Babies, Too!" *Medical Opinion* 3 (November 1974): 38–40, 43.
16. Barbara Hall, "Changing Composition of Human Milk and Early Development of an Appetite Control," *Lancet*, 5 April 1975, 779–781.
17. Malcolm Martin and Arline L. A. Martin, "Obesity, Hyperinsulinism, and Diabetes Mellitus in Childhood," *Journal of Pediatrics* 82 (1973): 192–201.
18. Richard Stiller, *Habits: How We Get Them, Why We Keep Them, How We Kick Them*. New York: Thomas Nelson, 1977, 85.
19. Leonard Cammer, *Freedom from Compulsion*. New York: Simon & Schuster, Inc., 1976.
20. Stiller, op. cit., 87.
21. Richard F. Spark, "Fat Americans," *The New York Times Magazine*, January 1974, 10.
22. Richard B. Stuart, *Act Thin, Stay Thin*. New York: W. W. Norton & Co., Inc., 1978.
23. Susie Orbach, *Fat Is a Feminist Issue*. New York: Paddington Press, Ltd., 1978 (also New York: Berkeley Publishing Corporation, 1979).
24. Grace Meynen, "Behavior Therapy with Groups of Obese, Female Dieters," Ph.D. dissertation. Illinois Institute of Technology.
25. "Study Reveals Behavior Modification Increases Weight Loss in Group," Diet Workshop news release, September 17, 1975. Diet Workshop, East Meadow, NY.
26. Albert Stunkard, "Studies on TOPS, A Self-Help Group for Obesity," (National Institute of Health, Conference on Obesity, Bethesda, Maryland, October 2, 1973).
27. Albert K. Stunkard (ed.), *Obesity*. Philadelphia: W. B. Saunders, 1980, 328.
28. Shirley Simon, *Learn To Be Thin*. New York: Berkley Windhover, 1976, 112.
29. Theodore Isaac Rubin, *Forever Thin*. New York: Bernard Geis, 1970, 116.
30. Frank J. Bruno, *Think Yourself Thin*. Los Angeles: Nash Publishing, 1972.
31. Stuart and Davis, op. cit.
32. Edwin Bayrd, *The Thin Game*. New York: Newsweek Book, 1978.
33. Stiller, op. cit., 48–52.
34. Ronald Jay Cohen, *Binge!* New York: Macmillan, Inc., 1979.
35. Edwards, op. cit., 161.
36. Bruce Lansky, *Successful Dieting Tips*. Deephaven, MN: Meadowbrook Press, 1981.
37. Theodore Isaac Rubin, *Alive and Fat and Thinning in America*. New York: Coward, McCann & Geoghegan, Inc., 1978.
38. D. Balfour Jeffrey and Roger C. Katz, *Take It Off and Keep It Off*. Englewood Cliffs, NJ: Prentice-Hall, Inc. (Spectrum), 1977, 189.
39. Jean Allen and Emily S. Mix, *Build a Better and Slimmer You*. New Rochelle, NY: Arlington House, 1977, 101–102.
40. H. S. Judd with James M. Terrill and Evelyn Langenwaler, *California Weight Loss Program*. New York: Simon & Schuster, Inc., 1974 (also Pocket Books, 1979).
41. Anna Auersbacher, "Obese Patients Sign Contract, Shed Pounds or Lose Dollars," *Medical Tribune*, March 17, 1982.
42. Michael J. Mahoney and Kathryn Mahoney, *Permanent Weight Control*. New York: W. W. Norton & Co., 1976.
43. William H. Redd and William Sleator, *Take Charge*. New York: Random House, 1976, 52.
44. Jack D. Osman, *Thin from Within*. New York: Hart Publishing Co., 1976.
45. Alberto E. J. Cormillot, *Thin Forever*. Chicago: Henry Regnery, 1976.
46. Henry A. Jordan *et al.*, *Eating is Okay*. New York: Rawson Assoc., 1976.
47. Art Ulene, *Feeling Fine*. Los Angeles: Tarcher (St. Martin's), 1977.
48. Leonard Pearson, Lillian R. Pearson, and Krola Saekel, *The Psychologist's Eat-Anything Diet*. New York: Peter H. Wyden, Inc., 1973, 5.
49. Mary Catherine Tyson and Robert Tyson, *The Psychology of Successful Weight Control*. Chicago: Nelson-Hall, 1974.
50. Walter H. Fanburg and Bernard M. Snyder, *How To Be a Winner at the Weight Loss Game*. New York: Simon & Schuster, Inc., 1975 (also New York: Ballantine Books, 1976).
51. Joyce Brothers, *Better Than Ever*. New York: Simon & Schuster, Inc., 1975.
52. Franklin D. Cordell and Gale R. Giebler,

Psychological War on Fat. Niles, IL: Argus Communications, 1977.

53. Bob Schwartz, *Diets Don't Work!* Galveston, TX: Breakthru Publishing, 1982.
54. Stuart Berger with Marcia Cohen, *Southampton Diet.* New York: Simon and Schuster, Inc., 1982.
55. John E. Eichenlaub, *A Minnesota Doctor's Guide to Weight Reduction and Control.* Englewood Cliffs, NJ: Prentice-Hall, 1977.
56. L. Melvin Elting and Seymour Isenberg, *You Can Be Fat Free Forever.* New York: St. Martin's Press, 1974 (also New York: Penguin Books, 1975).
57. Robert Linn, *Staying Thin.* New York: G. P. Putnam's Sons, 1980, 216–218.
58. Larry Goldberg, *Controlled Cheating.* New York: Avon Books, 1982.
59. Edward M. Marshall, *The Marshall Plan for Lifelong Weight Control.* Boston: Houghton Mifflin Co., 1981.
60. William Rader, *Dr. Rader's No-Diet Program for Permanent Weight Loss.* New York: Warner Books, 1981.
61. Albert J. Stunkard, *I Almost Feel Thin!* Palo Alto, California: Bull Publishing, 1977.
62. Eric Berne, *Games People Play.* New York: Grove Press, 1964 (paperback, 1967).
63. Frank J. Bruno, *Born to be Slim.* New York: Barnes & Noble Books, 1979 (originally published as *Weight Loss for Everyone the TA Way.* New York: Harper & Row, 1978.)
64. Frank T. Laverty, *The O.K. Way to Slim.* New York: Grover Press, 1977.
65. Elyse Birkinshaw, *Think Slim—Be Slim.* Santa Barbara, CA: Woodbridge Press, 1976.
66. Alan Dolit, *Fat Liberation, The Awareness Technique.* Millbrae, CA: Celestial Arts, 1975.
67. Frances Meritt Stern and Ruth S. Hoch, with Jean Carper, *Mind Trips To Help You Lose Weight.* Chicago: Playboy Press, 1976.
68. Donald L. Wilson, *Total Mind Power.* Los Angeles: Camaro Publishing Co., 1976.
69. Peter G. Lindner, *Mind Over Platter.* North Hollywood: Wilshire Book Co., 1978.
70. Birkinshaw, op. cit.
71. Denise Denniston and Peter McWilliams, *The TM Book.* Los Angeles: Price/Stern/Sloan Publishers, Inc., 1975.
72. Ibid.
73. Peter McWilliams, *The TM Program.* Greenwich, CT: Fawcett, 1976.
74. Harold H. Bloomfield *et al.,* *TM: Discovering Inner Energy and Overcoming Stress.*
75. Richard Tyson and Jay R. Walker, *The Meditation Diet.* Chicago: Playboy Press, 1976 (also New York: Fawcett, 1977).
76. Ibid.
77. Ibid.
78. Ibid.
79. Ibid.

FASTING IT OFF

1. Judith H. Dobrzynski, *Fasting, A Way to Well-Being.* New York: Sovereign Books, 1979.
2. Jack Goldstein, *Triumph Over Disease.* New York: Arco Publishing Co., 1977.
3. D. R. Young, *Physical Performance, Fitness and Diet.* Springfield, IL: Charles C. Thomas, 1977.
4. Frederick W. Smith, *Journal of a Fast.* New York: Schocken Books, 1976.
5. Eric N. Rogers, *Fasting: The Phenomenon of Self-Denial.* Nashville: Thomas Nelson Inc., 1976.
6. Dobrzynski, op. cit.
7. Allan Cott, with Jerome Agel and Eugene Boe, *Fasting: The Ultimate Diet.* New York: Bantam Books, 1975.
8. Ibid., 58.
9. Allan Cott, with Jerome Agel and Eugene Boe, *Fasting as a Way of Life.* New York: Bantam Books, 1977.
10. Stanley J. Rzepela, *Zip Diet.* New York: Vantage Press, 1978.
11. George F. Cahill, Jr., "Starvation in Man," *New England Journal of Medicine* 282 (19 March 1979): 668–675.
12. "Crash Dieter's Hair Loss," *Journal of the American Medical Association* 235 (2 February 1976): 476.
13. Salem Kirban, *How to Keep Healthy & Happy by Fasting.* Huntingdon Valley, PA: Salem Kirban, Inc., 1976.
14. Ernest J. Drenick, "Weight Reduction by Prolonged Fasting," *Medical Times* 100 (January 1972): 209–229.
15. Garfield G. Duncan *et al.,* "Intermittent Fasts in the Correction and Control of Intractable Obesity," *American Journal of Medical Science,* May, 1963, 515–520.
16. Garfield G. Duncan *et al.,* "Correction and Control of Intractable Obesity," *Journal of the American Medical Association* 282 (28 July 1962): 309–312.
17. Garfield G. Duncan *et al.,* *American Journal of Medical Science*, op. cit.
18. Berger *et al.,* "Verlaufsuntersuchungen zum Langzeiteffekt der Nulldiat,"

238

Deutsche Medizinische Wochenschrift 101 (16 April 1976): 601–605.

19. Drenick, op. cit.

20. Jean Mayer, "Should You Starve Yourself Thin?" *Family Health/Today's Health*, February 1977, 24–26.

21. Shirley Ross, *Fasting—The Super Diet*. New York: Ballantine, 1976.

22. *Obesity and Health*. (PHS Pub. No. 1485) Washington, D.C.: USGPO, 1966, 56.

23. Fredrick J. Stare, "The Diet That's Killing Our Kids," *Ladies' Home Journal* 88 (October 1971): 70.

24. Amy Gross, "Chewing Your Way to Health, Sexual Vitality, Peace…and a Lot of Other Things, Too," *Mademoiselle*, April 1971, 279.

25. Stare, op. cit.

26. U. D. Register and L. M. Sonnenberg, "The Vegetarian Diet," *J. Amer. Diet. Assn.* 62 (March 1973): 253.

27. Associated Press, *Chicago Daily News*, 21 September 1977.

28. A. Howard and I. McLean Baird, "The Treatment of Obesity by Low Calorie Semi-Synthetic Diets," *Recent Advances in Obesity Research*. London: Newman Pub., 1975.

29. Cited in *Bulletin of the Walter Kempner Foundation*, Vol. 4, No. 1, Durham, NC, June 1972.

30. Walter Kempner, "Radical Dietary Treatment of Hypertensive and Arteriosclerotic Vascular Disease, Heart and Kidney Disease, and Vascular Retinopathy," GP 9 (March 1954): 71–93.

31. Walter Kempner, "Treatment of Heart and Kidney Disease and of Hypertensive and Arteriosclerotic Vascular Disease with the Rice Diet," *Annals of Internal Medicine* 31 (November 1949): 821–856.

32. Walter Kempner, Ruth Lohmann Peschel, and Clotilde Schlayer, "Effect of Rice Diet on Diabetes Mellitus Associated with Vascular Disease," *Postgraduate Medicine* 24 (October 1958): 359–371.

33. *Bulletin*, op. cit., 45–46.

34. "McCall's Diet of the Month. April: Remember the Rice Diet?" *McCalls* 97 (April 1970): 32–34.

35. Kempner, *Annals of Internal Medicine*, op. cit., 821.

36. Ibid., 76.

37. "Diet Changes Found to Lower Levels of Glucose, Insulin," *Diabetes Outlook* 13 (July-August 1978): 3.

38. Kempner, *Annals of Internal Medicine*, op. cit., 821.

39. "A Mini-Dictionary of Diets," *Epicure*, Summer 1973, 56.

40. T. H. Fehrenbach, *This Kind of War*. New York: Pocket Books, 1964.

Index